AFFIRMING LIFE

by
Rabbi Seymour J. Cohen

AFFIRMING LIFE

by
Rabbi Seymour J. Cohen

KTAV PUBLISHING HOUSE, INC.
Hoboken, NJ
1987

Library of Congress Cataloging-in-Publication Data

Cohen, Seymour J.
  Affirming life.

  1. High Holiday sermons. 2. Jewish sermons—
United States. 3. Sermons, American—Jewish authors.
I. Title.
BM746.C64   1987   296.4′2   86-21342
ISBN 0-88125-112-7

Manufactured in the United States of America

This Silver Jubilee volume is dedicated to our grandchildren

Dov Philip Grossman
Ariel Hayim Grossman
Michelle Sarah Cohen
Susan Ellen Cohen

whose beautiful lives give meaning to the promise of the
Psalmist:
"You shall see your children's children."

Table of Contents

Introduction

This year marks the Silver Jubilee of my ministry to the Anshe Emet family. Among the most rewarding experiences of these twenty-five years has been the renewal of the Anshe Emet Publication Fund. This unique instrument has enabled the issuing of a number of significant texts. Through the efforts of devoted friends, studies in various phases of Jewish literature have appeared. My efforts have been primarily in the fields of Jewish ethics, contemporary social concerns, and homiletics.

I am grateful to Eleanor and Jules Green for the magnificent gift which made this volume possible. Their subvention is an act of devoted friendship and faith. They have been constant in their loyalty over the years.

This ingathering of the sermons and essays I have given since 1961 may serve as a creative vehicle in spreading knowledge of our faith and people beyond the bounds of Anshe Emet. It serves as a permanent record of my efforts in the synagogue pulpit and in other forums.

In abiding love, Naomi and I have dedicated this study to our young grandchildren in gratitude for the past and in hopeful anticipation for their future.

The sermons, in the main, first appeared in the *Anshe Emet Bulletin.* The essays were published by the Rabbinical Assembly in both its Annual Proceedings and *Conservative Judaism.* The study of Negro-Jewish Relations was first published by the Synagogue Council of America for the historic National Conference on Religion and Race held in Chicago in Jan. 1963. I thank Schocken Books for permission to reprint an essay edited by Rabbi Jack Riemer in *Jewish Reflections on Death.* This first appeared in the *Anshe Emet Bulletin* and in a revised form in the Riemer anthology.

My gratitude is expressed to Ms. Ingrida Hernandez for preparing the typescript. To Mrs. Naomi G. Cohen, my beloved helpmate and co-worker, and to Ms. Hernandez my thankfulness can never fully be articulated. Their diligence in guarding this text from error and their constant concern about a fully correct printed text have been most encouraging.

This publication completes a cycle of seven volumes published over the years. May God grant all of us the health and strength to continue to bring other works to the light of day, helping both reader and author to find their way in a world that is marked by gnawing perplexity and hopeful promise.

Seymour J. Cohen

10th Day of Av, 5746
August 15, 1986

High Holidays

Compassion

SELIHOT, 1980

"I pleaded with the Lord at that time."

Deut. 3:23

The classic scriptural commentator Rashi makes the observation that all forms of the verb *hanan*, to plead, signify a free gift.

Compassion is shown to us by God as His free gift. Compassion is the *leitmotif* of our High Holiday prayer service. From the onset of our Selihot prayers to the final moments of Yom Kippur, this basic attribute of God—that He is compassionate and wishes us to be compassionate—is repeated. While it is true that we have a heavy emphasis in our faith upon ritual, there are times when law and ritual practice alone can lead to self-righteousness and even to callousness. What a person needs—and this is stressed by our prayers—is the encouragement of humaneness and the opening up of human possibilities.

We need not be compassionate to all. "He who is compassionate to the cruel, will, in the end, be cruel to the compassionate." We need not be kind to a Hitler or a Khomeini.

Compassion is an expression of ethics and must be accompanied by a search for spirituality. To be compassionate is a reflection of our character training. To be compassionate is to have a special concern for the sensitivity of fellow human beings. We must try to better our community. We must show love, sensitivity, humaneness, compassion for all persons. Only by continued self-examination, by a heightened sensitivity to the needs of others and to the potentialities of ourselves, can we find the source through which we can improve our own character.

My words are said on the eve of the New Year. I had learned that

3

a fine congregation in California is establishing an Ethical Action Committee. Most congregations have appeals for monies on the High Holidays. This congregation was appealing in the spirit of scripture, "You take the money and give me the soul." This, of course, is a paraphrase of the Biblical statement where one of the personalities said, "Give me the persons and take the possessions for yourselves." We might paraphrase this as meaning that while it may be necessary to have an appeal for funds, we also have to make an appeal for souls. The congregants were asked to take on special duties—reading for the blind, acting as foster parents, contacting the elderly or infirm on a daily basis, talking to the shut-ins who are now so large a part of the American landscape. What we need is to further the ethical qualities of our people, to advance the traditional devotion for human freedom, to enhance family life, to guard our tongue, to plan for humaneness for the poor and the elderly.

A remarkable thing was that the rabbi of this congregation told me that in a rap session with his high school youngsters, he asked for a character description of the Jew. The response sounded almost like a page from "The Merchant of Venice" or "Oliver Twist." Jewish youngsters responded that Jews were hard-driving, vicious, competitive, and materialistic. While at Harvard this summer, I saw a rerun of the Canadian film, "The Apprenticeship of Duddy Kravitz." The young man was a composite of all these negative factors.

Compassion means to share. Just as companion means one who shares our bread, compassion means one who shares our feelings, our pity, our suffering. As we go through our prayers on the holidays, we read the moving prophetic section on Yom Kippur. "Is such the fast I desire? . . . Do you call that a fast, a day when the Lord is favorable? No, this is the fast I desire: to unlock the fetters of wickedness. . . . It is to share your bread with the hungry and to take the wretched poor into your home. When you see the naked, to clothe him, and not to ignore your own kin . . . and offer your compassion to the hungry" (Isaiah 58:5). It is interesting that some Hebrew manuscripts read, instead of "offer your compassion to the hungry," "offer your bread to the hungry."

God, Himself, promises to be compassionate. "Truly, Ephraim is a dear son to Me, a child that is dandled! Whenever I have turned against him, My thoughts would dwell on him still. That is why My heart yearns for him; I will receive him back in love" (Jeremiah 31:20).

Compassion for our children is needed in every stage of life. Each stage has its own problems. The crises of infancy differ from those of puberty, which in turn differ from those of adolescence. An old Yiddish expression has it: "Little children, little woes, big children, big woes." Even when our children are grown tall and have families of their own, there is still need for compassion.

Why do we think of compassion? In confusing times like the present when our own problems become so weighty, we lack patience, feeling, and compassion for others. We need to have compassion for the ill. Some of us do not have the inner strength to visit the sick. We must have compassion for those who are suffering because of our changing economic life. Inflation affects all people. We must realize that many have less than we do.

Compassion is needed for the loser in the ballgame as well as for the defeated candidate in an election. A great journalist once put the choice confronting Americans as being a decision for a competitive society or a compassionate one. "Compassion is that rare thing which partakes of the sacred." Compassion means being sensitive to the needs of others. Competitiveness means looking out for one's self. Compassionate people love their neighbors as themselves because they are part of their neighbors.

There are many philosophers who were opposed to compassion. The great Spinoza thought that if man were compassionate, he would be imitating the ways of God. How can you imitate the ways of God if you do not believe in God? Spinoza's thoughts inspired Neitzche, who wrote that "A man loses power when he pities. . . . Pity thwarts the law of development which is the law of selection. . . . Nothing is more unhealthy than pity."

It is important for us to be empathetic, not judgmental. This world was created out of compassion. God, Himself, sought to reveal His compassion. If the world had not been created, to whom could He reveal this great quality?

We are all building a new world. May the quality of compassion be a mighty part of it. Our prayers ask for God's compassion. We repeat the 13 attributes of God that begin on the theme of His mercy. We hope that God, with His superior strength, will overlook our shortcomings and have compassion, even when merit is lacking.

Our age, tragically, has witnessed a lost sense of compassion. How can we explain the closing of the gates in the 1930s to German-Jewish refugees? How can we watch the showing of "The Voyage of the Damned"? How can we explain the tragedy of Biafra—of a hundred Biafras?

The absence of compassion is one of the saddest commentaries on contemporary people's lack of moral judgment. Why moan about what is happening in Asia or Africa or Central America when we are mute concerning the tragedies next door? Compassion is the hallmark of the Jew.

A Second Birth

ROSH HASHANAH EVE, 1981

One of the most remarkable testimonies to human faith and endurance is *Anne Frank: The Diary of a Young Girl.*

Hiding with seven other people in a secret nest of rooms in Amsterdam, she compiled a remarkable testament to life. Her small group of Jews were in constant danger of being discovered by the Nazis. This ultimately happened and Anne was deported to a concentration camp where she died several moths before V-E Day. She left behind a statement to the world. The Nazi soldiers who found her papers did not realize that this document was a priceless and immortal treasure. They did not realize that the little diary was "a story of great adventure which was to symbolize a triumph of the human spirit."

In her diary, Anne wrote that she felt that something within her was changing. Moving from puberty to adolescence, she noted, "I think what is happening to me is so wonderful, and not only what can be seen on my body, but all that is taking place inside. I never discuss myself or any of these things with anybody; that is why I have to talk to myself about them."

Anne felt that she was emerging as a fuller human being. She was being born a second time. Anne Frank the child was becoming Anne Frank the person.

Obviously, when we speak of birth, it is a metaphor; it is more than physical birth. There is the birth of an idea. There is even the birth of a style of music we call "the birth of the blues." When we discover resources within ourselves that we did not realize were present, this is a second birth.

A magnificent scholar, living in Rehovot, gave us a legacy of spiritual insights. His name is Rabbi Elimelech Bar Saul. He made the great point that there are two types of birth for a person. The first happens without our being able to control it—when our mother gives birth to us. The second birth comes from ourselves, from our own thought processes as they develop. The birth of a child is the result of the love of two individuals, a father and a mother. The birth of a mature person comes from his or her own volition. A babe's birth is accompanied by the pangs of child birth. A birth of a mature person is blessed by the pangs of creativity. A babe's birth is a relatively short process: conception, gestation, delivery. All take place in a little over nine months. The birth of a mature human being continues all the days of our lives. A babe's birth is essentially a physical experience. The mature person's birth is the unfolding of a soul. The babe moves from the shelter of the mother's womb to the exhilarating air of the world. The birth of a mature person is the revelation of one's character through the purposeful type of life. For the Jew, that life is marked by the study of the Torah and the keeping of God's commandments. That is why the rabbis said, "Whoever keeps the Torah with integrity, it is regarded as if he had *created* himself. He opens for his soul the gates of new life."

People, by creating themselves, become partners with God in the act of creation. Whoever does a good deed, it is as if that person had kindled a lamp before God, as if that person had revived his or her own soul—also called a light, for it says, "The spirit of man is a lamp of the Lord."

This day in the calendar of our people is concerned, to be sure, with physical birth. In one of our most important prayers we say, "This day is the birthday of the world. Today the world is born." This day the Lord took note of Sarah as He had promised. He did for her as He had spoken. Sarah conceived and bore a son to Abraham in his old age. This day we think of the barren Hannah who prayed, "O Lord of Hosts, if you will look upon the plight of Your servant, if You will not forget but remember me and give Your servant a son, then I will dedicate him to the Lord all of the days of his life." This day not only was the world created, but the patriarchs were born; not only Isaac, but also Abraham and Jacob. This day was not only a day of physical birth, but the rabbis say it was a day when Joseph was born anew, when he went forth from prison. According to one account, on this day the bondage of our ancestors came to an end and six months later they were redeemed.

The theme of a second birth differs from the concept of a reborn Christian, who depends upon another power to remake her or him. We must rely upon ourselves. Who helps us to be born the second time? Our parents, our teachers, our friends, even our enemies, as we react to what they have in store for us. Books help us to be born anew, to become what the rabbis called *adam bifne atzmo*, a person vis-a-vis himself. The theme of the second birth runs throughout our lifetime and throughout the year. Somehow, because of the awesomeness of this season, because of the mystique of this time of the year, we are able to understand what the Psalmist meant when he wrote, "This shall be written for the generation to come; and a people that shall be created shall praise the Lord" (Psalm 102:19). Is another people still to be created? A rabbi explained that the words referred to the generation of Mordecai who almost perished but who were, by the act of being spared, created anew.

A second birth is possible for all of us. It will be accompanied by anguish and pain. It requires us to turn our backs on what we thought was so gratifying and satisfying but was really a vapid existence. On this day of the birth of the world, let us help bring forth a new personal world.

Our Generations

ROSH HASHANAH EVE, 1979

This evening we think of parents and children. Both the matri-archs and patriarchs of our people had a special relationship with this day. This was the time when Sarah was remembered. This is the day when Isaac was born. We remember, on this day of remembrance, Hannah pleading for a child. We remember this day the desperate Hannah who vowed, "O Lord of Hosts, if You will look upon the suffering of Your servant, if You will not forget but remember me and give Your servant a son, then I will dedicate him to the Lord all of the days of his life." Hannah conceived and later bore a son. She named him Samuel (Shmu-el), for she said, "I have asked the Lord (sha'ul me'el) for him."

Our generation is deeply concerned with children. The philoso-pher John Dewey observed that the great discovery of the twenti-eth century was the child. For our neighbors, this was not always so. We think of children as being the objects of tenderness, coddling, and love. Yet a great study of medieval history demon-strates that, "Of all the characteristics in which the medieval age differs from the modern, none is so striking as the comparative absence of interest in children." Evidence of this is shown by the fact that children are depicted in art by a mother who is holding the child stiffly away from her body. The thought is offered that because of the unfavorable conditions of the time, maternal love could atrophy. The medieval infant mortality rate went as high as two out of three children. There was a suppression of the invest-ment of love for a tender babe who might be taken away. There is another thought which is advanced—that life was cheap and that this accounts for the relative emotional blankness of a medieval infancy. Medieval people had a casual attitude towards life and suffering.

We live in an age of concern for children. This is the twentieth anniversary of the Declaration of the Rights of the Child. All over the world men and women and children are observing the twentieth anniversary of the adoption by the United Nations, on November 20, 1959, of this Declaration. Children are entitled to special protection. They must be given opportunities and facilities to develop physically, mentally, morally, spiritually, socially. Children are entitled, from birth, to a name, to nationality. They have to belong to some country; some country has to be concerned about them. If children are handicapped, mentally or physically, they shall receive special care. Education must be universal.

Our children need not only the protection of the Declaration of the Rights of the Child; they need also the right to grow up Jewishly. Their parents must be alert to what must be done for them. Scientists tell us that children have innate abilities. The sad thing is that many of them are not realized.

The August 1979 issue of *Natural History* pointed out that infants and very young children who have not yet learned to talk, can recognize differences in the nature of speech sounds. Infants a month old seem to be able to distinguish between pairs of sounds that linguists call voiced and unvoiced consonants. Sounds come from different parts of the mouth. The ga-ka comes from the back of the mouth; the ra-la and da-ta pairs, from the back of the teeth. The ba-pa comes from the front, using the lips. Japanese children, a study showed, can, at a tender age, distinguish the ra-la that Japanese adults find so difficult to articulate. Since there is no difference between this pair of sounds (the ra-la) in the Japanese language, the children of Nippon lose the capacity to tell the difference as they grow older. The natural ability and innate talent fall into disuse.

What does this mean to us? We talk of the rights of the child, but we must think of the responsibility of the parents. How can children appreciate the beauty of the Sabbath if they have never experienced a Sabbath at home? A Sabbath demonstration in religious school is not enough. What does Shabbat eve mean to youngsters if there are no Sabbath candles on the table and the Kiddush is unheard? There are no examples set for them. They have never seen a real Sabbath. How can one expect them to grow up Jewishly, to develop spiritually? They are like the Japanese child, who has the innate ability to make every sound, but never having heard it loses that skill. There is within all of us the power to grow. This is what Rosh Hashanah means. It is a springboard to growth.

There is a very sad book that has appeared on the bookstalls of our nation. An author writes about his father who was a confidence man. *The Duke of Deception: Memories of My Father* is a touching book. The father claimed that he was a W.A.S.P., had studied at Groton and Yale, and had enrolled at the Sorbonne. He claimed that he had been in the R.A.F. in World War II. The fact of the matter is that it was all a charade. The author's father was an intelligent man, but he flunked out of every school he attended and he never wore any nation's uniform. The father was a Jew but didn't like the idea. Some ten years before, when the son wrote a novel called *Bad Debts*, he explained to his father that it was a fictional work. Before publication, the son tried to justify himself to the father and used these words, "The problem is: Be careful who you pretend you are, lest you wind up becoming your pretense. . . . Who you in fact are is someone far greater than the person you have, from time to time, pretended to be."

All of us, from the youngest lisping babe to the grey beard, is potentially a greater person than the individual we have pretended to be.

It is not only our parents who have not done enough. Our schools merit some candid examination this day. Children learn by copying the activities of their parents. Nothing is more tempting to normal children than to emulate their parents. They pretend to be grown up when they imitate parental life activities, wear their clothes, mimic their gestures. What parents are unable to achieve, is supplemented by the school. Teachers, knowing that children wish to imitate, must set themselves up as positive exemplars. The teacher is a parent-surrogate. Children recreate in the school experience what they once imitated in their parents.

I had a talk this week with a great educator who pointed out to me some of the deficiencies of American education. In a new book, *America Revised*, Frances FitzGerald tells of what has happened to the teaching of history. "There has been a watering down of the quality of our textbooks. We have taken away any sense of America. What is remarkable about (recent) American-history texts, compared with those of the past, is the sense of uncertainty they show. The central questions about identity and value are not in our current books. Some textbooks are good, but others, on the whole, have an astonishing dullness." For a foreigner to read American history books, he or she would have to conclude that

American political life was completely mindless. FitzGerald compares the treatment of one American president in the 20's and shows how "the characters of American history have grown small and pale."

We cannot blame everything on the schools. All indications show that the ability to read and write has declined over the past decade. There are several reasons, among them the decline of parental discipline and the omnipresence of television. FitzGerald concludes her study of our history textbooks by saying, "We not only close off the avenues of thinking about the future, but we deprive American children of their birthright."

If you think I have overstated my case, take a copy of the August 6th issue of *Newsweek* into hand and read the feature, "Where Have All The Heroes Gone?" We no longer emphasize the heroes who helped to make our republic. The writer went to the Alamo in Texas. He brought a gift T-shirt for his daughter, who attends a very fashionable and very expensive private school. Excitedly he told about his experiences in Texas. The child accepted the gift with a polite, bemused smile and then said, "I never heard of the Alamo."

I think that what has happened with history textbooks has happened in most Jewish schools. We feed our children pablum instead of a sturdy diet.

The story is told that Elijah was walking by the seaside. He met a man who made fun of him and mocked at his words. Elijah said to him, "What will you answer to your Maker on Judgment Day (Yom Hadin)?" The man responded, "No one gave me the knowledge and understanding to read and to study." Elijah said, "What is your work?" The man said, "I am a fisherman." Elijah said to him, "Who taught you to take flax, make nets to throw into the water and bring up the fruit of the sea?" The fisherman answered, "This knowledge I got from God." Elijah responded, "For all of these skills you admit knowledge from heaven, but for the words of Torah which are very close to you, you do not have understanding and knowledge." Immediately the fisherman began to cry until Elijah told him, "Let it not grieve you for all can return in repentence, but it depends upon your own deeds and your own ability."

All of us must help each other grow. Parents their children, teachers their students, and we are duty-bound to help our fellow human beings develop. We must appreciate that we are, in fact, greater than the person we have pretended to be. This can be the day of a new spiritual life, a life that will bring greater gratification and a deeper satisfaction than we have ever known.

Binding Our Wounds

ROSH HASHANAH EVE, 1985

This has been a year of remembrance, remembrance of humanity's folly. This time forty years ago marked the end of World War II. V-J Day, victory over Japan, in August followed in the wake of victory in Europe in May. That year, the Atomic Age began with all of its unspeakable dangers.

This year, I had the occasion to visit the Vietnam Veterans Memorial in our nation's capital, a tribute to the 58,000 persons killed or missing in our country's longest war. I came to the memorial as thousands do each day. Carved in black granite are precious names. The memorial is close to the sacred places of American society. When it came to picking a designer, a special selection committee was appointed. Their final choice was a young Chinese-American sculptor, Maya Lin.

The members of the committee were outstanding architects and sculptors from all over the country, including one Chicagoan. A statement informing competitors as to the purpose of the Vietnam Veterans Memorial was issued. Its stated purpose was "to recognize and honor those who served and died. It will provide a symbol of acknowledgement of the courage, sacrifice and devotion . . . of those who are among the nation's finest youth." The statement went on to say, "The failure of the nation to honor them only extends the national tragedy of our involvement in Vietnam." The memorial was to contain no political statement about the war or how it was fought. "It will transcend those issues. The hope is that the creation of the memorial will begin a healing process, a reconciliation of the grievous divisions wrought by the war."

That hope is at the heart of this day, when a people who are

created anew praise God. We need healing and we need reconciliation. We need healing within our very beings, for most of us are
torn apart by contending forces. Our classic thinkers understood
this tug of war quite well. A 13th-century writer said, "Whom can
I accuse, of whom revenge demand, when I have borne deep
suffering at my own hand? Other hearts have held hatred for me,
but my own heart hates me more than anyone knows." Are we
self-destructive? The poet asks, "Whom can I blame, how can I
function, when I am the source of my own destruction?" We must
learn to bring peace to our hearts. The rabbis said that "He who
wishes to be a good person, let him study the art of proper
relationship to himself."

As social beings, we live in a wider world. We are not isolated
but must have a relationship to other persons. Here, too, we need
a healing process, the working out of reconciliation. The relationship between people and their fellow human beings is important.
Surely we must say, "Heal me, O Lord, and I will be healed." But,
at the same time, we must be able to work for healing with our
fellows.

There is a hunger for wholeness as our society moves from
traditional forms to modernity. There is a search for wholeness,
to join the fragments of human life and the dualities of human
thought together. There is a need to unite.

The process of healing and reconciliation extends in another
dimension, the dimension of one's relationship to God. It is
interesting to report that Maya Lin's design was accepted only
after great controversy. There was harsh criticism of her efforts.
The impressive black granite was labeled "a black gash of shame,"
"a wailing wall for future anti-draft and anti-nuclear demonstrations." Changes were made to appease those who were unhappy
about the design. On the day of the dedication, a young veteran
wearing a purple heart accosted the sculptor and began shouting
accusations: "Why did you do such a thing? This is a memorial to
you, not to us." Wiser and cooler heads prevailed. Three young
men in green berets moved in on the angry veteran and urged him
to "cool it." The sculptor went back to her hotel and wept. It was a
shattering confrontation.

The memorial is now part of our capital's landscape. Veterans
and their families in the thousands visit each day. They leave
their flowers; they touch the names; they look about for comfort.

The memorial is now the second most heavily visited tourist attraction in Washington, next only to the White House.

Far beyond what has been achieved in the granite memorial, in the statue of the three veterans, is the basic purpose of the memorial: to serve as the beginning of a healing process, of a bringing together through the working out of reconciliation of the horrible divisions caused by the war.

Annually, we have a day devoted to healing and reconciliation. May we take the road that leads to a unity within, to a unity without, and to a sense of oneness with the One.

What Really Counts

ROSH HASHANAH EVE, 1982

Several weeks ago, an important article entitled "Rationing Medicine" appeared in our nation's press. Written by Harry Schwartz, a former member of The New York Times Editorial Board and writer-in-residence at Columbia University's Medical School, it made some very dire predictions about the future of medical care.

The article itself was a reaction to a Supreme Court decision denying a deaf eleven-year-old a full-time sign-language interpreter to help her at school. The decision, as reporter Schwartz read it, laid down a principle for rationing scarce social services for those who need them but cannot afford them.

A new principle was introduced by the writer, a principle that could be called "cost effectiveness." Instead of considering costs as being only one of the tools that permit us to judge the overall value of a medical service, cost effectiveness becomes an end in itself. Schwartz proposed the following:

"*No person shall be provided with (free) medical care worth an aggregate of over $1,000,000 in a lifetime or over $100,000 in any 18-month period.

*No person shall receive more than one (free) transplant of any kind (heart, lung, kidney, etc.) per lifetime."

With callousness, from my point of view, he added:
"*No (free) major surgery shall be done on any person 75 years or older. Admission to (free) hospital care shall be denied to persons 85 or older.

*No (free) intensive care shall be provided infants born weighing less than three pounds or having a major anatomic anomaly of the central nervous, cardiac, respiratory or gastrointestinal systems."

Schwartz goes on to say, "Our society is simply not rich enough to give every handicapped or sick person every bit of help that is technically possible." The deaf girl for him is "the symbol of the austere future ahead of us all."

The reporter believes that health care and other vital services can be rationed on the same cost-benefit basis as other services. If a patient is well up in years or is a tiny preemie with anatomical problems, why expend thousands of dollars on medical care? Talking of the old, he asked, in a sense, "How many years do they have to live? What real service are they to humanity?" I label this "cost euthanasia," and I wonder about its ethical merits.

In medicine, whether on a battlefield or in an emergency room, physicians practice triage. The physician in charge determines who should go first, in terms of medical care. When penicillin was discovered, just prior to World War II, it became a very important healing drug. Among the first of the antibiotics, it was used in battlefields throughout the world. But how and when was it used? If a soldier appeared to be so mangled that he would never be fit for fighting, his needs were put aside. Penicillin was given to those who seemed likely to be restored to active duty.

Schwartz's column drew many answers. A woman said that she knew of a ninety-year-old stroke victim—originally considered a hopeless case. Six weeks after his stroke he recognized his family and nurses. He started to speak, could hold a cup in his hand, and tried to feed himself. The patient owes much of the opportunity to life to the dedication of all who worked with him—his family, his physician, his therapist, his nurses. The patient may never leave the hospital, but he has maintained his dignity and humaneness. All who have been involved have been given a chance to be their better and more tender selves.

From the point of view of dedication to the principle of cost effectiveness, all this is a waste. An older patient is entitled to nothing. Care for a ninety-year-old person is not cost effective. Granted that we live in an age where hospital bills have soared beyond our wildest imagination. But I think of our prayer, "Cast us not away when we are old. When our strength is gone, do not abandon us." Who shall live and who shall die? Who decides that an old man or an old woman is expendable? Who is the gatekeeper who determines who shall enter the inn and who shall be kept out? The future is austere only if we refuse to make human needs our first priority.

Our society is youth-oriented. No one can deny that the theme of children being born and reared is the major thrust of our festival of renewal. Remember that along with an Isaac, there were an Abraham and a Sarah who miraculously bore him when both parents were very old. The Bible is trying to tell us something. We must be concerned about our youth, but we must not forget the generations that preceded us who brought us to this day. If one deals with cost effectiveness as our sole principle, Abraham at a hundred was not a candidate for the expenditure of funds, nor was Sarah.

I recall reading Max Lerner, the great student of American society now retired from teaching at Brandeis. He made the point that we start to die when we are born, but we can retain the love of life until we pass away. The years count less than the health of mind. Some people are senile when they are young, and others remain young in spirit while they are old in years. I know members of our congregation who are well into their 80's and 90's who do not permit even physical disability from preventing them in functioning day by day in a most creative sort of way.

It would be well for us to rid ourselves of the youth cult that has distorted perceptions of ourselves as aging. What has plagued the older citizens of the community has been not their years, but the image of society that advanced years mean a diminution of work, play, action, activity, and a hunger for life.

On Yom Kippur, I will speak on the theme of loneliness. It is greater among the young and the middle-aged than among the aged. Time is not only a destroyer, damaging brain cells, but it is also a preserver. It gives the aged the ingredients of judgment and enjoyment.

Age has its moments of grandeur. There are some who say that when you grow old, it is hard to think big. I remember that there have been heads of state who have served well into their 80's. There are active members of our Congress who function well even though they are more than fourscore years old. In the history of thought and art, there have been numerous examples of the greatest conceptions that have come late in life rather than in an earlier moment.

My great teacher, Abraham Joshua Heschel, once wrote, "The test of a people is how it treats the old. It is easy to love children. Even tyrants and dictators make a point of being fond of children. The affection and care for the old is the measure of civilization. What we owe the old is reverence. All they ask for is consideration. What they deserve is preference. All they ask for is equality."

In the Ten Commandments, God did not say, "Honor Me, revere Me." Instead, He said, "Honor your father and your mother." There is no reverence for God, but a reverence for the aged.

We of our congregation, we of our community, we of our state, and we of our nation are now at a critical point in the development of American society. What we will do for the older members of our community, of our city, state, and nation will be the touchstone of our humanity.

History or Hysteria

ROSH HASHANAH, 1979

Today is the New Year, our day of remembrance. Our theme deals with history.

Henry Ford I, great manufacturer of automobiles, knew more

about technology than social science. He once said, "History is more or less bunk." He dabbled in pseudo-historical forgeries. He reprinted the notorious "Protocols of the Elders of Zion," which the Nazis used to justify their murder of Jews.

Ford grew older and perhaps wiser. He built a museum in Dearborn and erected Greenfield Village, a restoration of an older America. There he emblazoned on an iron sign, "The farther you look back, the farther you can see ahead."

People are afraid of the past. History doesn't have happy endings. History is Janus-faced; one side tells of human achievement, the other of human defeat. We must know the past. The horrible tragedy of hundreds of people taking their own lives in Jonestown, Guyana, caused many to think of similarities of our age with an age gone by. Is it a growth of fanaticism that we are witnessing? Fanaticism is but a despairing admission that one can no longer believe in anything.

Human beings are living through difficult events. Terrorism has grown, violence is rampant, there is upheaval in Iran and insensitivity to the boat people. The world has gone through a Holocaust that marked a new low in human depravity. Most of us have lived through years when two of the most powerful nations in the world, Germany with Hitler and the Soviet Union with Stalin, were ruled by men who were insane. This century has witnessed an assault on our senses.

Many of you have read Barbara Tuchman's *A Distant Mirror*. We can see her skillful analysis of an age that lost hope. The fourteenth century was one in which people lost confidence in their ability to build a good society. Our age is witnessing a similar failure of nerve. There are symptoms of self-doubt. A murky mysticism usually wafts in during a period such as this. Hopefully, after the darkness and gloom, there will be light.

This is a day of remembrance. History tries to make us differentiate between the good and the bad, between the desirable and the undesirable. Historians provide us with the selectivity of memory.

Set within this framework, I would like to recall that this year, 5739, marks the end of a decade. We stand on the threshold of a new decade. Though many things have happened in the last decade, there are two central ideas that merit our discussion.

One central fact is the the changing position of Israel in the world. Israel is beleaguered. Support of Israel in the United States is shrinking. Political support by European nations is melting.

There is a conscious scheme to de-legitimatize Israel. A recent study, *The Jewish Emergence from Powerlessness*, focuses on the gradual emergence of our people from total political powerlessness, a development stretching over nearly one hundred years and culminating in the founding of the state of Israel.

Some years ago, I spoke of our enemies turning the clock back, throwing us back to the medieval ghetto. Hitler took away our human rights and declared us a sub-human species, fit only for destruction, root and branch. At the United Nations, during this decade, we have witnessed the passage of a resolution that equated Zionism and racism. The United Nations, which had been called into being after Hitler had been smashed, now is a stacked deck of cards in which Israel's enemies are at liberty to adopt any resolution unfavorable to her. The ambassador of Israel, Chaim Herzog, spoke on this false identification of Zionism and racism on the very anniversary of Kristallnacht, the night of the broken glass, that horrible night when Hitler's stormtroopers attacked Jewish communities in Germany, burned our synagogues, burned our Holy Books; when heads of families were taken away, many never to return.

The United Nations, which began its life as an anti-Nazi alliance, has become a world center of hatred and ignorance. The melancholy truth is that the candles of civilization are burning low. The world is being ruled not by capitalism or communism, but by a false lexicon of cliches.

Yassir Arafat has found new allies in this country. Israel is being pushed by elements in our administration and State Department towards negotiations with the PLO. The PLO calls for the destruction of the state of Israel. The PLO rejects any form of compromise on the Palestine issue. Yassir Arafat has stated his position: "There will be no other presence in the region other than the Arab presence." No one else is entitled, from the Atlantic Ocean to the Persian Gulf, to enjoy self-determination. Look at the tragedy of the Kurds. Consider the butchery of the black population in Sudan. Think of the peril of the Christians in Lebanon.

Yassir Arafat, murderer of Munich, Maalot, and Ben Yehuda Street, has met with the prime ministers of West Germany and Austria, Helmut Schmidt and Bruno Krieski. The PLO has won support from a part of the American black community, who, in a desperate mood, have latched on to the resignation of Andrew

Young. Young, who said, "I didn't tell a lie, I only told part of the truth," is a morally fractured man.

This decade began with the horrible war of attrition. Israeli positions along the Suez Canal were shelled day and night. How can one forget the Israeli press with the photos of young soldiers who had lost their lives? This decade has been the decade of the Yom Kippur War. How much do we have to comment on that experience which is still so fresh in our minds? Inflation in Israel is rampant, with a 98 percent rise in food costs during one year.

History, which can be full of despair, also has its affirmative side. There have been powerful beginnings of a breakthrough in Israeli relations with the Arabs. Think of the visit of Anwar Sadat on November 19, 1977. A few months later, Mrs. Cohen and I were part of a small group of American Jewish religious leaders who were received by Sadat. In the spring, I had the honor of being at the World Council of Synagogues when word was flashed that President Jimmy Carter had succeeded in winning an Israeli and Egyptian agreement to a peace treaty. The electrifying word came to us as we were reading the Megillah in the Conservative Synagogue on Agron Street.

There are occurrences in history that are unique. The president of Egypt and the prime minister of Israel have met with each other. This is a difficult time for them. Their own personal security is in danger. The events of Camp David remind us of the verse in the Song of Songs, "My beloved knocks." An unexpected knock is heard at our door. A knock requires a response. Hopefully we are moving to a more peaceful Middle East.

This is the first High Holy Day following the signing of the peace treaty on the lawn of our White House. It is a day of remembrance, it is a time of rejoicing.

My second area of concern deals with the mood of America. It can be captured in the simplest of ways by a menu I saw in Montreal. The menus are in French and English. It offered sandwiches served on black bread and *salade verte*. When I read the English part, I laughed and then I cried. It read: "Sandwiches served on black bread and greed salad." The typesetter had substituted a "d" for an "n." This last decade has been a time of the growth of greed, of self-concern. Yes, we have been taught, "If I am not for myself, who will be for me?" But there is a second part to Hillel's statement: "If I am for myself alone, what am I?"

Our age has been labeled as the "me generation." It is not a question of simple selfishness. Individuals place a supreme value on their own importance. Meism, in a sense, is healthy. People should be concerned with their physical well-being and care about their personal capacities. Exercise is healthy, dieting is healthy. But Meism is destructive. There is a difference between self-love and self-esteem. It is destructive to be caught up in self-love. Why has this decade witnessed such a growth in this pattern of absorption with the self? People have too many decisions to make; too many events crowd in. They turn inwardly to themselves as a sort of defense against a difficult world. One of the casualties of this Meism is marriage in America. How can two people who are so preoccupied with Meism share space with one another?

The Greeks told of a young man, Narcissus, who fell in love with his own reflection. Unfortunately, the reflection did not reciprocate and Narcissus was turned into a flower. Some years ago, a college president spoke to her students. She dealt with some of the problems that face a school administrator. Her theme was privatism, the attitude of "count me out." Privatism is the mood of being uncommitted to anything, of taking no part in anything, of being primarily devoted to personal gratification. Privatism is a modern word, but it reflects a frame of mind that is as old as time. The rabbis taught, "When the community is in distress, one should not say, 'I will go home, eat and drink, and peace will be upon my soul.' "

One best seller of this year has been Christopher Lasch's *The Culture of Narcissism*. The new narcissist is liberated from the superstitions of the past. He looks for new kicks and new cults. He is afraid to give of himself, to be involved with another. There is no hope or interest in the future. Lasch, a historian, joins a sense of the irrelevance of history and mates it with the bleakness of our era.

I find that Lasch tries to force too many different manifestations of life into his rigid ideological framework. Lasch rarely speaks of a better world. He is totally involved with decadence. In sum, having lost communion with the past, the "me generation" feels no responsibility for the future.

The devaluation of the past has become one of the most important symptoms of our cultural crisis. A denial of the past embodies the despair of a society that cannot face the future. After

the political turmoil of the sixties, Americans have retreated,
pulled back, to purely personal preoccupations.

Who needs recollections of the past, what lessons does history
have? A modernist once said to T. S. Eliot that the poets of the
past were no longer worth reading since we knew so much more
than they did. "Yes," was Eliot's famous retort, "and they are what
we know." It is in the dustbins of history that we may rediscover a
nourishing diet.

This is the anniversary of Woodstock, one of the most
heathenistic experiences ever recorded in American life. What has
happened to the Woodstockists? In a survey taken, a young
occupational therapist who reveled in the high spirits of Woodstock and considered herself a committed political activist, says,
"I am more selfish, when I have time off I'd rather play tennis than
go to a march. Ten years ago, I had to belong to political organizations to feel that I fit in. Now, I don't need other identities to
express myself. I know what I want and I can make choices based
on my experiences. I'm happier because I have more control over
my life."

To live for the moment is the prevailing passion. Do not mull on
your predecessors, forget posterity, "live for yourself," is the credo
of this new mood. We are fast losing the sense of historical
continuity, the sense of belonging to a succession of generations
originating in the past and stretching into the future. The "me"
society is concerned only for the moment. "I have only one life to
live," is their credo. Commercials ring out: "You can only go
around once in life, so you have to grab with all the gusto you
can."

Plagued by anxiety, troubled by worry, the psychological individual of our decade seeks only "peace of mind." It appears to
represent the best way of coping with life's tensions. There is a
pathological need to fill the hollow of our inner being. As we do not
have sufficient sense of selfhood, there must be a constant reaffir-
mation of our existence by seeing ourselves in others. We wait for
signals of approval from others concerning our conduct. One
observer noted that people seem to look at their reflection in store
windows, in revolving doors.

Narcissism is found in every strand of our society. From the
political world, from the halls of Congress, we hear similar confes-
sions. Congressman Peter Rodino, who served as chairman of the

House Judiciary Committee that prepared the impeachment charges against President Richard M. Nixon, said: "Political officials at all levels are less secure and confident in this long, post-Watergate era. Elected representatives generally are far more preoccupied with survival than they are concerned with leadership. In more than thirty years in public office, I have never been more aware of an 'every-man-for-himself' atmosphere."

The Joffrey Ballet performed at Ravinia this summer. There were several offerings. One, called "Trinity," summed up an aspect of the hopeful 60's. The other, "As Time Goes By," looked deeply into the fragmentation of the 70's. "Trinity" includes handholding and circle dances, but in "As Time Goes By" the bodies of the ballet company never even dance together. "As Time Goes By" cuts inwardly and alone.

Where do we go from here? Rosh Hashanah is a time of affirmation. We borrow a lesson from Arnold Toynbee, the great English historian. Toynbee developed the idea of the rhythm of challenge and response. Difficult conditions rather than easy conditions produce great achievement. Nations fail and fall, not because of material weaknesses, but because of complacency and a failure to meet new challenges creatively.

In a marvelous new book, *Yesterday, Today and What Next?* the point is made, that historians often ask themselves whether one can make sense of historical study. Yes, one can make sense of history. History is intelligible if one moves from a study of human nature to an affirmation of God's role in history.

We began with Barbara Tuchman's fourteenth century, which was a bad time. The next fifty years of the fifteenth century were even worse. Then, by some mysterious chemistry, energies were refreshed, ideas broke out of the mold of the Middle Ages into new realms, humanity redirected itself. Seeds have to rot in the ground before they can produce growth and flower. Great political developments took place; men sailed forth, leaving Europe to find a new world. Printing, a great cultural leap forward, made it possible for all to be learned.

A Century of an Enigma

ROSH HASHANAH EVE, 1983

This is a festival of birth and childrearing. This is the time when the world was created and when a new world—with each newborn child—comes once again into being.

Bringing up children is not an easy undertaking, but it is the most rewarding vocation. Recently, someone asked me what my number one priority in life was. I replied my wife, my family. More important than my sacred calling, more significant than any undertaking in which I can become involved is my family.

Rearing children is not easy. I recall an interesting statement I want to repeat on this day of candor and intellectual honesty.

A writer, in a lurch typical of a child lashing out against a parent, wrote a letter to his father. The letter was never sent but was published years later by a good friend of the author. The writer meant it as a final settlement with his father, an explanation for his way of life. "I found equally little means of escape from you in Judaism. Here some escape would . . . have been thinkable, but more than that, it would have been thinkable that we might both have found each other in Judaism." He continues with words that sear like fire: "But what sort of Judaism was it I got from you? As a boy, I could not understand how, with the insignificant scrap of Judaism you yourself possessed, you could reproach me for not . . . making an effort to cling to a similar insignificant scrap. It was indeed a mere scrap, a joke, not even a joke. On four days in the year you went to the synagogue, where you were, to say the least of it, closer to the indifferent than to those who took it seriously. That was how it was in the synagogue. At home it was, if possible, even more miserable, being confined to the first evening of Passover, which more and more developed into a farce, with fits of hysterical laughter. There was the religious material that was handed on to me. . . . How one could do anything better with this material than get rid of it as fast as possible was something I could not understand; precisely getting rid of it seemed to me the most effective act of 'piety' one could perform."

This letter might sound like a complaining son rebelling against a father who was concerned that his son rejected the faith and sought other forms of spiritual expression. This passage is hard to take, but it is even more difficult when you realize that it was written by one of the greatest writers of the 20th century. His name was Franz Kafka. Kafka was the author of *The Trial*, *Metamorphosis*, *The Castle*, and other works that have concerned and disturbed millions of readers around the world. Kafka died a young man. He asked that his literary remains be destroyed. A faithful friend, Max Brod, brought much of his work to the light of day.

Kafka is difficult to understand; he is illusive, ambiguous, and mysterious. He influenced many writers of this century. Simone de Beauvoir said, "Kafka spoke to us about ourselves. He revealed our problems to us." The search for the meaning of his fictional world continues unabated.

In his attempt to re-enter the Jewish fold, Kafka had an awakening of Jewish ethnic consciousness. He saw Yiddish actors entertaining in Prague. He visited some synagogues there. He made attempts to study Hebrew. He was drawn to the Jews of Eastern Europe when he saw refugees fleeing to Prague during the battles in Galicia. He was attracted to the Zionist ideal—not as an aspiration but as an inspiration. He tried to learn more about the Kabbalah, about Jewish customs. He was interested in the *halutz* (pioneer) movement.

There is much we can learn from Kafka's life. His candor in dealing with his father is something we can take to heart on this Rosh Hashanah eve. I can only plead for your loyalty and try to arouse your religious consciousness.

Kafka had much to say. He was a profound, deeply troubled, and lonely man. He was obsessed with death, repulsed by sensuality, and perplexed in his identity as a German-speaking Jew living in Prague. If there was a dominant theme, it was that of a highly personal struggle with circumstances. His loneliness shaded his writings. His troubled relationships with his father colored his thinking. His horror of tyrannical as opposed to nurturing authority left its everlasting imprint upon his writings. Kafka articulated the sense of hopelessness that typifies much of the writings of this century.

Kafka was an outstanding mythological writer, of the same stature as Dostoyevsky, Balzac, Malraux, Camus, Sartre, and De Beauvoir. Camus found in Kafka the ambiguity he deemed essential to expressing the true nature of humanity's situation in the world. "All of Kafka's art lies in forcing the reader to reread." With each successive examination, we open another door into the chamber where understanding may be found.

When all is said and done, Kafka will be remembered as the spokesman for a despairing attitude towards human existence. But on a day such as this, with all respect to this great master, can we live out our lives in a world without hope? It is important for us to think, in the midst of prevailing pessimism, of the positive aspects of the human experience. Much strength can be derived from reading Barbara Tuchman, that noble writer of human history. She could have become the chronicler of despair, but she insisted that the historian's role is to turn from a historian to a prophet. She has written about war and peace. She knows the problems of our century. "Let us remember that the history of the human race has its peaks and its troughs. Man has missed the mark frequently, but he has also conquered outer space. He has achieved artistic creativity, he has fought for liberty." These positive qualities are important to remember, particularly as we begin a new year.

Our epoch is a difficult one. There are elements of naivety and stupidity in our age as there have been in every age. There is corruption and cruelty. But side by side with that there is wisdom, courage, and benevolence. There are the flaws, the shortcomings, but there is also the possibility for valor, for virtue, and for happiness. A gifted spirit said, "This age keeps turning to look back on Sodom, but we have no view of the mountain of God." It is important for us to keep our balance and to hope. When Benjamin Franklin passed away, a great countryman said, "He pardoned the present for the sake of the future." Hope is a political, economic, and historic reality.

We think of Kafka and his vain struggle to be Jewish. We think of Kafka and his despair. We struggle to find a glimmer of hope in our troubled world. Hope exists. Hope sustains us. Let us think of the future and work for a good future, a hopeful future for ourselves, our children, and all humanity.

Memory

ROSH HASHANAH, 1981

This is an era in which many are involved in roots. We want to know more about our ancestors. We want to have a warm feeling of belonging. Irving Howe's *The World of My Fathers* was a tremendous success.

A few months ago, I was struck by a new book that was not concerned with memory and with roots. On the contrary, this work was absorbed in what the author called *A Generation Without Memory.*

Her name, Anne Roiphe, was well-known to me. On the eve of Christmas 1978, she wrote a rather exciting article that justified the observance of Christmas in the Jewish home. Blood pressures boiled. Letters to the editor of the *New York Times* came in abundance. Many of her friends were upset that she had gone to America's most prestigious newspaper to ventilate her feelings. After the smoke settled, Anne Roiphe's reputation as a journalist and novelist was established.

Her article was basically an observation of life on the assimilated plain. Her family was a secularist one. They had a nominal affiliation with a synagogue, and she received a minimal type of Sunday School education. So dim was her memory of her lessons that when she wrote about Hanukkah in the article, she mixed up the Syrians, who invaded Palestine and defiled the Jerusalem Temple, with the Romans who came a century later.

Anne Roiphe has tried assimilation. Yet, as I read her, I felt that she was trying to come back to the fold, for there are elements in her psyche, factors in her background and in her Jewishness (which she knows little about) that persist in haunting her. In *A Generation Without Memory,* we read of the *crie de coeur,* the anguish of the heart of a person who is caught between two worlds. Like a vast part of the American Jewish community, she is a typical member of a generation without memory.

The work stirs up great passion. "What then is wrong with this assimilation?" she asks. She answers her own question by saying, "There must be something wrong if I am willing to suffer the pity of a distinguished rabbi's wife and not fight back."

How does she look at the world? She doesn't think of the world in terms of Jewish or non-Jewish. She says, "I do not feel the temptation to value the life of an East European Jew over that of an Arab or a Cambodian. I do not need to be surrounded by Jews." Not only does she have manifestations of a spiritual amnesia, but she doesn't have the visceral reaction that most Jews have when it comes to the fate and the destiny of other Jews. We know from the 1967 War and the Yom Kippur War that many people who had no identification whatsoever with the Jewish community felt at one with embattled Israel.

As I read Ms. Roiphe, I was reminded of a famous Communist leader, Rosa Luxemburg, who was born in Poland but did most of her work in Germany. She said, in effect, "Why do you come with your particular sorrows? I have no separate corner in my heart for the ghetto. I feel at home in the entire world, wherever there are clouds and birds and human tears."

Anne Roiphe is a woman in search. She describes what it means to be involved in the assimilation process. If the people closest to you are friends rather than relatives, then you find your strength in the ties of friendship rather than of kinship.

She describes her lifestyle. "We have turkey and cranberries for dinner (this is a Christmas dinner for the family and friends), there is an angel on top of our tree. For years, we have read aloud 'A Child's Christmas in Wales' by Dylan Thomas." This reading is a kind of liturgy for her, for poetry and excellent prose are things she honors.

Yet, with all of her experimentation with assimilation, there is still a mysterious quality of being a Jew that draws her back. She protests that being a secular human being appears not to affect the moral cause at all; yet she is involved in all kinds of activities. People have tried to win her back. The pediatrician who takes care of her children had her over for the Passover seder. To buttress his arguments, he also invited a Seminary professor and his wife to the seder so that the answers to her questions might be all the more authentic. Then she writes, "I believe, on balance, that the well-being and happiness of my family would have been better supported within the wealth of the Jewish past. If I had had a deeper Jewish education, I could return to it now. . . . As it is, our universalism—once my joy, my breakthrough toward freedom—becomes my burden."

Our lady of *A Generation Without Memory* is indeed an anguished and tormented soul. With all of her gift of literary expression, there are, to use the Biblical phrase, "twins that are wrestling within her": the desire to be an assimilated person and the desire to be a Jew.

She believes in political action, but it doesn't have to be on behalf of Israel. This is a posture typical of many of our so-called "liberated" Jews. I admire her beneficent world view—for we have known all too well the experience of a world that stood silent. It doesn't have to be a protest against Soviet policy. "I mean the kind of moral and political activity for the oppressed and silenced of the world that involves some sacrifices of personal comfort." This is all-important to her. Tragically, it reminds me of Rosa Luxemburg, who met her death at the hands of right-wing elements in Germany in the early 1920s.

Anne Roiphe is, on the one hand, an assimilated Jew, but on the other hand, a person who says, "It might make it possible for this assimilated Jew to go back to her nation and life there, but the mind does boggle at the specifics of the route." She wants to come home, but she doesn't know how.

A strange person—bitter about the neighboring Reform congregation of her city, she is still affiliated with a Conservative congregation. She does not want to give Hitler any posthumous victories, to use the great phrase of Dr. Emil Fackenheim. But then she asks the question, "How can secular Jews avoid handing Hitler this victory, if not in their own lifetime, then in the lifetime of their children?" She is concerned about her children. They have been so washed out as to have reached near invisibility. After writing this in the book, she enrolled her children in the same religious school she attended as a child.

What is crucial is the fact that here is a tormented soul who is half in and half out. The title she uses, *A Generation Without Memory*, seems to point out that one must have roots, one must have background, one must have memory, one must labor to give oneself a correct perception of life. Only if we see our continuity with the past do we see ourselves as a link in the chain of the future.

Memory is all-important. Memory is not the enemy of inspiration or of free thought.

What is the importance of memory? What is life without the strength of roots? What is life without the pride of history? What is life without the warmth of memory? What is life without the ennoblement of culture? What is life without the fellowship of community? What is life without a link to eternity?

At the same time that *A Generation Without Memory* appeared, another very unusual work was on the bookstalls of our nation. It was written by a butcher. Many years ago, a humble soul from the Lower East Side of New York, on the first Yahrzeit of his daughter's untimely death by suicide, decided to write down his experiences in Yiddish. The work remained in manuscript for forty years until it was retrieved by a granddaughter. To me this particular work, *The Journeys of David Toback,* is among the most stirring works I have ever read in my life. It is not about a generation without memory, but rather about a generation that chooses to remember.

Carol Malkin, by taking her grandfather's handwritten Yiddish notes, translating them into English, and editing them, did a great service to us. Remember, from 1881, a hundred years ago—when the terrible May Laws of the Czar, which placed tremendous pressure upon the Jewish community, were promulgated—to 1924, a million Jews came to America. David Toback wrote of those who died in the pogroms during the early years of this century. He told of those who managed to live until the Nazis came. He wrote of the fate and fortune of our people. In telling his story, he was saying Kaddish for all that life he had once shared. He honored the dead and, at the same time, through an act of memory, refastened the ties with the living.

This is an exciting work in which his granddaughter has maintained the continuity of Jewish consciousness. David Toback was a man who had lived in the backwoods of villages of the Ukraine. He knew mostly peasants until his Bar Mitzvah. He had a brilliant mind. He went to Proskurov, a city near Kiev, a city in which my father-in-law was brought up. He describes what life was like in the pale, the limited area of Jewish settlements to which the Czars had forced our people. He was a student at the yeshivah.

He tells unusual stories—of a cantor and his choir whose singing was so beautiful that a Russian Czarist general asked that they participate in his funeral service. Finally, he sought to enter America. At Ellis Island he was refused admission because he had insufficient means. Someone said, "Try Philadelphia." He went back to Brussels, because he had been told that from Brussels one could sail to Philadelphia, and there the immigration authorities were kinder.

In America, David Toback became another Joseph, the provider. You remember how Joseph went to Egypt ahead of his family and provided for them and made it possible for them to come to Goshen. David Toback is one of a multitude of little Josephs who went ahead to bring their families out of the bondage of Eastern Europe, and, as the Holocaust was to prove, to secure the survival of our people. But it was only with great anguish and great pain.

In a final paragraph, he expresses the feeling that perhaps his notebooks will reach and help his grandchildren. This man, whose soul continued to be tested and continued to be saved, has left us a beautiful memoir. We see a world that is no more, but a world that helped to shape each one of us. As I read *The Journeys of David Toback*, I reminded myself that this was not a question of nostalgia but rather an appreciation of memory.

As we stand this day before God and humanity, do we have the religious faith of a David Toback? There was religious meaning to his journey. He had an abiding sense of a hundred generations of Jews and our God who stood behind him and whose Torah continues to guide us. Can we turn our backs on those who suffered and gave of their very lives that we reach this day?

One of the greatest teachers on the American Jewish scene traced the odyssey of our people. It was a memorable address, given just eight months before the thunderclouds of annihilation broke out over the world. The year was 1939.

"I stood with Abraham in his lonely vigil and read the destiny of my people in the stars. With Isaac I built the altar of a patriarch's stern faith and ultimate sacrifice." And then, moving age by age, he came to the present. We are now standing in the present. This is the day when we must remember the myriads of men and women, small and great alike, who made possible our continuity.

"And now I see the night descend again," the speaker said, "and into the dark and the storm my people are wandering forth again. Shall I leave them now? Can I leave them now? Shall I part company with this immortal band? They have become too dear and precious to me. The urgency of their pilgrimage is now coursing through my own blood. Their beckoning is now the shrine of my quest" (Rabbi Abba Hillel Silver).

We have looked at two literary efforts. The anguish of a troubled soul seeking identity and the religious meaning of life. We have gone along on the journey of David Toback, from the despair of Europe to the promise of America.

This day we stand before God and humanity. Shall we part company with the 3,500 years of Jewish history? Or, shall we remember, in a positive way, all that is dear and precious to us? The memory of a hundred generations demands an honest answer of us. May the response be an affirmative pledge that their experience is now part of us, that their sacrifices were not in vain, that their hopes were for us and for the generations to come. On this Rosh Hashanah—a day of memorial, rededication, and rebirth—we proudly proclaim, "They live within me and I will maintain their sacred trust forever."

Today's Child

ROSH HASHANAH, 1982

This morning's Torah reading deals with the birth and upbringing of children, Isaac and Samuel. In another great passage of Scripture, the question was asked, "What shall be done to the child that is born to us?"

A number of important studies have indicated that we are not dealing fairly with children in our society. Children are being robbed of their childhood. They are being dealt with on adult agendas. They live under the tremendous impact of television.

The history of childhood is a nightmare from which we have only recently begun to awaken. The further back in history one goes, the lower the level of children and the more likely children are to be abandoned, beaten, terrorized, or abused.

Dr. Leon Keyserling, distinguished economist, spoke of the national daycare crisis. He recommended that comprehensive development daycare be made available to all families who wish their children to benefit from such services. Daycare should be provided without charge to the children of low-income families, with fees scaled to income for others. Daycare should not be regarded as welfare service, but as needed by families at all income levels.

A full decade has passed since Dr. Keyserling spoke. In the meanwhile, there has been an accelerated number of women entering the work force and a rapidly increasing population of pre-school children. Only one-half of the nation's three- and four-year-olds are now enrolled in some form of daycare or nursery program.

Childhood is becoming at home in the world. Does a social space for childhood still exist in our age?

Today's child has become the unwilling, unintended victim of overwhelming stress, the stress born of rapid, bewildering social change and constantly rising expectations. Today's pressure on middle-class children is to grow up fast, and it begins in early childhood.

Pressure for early academic achievement is but one of the many pressures on children to grow up fast. Children's dress is another. When I was a boy, youngsters wore short pants and knickers until they began to shave. Girls were not permitted to wear makeup until they were in their teens. Today, even pre-school children wear miniature versions of adult clothing. Children feel that they must wear designer clothes because they are judged by clothes, not for themselves.

There are other pressures. Many children travel across the country, at times the world, alone. This phenomenon is a direct result of the increase in middle-class divorces and the fact that one or the other parent moves to another part of the country.

Everywhere you look, the behavior, language, attitude, desires, and even the physical appearances of adults and children are becoming indistinguishable.

The pressure to grow up fast, to achieve early in the areas of sports, academics, and social interaction is very great in middle-class America. It is reported that a hotline in our area provided by a Chicago psychoanalyst, receives some 150 calls per month from youngsters who are thinking about committing suicide.

When Freud was asked to describe the characteristics of maturity, he said, "lieben und arbeiten—loving and working." A mature adult is one who can love and allow himself or herself to be loved, and who can work productively, meaningfully, and with satisfaction. Most adolescents, and certainly all children, are really not able to work or move in the mature way that Freud had in mind. Children need time to grow and to develop. Hurrying children into adulthood violates the sanctity of life by giving one period priority over another.

Children grow up and become students in universities and colleges. As such, they face a tremendous burden. The need for expanded educational opportunities is clear. Access to college is indispensable. Many students cannot attend college without some form of public aid. I was shocked to read the report of Dr. Derek Bok, president of Harvard. He arranged for a meeting with one of President Reagan's deputies to discuss the problem of student aid. To bolster his argument, he invited his counterpart from Princeton to join him. "We were told, even before we entered, that we were fortunate even to receive an appointment in an unusually hectic week and that we could stay *no more than fifteen minutes.*" Imagine the level of respect and appreciation for education we have reached in our society when a White House aide can have the colossal chutzpah to allow the president of Harvard or Princeton an interview of fifteen minutes, or 900 seconds. Adam Smith said, two centuries ago, "The wealth of a nation depends upon the skill, dexterity and knowledge of its people."

The rabbis taught us, a long time ago, "Be careful in your handling of the poor for the Torah has to come forth from them." In medical schools, tuition has reached astronomic proportions. Undergraduate and graduate school students are going to less costly schools rather than to the type of schools that would develop their special skills.

The answer to the question which began our discussion, "What shall be done to the child that is born to us?" can surely be: Let them grow up slowly, without haste and let them have the best possible type of education that will enrich the life of all humankind.

Caves of Destiny

ROSH HASHANAH, 1983

Mount Moriah, how awesome is this name. Mount Moriah, the ultimate testing ground of Abraham's faith in the One God. Mount Moriah, where an old man who had been told, "Through Isaac will your seed be called" was tested in the supreme test, one that has been studied and re-studied throughout the centuries.

The ascent to Har Moriah is a central theme in the observance of Rosh Hashanah which we commence this day. We relive Abraham and Isaac going to the mountain of the Lord.

Beginning in the summer of 1967 in the city of Jerusalem, which had been divided since the War of Independence in 1948, I went up to Mount Moriah as a pilgrim on a number of occasions. I entered the Dome of the Rock, the mosque built by Omar, and there in the center of the mosque I found a magnificent outpouring of rock. That rock was the place upon which Isaac was to have been sacrificed.

In mountainous terrain, you frequently run into caves. The Dead Sea Scrolls were discovered in the caves around Kumran, near the Dead Sea. In this great rock that is within the mosque, there is a cave. There is an affinity between caves and humanity's growth. Something happens to a person in a cave. Today I will speak about caves and the intensity of religious experience; caves and the expansion of knowledge; caves and the spread of information; caves and the mood of anticipation; caves and the spirit of hope.

The cave on Mount Moriah has a flavor all its own. It has been visited by many people for hundreds and hundreds of years. Some have come as tourists armed with cameras; others have come to pray. The guidebooks tell you about this particular cave. It was artificially made to create a place within the great rock for private meditation. It is almost square in shape, 22 feet long and 21 feet wide, and is about the height of an average individual. What is particularly exciting are the legends—and life is a tapestry spun of legends.

A number of great spirits prayed there in the past: King David,

Abraham our father, the angel Gabriel. It was the place of prayer
of Elijah the prophet, and, according to a Muslim account, the
head of Mohammed pressed against the wall and left a mark. It is
the place where Solomon the king prayed for wisdom for himself
and all humankind.

The cave of prayer is important. People grow when they pray,
they do not become suppliants cringing before their Divine Master. In prayer, people become giants, for they have grown spiritually in establishing a dialogue with their Creator.

A cave played another role. The famous parable of the cave
found in Plato's *The Republic* illustrates the progress of the
human mind from the lowest state of unenlightenment to knowledge of the good. The image was probably taken from mysteries
held in caves representing the underworld through which the
candidates for initiation were led to the revelation of sacred
objects in a blaze of light. In its bare details, there is a cave with
an entrance open to the light. There is a long passage from the
opening to the cave itself. Here men have been chained from
childhood by the leg and neck so that they cannot move and can
only see what is in front of them, for the chains will not permit
them to turn their head. At some distance higher up is the light of
a fire burning behind them, and between the prisoners and the
fire is a screen so all they can see are images and shadows. One
man finally manages to go forth. When he sees the sun, he
realizes that it, not the fire, is the true source of light.

What Plato was trying to bring forth in his cave allegory was the
symbolic movement of humanity towards knowledge, the idea
that people rise towards knowledge when they ascend. Once that
blessed stage is achieved, the man goes back into the cave to
make certain that those who have not been able to free themselves
will be helped to see true knowledge. "All must be made to climb
the ascent to the vision of goodness which we call the highest
object of knowledge," Plato believed, "and when they have looked
upon it long enough they must not be allowed to remain on the
heights refusing to come down again to the prisoners or to take
any part of their labors." The cave of Plato taught that people
must ascend towards knowledge. That is what we attempt to do
today—surely to be stirred by our prayers, but also to become
better informed as Jews and as citizens of the world with the
knowledge of the true essence of the human experience.

We have heard of the cave of prayer. We have grappled with the concepts of the cave of knowledge. But there is another interesting experience of human growth that came to my attention a few months ago.

Although primitive people began to use memory and to appreciate the gifts of the brain, it was only in the great experience of cave art that they reached a new stage of intellectual, spiritual, and aesthetic development. There was no foreshadowing of this particular experience. In a most spectacular way, a great artistic drama began to unfold. Humankind went through a relatively sluggish evolution that has been described by some as "almost unimaginable monotony." Then all of a sudden art burst forth, culminating in one of the most exciting experiences in human history—the great cave paintings of Western Europe, most of which have been found in France and Spain.

I read a description of these caves which suggested that our ancestors may have started to paint and sculpt as a way of coping with expanded knowledge and growing population. People had to communicate, and the cave paintings represented a great attempt to transmit to the next generation what people had experienced. Humankind is not born once. Humankind is born over and over again. Every forward thrust in technology, spiritual growth, and aesthetic appreciation is a new beginning, a time of birth.

People had not learned to write as yet, but they had to move forward in the evolutionary scale. They had to transmit information to fellow human beings. To insure that the information would be absorbed, they had to create peak excitements by using every possible device to transmit the message, including singing and dancing. These early people who left us this exciting art form were concerned that what they had experienced would be passed on to others.

The art of the caves plays a major role in telling us how information was transmitted from generation to generation. It has a great sense of planning. A scholar from the University of Paris who visited the caves thought he would find "cultural chaos . . . works scattered over the walls in disorder by successive generations of hunters." Instead, he found something considerably more complex and not that personal. Every cave was a composition in itself, the result of a master plan conceived in great detail according to a group effort and in response to group needs.

It is remarkable that there are any monuments of this era at all.

Why did people come to caves, live in them, and make paintings of animals—not in their normal domicile but in places that were dark, secret, remote, hidden? What power did the hunters believe they got from these paintings? Jacob Bronowsky, the distinguished scholar of culture, offers his viewpoint. "I think that the power we see expressed here for the first time is the power of anticipation, the forward-looking imagination." The cave decorated with art was not only intended to communicate. It also helped people record their anticipation, their expectancy. The paintings served as a kind of telescopic tube of information. They direct the mind from what is seen to what can be inferred. The ability to visualize the future and to plan to anticipate it is all-important.

In his magnificent *Ascent of Man,* Bronowsky said that the people who made the weapons and the people who made the paintings were doing the same thing—anticipating a future as only human beings can do, inferring what is to come from what is here. He tells of an illustration that is found in the caves at Santander, Spain. All over the walls are found prints of the human hand. What these prints tell us is, "This is my mark. This is a human being." On this birthday of the world, birthday of humanity, we think of this magnificent statement.

People have many unique gifts, but at the center of them all— the root from which all knowledge grows—lies the ability to draw conclusions from what we see to what we do not see; to move our minds through space and time and to recognize ourselves in the past on the steps to the present.

We are living in a difficult age. We live in a time when there is a threat of doomsday. Humanity's capacity to wipe out life on earth is with us, and we see the absurdity of destruction. Flora Lewis of the *New York Times,* who visited the Spanish caves of Altamira, reflected, "Visiting the silent caverns makes it less depressing to consider that learning some elaborate technical skills hasn't advanced human wisdom all that much yet. On the contrary, the capacity to invent so much, to gain awareness of the earth we have populated, combines with the early capacity for grace displayed in the paintings to bring renewed assurance." Yes, humankind has a knack for awe, but humankind also possesses a capacity for survival.

From our cave experiences, we have learned the importance of a place for prayer, of the ascent of knowledge, of the need to develop instruments to communicate and to keep fresh our mood of anticipation. But what is most important, we have learned to maintain our hope that humanity will yet see a better day, a day of which the prophets foretold: "God's name will be one, mankind will be one and tranquility will be the order of the world forever."

Memories

ROSH HASHANAH, 1984

Lyrics of popular music can convey profundities of thought. Think of the line in *Showboat*, "I'm tired of living and scared of dying."

Back in the 1930s, T. S. Eliot wrote a book called *Old Possum's Book of Practical Cats*. A few years ago, this work became the core of a musical. The music was engaging, but one musical interlude was captivating:

> Memory, all alone in the moonlight
> I can smile at the old days
> I was beautiful then
> I remember the time I knew what happiness was
> Let the memory live again

> Daylight, I must wait for the sunrise
> I must think of a new life
> And I mustn't give in
> When the dawn comes tonight will be a memory too
> And a new day will begin

> Like a flower as the dawn is breaking
> the memory is fading

> Touch me, it's so easy to leave me
> All alone with the memory
> Of my days in the sun

Another version of the libretto has these words:

> Daylight, I must wait for the sunrise
> I must think of a new life and I mustn't give in
>
> A new day has begun, a new day now for ev'ry one
> Yes, a new day has begun, a new day now for
> ev'ry one.

Memory plays an important role in human history, whether it be a private memory or the recollection of a people. We place great emphasis upon the element of memory. The role of memory affects the destiny of the group, not alone by its prior experiences but also by the nature of that which it selectively chooses to recall.

Sigmund Freud once said that "Nothing is past or forgotten." Every individual's experience leaves permanent "memory traces." The recall of these memory traces is affected by the intensity of our associations with it. Over the centuries, learned men and women have developed elaborate schemes to assist recall—diagrams, rhymes, and picture alphabets. In our own age, scientists seek for models of artificial intelligence as they strive to develop machines with the ability to encode, store, and retrieve information. It is important to remember who we are. It is essential to remember what we choose to forget.

King David was a unique personality who had achieved many things. He had broken the yoke of the Philistines; he had boldly moved into neighboring lands to expand the borders of his country; he had united his people; he had captured a capital—the city of Jerusalem—that had been defended by the Jebusites for many centuries. But when we recall his career, when we lovingly think of him, we speak of him as the author of the Book of Psalms, as the sweet singer of Israel who was constrained to awaken each night at midnight and play upon his lyre until the coming of the dawn. He was idealized as a just ruler. He was to become the ideal ruler of the golden age to come. "The days are coming, saith the Lord, that I will raise up to David a righteous scion and he will reign as king and prosper and do justice and maintain righteousness in the land."

Let us consider our memory of Elijah. One can think of him as a rough and ready man who took on King Ahab of Israel; a man who ran for many miles by the chariot of the monarch; a man who said, "Shall you slay and also inherit?" He threw the cup of morality into the very faces of Ahab and Jezebel. When we recall Elijah now he is the angel of the Covenant who comes to the induction of every Jewish lad into the faith, who is present at our seder table where a special cup of wine is prepared for him. We sing of Elijah as we think of Messiah at the end of the week when Sabbath has come to an end and we recite our Havdalah and say, "Elijah the prophet, Elijah the Tishbite, come speedily in our own day."

Ahad Ha'am, the great philosopher of the early part of the twentieth century, drew a sharp line between the Moses of history and the Moses of memory, "whose image has been enshrined in the hearts of the Jewish people for generations and whose influence on our national life has never ceased from ancient times to the present day."

Memory is important in the life of all people. Laws were preserved by memory before they were preserved in documents. The collective memory of the community was the first legal archive. Daniel J. Boorstin, in his monumental *The Discoverers*, cites the English common law as being "immemorial" custom that ran to a "time whereof the memory of man runneth not to the contrary." Among the British as well as the Gallic Druids, there was the committal of all their laws as well as learning to memory. Ritual and liturgy were preserved by memory, of which priests were the special custodians. Religious services were ways of imprinting prayers and rites on the congregation. The prevalence of verse and music as mnemonic devices attests to the special importance of memory in the days before printed textbooks. In our prayer service this very day, the key, the heart of our prayers is in our prayers of recollection, the collective memory of the Jewish people. The Jewish people never forgot its humble origins. We never lost consciousness of the gray dawn of our people's past which took place not in the land of Israel but in Ur of the Chaldees and in Aram, modern Syria. We did not begin our saga from the days our ancestors came into the land under the leadership of Abraham. We remember that his grandchild, Jacob, was a wandering Aramean and to this day we recall that experience at our seder table.

Professor Byron Sherwin, in a forthcoming volume on Jewish ethics that he is co-editing with me, points out that in the writings of Judah Ha-levi, "the surest foundation for faith is not abstract philosophical speculation but concrete human experience." On this day of creation, it is important for us to be mindful of the fact that God did not begin the Decalogue by saying, "I am the Lord your God who created heaven and earth." No one witnessed the creation of the world. No human being was present. The Ten Commandments begin with the statement: "I am the Lord your God who took you out of the land of Egypt." The striving for freedom, the revelation at Sinai, and other important and unimportant events in the collective memory of the Jewish people were conveyed from generation to generation down to our own time.

Our faith is founded on memory. In the historic experiences of our people, we find our strength. Through memory of the past and its internalization by recollection and ritual, we encounter the notion that Jewish faith is predicated upon memory. In our liturgy, there is always the notion of memory. The great historian, Professor Hayim Josef Yerushalmi of Columbia University, called his latest book *Zakhor.* Faith in the present is expressed by our recollection of the past. The events of the past become part of us who live in the present. In every generation, remember the words of our sacred literature: we regard ourselves as though we personally went forth out of Egypt.

Memory was important to our people. It is significant to most people. In Greek mythology particularly, memory was regarded as the mother of the muses. More was meant by this than merely that a poet must remember a song or poem in order to perform it. Poetry was an act of reminiscence designed to elicit a response in the memories of each of the members of the audience.

Among the memories our people have borne with them in the baggage of recollection is the memory of what happened to us in Egypt. The experience of Egyptian slavery lasted only for a few hundred years, but this unfortunate phase of our people's past left an indelible mark upon the psyche of the Jewish people. It gave us a compelling feeling for social justice, a sympathy for those who are downtrodden. It was not only for the Jewish people that we have concern. We are moved by our memories to have a sense of responsibility for the downtrodden of all the world.

Another great factor in our people's recollection was the experience of the desert—dangerous and yet at the same time liberating. The desert was both the site of the revelation of the Ten

Commandments and the place where the mettle of the Jewish people was tested. The desert was the site of the consolidation that finally emerged after horrendous experiences of controversy and internal strife. Another important memory was the memory of the covenant, the agreement between God and His people that remains constant as an everlasting blessing.

This cluster of past memories—memories concerning the painful times of slavery, of liberation, of the wanderings in the desert—remained with our people forever. In connection with these memories, it has wisely been observed that "a conscious effort was made to keep alive the memory of those experiences and to pass them on from generation to generation; to advise our children to transmit the word of what had happened to us." We keep alive the memory of the slave experience to move us to a life of greater humanity and to being God-like, gracious, and compassionate (see Psalm 111:5). The saddest affliction that people suffer is not to remember. We emphathize with the families of those who have a condition like Alzheimer's.

Memory and our regard for it does not mean that we must recall everything. It is recorded that when Simonides offered to teach the Athenian statesman Themistocles the art of memory, Cicero reports that he refused. "Teach me not the art of remembering but the art of forgetting." As important as memory is, there are things we must try to forget. Just as one cannot overload electrical lines, one cannot overload the lines of recollection. Dr. Daniel J. Boorstin describes the evolution of memory as an art, but makes the all-important suggestion that in our age of information overload, forgetting may *"become more than ever a prerequisite for sanity."* William James, the great Harvard psychologist, wrote, "In the practical use of our intellect, forgetting is as important a function as remembering. . . . If we remembered everything, we should on most occasions be (as) ill off as if we remembered nothing."

We begin the section on *zikhronot*, memories, by first acknowledging our faith in God, by proclaiming that He is the master of heaven and earth. Otherwise our memories are fatuous dreams that have no real meaning.

We begin with remembrances, passages that goad us to reflection. We conclude this great section of our Mahzor by proclaiming that some day the shofar will be sounded, the shofar of freedom, liberation from pain and sorrow, for our people and all of the peoples of the world. We are grateful to those who preserved the memories that can lead us all from the lowlands of strife and struggle to the high places of moral victory and spiritual triumph.

Joyfully and triumphantly we sing:

A new day has begun, a new day now for ev'ry one
Yes, a new day has begun, a new day now for ev'ry one.

Affirming Life

KOL NIDRE, 1985

In Eastern Europe, it was a cherished custom for families to gather together for the High Holiday season. Prior to Yom Kippur, women of all ages would stand together around the family dining-room table rolling long wax candles. Each member of the family was given a *gezuntlicht*, a health candle; others, who had lost relatives, were given a *neshomelicht*, a soul candle. The emphasis on the health candle was to underscore that we are a life-affirming people. Were it not for this faith in God and belief in life, it would have been difficult for the Jewish people to persevere through the generations. Even in our moments of greatest despair, of personal and collective tribulation, we have affirmed our belief in the loving and living God.

I would like to relate some experiences, taken from our religious sources and general literature, that underscore our belief and faith in the living God—even in extreme moments.

During the war, the mettle of the Jew was tested. A writer by the name of Abraham Sutzkever composed poetry as an underground fighter crawling through the sewers under the Vilna ghetto. He managed to elude the Nazis and wrote while fighting with the partisans in the forests of Lithuania. In a press interview, he related how he even wrote a life-affirming poem while inside a coffin. "If I didn't write, I wouldn't live." He felt that as long as he was able to write he could fashion weapons of life against death.

Sutzkever's weapons of words, written in Yiddish, have made him one of the great Yiddish poets of our generation. Some years ago, some of his poetry was translated into Hebrew. Marc Chagall illustrated one of Sutzkever's works. It is truly a treasure to behold—with the magnificent expression in words and the splendor of the pen sketches. Sutzkever was able to change his painful experiences into poems that vibrate with life and reaffirm the saving richness of human experience.

One of the most difficult events in his life, which could sear the soul of any man, was when he and the other Jews of Vilna were herded into the ghetto. A young scholar and Sutzkever were ordered to dig their own graves. They thought that this was in preparation for their execution, but it turned out to be another Nazi act of sadistic brutality. In the midst of digging, Sutzkever was stunned when his shovel cut an earthworm and both of its halves remained alive. Later he took this experience and recalled how, when faced by death, he was given hope for life by the quivering worm. "If a worm doesn't succumb to this cut, am I less than a worm?" Sutzkever understood that life was greater than death.

The strong affirmation of life, which I believe is at the heart of our Jewish theological system, was underscored in another dimension some months ago. A young writer, Amy Kempel, issued a small volume of short stories called *Reasons To Live*. The stories affirmed that all of life's experiences give one a reason to live. Even if they appear to be negative, one can transform them. A modern writer once said, "One should . . . be able to see things are hopeless and yet be determined to make them otherwise." There is a reason to live. There is a reason to affirm life. As we recall the trials, tribulations, and falls that each of us undergo, we still have the strength to persevere. Kempel's characters face all sorts of difficulties but are not overwhelmed. They keep searching for reasons to live. One of the ways in which her personalities cope with life—which has been a Jewish characteristic—is by making jokes.

The Jew has always been strengthened by the words of the Psalmist, "I shall not die but live and declare the works of the Lord" (Psalm 118:5). We carry on for a purpose: to declare the glory of God, to reaffirm His oneness. We steady ourselves, even in years of fleeing and running, by writing and creating. We must grasp on to the smallest, most positive elements in an otherwise despairing situation. We carry on, as a young writer of our time has shown us, because there are reasons to live.

Out of the torment of Hitler's camps have come great moments of courage. During a cold night in a Nazi camp, the air was broken by a brutal command to empty out all the barracks. The prisoners were taken to a large field. In the middle were two huge pits. The commander spoke harshly, "Each one of you dogs who values his miserable life must jump over one of the pits and land on the other side." One can imagine the terror that broke forth. Among the thousands of Jews on that field were a Hasidic rebbe and a freethinker. They had met in the camp and developed a deep friendship. The freethinker argued that it could not be done. "Let us sit down in the pits and wait for the bullets," he said. The rebbe, a frail man in his fifties, said, "We are jumping." When they opened their eyes, they were both alive on the safe side. The freethinker said, "Rebbe, we are here, we are alive. There must be a God in heaven. Tell me, rebbe, how did you do it?" The rebbe, Rabbi Israel Spira, said, "I held on to my ancestral merit, to the coattails of my father, grandfather, and great-grandfather. Tell me, my friend, how did you reach the other side?" "I was holding on to you," replied the freethinker.

Some of us hold on to the faith of our ancestors. Some of us are sustained by the faith of others. But what we all need is an overwhelming faith that can carry us over the pits of life.

What Counts

KOL NIDRE, 1984

The central themes of Rosh Hashanah and Yom Kippur are cited in Scripture: "Remember the days of old, understand the changes of the generations" (Deut. 32:7). On Rosh Hashanah we speak of memory, on Yom Kippur we speak of change.

The rapidity of technological change is illustrated in the life of my octogenarian father-in-law. He left the village of his birth in a horse and buggy and now lives in the shadow of the space shuttle.

One of the most gripping moments in the liturgy of Yom Kippur is called the *Avodah*, the service par excellence. We re-enact the *Avodah* tomorrow, and we recall the lines of the various portions of the service where the high priest carried out the instructions of the Torah reading. One of them was connected with counting. So that the high priest would not confuse himself, he would count: one, one and one, one and two, one and three, and so on.

Parents are "uptight" in making certain that their youngsters have computers so they will not be left behind in the computer age. The percentage of public schools with at least one microcomputer has grown dramatically in the last few years. In elementary schools, it has gone from 11 percent in 1981 to 62 percent in 1983, while in high school it has gone from 43 percent to 86 percent during the same period. Even young children can acquire rudimentary computer skills. For a six-year-old entering school today—who will go to work for the first time in the 21st century—and for a nation depending on those children to be the workforce of the future, computer education cannot be thought of as an optional course or a luxury. It is nothing less than a necessity.

Possible home applications will increase when greater access to electronic libraries becomes available. The libraries of the future may have no shelved books at all, only banks of terminals.

The drop in the cost of home computers is rapidly spawning a generation of young, even pre-school, children who are fully conversant with the new technology. There is something disturbing, although almost comic, about a tiny child seated at the keyboard of a computer, bolstered on a pile of telephone books, and moving little fingers across the hardware with the absorption of a scientific expert on the verge of a breakthrough. There is danger that the technology of the traditional role of book and teacher may be supplanted. There is danger that the computer will usurp the role of the book.

An English reporter developed the notion that by the year 2000, education in the home is predicted to take over the primary school teacher. The home will be for work and the school for play. Children will need to go on outings and field trips and, above all, they will need to interact and acquire basic social skills. An

English professor, Dr. Michael Shallis, describes the perils computers have for children. "The danger of computer-assisted learning, especially for the primary school child, lies not in the depersonalized teaching relationship but in the form of instrumental thinking that the computer imposes on its user. The computer encapsulates a mechanistic uniformity of thought and imposes on children an adult mode of thinking that acts as yet another means of preventing children from being children."

Critics of the computer age see dangerous consequences of this dependency of people upon machines. An economist warned that "as machines become more human, men will become more like machines." We delegate to things that which belongs to people. The social atmosphere in which we work and live is being affected by these machines. The opportunities for human beings to respond humanely toward one another are lost when each is treated, not as an individual with a unique history and unique problems, but as an identification number to which is attached a vector of quantified data. As our society moves toward the conviction that there is nothing important in the human condition that cannot be quantified and fed as data into a digital computer, the positive qualities of Western humanism may well be lost. Consider the following quotations on the importance of the human dimension. "Where is the wisdom that we have lost in knowledge? Where is the knowledge that we have lost to information?" (T.S. Eliot). "Perfection of means and confusion of goals seem—in my opinion—to characterize our age" (Albert Einstein).

Are the critics right? Does the computer threaten the values of a humane society? Electronic technology is not yet well enough understood for its potential for good or ill to be properly evaluated. Merely to rehearse the number of jobs lost to automation is to commit the same error that is charged to the computer itself—to mistake a quantitative analysis for a qualitative one.

No one can deny that there is need to put much of our information on computers. I recall a conversation at Oxford University this summer with a librarian who told me how overwhelmed the library is with printed books for which there is only a fixed amount of space.

Artificial intelligence is a subject that commands enthusiasm from its more ardent advocates. It raises substantial criticism from those who are more reserved about its future potentialities.

We can create artificial intelligence; we cannot create artificial feelings.

One of the most interesting phases of the computer life is the attempt to create artificial intelligence—the notion of putting together hardware and programs to create new thinking entities, machines that will rival human beings. The classical Pygmalion theme was used by George Bernard Shaw in the famous play that became a motion picture. Pygmalion tells of a master craftsman so skilled as a sculptor that he fashioned the perfect likeness of a human woman and then fell in love with his own creation.

Artificial intelligence is a subject that generates a great deal of heat and some very high-pitched rhetoric. Our contemporary task is to come to terms with the new electronic technology, a task that permits neither a complete rejection nor blind acceptance of the computer metaphor. Artificial intelligence is the science of making machines do things that would require intelligence if done by people. While others applied computing techniques to engineering and business, artificial intelligence experts spoke of replacing the human mind with more efficient electronic models, of creating nothing less than a new species on earth.

The creation of "artificial" beings is sanctioned and encouraged by classical Jewish sources. As a creator, the human being is most human. Through creativity, the human being expresses his or her godlike qualities. Creativity expresses an attribute that we derive from God and that we share with God. Therefore, creativity can be a means of achieving communion with God. Human creativity can provide an entry to an intense religious experience. Creativity is a double-edge sword. The creative endeavor is replete with dangers.

The creation of artificial life does raise moral problems. Gershom Scholem spoke brilliantly at the inaugural ceremonies for the computer of Rehovot. His essay *The Golem of Prague and the Golem of Rehovot* is a classic.

The already overwhelming and still rapidly expanding presence of computers leads many people to believe that computers must be the universal answer to all our difficulties. If we process fast enough, store sufficient data, and have "intelligence," nothing seems impossible. As with any proposed panacea, however, we need to be reminded that *nothing* is that good.

Some voices are being raised, but the problem lies in making them widely heard. A great writer said, "There are three aspects of human thinking that computer programs lack: people grow and learn, human thinking is passionate and emotional, and people operate from complex motives. A computer program, by contrast, does not grow, has no emotions, and is monomaniacal in its singlemindedness." We need a dialogue to extract the greatest benefits from our discoveries without sacrificing human values.

It has been observed by one of the fine thinkers of our age, Norman Cousins, that "We are turning out young men and women who are superbly trained but poorly educated. They are a how-to generation. . . . They know everything that is to be known about the functional requirements of their trade but very little about the human situation that serves as the context for their work."

Let us conclude with a fundamental question: What really counts in this life? It is the kiss of a child, the embrace of a lover, the affection of a parent. In the long run, more than the physical possessions we have, these intangibles are what give us contentment. Through these moments of tenderness, life becomes worthwhile.

Loneliness

KOL NIDRE, 1982

We have come to pray. Some, when asked where they were going, answered, "To shul." The Jewish house of prayer is a schoolhouse. Others responded, "I am going to the synagogue" or "I am going to the temple," which is a takeoff from the 19th-century revival of the ancient Temple in Jerusalem. Every house of worship is the temple of the Lord. Regardless of where you feel you have come, it is important to remember that for 2,500 years Jews in every part of the world have gathered together to find strength and to partake of the fellowship of other human beings.

During the Middle Ages, some synagogues were built like fortresses. We have the record of one in Zholkva, in the Ukraine, to which Jews fled on numerous occasions. That synagogue, built in 1687, was destroyed by the Nazis in 1941.

This summer, Naomi and I had the opportunity of visiting both Brussels and Paris. In Brussels, it was hard to get into the synagogues because of security measures. In one little synagogue, there was an announcement on the bulletin board that read, "On leaving the synagogue, go in small groups. Do not try to draw attention to yourself. Do not pick up any packages which you may find on the road." In another synagogue where we worshipped, they had a closed circuit T.V. monitor in order to see exactly who was at the door.

The role of the synagogue is to give strength in an age in which men and women are lonely, in which they are "locked in the solitude of their own hearts." I was stirred to read some words by Yehuda Amichai on the theme of loneliness. He speaks of his perception that the whole of human society is composed of lonely people rocked by inner unrest in an alien world. God's footsteps are no longer heard; life has lost all points of reference; people can no longer band together. Amichai, in his short story "The Times My Father Died," tells of a visit to a cemetery. "Every grave bears a name. . . . No one knows where Moses was buried, but we know where he lived. . . . Today, everything is the other way around. We know where the graves are, but we live lives which are unfixed and unknown. We change, we shift, but the only thing we know is where the graves are."

Loneliness has been studied by scientists and mental health professionals. The results of their research reveal that "the physical and emotional consequences of loneliness pose greater dangers than anyone thought." Loneliness affects all ages. Adolescents appear to be more plagued by loneliness than anyone else. Old people—and this is remarkable—may be less so affected. Loneliness is experienced in rural as well as large metropolitan areas. It is not that people have become more isolated. On the contrary, electronic communication and jet transportation have made it possible to stay in closer contact than ever before. We need but dial a number to reach a loved one who is many miles away.

The breakdown of family life is revealed clearly by the 1980 census, which points out that almost one-fourth of our population live by themselves. A large number of people under forty have chosen not to marry or have never been asked to marry. Many of those who are alone are divorced, separated, or widowed. We have spoken and written about the unique situation of children in the single-parent home.

Tonight is not a study session in well-being. Tonight is an experience in trying to heal, "to bring balm to the daughter of our people." If it is true, as one scholar pointed out, that "the rise of human loneliness may be one of the most serious sources of disease in the 20th century," then we must do our share to strengthen the feeling of community. We are not merely a group of men and women who have associated themselves with a congregation, who feel comfortable in the pews of Anshe Emet listening to familiar voices chanting to us and speaking to us. We must understand and appreciate what a synagogue is. We must have the ability to reach out to each other, both in times of sickness and adversity, and in times of good health and prosperity. You surely remember the story of the rebbe and the hasid. When the rebbe asked the hasid how Moshe was getting along, he was answered, "I don't know." The rebbe responded, "You pray under the same roof, you serve the same God and yet you do not know whether Moshe is in good health, whether he needs help, advice or comforting?" We are banded together as people of truth. To live a life of truth is the very core of our purpose for being here on earth. We must learn to share and really care—not to talk about our concern, but to be really involved. These are not limp phrases; these are cries of the heart.

The idea of community is vital. The breakdown of community has occurred throughout our society. While there are those who hail the secular city where one can live alone and undisturbed, others are concerned that with the release from the linkage of family, faith, and friends we face destructive times. No one is alone when seeking and winning the fellowship of other human beings.

In his book *New Rules*, Yankelovitch, the famed pollster, talks about community. "The idea of community is precious to people. The idea of community invokes in the individual a feeling that here is where I belong, these are my people. I care for them, they care for me, I am part of them. I know what they expect from me and I from them. They are my concerns. I know this place, I am on familiar ground, I am at home."

When this congregation will be able to think in this spirit as a religious community, we will be carrying out our historic purpose. We will become a true community, unselfishly concerned with each other's tasks and needs, and freely expressing joy and friendship.

In the Torah (Leviticus 9:5), the dedication of the Sanctuary is described: "They brought to the front of the Tent of Meeting the things that Moses had commanded and the whole people came forward and stood before the Lord." The Hebrew word "came forward" is significant. It means "to come closer to one another." When the community learns to become closer to one another, then they stand before the Lord.

May closeness and a feeling of deep concern for fellow congregants be the hallmarks of this synagogue.

What Is Courage?

KOL NIDRE, 1981

These have been fast moving days since the assassination of Egyptian President Anwar Sadat earlier in the week. Robert Frost once said, "Courage is the highest virtue that counts most. Courage to act on limited knowledge and insufficient evidence— that is all any of us has, so we must have the courage to go ahead and act on a hunch. It is the best we can do."

Anwar Sadat was a man of courage. Like all human beings, he played many roles in the course of his career, some of them consistent and others contradictory. It took great courage to go to Jerusalem to start the peace process. I recall meeting with him in February 1978 together with a group of American Jewish religious leaders. He seemed to be a man of great dynamism who was determined to take history by the forelock and to change its course.

We need courage, we need internal fortitude. Some day there will be fulfilled the words of Isaiah, "In that day, Israel shall be a partner with Egypt and Assyria as a blessing on earth. For the Lord of Hosts will bless them saying, 'Blessed be my people Egypt, my handiwork Assyria and my very own Israel.' " The death of any human being diminishes me, but we live in faith in the One God who will some day recreate a united world.

I am concerned with trying to define and refine the mood of courage. An American writer said that courage is present in going into the unknown. There is a special type of courage that we as Jews need. When the President of the United States opens a barrage in his attempt to secure approval by the Senate and the House of the sale of billions of dollars' worth of arms to Saudi Arabia, a country that is determined to destroy the Jewish state, we need courage not to be afraid of responding.

In an important policy statement, the President lashed out, saying, "It is not the business of other nations to make American foreign policy." The members of the House and the Senate who are opposed to the sale of the AWACS planes are doing it out of concern for America and not in response to the prodding of another nation. While the President did not quite say "choose Reagan or Begin," there were, to use the phrase of the *New York Times* editorial, "repugnant implications" in his prepared statement. This is a hard ball game in which we are now caught up. As a senator, Carl Levin of Michigan, stated openly on the floor of the United States Senate, there are "nasty undertones."

Mr. Reagan's foray was joined a few days later by Richard M. Nixon who, in a bluntly-worded statement in support of the AWACS sale, said, "If it were not for the intense opposition of Prime Minister Begin of Israel and parts of the American Jewish community, the AWACS sale would go through." There is an orchestrated effort at intimidation. We are warned that opposing the President and the sale of AWACS will be harmful to the Jewish community. These statements have to be stood up against, refuted, and answered. This requires a great measure of courage. I can understand the President's involvement, but I am shocked at Mr. Nixon's comments—considering his background, with all the demerits against him. One wonders where he got the audacity to speak.

Like Isaac, we are being tested. During the struggle to establish an independent state, we were accused of dual loyalties. Justice

Brandeis refuted this nonsense. He wrote that American and Zionist ideals reinforce one another. "The men and women that we have lost in America's wars, our great contributions to science and industry, to business and labor, to education and the arts, testify to our faith in America." We serve notice that we will not go back to a sense of insecurity. We feel that the interests of Israel and America coincide on most occasions, but where they do not coincide and there is temporary strain, we look forward to a time of healing.

The highest morality in life is survival. "And you shall live by them." Only then can we be moral or immoral—even if our friends do not fully understand our motivation. Only people on the firing line, whose survival is threatened, have to insist on the first principle of morality—to survive, even if this causes a temporary breach of friendship. If we do not survive, we cannot be friends.

It takes courage to respond in a democracy like ours. One also needs courage to oppose a police state. I was reading some of the background material that will be presented at the end of October to the World Psychiatric Association. Russian dissidents—whether they be political, religious, or economic—are falsely diagnosed as being mentally ill and are placed in mental asylums. A Russian general, who has managed to come to the United States, wrote of his experience. "People like myself are declared insane in accordance with the elementary philistine logic: 'Can a general who opposes the government be sane?' "

There are other forms of courage. There is the courage of ordinary people who live out their lives in Israel, who go into marketplaces and have to make sure not to kick a tin can that may have explosive material within it. There are those who live on the northern border of Israel who are subjected to rockets coming from Lebanon. There is the remarkable courage of the Holocaust survivors who came to Israel in June, who submitted themselves to the reopening of wounds that had been healing since World War II. Elie Wiesel wrote at that time, "Everyone of us here is surrounded by invisible parents, vanished children, friends who left us behind to remember their names, their faces, their fears, their eyes." He asked, "Have we acted as true witnesses? It is with fear and trembling that we reach the conclusion something went wrong—for our testimony was not received. The world which surrounds us is filled with suspicion, violence, hatred and terror."

Heroes, courageous people, are different from celebrities. We confuse heroic with being famous. You don't have to be famous to be a hero, and being famous does not make a person heroic. People can be courageous morally, people can be brave physically, and people can be heroic intellectually. A person who responds in an unexpected emergency is a hero. Judge Benjamin Cardozo, while serving on the New York State Court of Appeals, wrote, "Danger invites rescue." Emergencies make us courageous. "Suddenly and without warning," Edmond Cahn said, "the rhythm a man is accustomed to in his daily life will break into a wild clang, like an alarm bell, beat out a frantic summons to action and then, just as quickly, subside to its normal tempo."

I remember my older brother and I walking along a country road on a farm. Suddenly a runaway team came in our direction. My brother threw his body over mine so that I might be protected from the horses' hooves. We find out who we are in moments of testing. We find out what kind of moral beings we are and whether we really feel for other persons who move about us. Milton Meyerhoff wrote that "Trust in the other to grow and in my own ability to care gives me courage to go into the unknown, but it is also true that without the courage to go into the unknown such trust would be impossible."

Courage means being the kind of person who does not run away when physical, moral, or intellectual bravery is called for. An instance that immediately comes to mind is the woman whose husband passes away and leaves her to raise young children by herself. This is a quiet, durable heroism that consists of facing up to whatever the world puts before us and refusing to give up. This is the courage of the ordinary. This is the courage that many a student of the Bible saw in the experience of Elijah. Elijah looked for God and then had a sublime experience—there was wind, earthquake, fire, and, finally, a still, small voice. The small voice of the courage of the ordinary is more powerful than the storm, earthquake, or fire.

It is good to end on a story. Jonah was sent on a mission. He turned to God and said, "You've made a mistake. I'm not courageous enough to go to Nineveh. I want to go to Tarshish, the other direction." Jonah's action was an act of defiance. He tried to flee "from before the Lord." While the sailors were crying, Jonah was trying to sleep in the innermost part of the ship. Jonah tries to run away, but, as this small book unfolds, God's pursuit is successful and Jonah is brought back. Jonah, who was afraid to speak God's word, becomes Jonah the speaker, Jonah the courageous one.

A great poet of our age has asked, "What is our innocence, what is our guilt? All are naked, none is safe and whence is courage?" That is what we must ask ourselves. How does one become heroic? What must we do to become the kind of durable people who do not give up? We must practice not giving up. We must try to achieve courageousness in all we do. If we can instill this in ourselves and transmit it to our children, we will produce generations of human beings who are "clear-headed" and "full-chested"; who will have the courage to talk back to princes and to presidents, to stand up to kings and ordinary people. In the language of tomorrow's Torah reading, we will be able to "stand alive before the Lord."

On this Kol Nidre night, on this Yom Kippur day, we hope that we will produce offspring who will be clear-headed and full-chested, who will have learned that only with courage—courage at times in battle, courage in political controversy, but, what is most important, courage of the ordinary—are we able to build the gratifying life. Generations to come will bless us for having realized here on earth, the true testing place of all, what it means to be courageous.

Never Despair

KOL NIDRE, 1980

The notes of Emanuel Ringelblum's diary depicted life in the Warsaw ghetto during the Nazi occupation. He mentions that "In the prayerhouse of the Hasidim from Bratslav, there is a large sign: 'Jews, never despair.' " There was more to this plaque which merits being repeated. Written both in Hebrew and in Yiddish, it spoke of a number of elements of life. As I hold Ringelblum's diary in my hands, I feel that "This is the law of the burnt offering" (Leviticus 6:2).

In an age like ours—which seems to hover on the brink of despair, where there is so much difficulty in both the private and public realms—it is good for us to listen to the words of Reb Nahman, the great Hasidic teacher of the end of the 18th century. He proclaimed, "Gevalt, do not despair." He went on, "There is no such thing as despair." He said these words with such resolve that he taught his followers and successive generations that one should never despair, regardless of how heavy a burden of life one must carry. The words he used were among the last statements he gave to his followers, for he died only a few months later. But, as his biographer Arthur Green describes him, "He died without again having fallen into the abyss of despair."

The example of his life has been an inspiration to the Hasidic community, which revered him. The Bratslaver Hasidim, who continue to this day, are known to the world as "Dead Hasidim." In all the Hasidic world, they were the sole group who did not seek a successor to their original master. This relationship between the memory of Reb Nahman and that of his disciples was a unique one. This man had suffered the anguish of a tormented career. His leadership was unappreciated outside his immediate circle. But he never committed himself to despair, he never permitted himself to give in.

Reb Nahman said other things. He spoke of joy. He spoke of it as a great commandment in which one must be engaged at all times. What is the meaning of joy? It is a mood into which one places oneself with all of one's being, with all of one's strength. There is always the danger, Reb Nahman said, of a person being sucked up into melancholy, being drawn into sadness because of the events of life. All of us have our share of affliction. All of us have our personal sorrows. All of us are buffeted by the conditions of the world. All of us are tormented by that which happens both privately and publicly. But Reb Nahman said, when he spoke of the world which is at times a vale of tears, "Yea, though I walk through the valley of the shadow of death, I fear no evil." We encounter evil, but we are not to fear it. He urged his followers to be joyous and content.

To be sure, Reb Nahman had a sense of joy. Those who have

studied his life describe his dancing. Reb Nahman's dancing was aimed, in one case, at trying to change the will of the czar in distant St. Petersburg. The czar had issued an evil decree against our people and Reb Nahman was trying to overturn it.

In Reb Nahman's approach to life, the goal of life is sacred joy. Can this sacred joy be achieved when there is so much suffering in this world? Reb Nahman said that the only authentic joy is that when people confront the dark side of life, they reach out to drag it into the orbit of joy. Simply, joy may be found in facing sadness. But there is a higher form of joy, which is depicted in a parable told by Israel Baal Shem Tov. When people are joyous, they grab a man from outside their dancing circle. They take one who is sad and force him to dance. What happens is that with joy that person, too, becomes happy and his own sadness stands off on the side. The sadness has been transformed. Grab hold of the suffering, force it to join you in rejoicing. Dance can become a weapon in the struggle against melancholy and depression.

Reb Nahman spoke of another important factor, and this was the element of *hitbodedut*. *Hitbodedut*, being in solitude, is not a new teaching in our ethical system. Being alone is one of our highest qualities. We are so caught up with other people that we fail to have time for ourselves and for the consideration of the needs of our own being. The *New York Times* (August 19, 1980) spoke of the fact that "Solitude Emerges as Blessing in Research on Adolescence." Solitude, whether it is the pain of loneliness or the pleasure of autonomy, plays an important role in adolescent life. Frequently, solitude enables teenagers to be more comfortable in dealing with others. Based upon a study of 75 student volunteers from high schools in Chicago, two psychologists found that youngsters spent more than a quarter of their waking hours by themselves. The students reported that they were in better spirits than when with others. While the research on the positive effects of solitude is still in the early stages, there are definite indications of how important being alone is in the lives of people.

Reb Nahman said, "When everyone is standing around me and I am seated in their midst, that is when I practice *hitbodedut*, the aloneness which is required for private conversation with God." Though he was in the midst of a crowd, he was able to commune with God. This lonesome act of *hitbodedut* was described as the most important activity of the master and his congregation. How else can one reach out for God? How else can one be close to the Almighty? This is a great goal for which people must search. "I have been told," Reb Nahman said, "that no person, however great or small, can do what he truly must except by means of *hitbodedut*. Though it may appear to you at first that no change is taking place in your life when you practice this aloneness with God, a person who has a regular life with God in this way is, over time, so transformed that a skilled observer may recognize it in him and distinguish him from others. Only patience and constancy will bring one to such reward."

Reb Nahman compared the effects of his practice of *hitbodedut*, aloneness, with the classic example of Rabbi Akiba, who related how there was a hard stone upon which drops of water fell until the stone had a hole bored into it. The heart of stone can be worn away by constant prayer. This claim—that the core of religion lies in the inner life of the individual—is unique, observers tell us, in the history of Judaism. *Hitbodedut* has been a Jewish philosophical theme for almost a thousand years, but the important thing is that religion, in one of its significant dimensions, is an inner aloneness with God. Humans pour out their personal being before the Almighty. For a people who have known the collective study of the tradition, for a folk who have been active in our way of life, this emphasis upon *hitbodedut*, upon private searching, represents a special dimension.

Reb Nahman said other things. "If you believe that people can upset, make trouble, believe too that what they have done can be repaired." There are problems and difficulties in life, but Reb Nahman said, simply but profoundly, "There is nothing so whole as a broken heart."

As a mystic, he believed that the ultimate truth in the universe is the oneness of God. It is hard to bring people to such an awareness, but the beginning of the road back to God is when one is prepared to stand in full confrontation with the mystery and loneliness of God himself.

Reb Nahman's statement, as recorded on the Warsaw plaque, ends with the powerful words, "Know that the world is like a narrow bridge and that man has to cross over that narrow bridge. But, what matters above all is not to be afraid as one walks over it." These words became the words of a popular Israeli song after the Yom Kippur War.

What was Reb Nahman trying to say in all these statements? He was trying to raise our sensitivity. He was trying to intensify the awareness of his followers. He was trying to teach us that through being alone, one can overcome some of the problems of life.

Reb Nahman spoke of the majesty and the beauty of each soul. Everything in God's world, whether it be a tree or a song or a blade of grass, proclaimed the oneness of God. Yes, God seemed to be absent, but it was one's duty to seek out His presence. People have to transcend the self; they have to search for God until the very last moment.

Reb Nahman was a great spiritual personality despite the fact that he was far from a satisfied individual. There is a message which his life can transmit to us. There are higher goals which he has placed before us. All too frequently we think that we cannot achieve more than we have in the past.

In the July issue of the *Smithsonian Magazine,* there was an interesting discussion of how sports scientists train athletes to defy old limits of achievement. They analyze the nervous system and the muscles. They use treadmills, test tubes, and computers. Researchers are trying to learn what it takes to break old records, how outer limits can be penetrated. What is possible in the physical world is possible in the world of the spirit. We do not have to be satisfied with what we have achieved. We must look for higher attainment.

Martin Buber wrote about the Hasidic way of life. The Hasidim tried to take people out of their moribund stage, they tried to get people to actualize themselves, to fulfill themselves, to see the total picture. Man, they cried, don't brood, don't talk about the limits of human performance, don't think that you can't be better in the year that is to come than in the year that has passed. The important thing to remember and to know is that man has to pass over a narrow bridge. It is very, very narrow, and the important rule, the essence, is: do not be afraid, you can do it. Man is not to be afraid as he walks over the bridge to the other side where great potentialities remain to be realized.

Tomorrow's Synagogue

YOM KIPPUR, 1979

"Jerusalem is a cradle city rocking me . . . I
am a Jerusalemite. The dust is my con-
scious, the stone my subconscious."
—Y. Amichai

Our service this day, and every day, is related to Jerusalem. At
the end of Neilah, we will conclude with the grand affirmation,
"Next year in Jerusalem."

If one goes to the Kotel, the Western Wall, one sees an interesting grotto. The grotto is not a natural one, but rather one built
into structures that are above it. This grotto was known a hundred years ago, when it was identified by the British archaeologist
Sir Charles Wilson. One can see the arch of the bridge that led
from the Temple Mount to the upper city. For many years, the
entrance to Wilson's Arch was sealed by small buildings that had
been added by the local residents. After the 1967 war, the buildings were removed so that the Western Wall might be seen in all its
grandeur and an entrance afforded once again to the site of
Wilson's Arch. In the midst of the arch area, there is an archaeological shaft cutting through many layers of historic development.
One goes down thousands of years in Jerusalem's history. Our
City of Eternity was built layer upon layer, one conqueror's destruction becoming the foundation stone for the next builder's
activity. "The stone which the builders rejected is become the
chief cornerstone."

As I hold my Mahzor in hand, I clutch a book that has been
examined and re-examined by the generations. On Yom Kippur, I
approach the Mahzor. It contains the story of the synagogue, the
account of Jewish worship throughout the centuries. Public
worship is part of humanity's spirit. Surely we can pray privately,
but when we pray with the many, there is a heightened experience. "In the abundance of people is the King's glory." Public
worship expresses the sanctity we feel in the bond of shared
humanity.

Where did our saga, our prayer begin? What is the lowest layer of our archaeological find? Surely it was Abraham and Isaac on Mount Moriah, just a few feet away from the archaeological shaft. The Mahzor recalls our ancestors praying in the desert. Freed from Egyptian bondage, they were commanded to build a tabernacle, a portable house of worship—portable, perhaps as a prefiguration of the fact that the Jew would be on the march throughout history. Not the wandering Jew of the hating myth-makers, but the victim of their distrust.

From worship in the desert tabernacle, our ancestors moved into the land of Israel. There they built a great temple in Jerusalem, the glory of all the earth. On Yom Kippur, there was a continuous worship of God. The highest moment during the long night and day was the *Avodah* service, when the high priest conducted the special ritual practiced only once during the year. "How glorious the Kohen Gadol emerging from the Holy of Holies. He was like the morning star appearing through the clouds, like the sun reflected on God's temple."

From that point of time, the first exile of our people began. It was then that the first synagogue was built. The history of the synagogue from that time on is well known to us. Before us, there flashes the memory of the Alexandrian synagogue, which was so huge that messages had to be sent from one end of the sanctuary to the other by the waving of flags so that people would know when to recite the word "Amen." We think of the synagogue of Toledo, Spain, now converted into a church called "El Transito." Its Hebrew inscriptions are still found along the fresco walls of the sanctuary. We think of the Altneuschul synagogue of Prague, the oldest synagogue built in the Gothic style. The Spanish Jews called the synagogue *Eshnogah*, "fire and light."

Our Mahzor reflects the synagogues of the Jews who lived through the Holocaust. They maintained the tradition of prayer during the most difficult era ever experienced by the Jewish people. No one could hold them back. The lash of the enemy, the threat of annihilation, did not prevent Jews continuing to worship. They worshipped in bunkers, they prayed in cellars, they met in underground tunnels, they prayed even in the sewers of the cities of German-occupied Europe. Though Jewish tradition says that one can only pray to God in a place that is clean, the impulse to pray was most compelling. The Germans decreed that there was to be no Jewish public worship, but Jews prayed from memory. They copied down the words of the Mahzor that they recalled, and passed them one to another.

One of the great rabbis who survived the experience of Auschwitz tells how he went from cell block to cell block with a shofar in hand. The danger was great, but he insisted upon carrying out the commandment of sounding the prescribed number of *Tekiot*. Rabbi Zevi Hirsch Meisels, in his classic responsa (questions and answers) that he recorded during the Holocaust period, told of one experience in which a group of 1,400 boys who had been condemned to be sent to the crematorium, were sequestered in one of the cell blocks. They learned that the rabbi had a shofar. They pleaded with him, "Rabbi, rabbi, come, for God's sake; have pity on us; let us hear the sound of the shofar in our last moments." The rabbi carried out their request though in great personal danger.

I think of the synagogues of the Bar Lev Line along the Suez Canal, in which the soldiers prayed on Yom Kippur Day, 1973 as they were being assaulted by a powerful Egyptian army equipped with the newest Soviet armaments. After the 1973 war, I was in the Golan Heights, where I saw a temporary army chapel. It was in a small building, and there was a simple reading stand supported by two munition boxes, one, manufactured by the United States Army, which had been used by the Israelis, and the other, bearing a Russian legend, which had been used by the Syrians. Our Sefer Torah, our Book of Peace, was read from this makeshift table.

This is the account of the synagogue of yesterday. But what of the synagogue of today, and what is its relevance to us in this hour? What direction must the synagogue take in the future? The synagogue of today must reflect our new needs.

A strange and paradoxical experience has happened to modern man. Great thinkers in American society placed an emphasis upon the individual, saying that "the individual is to be the bearer of civilization" (John Dewey). But the tremendous emphasis that we placed on the unique role of the unfettered individual has proven to be an empty promise. Our age is one that is marked by the loneliness of the individual. The individual feels the emptiness of the crowd. Most individuals are reaching out for warmth of others.

Some months ago, I was privileged to hear Rabbi Harold M.

Schulweis, one of the most distinguished rabbis on the American scene. He spoke before the Rabbinical Assembly Convention in Los Angeles. He described how this mood of the lonely individual affects even some of the best minds of our time. He quoted the most distinguished Orthodox rabbi in America, J. B. Soloveichik, noted for his rabbinic scholarship and mastery of philosophy. Soloveichik wrote, "I know that I am perplexed. . . . I am given to panic, I am utterly confused and ignorant. . . . I am lonely. Let me emphasize, however, that by stating that I am lonely I do not intend to convey to you the impression that I am alone. I, thank God, do enjoy the love and friendship of many. . . . I am lonely because I feel rejected, thrust away by everybody, not excluding my most intimate friends."

A number of writers have written in a similar vein. We have had the privilege of meeting Abraham Joshua Heschel. His words still ring from this pulpit which he graced on several occasions. The Jewish soul is unsatisfied. There is a famine in the land. The synagogue of today does not truly satisfy the needs of our people. The rabbis declared, "If a flame among the cedars fall, what avail the hyssop, the little lichen, on the wall?" (Mo'ed Katan 25b). If the great scholars of our people, the sensitive minds of Israel, bemoan our discomfort, what can we say of the concern of the individual Jew? If the shepherds are lonely, how do the sheep fare?

It is good to feel our individual being, but there are mighty personal problems that weigh heavily upon every Jew in this synagogue. There are limitations of career. Outer prosperity and inner emptiness bothers our people. Some have made it and remain unsatisfied. Others haven't made it and feel deficient. These individuals look to the synagogue for guidance and for warmth. The other day, Mrs. Cohen and I, on very short notice, flew down to Pittsburgh to attend the funeral of a former neighbor, the mother of six and grandmother of three, who had passed away at the age of 52. What do we do for our people, not during the day of the funeral or the week of the Shiva, but during the months of emptiness and the years of grieving?

A late medieval rabbi, Maharsha (1555-1631), pointed out that there are three types of relationships in the realm of human experience. There are laws between the individual and God. There are rules regulating the conduct between people. There is the relationship between individuals and themselves (Commentary on Baba Kamma 30a).

One of the realities that concerns us very deeply is what is happening to our young people and how they are being attracted to the various new secular religions that have cropped up in America. In our Kol Nidre liturgy, we use a special formula that says that we are permitted to pray with the *Abaryanim*, with those who have sinned. It also means with those who are missing, those who are not with us. We are permitted to pray for those who have missed the mark, and we miss them. So many of our young people are being attracted to these secular religions.

Walking down a main thoroughfare, a man came over to me with a pamphlet on scientology. He presented it with the force of a determined missionary. One reads of the various groups that function in our city: "The Inner Light," "Consciousness Experience," "The Moment of Enlightenment." There are many other such groups and they attract our young.

People want the synagogue to be a setting in which they can relate to other individuals. We are instructed in Proverbs that a man must unburden his heart. "If a person has care in his heart, let him speak it out to others, he should not keep it to himself" (Proverbs 12:25).

If I ask myself what should concern the synagogue of today and tomorrow, my answer would be to help feed the hungry and clothe the naked, both physically and emotionally. The hunger of our people these days is not for bread alone, but for a faith in God based upon the fellowship of humanity. The Jewish community has not mastered an ability of satiating this hunger. Our relationship with one another is superficial, it is skin-deep. Our compassion for one another is limited. We talk of the synagogue *Mishpacha*, but how much sharing of feeling do we really have, how close are we to one another at our various gatherings and assemblies, at our services?

Every era has its own problems, every individual is weighted down by anxieties, but we must learn to feel for other individuals. Reb Moshe Leib of Sasov learned to love men from a conversation between two peasants sitting in an inn, drinking. One said to the other: "Tell me, do you love me or don't you love me?" The other responded, "I love you very much." But the first replied: "You say that you love me, but you do not know what I need. If you really loved me, you would know."

Many Jews want to hear God's word, but they also want to hear the word of another Jew, a word of understanding, of feeling friendship. Most Jews, both within the synagogue walls and beyond, are not at ease with the institution we have built in this country. There is not enough meeting, there is not enough interaction, there is not enough fellowship. This is not a task for the rabbi alone. Please do not paint the guilt on the professionals, on my colleagues, on those who give full-time to Jewish service. It is a responsibility of each one of us.

The synagogue of today and tomorrow must find ways of satisfying the hunger of our people. It was wisely said that, "A Jew can best be defined by what hurts him." With Jeremiah of old we can cry, "Why has healing not yet come to my poor people?" Our responsibility is to help bind up our people's wounds. Our old will find warmth in the synagogue, our young people will find their strength. As we read in the Haftarah last week, our sons will return to our borders.

A great student of religion, Professor Mircea Eliade of our University of Chicago, spoke of his students and said, "They want unconsciously to find something meaningful but don't want to look in their own traditions." Then he offered the hope that some day these students and these young people will be led back to find a place for themselves within their own religions.

To demonstrate his point, Professor Eliade related a Hasidic tale that in Cracow, a rabbi dreamed several times that an angel told him to go to a distant city where he would find a treasure in front of the palace. When the rabbi arrived at the distant city, he told his story to a soldier who caught him digging. The sentinel told the rabbi that he, too, had had a dream in which he was told to go to the rabbi's house in Cracow where there was a treasure buried in front of the fireplace. The rabbi went home, dug up his fireplace, and found the treasure. Professor Eliade said that this means that the spiritual treasure is there with you, in the heart, but you have to go somewhere else, to another teacher outside your tradition, to find the treasure. To find yourself, you must go to a stranger.

This is where the professor ended his talk. We add this thought:

Our sons and daughters will return, they will seek the fellowship of the synagogue when it is a fount of meaning, an institution that cares, a place that vibrates with concern, that bears a message of faith and hope.

The Caring Heart

KOL NIDRE, 1983

When was Jonah called to his ministry as a prophet, when was he told that he would have to be the messenger of God's word? An old tradition has it that Jonah's call occurred on the second day of Sukkot. In a rarely cited text in the Jerusalem Talmud, we read that "Jonah was among the pilgrims who came to Jerusalem. He was partaking in the joy of the celebration of the water libation (the pouring of the water) when the Holy Spirit came upon him." While this legend had Jonah called into service on Sukkot—in a time of joy, in an hour of abundance, thanksgiving, and celebration—tradition is that we read the Book of Jonah, not in acknowledgment of affluence, but rather in a mood of austerity—when we are fasting, when we are hungry, when our head is logy from an almost 24-hour-long abstinence from food, drink, and earthly pleasures.

What was the change in practice trying to tell us? You can only feel for your fellow human beings when you stand in their shoes. Do not judge them until you are in their place. You can only feel for your fellow human beings, appreciate their hunger, their deprivation, when you yourself are hungry. That is why on Atonement Day we read from Isaiah that we are to share our bread with the starving.

Many points are motifs of instruction on this day, but we are summoned essentially to our responsibilities as moral and sensitive human beings. This is a day of instruction, this is a day of education, this is a day of morality and character building.

During this last year, there have been a number of important studies dealing with significant aspects of American education. Last April, a monumental report was addressed as an "Open Letter to the American People." Called "A Nation at Risk," it was a report to the nation and the Secretary of Education by the National Commission on Excellence in Education. A moment ago, I mentioned that this was a day of moral sensitivity. But as I read the report and similar studies, and as I read the many efforts to define the problems facing American education and to provide solutions, the one element I missed was the element this day attempts to teach: how to feel for your fellow human beings, how to develop sensitivity and moral concern.

In a rather long report, there is a brief message to parents and teachers: "Help your children understand that excellence in education cannot be achieved without intellectual and moral integrity coupled by hard work and commitment. Children will look to their parents and teachers as models of such virtues." As far as I am concerned, this is far from being enough. The critical point lacking in that understanding of our society is to be found in the moral dimension. The seeds of discontent with American education were not, as has been observed, "sown in academia." This counter-revolution sprang from a dissatisfaction among the people generally—parents who saw that their children, after being exposed to eight to ten years of basic education, still could not read or write or do simple sums.

The basic thrust of the report "A Nation at Risk" is this: "Our once-unchallenged pre-eminence in commerce, industry, science, and technological innovation is being overtaken by competitors throughout the world. This report is concerned with one of the many causes and dimensions of the problems, but it is the one that undergirds American prosperity, security, and civility. The risk is that history is not kind to idlers. The time is long past when America's destiny was assured simply by an abundance of natural resources and inexhaustible human enthusiasm." The burden of this approach seems to be that it is the pragmatic thing that we have good schools. Unless we have good schools, we cannot have an affluent society.

This worry about the fact that the educational foundations of our society are being eroded by a rising tide of mediocrity that threatens our very future as a nation and as a people concerns me. I care that, "If an unfriendly foreign power had attempted to impose on America the mediocre educational performance that exists today, we might well have viewed it as an act of war." But there is more to life. And *that* is the message of Yom Kippur: life is measured in a spiritual and ethical dimension.

I studied a document on higher education by a professor of the University of Chicago. He wrote about the effects of the music to which our youngsters listen. "There is now one culture for every-one, in music as in language. It is a music that moves the young powerfully and immediately. Its beat goes to the depth of their souls and inarticulately expresses their inarticulate longings." The professor was not happy with the rock music that is so much a part of our time. Its success was the result of an amazing cooperation between lust, art, and commercial shrewdness. With-out parents realizing it, their children were liberated from them. Professor Allan Bloom begins with this powerful statement: "Stu-dents in our best universities do not believe in anything, and those universities are doing nothing about it, nor can they." He goes on to speak of the new language of our time, which subtly injects into our system the perspective of "do your own thing" as the only plausible way of life.

American education needs training for character. But are our universities capable of transmitting an ethical message? Let me cite a few examples, culled from the reading of the last year.

I am concerned with business ethics. I have lectured and published on that theme over the last twenty years or so of my ministry here at Anshe Emet. Among the many volumes in my library on this and other moral issues is a fine study called *Beyond the Ivory Tower.* It deals with the social responsibilities of the modern university, and contains the statement, "This book is the first to examine in detail the university's many ethical and social responsibilities." Listen to the topics that are treated: "The Moral Development of Students," "The Social Responsibilities of Research," "Accepting Gifts." That is the statement. But what is the reality?

I was surprised to read in *Newsweek* of June 6 of this year how that very same university, whose president gave so magnificent a statement on social, moral, and ethical development, sponsored a conference on "Video Games and Human Development." There are some who are concerned about these video games. I am concerned as a grandparent, as a parent, as a teacher. While the games are helpful in some instances, they stir up other youngsters with negative results. The most startling statement in the article was made by a university official, the librarian, who said that while the video-game manufacturer had suggested the symposium and paid $40,000 to finance it, the absence of any antigames spokesperson was completely coincidental. *Newsweek* went on to observe that, unfortunately, the one-sidedness of the conference served to undermine the credibility of many worthy observations proffered by researchers who admit that we are just beginning to understand the effects of video games on the human psyche. In the closing hours, the panelists even broached the sensitive question of how poor children will be able to compete with wealthier children whose parents own Apple IIs. "Is this going to be a tool to divide the poor from the rich?" wondered an author and educator. But perhaps the most provocative question of the day that could not be erased was the feeling in some observers' minds that they had just spent several days playing someone else's game.

Can we expect our young people to take us seriously when our ethical mode of behavior does not meet the standards we write about, discuss, and are allegedly concerned with?

Another interesting episode occurred towards the end of July. A Nebraska engineering student was troubled. Many universities now offer courses on a profession and its ethical dilemmas. In my library, I have books on education and ethical questions, law and ethical questions, medicine and ethical questions. While this engineering student's textbooks mentioned bid-rigging, his courses taught little about this time-honored crime which is, unfortunately, found in many industries. A lawyer friend happened to be representing a company convicted of manipulating bids for state highway contracts. They spoke, and the result was creativity in the court. Instead of paying a simple fine, the lawyer proposed that the company be made to endow a chair of ethics at the University of Nebraska. The judge liked the idea. The cost of the chair was $1,500,000. The outcome was imaginative and, as one witty observer said, "certainly constructive." The magnitude of the fine in Nebraska made it a welcome gift. But should it go to a university? And who authorized the judge to decide? In the

Catholic Church in the Middle Ages there were what we call indulgences. A person could commit a crime, and all he or she had to do was to make a contribution to the papacy and the crime was absolved. One of the reasons why Martin Luther—whose 500th birthday occurs this year—was so indignant about the practice was that it was not moral. He forced a religious reformation in his church.

There is a drive in some quarters to bring values of education into our schools. It comes in an hour when society is faced with a breakdown of traditional values, when cultural and racial conflict are rampant and there is an increasing distrust of our political and social institutions. The schools should play a role in helping our young people clarify their values and make moral and ethical decisions. Permit me to cite one instance why I believe our young people are disenchanted with what is happening in the highest places in our land, in our schools, in our universities, and even in our national administration.

I read an editorial in the *Wall Street Journal* some weeks ago. You remember that we have been dealing in the last few months with the question of whether or not the President of the United States was privy to the briefing book of his opponent, Jimmy Carter. The editorial I read and that sent me for a loop was called "Ethicsgate." It began: "We are going to have to kill ethics before ethics kills us." Taken at first hand—and one must take the first line of any editorial at first hand—means that our society must give up all the great moral and ethical teachings that have developed over thousands of years of human experience. The editorial writer continues, "We came to this conclusion sometime in the last few weeks, though we're not sure of the precise moment." He cites, for example, the difficult findings of Seymour Hersh in his study of Henry Kissinger. Later, this is what we are told ought to be the proper way: "The point is that there's a kind of ethical absolutism that no human and no human institution can sustain. It's not necessary to abandon ethics to recognize that the real world will always be full of cut corners and uneasy compromises. If you set out to destroy a person or cripple an institution by dredging up every possible ethical question, you will always be able to find ammunition." And then the denouement. "At some point the untrammeled pursuit of virtue becomes irresponsible, even if it is not tinged with hypocrisy, as it so often is. We have developed the habit of unleashing moral absolutism to devour anyone who reaches the public spotlight. Then we wonder why the best men and women are not found in public life, why those you do find there are often curious personalities with a moth-like attraction to the flame."

To the editor of the *Wall Street Journal*, to those who think that we can atone for business sins by buying chairs at universities, to those who forget at a university conference to invite both sides to a dispute, I can but say: this is what Yom Kippur is all about—to bring into being a society in which the forge of ethics is hammered upon in such a way that the finest types of human beings emerge from our educational and religious experience. Socrates once said, "As long as I have breath and strength I will not give up . . . exhorting you and declaring the truth to everyone whom I meet, saying 'My good friend, you are a citizen of Athens, a city which is very famous for wisdom and power—are you not ashamed of caring so much for the making of money, for fame and prestige, when you neither think nor care about wisdom, truth, and the improvement of your soul?' " Socrates reproached those who undervalued the most valuable things and overvalued those that are less valuable.

We remember what Isaiah said: "Wherefore do you spend money for that which is not bread (for that which gives no satisfaction) and your gain for that which satisfies not."

The Restoration of Trust

SHABBAT HAGADOL, 1979

"And he shall turn the heart of the fathers
to the children and the heart of the children
to their fathers. . . . Behold, I will send you
Elijah the prophet before the coming of the
great, awesome day of the Lord."

Malachi 3:23,24

"The Department of Housing and Urban
Development has installed four gold-lettered
security doors. . . . They are useless because
HUD refuses to keep them closed and man
them with a full-time guard."

Chicago Tribune

Today is known as the great Sabbath. We read from the prophet
Malachi, "Lo, I will send the prophet Elijah to you before the
coming of the great, awesome day of the Lord. Elijah will reconcile
the generations. Parents will be reunited with children, children
will be rejoined in spirit with their elders."

This verse occurred to me as I was reading an unpleasant
article in a national magazine. Written by its editor, Richard
Reeves, it stressed the fact that America lives in an atmosphere of
fear. America's new motto is: "In surveillance devices we trust, we
do not trust in persons." The great day of the Lord will come when
there will be a restoration of trust and a feeling of mutuality, when
heart will speak to heart in a loving way, when people will trust
each other. The relationship of trust will be dramatized by the end
of conflict between the generations.

I have found it unpleasant to travel by air these days. Perhaps
the bias goes back to an experience I had. Two days after Purim,
1973, I was in the hospital getting a checkup. During the night,
my father passed away. At about 7:30 a.m., I was advised by my

attending physician that dad had passed away and that I had half an hour to get dressed. My family would meet me downstairs and we would make the 9:00 a.m. plane to New York. Fighting through the traffic, we got to the airport a minute or two before departure time. I simply couldn't get through the surveillance device. It kept ringing and I kept pulling out all kinds of things. Finally, I was taken into a corner, frisked, and then, as my son-in-law held the door to prevent the plane from leaving, was allowed to board. What do you suppose was the conclusion of the security guard? The answer came in his final question, "Do you have any cards?" The little metal tape on a plastic card had caused all the trouble.

I heard recently of three small boys, all under the age of twelve, being lined up against the wall at an airport in New Orleans. They spoke little English; their mother tongue was French. Finally, the eldest understood that the security guard wanted one of them to turn over a plastic flashlight that was shaped like a gun. The pilot, coming through at the same time, asked the guard, "Aren't you overreacting?" The guard said, "We've got our rules." The visitor coming to our country would be stunned by the number of starry-eyed men and women in various shades of police uniforms. A Southern newspaper closes its gates every night at 6:00 p.m. There is barbed wire around the tennis courts in Tucson, Arizona. One could go on and on.

Let me tell you another story, about an incident that happened to me in Chicago. This is from a letter—which, incidentally, still has not been answered—to a downtown department store. "May I make a modest suggestion to you for the improvement of the State Street store. . . . Yesterday, having finished a meeting at the Dirksen Building, my eye was attracted to a piece of luggage. As I was leaving for overseas in about a week, I needed another piece. Your store would not accept the credit cards I had and said that I could write a personal check provided that I could give two pieces of identification, preferably a driver's license and a recognized credit card. Upon producing my driver's license—which I carry next to my identification as Fire Chaplain of the City of Chicago and which is as big as the moon in size—I gave the sales person two identification cards. Before the transaction was completed, I was asked, quite politely, to do something which I have never experienced in a store before. I was asked for a fingerprint. I can understand that stores are ripped off, but after the presentation of two modes of identification—for a super sale of $14.95—is fingerprinting in the best interest of good community relations?" What has happened to our country? Why do we need books on *Managing Employee Honesty*? Part of the answer lies in the fact that religion has lost its discipline. Peer pressure, the pointing fingers of the community are gone. We are mobile and alone. So the land is full this springtime, not with the song of the dove, but with the cacophony of former FBI agents and fear hucksters who are promoting plastic identification cards, lie detectors, and one-way mirrors. They hope they can accomplish the same end as the moral law of the Bible. We are mistaken to think that we cannot trust our fellow human beings. It is faulty to believe, as some security people believe, that our country is in such a state of moral decay that the only thing that can save us is to increase our security precautions.

I read a touching story about an Air Force sergeant named Chamberlain. The 21-year-old son of an IBM security officer was driving in New Mexico. He was out of gas and out of cash; all he had was some checks from an out-of-state bank. No less than three banks and six pumping stations and stores refused to cash a small check. The young man slept in his car, the temperature dropped to six degrees below zero, and frostbite set in. A week later, both of his feet were amputated.

We need a trusting heart. We need to reconcile the generations and to restore our faith in our fellow human beings. We can do this in a host of ways, but essentially it must be done through religious faith and moral education. This, I think, is intended in the message that Elijah will bring.

Sabbath of a Great Man

SHABBAT HAGADOL, 1985

This Sabbath is our Great Sabbath, which comes on the eve of Passover. This Sabbath might be poetically called "the Sabbath of a Great Man."

Our festive joy has been diminished by the death of Marc

Chagall, who was born some 97 years ago in Vitebsk, a small city in Byelorussia. Vitebsk was a typical Russian city for its size. It was in the Pale of Settlement, a limited land area in which Russian Jews could live. Chagall was the most distinguished person to come from that place. There is a lovely gouache featuring a Chagall flight of fancy called "Night over Vitebsk." The central figure is a man in typical East European garb. When Chagall was born, Vitebsk had a population of about 65,000, of whom 35,000 were Jews. The Jewish community was going through the throes of change. It was a time of religious upheaval and revolutionary manifestations. In a family photograph, Chagall and his kinfolk are wearing Western dress and their heads are uncovered. One can feel that the artist—who is by nature antinomian, opposed to the rigidities of the law—was struggling to break loose.

One is reminded of one of the most majestic sections in our Bible, which Chagall loved to illustrate. King Balak was frightened by the hordes of Israelites moving towards the Promised Land. He sent for a seer by the name of Balaam and commissioned him to curse the encamped Israelites. Balaam was so impressed by the tents of our ancestors that he used a phrase that is the opening prayer of our prayer service, "How goodly are your tents, O Jacob, your dwelling places, O Israel." Among Balaam's words of tribute was, "There shall step forward a star out of Jacob."

Chagall was a true star in the full sense of the word. For seventy-five years, he dominated the artistic scene. Being so close to Passover, when we sing the final song of the Haggadah, we think of the many works of Chagall, which had as his signature not only his name but also a little kid somewhere in the creation—whether it be a mosaic for the First National Bank in Chicago or the mosaics and tapestries for the Knesset, the Biblical paintings in the Museum of Nice, the stained-glass windows of the United Nations building, or the stained-glass windows for Hadassah Hospital in Jerusalem. All of them show the strong influence of his youth in Vitebsk. Our own day school has graced the Cummings Gallery with the permanent exhibit of the lithographs of the Chagall Jerusalem windows.

We are reminded that the theme of the Jew as being a "fiddler on the roof" appears in several of Chagall's paintings. "The Wedding" is one of them. In the permanent collection of the Museum of Modern Art in New York and in the private collection of Joseph Randall Shapiro—parts of which are now on exhibit in the Chicago Art Institute—one can find this motif of the fiddler repeated.

Chagall was an identified Jew. Though he did not believe in ritual, his themes are infused with Jewishness. In a gouache entitled "The White Crucifixion," painted in 1938, one finds Jesus as a Jew, wearing a tallit about his torso, with Hebrew on the cross. There are refugees in small boats surrounding the Jesus figure. A Jew is fleeing with his possessions in a sack. There is a brown-shirted stormtrooper before the Ark. Flames issue forth. One can feel the shrieks of the dying and the horror of death. In a similar painting called "The Martyr," done in 1940, there is a fiddler near the figure of Jesus, as well as a goat and a typical burning village of Eastern Europe.

We are justifiably proud of Chagall, the star that stepped forward out of Jacob. He was forced to leave Vitebsk by the change in circumstances wrought by the Soviet Revolution. Chagall lived in America as a wartime refugee from 1941 to 1948. Some members of our congregation were personal acquaintances of his. Among them is the gifted poet Selwyn Schwartz, who spent considerable time with Chagall while he lived in New York. Schwartz published a creative poem in *Poetry Magazine* entitled simply, "Marc Chagall." I quote some of the lines that touched me deeply:

> See, the sound of yellow
> is a season of
> incendiarism. A blaze taller
> than leaves, and genesis impales
> martyrdom in the utlimate eye.

> See, the fish with the leaping violins
> invades the childhood's
> continent. . . .

> See, the ordained clock
> upon the cheek of its village. . . .

> And here,
> the moon renews the kiss of the evening . . .

the third eye blooms a historic tear.
This is Vitebsk's fever, indelible color,
the flawless purple of
grandfather's caftan.

After the seven years of refuge in America, Chagall returned to southern France. There he went on with his creativity until his death. At the final burial service, there was no religious expression save for the reciting of the Kaddish by one of his friends. Incidentally, this was similar to the funeral of the late Supreme Court Justice Felix Frankfurter. There, too, a devout Jew, Professor Louis Henkin, a former law clerk and now a professor at Columbia University, recited the Kaddish.

This is the season of promise and fulfillment. Chagall represented both. The road from Vitebsk to the French town of Vence was marked with much light—shed by his star.

Shabbat Hagadol

THE DAY OF THE LORD
1982

"Lo, I will send the prophet Elijah to you before the coming of the awesome, fearful day of the Lord. He shall reconcile fathers with sons and sons with their fathers."

Malachi 3:23

Elijah the prophet plays a major role in our Passover celebration. On the Sabbath immediately preceding our Festival of Liberation, we observe Shabbat Hagadol, the Great Sabbath.

Elijah is among the most popular figures in Jewish folklore. In the prophetic reading, there is reference to the special task of Elijah as the forerunner of the Messiah. Passover is the festival of ultimate Messianic redemption. In Nisan, our ancestors were redeemed from Egyptian bondage, and in Nisan the Redeemer will come at some future time. It was said that when the Lord brought Israel up from Egypt, it was through Moses the prophet. "By a prophet they were guarded" (Hosea 12:14). Moses was the first prophet. Elijah, who guarded them, was the second. As Moses redeemed our people in ancient times, so Elijah will help activate the process of redemption in the future. On Elijah's flight to Mount Horeb, he had little to eat or drink. The angel of the Lord touched him and said, " 'Arise and eat or the journey will be too much for you.' He arose and ate and drank. And with the strength from the meal he walked forty days and forty nights, as far as the Mountain of God at Horeb" (First Kings 19:8). This recalls to us the experience of Moses, who likewise lived without food and drink for forty days and forty nights.

Elijah comes to grace our Seder table. The cup of Elijah, which is filled to the brim, is a custom with many different origins. The imagery of Elijah is unique. A fiery chariot with fiery horses suddenly appeared as he was speaking to his disciple Elisha, and Elijah went up into heaven in a whirlwind. Tradition has it that he lives on in heaven but functions here on earth. Elijah has been described as *perpetu um mobile,* constantly in motion. He never rests or is silent. He is always taking up the cause of the afflicted and serving as the advocate of the oppressed. He does continuous acts of loving kindness, particularly for the righteous and the wholehearted.

It is interesting that Elijah is called "Elijah the Tishbite" or "Elijah the Gileadite." He has no family name, and no name is given for his father. He is known only by his personal name of Elijah. Elijah comes into the Jewish family observance at the very time we introduce a young boy into the covenant of Abraham, our father. He is present at every circumcision; he is the angel of the Covenant. He sits in a special chair. If one goes to some of the old synagogues of Jerusalem, one can see the chair of Elijah present.

Battler for Justice

When King Ahab put Naboth to death on trumped-up charges and took possession of his vineyard, Elijah, at the command of

God, confronted the king. In words that sear like fire, in one of the great statements of a demand for justice, the prophet said, "Thus said the Lord: Would you murder and take possession?"

Elijah was an unusual individual. He wore some kind of animal skin about him. When King Ahaziah's messengers were asked the question, "What sort of man was it who came towards you and prophesied things?" the messengers replied, "A hairy man with a leather belt tied around his waist" (II Kings 1:8).

Battler for God

In the great struggle with the pagan princes of Baal, it was Elijah who finally emerged victorious. Though vastly outnumbered, he was able to hold his own; for being together with God he became a majority. When the people heard the prayer, "O Lord, God of Abraham, Isaac, and Jacob, let it be known today that You are God in Israel and I am your servant," they acknowledged their belief in God and cried out, "The Lord alone is God, the Lord alone is God." If we look at our liturgical order of the year, this very statement is repeated seven times at the end of our Neilah service on Yom Kippur. I have the feeling that this particular verse, tied in with the recitation, with the Shema and the words, "Blessed be the name of His glorious Kingdom for ever and ever," was a statement of affirmation that the Messiah was about to come. In our prayerbook, we have a number of prayers with a Messianic implication in their recitation. This statement, "The Lord alone is God," I believe is one of them.

The Lonely Prophet

Professor Abraham Joshua Heschel wrote on the question of solitude, or of being alone. Very aptly, in his unique style, he asked, "Is not solitude a state needed to both imagination and contemplation?" Elijah lived alone. At times he lived on Mount Carmel, at times, on Mount Sinai. On another occasion, he lived on top of a hill. At times he was fed by the ravens. It was Elijah who heard the thunder and lightning and then the still small voice of God. The man of solitude, one of the ten men who are called "Man of God," Elijah was a lonely figure. Save for a limited circle of followers, he functioned almost by himself.

Elijah and Our Liturgy

In the liturgical expressions of our people, Elijah is remembered in the grace after meals. We ask that Elijah, may he be remembered for good, be sent to us by the All-Merciful One. We recall him in the blessings after the Haftarah. We remember him in the Havdalah service. We think of him at the Seder. We remember him on Rosh Hashanah and on Yom Kippur. Each of the holidays of the year, the students of our liturgy point out, have special prayers devoted to Elijah.

Elijah, the Harbinger of Peace

The most important assignment of Elijah is to be an instrument of peace, the great reconciler. The sages say, concerning Elijah, that his most important role is to bring peace and harmony in the world. They cite the words of the Haftarah for Shabbat Hagadol, "Lo, I will send the prophet Elijah to you before the coming of the awesome, fearful day of the Lord. He shall reconcile fathers with sons and sons with their fathers." This is not a simple task. Anyone who has witnessed interfamilial controversy knows how hard it is to put the pieces of a family that has been torn asunder together again.

Elijah's responsibility is that of serving as the forerunner of the Messiah. Peace must begin in the hearts of individuals. It can only be realized in the amicable relationship between members of the same family. Only when family unity is restored, only when parents and children are reunited and reconciled, can there be the beginnings of peace in this world.

Maimonides, in his classic commentary on the Mishna, speaks of that which destroys peace, and he attributes the breakdown of peace to the unrighteous and perverse act of causeless hate. The prophet Malachi had asked, "Have we not all one father? Did not one God create us? Why do we break faith with one another?" The prophet was speaking about the breakdown of faith and trust between members of the community. Elijah will come to heal the breach between people, to remove causeless hate. Peace can only be realized when the members of the community trust one another, when men and women respect each other.

There is a need for family peace. There is a need for community harmony. A third explanation was given by a rabbi who commented upon Maimonides, the Rabad of Posquieres. He explained that Elijah's task in bringing peace to the world meant bringing peace between Israel and the nations of the world. We who live in an era where the people of Israel, both in Israel and abroad, live in so isolated a condition, understand what this means. When there will be peace between Israel and the nations of the world, then the Messiah will come.

This is Elijah's duty—to clear the way for the great day of total peace. May it come in our children's time if not in our own.

Me or We

PASSOVER, 1985

It is a lovely custom of our people to make extensive preparations for Passover. It is not only the cleansing of the house that is important. Passover is a time to cleanse our souls. The cleansing of our souls means to take a fresh look, another perspective of life; to find out what is wheat, which can sustain us, and what is chaff, which is of limited value.

We prepare for the Seder by reading the Haggadah. It is a little book but a most meaningful one. The custom is that on Shabbat Hagadol, the Great Sabbath, we read to its midway point. Over the years, one line in particular has engaged my attention. There is mention of four children: one who is wise, one who is wicked, one who is simple, and one who does not know what to ask. About the first child there is a lot to say, but blessed are the parents who have good children. They are the greatest joy in life. The second child, the wicked youngster, concerns me. He asks, "What does this ritual mean to you?"—to "you" and not to "him." He removes himself from the community. This act is regarded as a denial of God's role in the Exodus. Our new Rabbinical Assembly Haggadah says, "Shake him up." Tell him, talk to him, explain how important it is to remember the community and to recall our share in the experience of redemption.

A few months ago, a distinguished physician in our city was testifying before a Senate committee. Senator Richard Lugar, who is the new chairman of the Senate Foreign Relations Committee, said, "Doctor, I disagree with what you have said about the President's statement during the campaign. I chastise you for having objected to the words, 'Are *you* better off than you were four years ago?' " I do not wish to engage in partisan politics, it is neither my predilection nor my forte. However, the physician's answer was interesting. He said, "Instead of the President saying, 'Are you better off than you were four years ago?' he should have asked, 'Are *we* better off than *we* were four years ago?' " What is the difference between "I" and "we"? The difference is that stressing the word "you" in the singular helps to strengthen the position of those who believe in the importance of "What's in it for me?" and not "Is the community in a better condition than it was in 1980?"

This stress on individualism has been studied over and over again. Our libraries are full of books concerned with individualism understood simply as "selfishness." A new study by five sociologists called *Habits of the Heart* speaks of what has been happening to the American people. The phrase "habits of the heart" was first used by Alexis de Tocqueville in his classic *Democracy in America,* published 150 years ago. Since the time de Tocqueville made his observation that Americans are highly individualistic, we have had other writers who have dealt with this same subject. De Tocqueville spoke of American individualism as being a mixture of adoration and anxiety. With each individual constituting his or her own moral universe, we find that our value system represents no more than the arbitrary preferences of each individual personality.

A recurring theme in contemporary literature is the isolation of individuals in our complex society. By stressing our individualism, by being addressed by a President who asks, "Are you better off than you were four years ago?" we find ourselves isolated both spiritually and emotionally from the community. We appreciate the role of the individual in Jewish life; we stress individual dignity. However, when a person becomes overly concerned and preoccupied with the self, we end up with a narcissistic situation. No single soul alone can satisfy his or her total aspirations. We are social beings. Our deepest fulfillment comes from our continued service within the framework of the broader community. We remember the statement of Raba, a 4th-century master, who quoted the popular proverb, "Either a companion or death."

We need a community to fulfill ourselves. The philosopher Aristotle once said, "Without friends, no one would choose to live though he had all other goods." It is true that we cannot depend completely on other human beings, however dear. We meet all of life's greatest tests alone. But we have to have the broader framework of the communty to help fulfill our individual destiny.

A community is important. You remember the Hasidic tale of a master who asked the Holy One to show him heaven and hell. In hell, he saw persons who could not bend their arms. Though surrounded by the most lavish and tasty of foods, they were starving because their arms did not permit them to place the food in their mouths. In heaven, people had the same unbending arms, yet each was well fed because they all fed each other. There is much sense to this account. If we devote ourselves only to our own needs, we are left empty and unsatisfied, but when we care for the needs of others we are satisfied and fulfilled.

We cannot join the "me generation." There is a great deal of truth in the focus on the rights of the individual. An individual is created in God's image and is sacred. But God put us into communities, and among these the community of the Jewish people is central. A community can be of help to us. It can galvanize our energies, it can permit us to mobilize our capacities for the common well-being. Many people choose to be moral loners. They make decisions about the lives of others that are based on a "privatist" ethic. The basic doctrine of the privatist ethic is: In the end you are really alone and you really have to answer for yourself.

In the study *Habits of the Heart* that I mentioned earlier, five scholars joined together in producing a study on individualism and commitment in American life. They believe in equality, but aver that individualism has damaged community life. The authors interviewed and studied 200 people ranging from blue-collar persons to therapists and community organizers, and reprinted some of the responses on growing up, worshiping, and politicking. The burden of this learned team is that the values of Americans have become increasingly individualistic, with self-satisfaction the prime element. "Individualism lies at the very core of American culture. As we have been suggesting repeatedly in this book, some of the deepest problems both as individuals and as a society are also closely linked to our individualism. We do not argue that Americans should abandon individualism—that would mean for us to abandon our deepest identity. But individualism has come to mean so many things and to contain such contradictions and paradoxes that even to defend it requires that we analyze it critically." This work is an attempt to reveal the inner understanding of Americans as a nation, as a people. The study explores the traditions Americans use to make sense of themselves and the society in which we live. Our authors demonstrate how our fierce individualism, while creating self-reliant heroes, also undermines our capacity for commitment to one another.

When we attempt to utilize a privatist ethic as our chief device for self-fulfillment, we are bound to fail, and we cut ourselves off from other men and women in making our decisions. We convert the knife—an otherwise useful tool—into a dangerous weapon. It is difficult to draw the balance between our private attachments and our public involvement. In an age when we are more and more dependent upon one another than ever before in the history of humankind, we must guard against being trapped in a posture of individualism. It is not good to be a moral loner. It is not good to ask, "What is this ritual to you? the community to me?" May we always have the strength to realize that in the shared friendship of others we find our strength, even in the most despairing of hours.

You Have to Feel Free

PASSOVER, 1982

We are grateful to God for taking us out of Egyptian slavery and permitting us to enjoy everlasting freedom. The key mood of *herut*, freedom, must be felt during the Seder. *Herut* is a mood of liberty. Even if a person drank the four cups of wine prescribed for the Seder service but did not feel free, he or she has not carried out the purpose of the Passover.

What does *herut* mean? It has both a negative and a positive meaning. To be free from another's mastery, from another's bondage. To carry out one's own free will. As a fine scholar explained, freedom means the ability to keep your own calendar, to master your own time. Jews had an experience of freedom while still in Egyptian bondage. They were told by God to observe two commandments. The first was to have a calendar of their own. "This month shall mark for you the beginning of months. It (Nisan) should be the first of the months for you." And, in a land where sheep and rams were worshipped, the Hebrew slaves were told to slaughter a paschal lamb before the very eyes of their oppressors. Several years ago, I visited the Temple of Karnak in Luxor, Egypt, and saw parallel rows of sphinxes with rams' heads that were worshipped by the Egyptians.

Herut is essentially a state of mind. The opposite of *herut* is slavery, *avdut*. Don Isaac Abrabanel, the scion of a famous Spanish family, served as one of the leaders of both Spain and Portugal prior to the Spanish expulsion in 1492. Despite the great service that he had given to his native land, he was driven, as were all of Spanish Jewry, into exile. In a famous commentary, *Zevah Pesah*, he noted that he felt the mood of freedom, for it is a matter of a person's inner spirit. Centuries later in another dark hour of Jewish history, during the Holocaust, a death camp inmate asked a rabbi whether he should recite the morning blessing thanking God that "You have not made me a slave." The answer that was given was, "Yes, you can recite it because in your mind you are a free man."

Herut is primarily freedom from the yoke of the master. There is no fetter restraining the exercise of our distinctive way of life. *Herut*, in a positive sense, means to be able to set one's own goals and try to realize one's potential. A free person walks upright and with dignity. This is the meaning of the word *komemiut*. We ask in our prayerbook, "Restore us upright to our homeland."

In our own time, much emphasis has been placed on removing discriminatory practices that inhibit the free growth of the human spirit. The Torah reading during Passover stresses and summarizes the mood of *herut* by saying that there must be one and the same law for the citizen and the stranger (Exodus 12:49). "Since the days of Moses," Heinrich Heine wrote, "freedom speaks with a Hebrew accent." There were times when this freedom was not completely realized.

On the First Day of Passover, the theme of freedom was discussed—how one must feel it within one's self, how freedom has to be internalized. The people had tasted freedom in Egypt when they used their own calendar and had the courage to follow their own culture. When they came into the desert, that newly acquired freedom was soon lost in the harshness of wandering.

There is a touching episode that describes how, when Israel went forth from Egypt, Moses had to reassure the people. Pharaoh had afterthoughts; he decided to go at the head of his army and try to bring the slaves back. The Israelites saw the Egyptian horde approaching. They cried to the Lord and then they spoke to Moses. "Was it for want of graves in Egypt that you brought us to die in the wilderness?" They railed against Moses. "Why did you take us out of Egypt? Did we not say, 'Let us be and we will serve the Egyptians, for it is better for us to serve the Egyptians than to die in the wilderness?' " The might of Moses in calming the people demonstrated itself once again. He told them not to be afraid. "Stand by and witness the deliverance which the Lord will work for you. . . . The Lord will battle for you; you hold your peace!" then the Lord said to Moses, "Why do you cry unto Me? Tell the Israelites to go forward."

Why were the Israelites afraid? Why did the great host of 600,000 people who went forth from Egypt with such a mighty demonstration of God's power, fear their pursuers? Why could they not fight for their lives and the lives of their children? Ibn Ezra, a great medieval commentator, answers that the Egyptians had been masters over Israel. This was the generation that had been trained as slaves, that had been subjected to the yoke of the Egyptians. They did not feel as free people do. Their very spirits had been crushed, their souls had been humbled. How could they now fight against their former masters? They were weak in spirit and not skilled in battle.

The generation that left Egypt had to die in the desert. They could not undergo the battle to conquer a new land. With the passing of the generation of those who went out of Egypt, it was possible for our people to enter Canaan. A new generation arose, a proud generation arose, a free generation arose.

Our century has witnessed the passing of the generation of enslavement and the rise of a new generation of freedom. One is reminded of the words of the poet Haim Nahman Bialik:

> *We are the mighty*
> *The last generation of slaves and the first generation of free*
>   *men*
> *Alone our hand in its strength*
> *Tore from the pride of shoulders the yoke of bondage.*

As we celebrate our Passover this year, a free generation that understands the spirit of *herut* is determined to remain free in the land of Israel. We are passing through one of the difficult hours of Jewish history. May God, in His goodness, strengthen the hands of those who are determined to enjoy *herut olom*, everlasting freedom.

Sidrot

The Moral Violence
of Our Time

1979

"The earth became corrupt before God. The
earth was filled with violence."

Genesis 6:11

The words we have cited are at the very beginning of Noah,
which we read today. God has seen how great was humankind's
wickedness on earth. "And the Lord regretted that He had made
man on earth and His heart was saddened."

The account of the Flood must be understood as a stern warning to humankind that immorality and improper social conduct
weaken the very foundations of society. Towards the end of this
week's Torah reading, the Bible uses a most unusual phrase in
expressing the divine promise. "Never again will I doom the world
because of man, since the devisings of man's mind are evil from
his youth, nor will I ever destroy every living being as I have done.
So long as the earth endures, seed time and harvest, cold and
heat, summer and winter, day and night, shall not cease."

The great medieval commentator Rabbi Moshe Ben Nahman,
known as the *Ramban*, placed emphasis upon the fact that
people are evil because of their youth. People sin because they are
immature. Mature persons know what they ought to do. They
understand how to differentiate between the proper and the
improper.

We think of the child as being the innocent one. Children
emulate what they see adults do. Imitation on the part of children
is part of the problems of our society.

93

Against this background we consider the account of the Flood. What was the violence that filled the earth? What was its nature and intensity? The violence as described by the rabbis was in doing petty things. For example, people would come to a shopkeeper and take a grape or a small melon off his stand. As the law does not concern itself with trifles, there was no punishable crime. The generation of the Flood were "scoundrels within the letter of the law." But what happens if a host of people do the same thing? The shopkeeper will ultimately lose whatever he possesses.

We as a nation suffer not only from great crimes but also from little crimes. It is tragic that these crimes are carried out in our schools. There has been a breakdown in the moral standards of American schools on every level, beginning with the elementary schools and reaching into graduate education. A special report was issued a few months ago by the Carnegie Council on Policy Studies in Higher Education. It dealt with both the positive and negative aspects of our schools.

There are many strong factors in American education. There are many who are committed to developing ethical values in our colleges. An educational leader like the president of Harvard University, Derek C. Bok, has spoken for years on the importance of teaching ethics in our schools. In his most recent presidential report, he stressed the fact that there was a crying need for the Harvard Business School to develop a deeper appreciation of the ethical dimensions of our society. He pleaded for the introduction of courses in applied ethics. He had the feeling that even if the courses turned out to have no effect whatsoever on the moral development of the students, these courses would still make a contribution. "There is value," he wrote, "to be gained from any course that forces students to think carefully and vigorously about complex human problems." The fact is that some schools are beginning to devote greater concern to the moral issues of our society. After President Bok's annual message was picked up by the prestigious *Wall Street Journal,* it was commented upon very widely and numerous letters to the editor were received.

The need for ethical teaching is great. In the physical sciences, it is possible to verify a proposition through observation. It is possible to use data to examine experience. However, when it comes to the realm of ethics, of making moral decisions, we find ourselves in a different situation. The president of another great university spoke of the crisis in higher education and stressed the fact that this crisis is just one reflection of the greater crisis facing our society.

What are some of the corrosive elements that are pointed out by the Carnegie Foundation report and other data which are readily available? There is, for example, an increase in the number of books stolen from university libraries. Grades have become inflated. We live in a land where there is a national mania for proper credentials. Unless you get good grades, unless you have a diploma, you cannot move along and rise the ladder to success.

Faced with a shortage of students, many schools are now recruiting older students, mature individuals. The '80s will be a decade in which we will have a shortage of college students and an abundance of space. We see throughout the country school buildings that stand empty or have been rented out to non-public schools. To attract students, there is misleading advertising by some institutions in the search for enrollment.

The other day I read an item that spoke about this problem. In the hunger to get students, there is an attempt to enroll foreign students who too often are hopelessly unqualified academically. There has been a demoralization of faculties. One faculty member complained bitterly about the ethical quality of many colleges and universities. He bemoaned the fact that in the administration of the universities, basic ethical principles are not being followed. There has been an attempt to silence faculty dissent.

What is the cause of the drop in enrollment? With the end of the draft, with the decreasing number of 18-year-olds, the inflated campus enrollments of the late 1960s and early 1970s have quickly declined. Institutions that over-expanded during this period are suffering painful withdrawal symptoms. Even tenured faculty members have lost their jobs, and many faculties have experienced demoralization.

Universities have promised students more than they can deliver. There are example after example of breaches in the ethical life. To keep students in universities, the student is made king. Some administrators are pressuring faculty to give students what they want. They are given essentially empty, though impressive-sounding, programs. At times, students find a situation where the university tells persons of limited ability that if they enroll in the particular school that is seeking students, their academic future is more or less guaranteed.

Just the other day, there was a long article in a national newspaper which stated that when it comes to brochures issued by colleges, many of them are adopting a posture of greater candor. "There are no warning labels, no ingredients listed on the package, no guarantees." But American colleges and occupational schools are "breaking new grounds with their own version of a truth in packaging movement—truth in catalogs and prospectuses." The goal: to prepare promotional materials that offer the students better information, to spare both the student and the college wasted funds and hard feelings later.

There is an expected drop of twenty-five percent forecast in the number of college people between now and the early 1990s. There is an intense competition among the schools to round up a student body. In some cases, insecure smaller institutions are paying bounty hunters to deliver up willing freshmen. The head of Barat College, in nearby Lake Forest, wrote, "Instead of just fancy pictures, we're trying to provide more accurate information." Barat, incidentally, is one of the pioneering better information institutions.

All of this is a source of great concern. In the very place where there should be justice and the training for the just society and the good life, we find injustice, we find violence. When society's most hallowed institutions stand in the dock and are accused of malpractice, all of us must be concerned—faculty, students, parents, and society in general. Our students must leave school better persons than they entered. The widespread cheating, the self-serving grade inflation, the theft of books, the reneging by students on their debts for educational loans, are all too widespread.

Some argue that the ethical failures being experienced in American education are due to the fact that our schools are no longer elitist, that they are no longer the exclusive province of the refined and better upper class. They charge that the admission of students of highly diverse backgrounds and of lower economic status may have weakened the fiber of the schools. The fact is that the corruption of the elite is no less prevalent. We are all too familiar with the fact that one of the outstanding political figures in America today was once censured by Harvard University because he cheated on an examination. This gentleman was not an underprivileged person, to say the least. Cheating on exams, stealing another student's experiments, cutting pages from a book, either to use oneself or to make certain that the next student doesn't have the reference work to study for an assignment—these are not desperate efforts by underprivileged children to survive. Such deeds take place in our most prestigious and most expensive institutions. The children of wealthy parents, intellectually gifted students, cheat not merely to hang on but rather to be in a position to compete for the best graduate schools and ultimately for the better jobs in our economy. The competition to be admitted to medical school, to law school, is a factor that drives some individuals to behavior that must be condemned.

The schools reflect our society, which has become morally aimless. Children are a mirror of their parents and their exemplars.

We need ethical teaching in the schools, but we must have ethical behavior in our homes. "As long as we look to the schools as catering to the transient interests of society and the job market," an observer said, "we run the risk of reaching the moon without knowing why. Of curing illness in the laboratory when there is still suffering in the field. In charting our course to the moon, we use the data of a variety of sciences. In charting our course to a successful future, we must have the data of the science of ethics."

Whatever else the future may hold, one thing is demanded of us: we must make choices upon increasingly complex issues. We can only expect to receive the right answers if we know how to ask the right questions. We must have an ethically-based approach to problem-solving. It is the only way in which we can truly prepare for the future. For all too long we have thought that the ability to lead more prosperous lives, to be better off in a material sense, would automatically make us better people. It seems that the reverse is true. "It may be that we must learn to be better people in order to realize the full potential of life." We must devote greater effort to enhancing the ethical dimension of our living. Otherwise the whole human drama has no meaning, no true vitality, and we will ultimately be swept away like the generation of the Flood.

There still is time, there still is a chance for us if we will understand that on every level of our society—be it in our schools, in our homes, in the market place—we permit ethical teachings to help guide our ways.

NOAH

The Comforter

1984

The Bible frequently gives the origin of the names of its heroes and heroines. Thus, Moses was given a name by the daughter of Pharaoh, who spied a little basket among the reeds and sent her slave girl to fetch it. The princess named the child Moses, saying, "It means: I drew him out of the water." The name Abraham means "the father of a great nation." Sarah means "princess."

What about the origin of the name of Noah? Noah had been born to Lamech and his wife, "and he called his name Noah, saying, this one shall comfort us concerning our work and the sorrow of our hands because of the ground" (Gen. 5:29). There is a play on words in the phrase "the name Noah shall provide us comfort." What was the comfort, the relief that Noah provided for humankind? Until he came, people had no agricultural instruments. Noah was the comforter: he invented the plow. Whether or not the tradition is correct is not as significant as the elements of discussion that it raises.

Throughout the history of humankind, there have been forward-looking men and women who have brought comfort to the earth. There are some who deprecate the value of a technological advance. There are others who point out our great dependence upon the comforters of civilization.

During the High Holidays, I went to great lengths in explaining the implications of our current technological advances in the world of computers. There is a vast debate raging as to the role of computers in our educational system. There are some students of life who are very "down" on television. I saw my first television set at the New York World's Fair in 1940. The war years prevented its commercial development, but once the war ended, a push was on to provide each home with a television set.

A distinguished writer, Jerzy Kosinski, born in Lodz and separated from his parents at the age of six, wandered alone in war-torn Eastern Europe. A most unusual writer, his *The Painted Bird* won the prize for the best foreign book published in France in 1965. Read these words of Kosinski, given to an interviewer: "Today, people are absorbed in the most common denominator, the visual. It requires no education to watch T.V. It knows no age limit. Your infant child can watch the same program you do. Witness its role in the homes of the old and incurably sick. T.V. is everywhere. . . . Language requires some inner triggering; television doesn't." This observation raises some fundamental questions as to the role of technology and the enhancement of human life.

When Isaac Bashevis Singer delivered his Nobel Prize in Literature lecture in 1978, he spoke of the problems we have with technology. He mentioned that a number of those who no longer have confidence in the leadership of our society look up to the writer, the master of words. In an age like ours, in which the nuclear sword of Damocles hangs menacingly over all of us, Singer made the point that men and women hope against hope that the people of talent and sensitivity can rescue civilization. He observed quite keenly that "There is no machine and no kind of reporting and no kind of film that can do what a Tolstoy or a Dostoyevsky or a Gogol did." Singer went on to predict that the pervasiveness of technology will drive humans ever more towards literature. He concluded his statement with this penetrating observation: "The more technology, the more people will be interested in what the human mind can produce without the help of electronics. If we have people with the power to tell a story, there will always be readers."

The debate will go on and on between the proponents of technology, the product of science, and the adherents of the humanities as expressed through gifted writers. Let us hope that our age, for the sake of our children, will produce comforters who will work in moving human progress in their unique and special way.

A famous professor of physiology at the George Washington University Medical Center in our nation's capital gave an unusual title to a paper she published recently: "After Science, A Song." "Although science has taught us many valuable lessons about the universe, it remains for communication to transcend the limitations of our scientific culture so that we may discover and exalt the power inherent in the relatedness of individuals to each other, to others, and to The Other." After science and technology, there must be the song hailing the human spirit.

NOAH

The Languages of Humankind

1978

The Bible is a reflection of Israel's view of the creation of the world and humankind's subsequent history.

With this week's Torah reading, we come to the account of the Flood. Many different cultures report a flood experience. The great divide between the Biblical account and that of other cultures is that in the Bible, human sin was the cause of the Flood. After the Flood, we come to an interesting description of how the various languages developed.

All the earth had the same language. As people migrated from the east, they came to a valley and settled there. They decided to make bricks and finally to build a city and a tower with its top in the sky, "to make a name for ourselves." God was concerned about this plan. He went out and confounded their speech and scattered them over the face of the earth. Each people now had its own language.

The attempt to account for the diversity of languages appears in widely scattered speech communities. There is a Choctaw Indian tale that reads almost like the Tower of Babel story. Beginning in the 17th century, Francis Bacon suggested the idea that a common language be developed. Nations would no longer misinterpret what their neighbors were saying. The common language might help end conflicts and wars.

In the 19th century, a Polish Jewish physician, Ludovic Lazarus Zamenhof, developed a language called Esperanto. As many as 100,000 used Esperanto at one time, but after the passing of years, this new common language has disappeared.

Some twenty-five hundred years ago, an Egyptian Pharaoh wanted to find the first language of man. He took two infants and placed them in the charge of an isolated shepherd. The monarch ordered that the babies should never hear a word spoken in any language. When the children were returned to the Pharaoh, he thought he heard them use the word *bekos*, which means bread in one of the languages of Asia Minor. So he proclaimed that that language was humankind's "natural" language.

The story is apocryphal. Children speak only when they hear other people speaking. Two infants reared in isolation from human speech cannot develop a language on their own. The language a child uses is what the child hears from others. Their language and their style and tone of using language are critical.

Words are all-important. In a significant modern play, one of the characters speaks of language: "Useless bloody things words are. Ronnie and his bridges! Words are bridges, he wrote, 'To get from one place to another.' Wait till he's older and he learns about silences—they span worlds."

The question which we must ask ourselves now is: Are our words bridges or are they barriers?

Words are an important reflection of our social and cultural life. Sir Walter Raleigh once said, "Morality colours all language and lends to it the most delicate of its powers of distinction." When any significant change takes place in the moral standards of the community, there is a shift in the meaning of even ordinary words. Language has preserved for us the movement of humankind's soul. It reveals the evolution of consciousness.

Over and over again in our ethical literature, the proper use of language is stressed. In Proverbs 15, we have examples in the following verses:

"A soothing tongue is a tree of life." (4)
"The lips of the wise spread knowledge." (7)
"How much better is a word in season." (23)

NOAH

An Added Letter
1982

One of the greatest moments in life is when an infant begins to speak. You wait for that moment and cherish its memory forever. The first sounds are like the blooming of a flower. Hopefully, an instrument of beauty will emerge.

Much has been written about speech. Language is a means to do something. Speaking is one of the many ways of "doing." A recent translation of the Bible reflects the opinion that originally the earth had the same language and the same words. This latter expression—*udevarim ahadim* in the original Hebrew—is important. The Bible relates how people of early times wanted to build a tower with its top in the sky. They desired to make a name for themselves. The Lord came down to look at the city and the tower that has been built, and said, "If, as one people with one language for all, this is how they have begun to act, then nothing that they may propose to do will be out of their reach." God decided to confound their speech "so that they shall not understand one another's speech."

The belief that there was once a time when all the peoples of the earth spoke one language was current in ancient Mesopotamia. A four-thousand-year-old tablet tells of a golden age when the whole universe, the people in unison, in one tongue gave praise to the god Enlil.

There is a magnificent insight on the expression "the same words." A commentator suggested that it can have two possible meanings. "The same words" in Hebrew can be vocalized not only as meaning "the same" but as meaning "words which unite," *devarim eehudim*. On the other hand, if you leave out the *aleph*, you have the words *devarim hadim*, "words which are sharp." The same tongue that can use language as a unifying force can turn language into a divisive force. It is said, "Life and death depend upon the tongue." Think of it. The word that means "one," the One God, is formed by putting together the *aleph*, the *het*, and the *daled*. But if you leave out the *aleph*, which is the symbol for the Name of God and His oneness, you have sharpness and bloodshed. It is said in Ezekiel, "Abraham was but one." In the *Shema*, we affirm "The Lord our God, the Lord is one."

Language used properly can be the tongue of unity. Language used properly can be the instrument of community.

LEKH-LEKHA

Departure and Destiny

1981

Abraham's life is encapsulated in one verse, the opening verse of this Sabbath's Torah reading, which says, very simply, "The Lord said to Abram, 'Go forth from your native land and from your father's house to the land that I will show you' " (Genesis 12:1).

The entire human experience is captured in a short sentence that traces a person's ascent from the point of departure to destination. Departure is all-important. For Abraham, it did not come easily. There is a lovely legend I learned when I was little about Abraham and the idols. When Abraham was twenty, his father fell ill. Terah spoke to his sons and said, "Sell these two idols for me." Haran carried out the wishes of the father, but if anyone asked Abraham for an idol, he would point out how silly it was for grown people to buy an idol that had been made that very day. On another occasion, Abraham broke all the idols belonging to the king. In a bold move, he placed an ax in the hand of one idol. When he was accused of being the guilty party and questioned about the motive for his deed, Abraham, tongue-in-cheek, responded, "I did not do it. Don't you see the largest idol with an ax still in its hand?"

The story may appear naive and simplistic, but it has tremendous implications. How do we learn to break, as Abraham broke, with the past? How do we have the courage to leave Ur of the Chaldees and go to the land of promise? How do we have the strength to listen to God's command telling us to depart for an unknown place? Departure and faith are all-important.

There were moments of breakthrough, moments of departure, in various cultures and civilizations. It is a striking thing to realize that breakthroughs occur when there has been a breakdown. When a civilization has reached a low point, then there is a possibility of breakthrough. When a man like Abraham is no longer satisfied with the message of idolatry and searches for the One God and is willing to become His first messenger, we have a breakthrough. This is a decisive moment in human history.

When we speak of a decisive change, we ought to ask ourselves, "decisive for whom?" Decisive for humanity, decisive in the fact that a new destination, a new destiny for human living is being sought. Those who break through do not find the going easy. Abraham passed through ten different tests. Those who make a breakthrough are despised, persecuted, ignored, and stomped upon. Yet, the world has a new message. New ideas, like new institutions, are invariably the work of minorities. They require time to spread, time to succeed. So it was with Abraham, and so it was with our people.

A breakthrough occurs when the idea and the ideal of rationality are brought forward. What was Abraham striving for? What have our people been striving for? To affirm the existence of a sense and destiny in historical events. What happens here on earth does not happen merely by chance, but is part of a divine plan.

Abraham went from his point of departure to seek his destiny.

The courage of his new beginning gave all of us great faith, great hope. His move from Ur to Eretz Israel was the most fateful breakthrough in our long history. It is the keystone of the entire Biblical experience. If you understand the secret of "Go forth from your father's house," a commentator once said, you will understand the rest.

LEKH-LEKHA

Wonder

1983

In Professor Abraham Joshua Heschel's great study on religious discovery, *God In Search Of Man*, he speaks of the decisive element of wonder and cites the Biblical text, "Lift up your eyes on high and see who created thee." This verse from Isaiah tells of one of the ways in which we can sense the presence of God in the world.

How did Abraham, the central subject of today's Torah reading, arrive at the understanding that there is a God who is concerned with the world? This theme is frequently found in Jewish thought. A medieval author of the *Sefer Hayashar, The Book of the Righteous*, said that one comes to belief in God through love. It is not through fear, but rather through love that we come to an appreciation of the Creator. That is why Abraham's offspring are spoken of as "the seed of Abraham my friend." We come closer to a knowledge of God through friendship.

According to the rabbis, Abraham may be compared to a man who was going from place to place when he saw a palace full of light. He asked, "Is it possible that there is no one who cares for the palace?" Finally, the master of the palace looked at Abraham and said, "I am master of the Palace." The Holy One, blessed be

He, looked out and said, "I am the Sovereign of the world. I am the Guide." It was in wonder that Abraham's quest for God began.

Jewish history begins with Abraham's quest. "If we fail to wonder," Dr. Heschel said, "we fail to respond to the present." This is the tragedy of so many. We dim wonder by indifference. We resist wonder, and life becomes routine. How magnificent is the world when people of faith have the ability to realize that it is filled with spiritual radiance. The world possesses so many marvelous secrets. The Baal Shem Tov, the founder of Hasidism, once said, "The small hand held against the eye hides it all. Just as a small coin held over the face can block out the sight of a mountain, so can the vanities of living block out the sight of infinite light."

Professor Heschel's great concern with wonder—or, to use another of his favorite expressions, "radical amazement"—is the chief characteristic of the religious person's attitude towards history and nature. So many people take things for granted. Dr. Heschel pleaded that we take to heart the verse of the Psalmist, "This is the Lord's doing. It is marvelous in our eyes" (Ps. 118:23). Wonder is the feeling of a philosopher. An awareness of the Divine begins with wonder. A Far Eastern thinker once said that wonder is the ability to look at things in a new way.

A great modern teacher, Sam Keen, wrote a marvelous book called *The Anatomy of Wonder*. He pointed out the reality that when the first astronaut circled the earth, it was an occasion for wonder. However, the subsequent voyages became occasions that interest us but no longer have the same quality of stirring us. Discoveries which a generation ago produced wonder at humankind's ingenuity now elicit only a yawn.

A modern commentator made the observation that there are those who seek knowledge about everything and understand nothing. It is wonder—not mere curiosity—a sense of enchantment, of respect for the mysteries of love for the other, that is essential to the difference between a knowing that is simply a garnering of information and techniques and a knowing that seeks insight and understanding. It is wonder that reveals how intimate is the relationship between knowledge of the other and knowledge of the self, between inwardness and outwardness. The starting point in the religious experience is wonder.

Let us think about the whole question of becoming excited about the process of living. Two weeks ago, I spoke about the

Garden of Eden, about the whole concept of an earthly paradise. I reviewed the outstanding study by the president of Yale University, A. Bartlett Giamatti, of the role of the paradise garden as a literary motif, with special reference to the great poetry of the Renaissance. The Garden of Eden concept ties in with our world view. The world, once an enchanted garden, has become disenchanted, deprived of purpose and direction.

The students of our vast school system who wish to keep growing need education for surprise. Education for surprise is important. We know a lot about the world and yet we must admit that there is so much we do not know. The larger the island of knowledge, it has been said, the longer the shoreline of wonder. Students ought to be asked questions like: Did anything surprise you yesterday? Did you have a sense of wonder?

Some years ago, *Newsweek* magazine made the following point in a study: "Perhaps ours is the strangest age, it is an age without a sense of strangeness of things. The human race has grown up and lost its capacity for wonder."

Growing up for many seems to be growing immune to astonishment. Keep alive your sense of wonder. It will make your life an exciting and religiously stimulating experience.

LEKH-LEKHA

"Let There Be No Strife"

1985

Scripture encompasses many human experiences. Among them are the friendships and rivalries that develop, sometimes in the most unexpected places, between relatives.

You remember how Abram prospered. He traveled from place to place and renewed each altar that he had consecrated before. Abram's party included his kinsman Lot. Unfortunately, there was not sufficient room on the land for the herdsmen of Abram and those of Lot. Abram did not want to have conflict. He said, "Let there be no strife between you and me, between my herdsmen and yours, for we are kinsmen." If one takes the Hebrew word by word, a profound point is made: Let there be no strife between you and me, for we are men who are brothers.

Conflict is never pleasant. Bitterness brings ashes to our tongues. If conflict between strangers is unpleasant, all the more so is it between loved ones and relatives. In contemporary English we use the phrase "sibling rivalry." Children of the same womb tear at each other, consciously and unconsciously. How sad it is for those who participate in this struggle between brothers and sisters. In Proverbs (27:10), we find a wise insight: "A close neighbor is better than a distant brother." There is also another insightful statement (18:24): "There is a friend more devoted than a brother."

Abram learned the art of dealing with controversy. He said, "Let there not be conflict between us." In the case of Lot, the solution was separation. "If you go north, I will go south; and if you go south, I will go north."

Just as there is the unfortunate conflict between brothers, a wider rift is also developing within the household of Israel, between those whom we call in one of our prayers "our brothers of the House of Israel." We pray for their well-being. We are concerned about their security. We are troubled about their safety. Yet, in various parts of the world the rift within the Jewish community is widening.

Let us consider the situation. Our text is implicit. When did this strife between the herdsmen of Abram and Lot take place? When the classic enemies, "the Canaanites and Perizzites, were then dwelling in the land." This part of the verse gives us more than a demographic setting, it tells us of the feelings between Abram's small band and the inhabitants of the land. It was a time of concern and of danger. It was a time when those who were relatives should have stood shoulder to shoulder. Instead, there was controversy within the small band of believers. They did not appreciate the point of working together with each other against those who threatened them.

I read a moving editorial in *Moment* magazine by Rabbi Harold Shulweis called "Divided We Fall." In the Los Angeles area, in our own city of Chicago, and in other larger and smaller centers of

Jewish population, increased conflict is breaking out on a host of different issues.

On a very serious level, we have the debates regarding who is a Jew. There is a continuing effort to deny the authenticity of conversions by non-Orthodox courts of law. In this controversy, the solution is not separation but rather an attempt to find a way of maintaining the cohesiveness of the household of Israel.

We spoke of the individual family, then of the household of Israel. But there is a wider human family—the family of the nations of the world. We are particularly concerned with the horrible ongoing struggle in the Middle East, which has poured out its venom through terror and boycott. I felt very badly about the 40th anniversary session of the United Nations General Assembly. Prime Minister Shimon Peres rose to speak and twenty-two Arab nations and their sympathizers in the Third World walked out. This same pattern of stalking out when an Israeli speaks repeats itself at international conferences and world gatherings. Peres used a simple but penetrating phrase when he said, "The sons of Abraham have become quarrelsome but remain family nonetheless." He made a bold proclamation: "The state of war between Israel and Jordan should be terminated immediately. Israel declares this readily in the hope that King Hussein is willing to reciprocate this step."

Abram of old said, "Let there not be strife between us." Our patriarch's descendant, Shimon Peres, pleads, "Let us face each other as free men and free women across the negotiating table. Let us argue but not fight. Let us arm ourselves with reason." Peres recalled the courageous visit of President Anwar Sadat to Jerusalem and the many positive things that resulted. With all the difficulties, Peres said, "Let us not allow gloom and doom to overshadow our worthiest accomplishments. Let us make our peace a success, a source of encouragement to others."

Different conflicts can be resolved in diverse ways. At times, separation is the best solution. At other times, in cases of community difficulty, a search for unity is critical. In the international arena, a continuous search for the ways of peace is the need of the hour.

Women's Changing World

1980

In November I am to deliver a major address before the biennial convention of the Women's League. My theme will be "The Changing Role of the Jewish Woman."

A discussion of the Jewish woman and mother frequently brings either a smirk or a smile. Our Torah reading tells of the first of our matriarchs, Sarah.

May I tell you of a model personality whose writings are recorded in memoirs she prepared for her children. They are what Rabbi Jack Riemer dubbed "a love letter from beyond."

The memoirs of Gluckel (1645-1724), who lived in the German town of Hameln, were begun when she was forty-four years old. She was a pietist, one who typified the highest ideals of our faith. She had given birth to fourteen children, whose financial and personal destinies she guided. She was a paradigmatic woman of valor.

Gluckel's memoirs are a rare account. She speaks about war, plague, pirates, and soldiers. She tells of the hysteria that developed about the time of Sabbatai Zevi (1666). She wanted to give her children a sense of their roots, so they would know from what sort of people they had come.

The book is engaging. It is interspersed with Hebrew words and phrases, snatches of prayers, quotations from the Bible and the Talmud. Gluckel reflects the ethical impulse of Judaism. Though she writes that the book is not to be a book of morals, she tells her children, "The best thing for you, my children, is to serve God with the heart, without falsehood and sham."

There is an element of humor. She tells of a young kinswoman. "The girl knew French like water," she writes. "Once this did my father a mighty good turn. My father, it seems, held a pledge of great value which he had made to a nobleman. The gentleman appeared at his house one day with two other toughs to redeem the pledge. My father gave him no concern but went upstairs to fetch the pledge while the teenager sat and played at the clavichord to pass away the time for the distinguished customers. The gentlemen stood about and began to confer with one another in French. 'When the Jew,' they said, 'comes down with the pledge, we'll take it without paying and slip out.' They never suspected that the girl understood them. When my father appeared, she suddenly began to sing aloud in Hebrew. 'Oh, not the pledge, my soul—here today and gone tomorrow.' In her haste the poor young lady could blurb out nothing better. My father then turned to the gentleman and said, 'Where is the money, sir?' 'Give me my pledge!' cried the customer. But my father said, 'First the money and then the pledge.' The gentleman spun about to his companions. 'Friends,' he said, 'the game is up—the wench, it seems, knows French,' and hurling threats they ran from the house."

Hear this beautiful observation on life: A philosopher was once walking along the street and meeting a friend asked him how things were going. The friend replied, "Badly. No one in the world has more sorrows and troubles than I." Whereupon the philosopher said, "Good friend, come with me to my rooftop. I will point you every house in the city and tell you the misfortunes and miseries they one and all conceal. Then, if you will, you may cast your own sorrow in with the rest and draw out any other you choose in its stead. Perhaps you will find one more to your liking." Together they climbed to the roof. The philosopher showed his friend the unhappiness that darkened one house after the other. He said, "Do now as I told you." But the friend replied, "In truth, I see that every house hides as much woe and hardship as my own, and perhaps more. I think I'll keep what I have."

Gluckel was a pietist type of Jewish woman, firm in our faith. Our mothers and grandmothers were cast in her mold.

Rahel Levin was born in Berlin in 1771. She was brought up in an Orthodox but uncultured household where Judeo-German was spoken. The Jewish intellectual elite of the community hoped to contribute to German culture. From the 1780s on, Jews and Germans mingled in the Berlin salons, where they exchanged opinions and influenced each other's religious expressions. By the time she was thirty, Rahel Levin had a salon on *Jagerstrasse* to which the most important personalities of the Prussian intellectual world, including Goethe, came. She married a Prussian Christian diplomat named Varnhagen, many years her junior. An outsider, she sought entry into the Christian world. She hoped to jump over the fence, by marriage in a church, to the wide world of universalism.

The most important study of Rahel Levin was written by Hannah Arendt, herself a great intellectual leader who fled from Hitler's Germany in the 1930s. Professor Arendt started her career as one very much involved in Jewish affairs and she, too, went over to universal concerns.

Rahel Levin's life shows the vast movement that some Jews made from a century before with a Gluckel of Hameln. On her deathbed, she said, "What a history! A fugitive from Egypt and Palestine. The thing which all my life seemed to me the greatest shame, which was the misery and misfortune of my life—having been born a Jewess." She fled from Judaism. "Everything is topsy-turvy, no Jew stays put; but, alas, I alone wretchedly stay where I am." If she would become a nobleman's wife, her disadvantages could be forgotten overnight; nothing would remain of Jewishness but a natural solidarity with all those who seek to escape from Judaism. She wanted to feel at home in the world, rather than be comfortable with her own people.

During this era, many Jews sought to escape from Judaism. They thought that the cause of humanity should be the prime cause of the Jew. They did not understand that a Jew can be a particularist and a universalist at one and the same time. Rahel Levin was a role-model for many Jews who sought to find their spiritual and intellectual fulfillment beyond the bounds of Jewish life. They thought that what could be achieved would be the neutral society.

In the salons like Rahel Levin's, there was more than encounters between Jews and non-Jews. Before this, the two groups had come together only for some practical concern. Now they were meeting for the sake of meeting itself. "The salons became part of an assimilating social framework dominated by non-Jewish culture. Participation in salon life generally led Jews to join the non-Jewish society outright, an act that meant embracing its religion and its church" (Professor Jacob Katz).

In modern times, we have had others who have redefined their Jewish identity. Another important figure who sought a universal solution was Rosa Luxemburg.

Rosa Luxemburg was born in Poland in 1871 but emigrated to Germany, where she became a leading figure of the extreme left. Arrested in 1919, she was gunned down by army officers. She was an internationalist and found national particularlism inimicable to socialism. She once rebuked a young correspondent for the latter's Jewish national sentiment. "Why do you come with your particular sorrows? I have no separate corner in my heart for the ghetto. I feel at home in the entire world, wherever there are clouds and birds and human tears." There was no room in her heart, she said, for Jewish suffering. There is a direct line from the apostasy of Rahel Levin to Rosa Luxemburg's desertion.

We move into our own century where most of the bars against Jewish women participating in education have been removed. Our interest today is focused on the 20th-century Jewish woman in America, participant in the great women's revolution. Part of this revolution began in Palestine before 1948.

One of our models for today's discussion is Rahel Yanait Ben Zvi, wife of the second president of Israel. Born in the Ukraine, she studied in France. She helped found the Labor Zionist Movement in Russia. She came to Palestine as a teacher and founded the first high school in Jerusalem. She played a pioneering role in the defense movement and the Women's Labor Movement. Rahel Ben Zvi was an editor as well as an activist.

What is most interesting about her is that, toward the end of her life, she moved back into the world of religious affiliation. Rahel Ben Zvi became a member of the group called "Seekers of the Way," the Israeli equivalent of our Reconstructionist Movement. A socialist to the very end, she sought to find a solution in both particularism and religious universalism.

As we discuss this century, I would like to deal with a phenomenon that is becoming a typical part of our landscape—the family in which both husband and wife contribute financially to its economic well-being.

Let me tell you about Dr. Rosalyn Yalow. She is a scientist, wife, and mother. In 1977 she won the Nobel Prize in Medicine. Only five women have won the Nobel Prize in Science, and three of them were married to their collaborators.

Dr. Yalow attended the same synagogue as my mother. The two of them—an 84-year-old lady and a Nobel Prize winner—would share a bit of Sabbath talk on a park bench in the Bronx. Dr. Yalow does her own marketing and maintains a kosher home. She is a person of great qualities. After her oldest child, Ben, was born, she nursed him while working fulltime. When the pediatrician objected to her working, she said, "Doctor, that's *your* problem."

When Dr. Yalow was seventeen, she read about Marie Curie, the French discoverer of radium, who became her model. She went to a city university, where her talents were recognized. Yet, though she had the best of grades, it was hard for her to get a graduate appointment. When her professor wrote to Purdue, the answer came back, "She is from New York, she is Jewish, she is a woman. If you can guarantee her a job afterwards, we'll give her an assistantship."

At one point, she was offered a post as a biochemist, provided that she become a stenographer first and get into graduate school through the back door. She became a graduate assistant of a professor at Illinois. When she received an A-minus in a particular course, her professor said, "Women do not do well in laboratory work." Dr. Yalow still insists that "The subtle discrimination was of no moment."

Dr. Yalow does not consider herself a feminist. She is not mad at the male establishment. At the Nobel Prize ceremonies, she said, "We still live in a world in which a significant fraction of people, including women, believe that a woman belongs and wants to belong exclusively in the home. That a woman should not aspire to achieve more than her male counterparts, and particularly not more than her husband. But, if women are to start moving towards their goal, we must believe in ourselves or no one else will believe in us. We must match our aspirations with the competence, courage, and determination to succeed and we must feel a personal responsibility to ease the path for those who come afterward." When asked about competing with her husband, a professor at Cooper Union, she said, "Women who feel that they can't compete with their husbands shouldn't compete with their husbands."

Dr. Yalow's career is inspirational. I think of our current situation with so many women engaged in careers who also have husbands and households. I am concerned as to what will happen to the volunteer capacities within our congregation when people are so preoccupied. Fifty-two percent of all college freshmen, forty percent of law school students, a third of medical school freshmen are women. If you project this reality into the future, you will find that women with careers have little time to serve in a voluntary way.

Today, people marry at an older age. The time of the birth of the first child is much later than has been recorded historically. There has been a fantastic increase of women with children under the age of six who are back in the labor force. What happens to these young children psychologically with the absence of mother from home? We have such a great need for good day-care centers.

Educated women, on the whole, are career-oriented. The more educated, the greater the desire to remain in purposeful work. There have been instances where the husband and wife make an arrangement—the husband goes to school first, then the wife goes to school, and they support each other mutually.

The following advertisement in a Jewish monthly magazine tells the case: "Two of us. . . . We're in a new age. The two-income family. Double digit inflation. Prices up. Interest up. Dollar down. Few of us can afford to buy and maintain a house on one salary. Plus a car or two. Sending our kids through college means spending our life's savings. That's why, as responsible parents, protection of our family income has become a major new concern. BOTH OF US COUNT. What if something happened to EITHER of us? Have we provided for each other? For our children? For their future? For continuing our standard of living? Face reality! Look into (life insurance). It's designed for the TWO OF US. Today, not many can do it alone. We need each other. Our children need US BOTH to protect and insure our way of life."

The prestige of voluntary work has decreased. There has been a major revolution in voluntary work. Why give twenty or thirty hours a week to a cause, if you can be working at a desk and earning income for a family in an age of spiraling inflation?

People who are in careers can be very helpful as mentors to those who are homemakers. Their expertise can be used in a host of different ways. I envision a new style Sisterhood and a new style Men's Club. They will have to be fashioned because of the dramatic changes that are taking place in our homes, in our careers, and in our time demands.

People need linkages. These links are important. People linked together in a comon cause have added power. The most vulnerable people in our society are those who are unlinked to families or institutions.

People need charismatic models, they need the example of a Dr.

Yalow or a Mrs. Ben Zvi. Our world is more crowded; yet there is a greater feeling of emptiness. A sociologist once said, "We are acquainted with more people, but we know fewer persons."

The tasks for all of us are here. Working together, we will build for a better Jewish tomorrow. These are indeed dramatically changing times and we must prepare for them.

VAYERA

The Judge of All the Earth

1981

Annually, we reread the Five Books of Moses. From time to time, I realize the importance of this repetitive act of piety. There is a new lesson that we seem to learn each time we take the Bible into hand. Somehow the Biblical lesson seems to meet a need of our time.

I read a striking statement by an editor of the *New York Times* describing what is happening to the poor and the underprivileged of our society. Budgetary considerations have become more important than human needs. The war against poverty has been turned into a war against the poor.

God heard the cry of the people of Sodom and Gomorrah. "I will go down to see whether they have acted altogether according to the outcry that has come to Me." God, the Great Judge, wanted to learn the facts for Himself. But the key word is *outcry*. The sin of Sodom was that its inhabitants had fullness of bread but did not help the poor or strengthen the needy. Then there is a powerful dialogue between Abraham and God. "Will you sweep away the innocent along with the guilty? What if there should be fifty innocent within the city?" The emphasis is on *within the city*. The phrase means involved—who are not only for themselves but for others. "If there are fifty such people, why should Sodom be destroyed? Will you then wipe out the place and not forgive it for the sake of the innocent fifty who are in it?" Then we have one of the great, great phrases of the Bible. *"Shall not the Judge of all the earth do justly?"* The question has found its echo in Shakespeare, who said, "O Thou that judgeth all things, stay my thoughts." Our own Declaration of Independence speaks of God as being the Supreme Judge of the world. God answers, "Yes, if there are fifty, I will forgive the whole place for their sake." And Abraham asks, "How have I the courage to speak to You, I, who am but dust and ashes? . . . What happens if there are only forty-five? What happens if there are only forty? What happens if there are only thirty? What happens if there are only twenty? What happens if there are only ten?" And God answers, "I will not destroy for the sake of ten."

I have always been concerned and disturbed by this passage. Abraham stopped at that point. He abandoned the plea for the people of Sodom. They are left to their own fate. Was it not possible that he should have continued to plead for nine, eight, for two, or even for a single righteous person? Or possibly even for a single not righteous person? But Abraham seemed to give up; he relinquished his power of responsibility. The question has been posed, but what is the possible answer?

In Jewish thought, the number ten is significant. In Jewish practice, we require a quorum of ten to be able to conduct a full sacred service. We prefer to have ten people present when a marriage is consecrated. The suggestion may be offered that ten represents a community. Unless Sodom had ten righteous people, it was not a community worth saving.

Surely we are concerned with the individual. Ours is a tradition which says that a person can proclaim, quite correctly, that the world was created for my sake. We say that whoever preserves a single life, it is as though he or she has preserved the entire world. But here we were concerned with a city. And the city can only be a city. There cannot be millions of Chicagos but only one Chicago. We have differences of opinion but one Chicago that is bound together in a sense of community.

"Perhaps you will find ten," and then he was silent. For when there are ten people, there is a possibility that these ten people will exercise influence. They will be able to call "halt" to the improprieties and shortcomings of the community. They have the ability to sanctify God's name. The proof text is "And I will be sanctified in the midst of the Children of Israel." The Children of Israel must be a community of the Children of Israel.

Our age has seen too much privatism. Our age has seen too much me-ism. Our age has seen too many people caring only for themselves. The text tries to convey the message that there must be a feeling of community.

A city, a state, a society, must rise above the individual and represent the will of the community. There is no purpose in life that can be achieved without society. For years, the great philosophers—men like Hobbes, Locke, Jean Jacques Rousseau—described the social contract in which individuals merge together to become a society—a society that can express the *general will*. It is a community which creates culture. It is a community which perpetuates ideals. It is a community that has an appreciation of life.

We are the seed of saints and martyrs. We are not Sodomites. We are the children of Abraham who shared his bread with the messengers of God and ordinary folk.

HAYE SARAH

All My Years

1982

There is an interesting cultural process that takes place within our society. Words from various languages have become part of American English. In different sections of the country, there are regional expressions that have been taken over from French, Italian, Spanish, German, and so on. Thus, the expression *l'chaim*, "to life," has become part of America's usage since "Fiddler on the Roof" appeared first on stage, later when its songs were heard on T.V. and radio, and, finally, when it became a motion picture.

When Sarah passed away, the Bible speaks of the lives of Sarah. "Her life span was a hundred and seven and twenty years"—as if to say that each part had a value all its own. The classical commentaries tell us, "As they were whole, so were her years whole." Obviously, in the course of a lifetime there are moments of grief and times of sadness, but Sarah regarded all of her life, even the most terrifying experience of the would-be sacrifice of Isaac, as being equal in goodness. Her career was a litany of gratitude. "They were all equal for good." This is the reason why the Bible starts the verse by saying, "The years of Sarah's life" and then repeats the expression about life, "These were the years of Sarah's life."

At the end of our Torah reading, there is another moving passage: "Abraham outlived Sarah by many years." Then the text uses unusual language, "And these are the days of the years of Abraham's life which he lived." Read carefully, "These are the days of the years of Abraham's life which he lived" has an obvious redundancy. The fact is that he lived; why repeat that reality? An answer is suggested that says, "What is the meaning of this repetition of language, 'which he lived'? It comes to teach us that all his life were days filled with life and they had nothing negative in them."

Our affirmation of life is part of the Abrahamic tradition. Sarah's life was a life for which she was grateful. Abraham's life was a life that found him thinking and doing affirmative things at all times. There are those who live life at its most meaningful level, but only for a part of their career. Abraham lived life to the fullest throughout his days.

Some people manage to live their lives only for a portion of their days. My attention was drawn recently to a new book called *Schindler's List*. Thomas Keneally writes about a man named Oskar Schindler who came to Poland during the Nazi occupation to make money. Something touched him, and he became one of the most dedicated rescuers of Jews. Instead of despoiling them, Schindler helped to save entire families. He put his own life into jeopardy. He functioned at terrible risk, feeding Jews and humanely keeping the SS from reaching them. For three years he manipulated Nazi officials. He slipped between seams of the Hitler death machine and saved human lives. For a short period of his life, he scored a tremendous triumph for humanity. After the war was over, Schindler apparently was spent. As has been described, "Schindler was not a strong character before the war, and he had a less distinguished life after it." The strange thing is, as his wife observed, he did nothing astonishing before the war and he was unexceptional afterwards. For part of the year he would go to Israel, where he would live off his Jewish friends whom he had saved. The rest of the year he lived in Frankfurt. After almost thirty years of unexceptional existence, he died in 1974. Part of his life was filled with life, but one could not say of him, as the Bible does of Abraham, that all of his years were filled with life.

We know of athletes who score one great victory and then live in the memory of that moment. There are novelists who write one best seller and then are never heard from again. In 1934, Henry Roth wrote a famous novel, *Call It Sleep,* dealing with Jewish immigrant life on New York's East Side about the year 1912. He produced a remarkable work, and then went to Maine to a farming life. A brief moment of greatness unmatched by other attainments.

Sarah and Abraham lived full lives. They met with many problems. They started their careers in Ur of the Chaldees and went as far west as Egypt. A goodly part of their days were spent in the Land of Promise. But at all times, they lived life to its fullest and at its most meaningful level.

TOLEDOT

Don't Use Food as a Weapon
1979

Ample food is a daily necessity. There is a strategic branch of combat called "economic warfare" in which you try to cut off the enemy's vital supplies. As important as strategic materials may be, food is of equal importance.

In our Torah reading, there is mention of the vital role of food. There was a famine in the land, like the famine in the time of Abraham (Genesis 26:1-3). Isaac was told by God to remain in the land and he would be blessed. Later, we read that Isaac sowed in the land and harvested a hundredfold. The verse ends, "And the Lord blessed him." Again, we read how there was a struggle about the water supply. What can one do if there is inadequate water? Isaac renewed the water wells his father had dug and which the Philistines had stopped up after Abraham's death. There was contention, harassment, and finally accommodation. Isaac called the place Rehoboth, saying, "Now at last the Lord has granted us ample space to prosper in the Land" (Genesis 26:22).

As I speak these words, our nation is locked in a difficult struggle with Iranian students in Teheran who have besieged the American embassy. It is to be hoped that by the time this appears in print, the situation will have been resolved in a satisfactory way.

I was stunned to read William Safire's column in the New York Times the other day. This man, who was a speech writer for President Richard M. Nixon, maintains the position that "We have a nonviolent weapon that will have an effect in Iran: food." He relates that 30 percent of Iran's food is imported, much of it from the United States. "We should now impose a food embargo on Iran, arranging with alternative grain suppliers like Australia and Canada not to take up the slack. The Soviet Union could not take up their grain shortfalls." This embargo, Safire recognizes, will not cause starvation in Iran, but will push up prices and contribute to the general unrest and will make the point around the world that a superpower is not necessarily musclebound.

Think of it, think of the callousness of this argument. Who will suffer? The poor and the indigent. Why? To make the point that America is not musclebound. I would rather spend my life being musclebound than being immoral in reducing another person's food supply. The fact of the matter is that Iran has already moved over to other suppliers. For months they have turned to other countries, perhaps in anticipation of the Safire-type of thinking. Iran has only a small order of wheat and rice and barley awaiting delivery, according to the Department of Agriculture. The American Farm Bureau, which traditionally opposed using food as a political weapon, has gone along with Safire's thinking. Long-

Affirming Life

shoremen have stopped a large order from going out of a Texas port.

Food embargoes are morally unacceptable. The first people to be hurt will be the average citizens of Iran. In no way do I sympathize with the Ayatollah Khomeini and his madman-like rule, but I am concerned about people. The mullahs and the other ayatollahs will eat while the average person will suffer a sharp reduction in diet.

Years ago (during the Korean War), I studied war economics. It was a time of the Cold War. Strategists encouraged making mischief by all methods short of war. "Don't get involved in direct conflict, use economic warfare, decrease the enemy's strength by cutting off the raw materials, his food and other items" *(Defense in the Cold War)*. Economic warfare aims at weakening the whole economy. The tragedy is that there is no distinction between the powerful and those who are innocent citizens.

Biblical morality protected against this indiscriminate conduct. Abraham challenged God, "Will you wipe away the innocent along with the guilty?" What does our tradition have to say about one's activity towards one's fellow beings? There are a number of classic sources that deal with this issue, with the moral posture towards one who comes to you for food. It is told of the great master Rabbi Judah the Prince that he, opening his granary in a year of scarcity, proclaimed that those who had studied could come, but those who were ignorant should not be admitted. A teacher by the name of Jonathan pushed his way in and said, "Master, give me food." Rabbi Judah said to him, "Do you have the credentials, have you studied the Bible, the Mishnah?" Jonathan said, "No." "If so," Rabbi Judah said, "how can I give you food?" The answer he received was, "Feed me as the dog and raven are fed" *(Baba Bathra 8a)*. So Rabbi Judah gave Jonathan some food.

This text is followed by another incident which stated that people who ask for clothing are to be examined to see if they are really needy, whereas applicants for food are not to be questioned but to be fed. What is the text that proves this? The magnificent statement of Isaiah, speaking of our duty to our fellow human being, which we read every Yom Kippur, "Share your bread with the hungry" *(Baba Bathra 9a)*. Food is precious, and it must be dealt with in that light.

War is a serious thing, but when a city is besieged, "You must not destroy its trees, they are trees of the field, human (like man.)" This was explained to mean that you may eat of a fruit tree, for humankind is the tree of the field (we are dependent on the fruit tree for food), but you cannot cut down a fruit tree to use for the siege. A great commentator, Nahmanides, offered the suggestion that if people go out and try to hide in the forest from the ravages of war, one must be concerned about them. "And there shall be a pavilion for shade from heat by day and for shelter and protection against drenching rain" (Isaiah 4:6). One must be concerned and considerate of the needs of human beings, even if they are enemies.

In the great code of Maimonides, there are rules of war. One is struck by the attitude of kindness towards the enemy. "When siege is laid to a city with the purpose of capturing it, it may not be surrounded on four sides. Only three sides should be sealed, the fourth was to be left open to give an opportunity for escape to those who would flee to save their lives." There was an ethic of warfare. "One who smashes household goods, tears clothes, demolishes a building, stops up a spring or destroys articles of food with destructive intent, transgresses the command, 'Thou shalt not destroy.' "

We do not know the complete story of the Shah, of our posture towards Iran in recent years, but at least we know that already in October a message was sent to our acting ambassador in Teheran telling him that the Shah might be admitted. President Jimmy Carter asked, "When the Iranians take our people in Teheran hostage, what will you advise me then?" There was heavy lobbying by friends of the Shah. It is too late to review the "who did what." The merits of asylum must be weighed.

In sum, what attitude must we maintain towards those against whom we are compelled to fight? The innocent ought not to suffer with the guilty. There is an ethical impulse in Jewish teaching that summons us to a heightened sensitivity for those who are on the other side.

Generations

1978

> "And these are the generations of Isaac, Abraham's son: Abraham begat Isaac."
> (Genesis 25:19)

Examining the text of Genesis, the opening book of our Bible, one finds at least a dozen references to the word *toledot*. For example, we read: "These are the generations of Noah" (Genesis 6:9), or, "These are the generations of Jacob" (Genesis 37:2). In most instances, the expression *toledot* is translated as generations.

Americans do not have a deep concern for the generations as compared to their European or Asian counterparts. The rapid mobility enjoyed by many Americans makes them forget their ancestors and their humble beginnings. Americans are usually concerned with the present generation and gloss over the contributions of preceding ones.

One of the greatest observers of American life was Alexis de Tocqueville, a Frenchman who visited our country in 1831. He wrote, after his study, that the United States might be best described as a place where *"each generation is a new people."* "The quality of concentrated change" affects the very nature of our society, he observed. The American Revolution had removed most of the props of colonial society. After 1791, with the adoption of the Bill of Rights, there was no longer an established church that dominated the religious scene. There was no hereditary elite who controlled society. Tocqueville stressed that "while aristocracy has made a chain of all of the members of the community . . . democracy breaks that chain. . . . Thus not only does democracy make every man forget his ancestors, but it hides his descendants and separates his contemporaries from him; it throws him back forever upon himself alone." The end result was that each individual was confined entirely "within the solitude of his own heart."

In sharp contrast to the mood that *each generation is a new people*, the Bible states proudly, "Children's children are the crown of old men" (Proverbs 17:6). Fathers are a crown, the Midrash tells us, to their sons, and sons a crown to their fathers.

Each generation has a specific mission, but that mission can only be completed by successive generations. Abraham was to go to a new land that God would show him, but Isaac was to take possession of the land by physical labor. Isaac was Isaac, but there was part of Abraham's promise uncompleted.

Each generation must understand that we have a higher goal, we have a higher mission that extends beyond our limited lives. The rabbis have a familiar saying, *Maaseh avot seeman l'vanim"*—the activities of the parents are a prototype for their children, they are a sign for their young. The past bequeaths us with unfulfilled tasks. "It is not incumbent upon you to finish the work or to desist from beginning it (for fear that you will never complete it)." Be assured in the blessing of the generations—they will come and complete your work as best they can.

TOLEDOT

Strong in Prayer—
Soft in Speech

1985

One of the great experiences of the Bible is the blessing of Jacob by Isaac, his father. Rebekah, sensing that the positive future of the Jewish people would be carried out by Jacob, arranged for him to receive the parental blessing.

We know the story since childhood days. Rebekah took the choicest garments of Esau, the older twin, and put them on Jacob, the younger twin. "And she covered his hands and the smooth part of his neck with the skins of the kids to make them feel like Esau's." Jacob said to his father, "I am Esau, your firstborn. . . . Pray sit up and eat of my game, that you may give me your innermost blessing." Jacob drew close to his father who, as he felt him, said, "The voice is the voice of Jacob, but the hands are the hands of Esau."

This statement tells us much about the character of the Jewish people. You might call it the *leit-motif* of Jewish existence. Jacob must symbolize the pleasantness of the properly expressed word. Jacob must epitomize the guarding of the tongue. Jacob does not descend to vulgarity, to coarseness, and to harshness. "Words spoken softly by wise men," we are taught in Ecclesiastes (9:17), "are heeded sooner than the scream of a lord in the manner of fools."

In a later incident in Genesis, when Jacob's sons are held by their brother Joseph whom they did not recognize, Joseph spoke harshly to them: "You are spies, you have come to see the land in all of its nakedness" (42:8,12). When the sons returned to Jacob, they said to him, "The man who is the lord of the land spoke harshly to us" (42:30).

The proper use of words is a great virtue. The rabbis thought of the word *kol*, voice, in different ways. One way was as meaning "the voice of prayer." When the voice of Jacob is heard in the synagogues, the hands of Esau cannot be successful. When the voice of Jacob is not heard, then Esau triumphs. One must be strong in prayer. When the voice of prayer is muted or even stilled as a result of our inability to transmit the significance of prayer, of Jacob's voice being heard, then the Esau element dominates.

On another level, the word *kol* signifies daily speech. The great master Maimonides recommended that our words be few but full of meaning. When a person's words are many and their meaning minute, only foolishness can issue forth. A person should not be hasty to reply or talk too much. At times, we think we have a reason to become angry. Wisely, Proverbs 15:1 teaches us: "A gentle response allays wrath. A harsh word provokes anger. The tongue of the wise produces much knowledge." The rabbis adhered to polite speech, *lashon nakeah.*

Language is the most astonishing of humanity's features. The sages were very careful to instruct their students in the proper use of language. They felt that whoever speaks excessively brings about sin. One must guard one's tongue. Words are not cheap. Jewish morality insists that words are very precious. A word is a commitment. It has a sanctity all its own.

In a classic legal instance recorded in the Mishnah, the rabbis expressed their strong disapproval of an act that does not involve even an obligation to pay by the laws of Heaven. The Mishnah teaches that there are two types of property, movable and immovable. A book is movable; a building is immovable. Movables are acquired by their actual removal into the possession of the buyer, not by the payment of the purchase price. Thus, if A gives B the money for some goods but the goods are still in A's possession, no legal transfer has been effected and either party, buyer or seller, can retract. After stating this rule, the Mishnah continues, "However, they (the sages) have said: 'He that exacted punishment from the generation of the Flood . . . will exact punishment from him that does not abide by his word.' "

It is interesting to observe that when Moses delivered his final address, the oration was called "the words of his song." The Jewish people were admonished: "Set your heart unto all the words for it is no vain thing for you because it is your life."

Our tradition has great belief in the efficacy of the soft-spoken word. A lovely interpretation of Proverbs 25:15, "and a soft tongue breaks the bone," says that the tongue of children studying the Torah, which is soft, breaks the force of sufferings, which are harder than a bone, and the sign for it is: *teshabber garem* (which is the equivalent of) *tinokot shel bet rabban gezerot ra'ot mebatelin* (school children overcome the evil decrees).

This is the voice of Jacob: prayers that are strong and speech and study that are soft.

The Way

1985

This Sabbath's Torah reading treats a critical period in the life of Jacob. It begins with the moving section on Jacob's flight and his dream of a ladder binding heaven and earth together.

Jacob the fugitive successfully escapes from his brother Esau. He seeks haven in the home of his mother's family in Haran. He is blessed with wives and children, but all doesn't go well. He yearns to return to his homeland. His difficulties with his father-in-law Laban accentuate the need for his return to Canaan. He hears God's command to return to his homeland and the place of his birth. A great parting ceremony takes place as he leaves Laban and his in-laws. They partake of a symbolic meal. As was the ancient custom, they erected a mound of memory. Laban, trying to leave the impress of his culture on Jacob, gives the mound an Aramaic name, *Yegar-sahadutha.* Jacob, faithful to his Hebrew tongue, calls it *Gal-ed,* the mound of witness. The Bible concludes the departure scene by saying "and Laban returned to his place and Jacob went on his way."

The great Hasidic master Rabbi Moshe Leib of Sasov commented that this parting of the ways between Laban the father-in-law and Jacob the son-in-law was a decisive moment in their careers. As long as Jacob was in the environment of Laban, he was affected by its corrupting lifestyle. When we are in the presence of honorable and wise people, we learn from their desirable qualities. If, on the other hand, we find ourselves in the presence of wicked people, we are tainted by them. The Psalmist has said, "With the pure, you show yourself pure. With the crooked, you show yourself subtle" (Ps. 18:27).

There is a vast difference between Laban leaving for his place and Jacob returning to his way. "Place" has many connotations. Among them is a fixed point, confining and constricting. Whereas "way" has an openness to it.

The moment Laban left for his place, Jacob was able to return to his proper way. He was able to go back to the path of truth, righteousness, and wholeheartedness. A commentator spoke of this great change by citing the verse "and Jacob went on his way and the angels of God met him." The moment Jacob realized that his life would now take a new direction, he was fit to meet with the messengers of God.

What was important in the way of Jacob? A late colleague of mine, Rabbi Ben Zion Bokser, taught that the Bible uses the word "way" as a synonym for life. The Bible encourages us to walk in the right way. "Happy are those whose way is blameless, who follow the teaching of the Lord" (Ps. 119:1). A great Hasidic master, Rabbi Dov Baer of Mezhirech, once taught, "A righteous man's career is like an open road," An individual's life is a spiritual journey, an odyssey of the soul. Why use this simile of the open road? A road helps us move from place to place, but our movement should be for positive reasons. We go from our circumscribed existence and bind ourselves to the lives of others. There are many who are afraid to move ahead and to bind their lives to the lives of others. They build fences about their lives, afraid to take the course of the open road.

VAYETZE

God Is In This Place

1978

"Surely the Lord is present in this place, and I did not know it!"

(Genesis 28:16)

This Sabbath's Torah reading contains one of the most magnificent descriptions in Scripture.

Jacob is fleeing from his brother Esau's wrath. Nightfall comes and Jacob rests with a stone as his pillow. He has a dream that a ladder is set on the ground, with its top reaching to the sky, and that God's angels go up and down on it. God gives him a promise: "Remember, I am with you: I will protect you wherever you go and will bring you back to this land. I will not leave you until I have done what I have promised you." Jacob awakes from his sleep and exclaims, "*Surely the Lord is present in this place, and I did not know it!*" Shaken, he says, "How awesome is this place! This is none other than the abode of God, and that is the gateway to heaven."

Frequently, we are not aware of the religious experience. Like Jacob, we are compelled to confess in the end that the Lord is present in this place and we did not know it. Sometimes it is because of the "I" *(anochi)*. We are so caught up in our own ego that we cannot acknowledge God's presence in our life. Sometimes we fail our children by not giving them sufficient religious grounding.

I have been reading some of the writings of Dr. Sigmund Freud. In the years between 1895 and 1899, he had worked out his theory of conflict between father and son. After extensive self-analysis, he realized the increasing effect of anti-Semitism upon the emotional life of the Austrian-Jewish community. This analysis surfaced both in his dreams and in his waking recollections.

Freud, in his earlier days, had had a deep commitment to politics. Born in 1856, he had gone through all the experiences of political hope and frustration that shaped the Central European Jewish community. In one decade there was a victory of liberalism; in the following, a crisis of liberalism. The liberal movement had changed in character and Freud had changed in reaction to it. He differed from his peers. Where they defined their tension with their fathers out of their demands for a new culture; Freud, according to some observers, defined his conflict with his father not in revolt against the values his father professed, but in criticism of his father's failure to live by them fully. I repeat this: *his father's failure to live by them fully.*

In recalling and retelling his dreams and memories of childhood, "he indicts his father for lack of courage as a Jew and for failure to encourage his children in intellectual pursuits." There is a remarkable account which I cite from Freud's *The Interpretation of Dreams.* Freud was taking a walk with his father. As they walked, they began to speak about the father's views on things of this world. He told Freud of an incident: "When I was a young man, I was walking one Saturday along the street in the village where you were born; I was well-dressed, with a new fur cap on my head. Up comes a Christian, who knocks my cap into the mud, and shouts, 'Jew, get off the pavement!' "—"And what did you do?"—"I went into the street and picked up the cap," he calmly replied. "That did not seem heroic on the part of the big, strong man who was leading me, a little fellow, by the hand." (Professor Simon thinks that the cap was a 'streimel,' the fur hat worn by Hasidim.)

Here and there, among our sensitive young people, we find criticism of our failure to live by our religious values. Groups of youngsters in a Hebrew high school department complained bitterly that they had never been exposed, as elementary school students, to religious experience. Young people who have gone to deeply observant religious day schools have protested that they learned the forms, they learned the commandments by heart, but it was all irrelevant. It was dry ritual. I sense that in many synagogues there is no real feeling of exaltation. How great is this verse, "The Lord is present in this place, and I did not know it." There is no response to the most dynamic element of human existence.

Freud was troubled by his religious identification throughout his life. At one time, Dr. Carl Jung and he were close associates. Later they split. Freud had a Jewish patient whom he was unable to help and asked Jung to take over the case. Jung was concerned with roots and racial consciousness. One day the patient told a dream of a long, dark tunnel. At the end of the tunnel, an old lady stood, and behind her was light. In the dream the old lady spoke and said, "Only he who is Jewish can pass through." This might mean that the patient was seeking his religious roots.

I know that many sensitive young people are searching for their religious heritage. It is our duty as parents and as teachers to realize that God is in this place, that we must be mature enough to say, "I know and I have been taught."

Loving God Through Gratitude

1984

Our Torah readings during these months relate mainly of the experiences of our patriarchs: Abraham, Isaac, and Jacob.

One commentator, looking at the word *vaahavta,* "and you shall love the Lord your God with all your heart, with all your soul, and with all your might," observed that the five Hebrew letters in *vaahavta,* "and you shall love," can be rearranged to spell the word *haavot,* "the patriarchs." The commentator then explained what each patriarch represented as his life's ideal.

Abraham loved God with all his heart. He was called by the prophet Isaiah, "Abraham, my friend." Abraham was the first of a long line of devout persons who stressed the love of God.

Isaac loved God with all his soul. He was prepared to surrender his life to carry out God's commandment. Do we not read in the Book of Genesis "and Abraham picked up the knife to slay his son"?

To love God with all your might is the mood of Jacob. Though the Bible says *m'oedechah,* is this not suggestive of Jacob's expression of gratitude and thanksgiving, *modeh?* He had said, "I am unworthy of all the kindness that You have so steadfastly shown your servant. With my staff alone I crossed this Jordan and now I have become two camps." Jacob was grateful. The river he had crossed when seeking refuge from his own brother would soon be crossed again. His circumstances had changed in twenty years. Now he had a family and had witnessed his physical possessions multiply.

As I read this saga of Jacob and his expression of thanksgiving, I am reminded of two events in recent weeks. One of the national networks showed a fictional series entitled "Ellis Island." Many of the characters in this depiction of the immigrant years at the beginning of the century went through Jacob-like experiences. My father, of blessed memory, came to this country with only $11 and the address of his older brothers. The immigrants who came were like coiled springs that had been pressed down for centuries. America finally gave them the opportunity to spring forward.

Stephen Birmingham wrote on the Jews of Sephardic and German origins. Now he has produced *The Rest Of Us*, a saga of Eastern European Jews who fled from the savage pogroms of Czarist Russia and who remained to prosper in the New World. Birmingham addresses the passionate ambition of the immigrants to succeed. There were, unfortunately, some whose reputations were sullied. In the main, however, the extraordinary success stories tell a magnificent tale.

Jacob knew how to be thankful. He remembered that a long time ago he had made a promise to the Most High. Just a week ago, we read of his vow, "If God remains with me, if He protects me on this journey that I am making, and gives me bread to eat and clothing to wear, and if I return safe to my father's house— the Lord shall be my God." Most critical is Jacob's pledge, "and of all that You give me, I will always set aside a tithe for You."

It is not enough to say, "Thank you, God. I am grateful, God. You have been good to me, God." One must, through positive deeds, express the mood of thankfulness. Abraham was the friend of God, Isaac was prepared to surrender his life, but it was Jacob who taught us how to be grateful and thankful.

Galut (Exile)

1979

There is a familiar rubric of the rabbis: what happened to the fathers is a foreshadowing of what will happen to their offspring. We read our Bible with that reflection in mind.

One of the most important factors in American Jewish history in the last six decades is the changing character of immigration to the United States. Job said, "From my own flesh I see." My own experience goes back more than half a century. Some of the images are blurred, while others are quite sharp. They are images of newcomers coming to this land, seeking new roots and finding their own way.

This morning our congregation is honored with the presence of one of the great Jewish scholars of America. I met him some forty-five years ago when he had been in this land for only a few years. His father had migrated from Lithuania, and several years later the family followed. They were among the last of the Eastern European Jews to come before World War II. We have to recall for a moment that a tidal wave of Jewish immigrants swept this country. It began around 1880, mounted in fury till 1914, and then receded with the passage of the oppressive immigration laws of 1922-24.

In the 1930's, I witnessed the coming of German refugees. I remember large wooden containers in which the remnants of entire family possessions were transported. The streets of the Washington Heights area in New York, where my grandparents lived and I went to high school, were filled with these well-constructed, large wooden containers. They brought the material remnants of a thousand years of Jewish life.

In my high school years, I met German Jews who came to America. I met them in college. One of them is now one of the most distinguished Orthodox rabbis of the Western Hemisphere.

I studied together with them in the Seminary in the early 1940's. Some of the distinguished rabbis of our community—Rabbi Herman Schaalman, Rabbi Karl Winer, Rabbi Ernst Lorge, the late Rabbi Frank Rosenthal—came to these shores in the 1930's. Some of the congregation who are worshipping today came at that time. The Ezra Congregation was established here at Anshe Emet by German Jewish refugees.

During the war, hardly a soul was able to move. The gates of America, the portals of freedom, were all but sealed. When the war came to a close, we had a vast influx of displaced persons. In 1956-57, following the Hungarian revolution, I participated in the movement of Jews from that country. I also participated in the movement of Jews from Egypt, for Nasser expelled most Egyptian Jews after the June 1956 war.

All during this period, slowly mounting in momentum, there was an immigration from Israel of Jews whom we referred to as *yordim*. The group that continued to come from Eastern Europe were those plucked from fire, from the Soviet Union. A handful of Jews have escaped from Iran, and I have met with them and helped them.

How have all these immigrants fared? What are the community's obligations to them? These items are uppermost on the agenda of the American Jewish community at the present time.

One thing we do know. Jacob, our father, taught us how to live. Jacob was the first of our ancestors who lived in *galut*, who lived for a long period of time in a foreign land. Most of Jewish history has been an experience in *galut*. What concerns us are the Soviet Jews and how some of them live in exile, either in the United States or elsewhere in the free world. Most of today's distinguished Russian writers, painters, and sculptors, Jewish and non-Jewish, have sought refuge in the West. The most famous of them, of course, is Alexander Solzhenitsyn, but there are many others. Some live in isolation. Others thrive in their new culture, but inwardly, though they are in *galut*, they still bear the seeds of Mother Russia within their hearts and minds.

The migration of Soviet Jews has mounted. The Kremlin has pushed into exile many, many people, including a great number of intellectuals. Their exodus is comparable to the mass departure of intellectuals from Nazi Germany in the 1930's. The Soviets have attempted to silence all dissent. They have opened their gates for a number of reasons, among them a desire to get rid of troublemakers. The Soviet artists who live abroad call themselves immigrants rather than exiles because they want to feel that they made their own choice between going West to the free world or going to Siberia.

The dislike of the word "exile" obscures an important truth. One observer remarked, "Everyone who leaves a homeland is in exile." Some of the reasons for expulsion are economic, political, or psychological. There is no difference whether one is expelled by physical force or makes a decision to leave without immediate pressure. The important thing is that when people are in their homeland, there is a language that is familiar to them, there is a style of life that they may call their own. We must empathize with these individuals.

One Soviet writer spoke of the nightmares of his existence. "The nightmare is awful, it's like losing your life. I first thought that when I wake up that it is true and I don't know what I will do because the only thing I can do is write in Russian." Exile is difficult for a creative person. "Here we are without our language, the streets, the pubs, the metros, all are silent. We live in a silent world. Silence is a good school, but it is also a difficult experience." The writer, torn from the roots of his homeland, finds himself in isolation. At times this isolation brings out the best, but at other times it is corrosive to creativity. The experience in the written word is mirrored in the experience in the arts. The artist in exile finds that feelings may become stronger. Though a long way from one's homeland, the images, the faces, the landscapes are still Russian.

A discussion on this subject was summarized by its title, "Alone Abroad." While some Soviet writers would live in isolation, others thrive in their new surroundings but inwardly still dwell in their homeland. A different approach to our question of *galut* was achieved by another generation of immigrants to the United States. This land has been described as "a nation of runaways." The history of our nation can be measured in a host of ways, but it is largely the account of how fast and how successfully our ancestors ran away from other lands. Our culture is still being molded by many who are refugees, fugitives, political pariahs. This century in which we live, with its horrible wars and famines, has meant that the history of escape and newly-won freedom cannot be closed just yet.

We must be grateful that American culture and world letters have been transformed by a writer like Thomas Mann, who began in pre-Nazi Germany and passed away in this country. In the interim, he won the Nobel Prize and wrote the magnificent "Joseph" cycle. Enrico Fermi decided to settle in this country just before World War II. He met with Albert Einstein, another refugee, and other atomic physicists, and was able to develop the atomic bomb that ended World War II. In the great dimensions of art, we have benefited from a host of men and women who have sought to live in America part or most of their time. We must think of Daniel Barenboim, Pinchas Zuckerman, Itzhak Perlman, and Zvi Zeitlin, among others.

Galut is a difficult process. The freedom hunters, as someone called them, have changed the face of America. Some have changed the outer face, like Walter Gropius, who taught a generation of architects at Harvard. Our own city has benefited from Mies van der Rohe. The inner face of America has been changed by Bruno Bettelheim.

Those who have chosen or have been forced to choose to live in *galut*, "the runaways," have changed us and helped reshape American life. Our father Jacob taught us to live in exile. His son Joseph, who followed him, understood this lesson and was among the most creative of all state builders.

VAYIGASH

Reach Out and Touch Someone

1980

In *The Holy Letter*, the unknown author states an important principle: "The matter is not as Rabbi Moses Maimonides, of blessed memory, said in his *The Guide of the Perplexed*. He was incorrect in praising Aristotle for stating that the sense of touch is shameful for us. Heaven forbid! The matter is not like the Greeks said. It smacks of heresy."

Some of the handwritten manuscripts spoke of Aristotle as being the accursed Greek. Others use very harsh language, always repeating the theme that the sense of touch is shameful for us. In checking through this matter, I found that Maimonides repeats this statement several times in his famous philosophical treatise *The Guide of the Perplexed*. What is behind the thinking of Maimonides? This great rationalist followed the teaching of some Greek philosophers that the sense of sight was more important than the sense of touch.

The great Danish Bible scholar and religious historian Johannes Pedersen explained the importance of physical touch. In a recent issue of *Signs, Journal of Women in Culture and Society*, there is a difficult passage by a French woman, Luce Irigaray, whose article is entitled "When Our Lips Speak Together." She stresses what Pedersen the Bible scholar emphasized, namely, the positive importance of the sense of touch. She writes, "How can I touch you if you are not there? It is to remind you, to remind us, that we can touch each other . . . to find ourselves and each other." Unless there is the sense of touch, persons "remain distant. . . . Touch yourself, touch me, you will see."

Pedersen went through the Bible, citing especially sections from the Book of Genesis. He explained the importance of physical contact. Isaac, when he gave the blessing to Jacob, sniffed his clothes and his body. Once they were in physical contact, once the father had touched the son, the father's soul could communicate itself to that of the son. Bodily nearness, the scholar wrote, is generally made more intimate by touch, most often by the laying of hands on the head of the person in question. You remember the blessing of Jacob who laid his hands upon the heads of Ephraim and Manasseh. Physical contact was essential. Greeting a person properly was all-important. When friends took leave one of the other, they blessed each other in order to confirm the friendship. Each gave to the other so much of the soul that the community could be maintained when they were separated.

Thus, Laban rebuked Jacob when he escaped. Why? Among the reasons that can be offered is the one that Jacob's flight deprived his father-in-law of the privilege of kissing his offspring and blessing them. The close bodily contact imparted in the kiss always pertains to the leave-taking. This example is found many times in the Bible. When Esau and his twin brother, Jacob, confronted each other after they had been separated by twenty years of misunderstanding, "Esau ran to greet him. He embraced him and, falling on his neck, he kissed him; and they wept." Later in the Bible, in Genesis, Joseph orders a chariot and goes to Goshen to meet his father. "He presented himself to him and, embracing him around the neck, he wept on his neck a good while."

Another example is found in Joseph's meeting with his brothers. "With that he flung himself on the neck of his brother Benjamin and wept and Benjamin wept on his neck. Then he kissed all his brothers, crying on each of them; only then were his brothers able to talk to him" (Gen. 45:15). Only after having a sense of touch were they able to have a true sense of brotherhood.

A commentator, Or Hahayim—a mystic whose works are beloved throughout the Jewish world—made the point that Joseph's words and crying were not believed by the brothers since they weren't sure what he was crying about or whether or not his words were sincere. But when he kissed them and cried over each one individually, that was a sign of true brotherhood.

Professor Jacob Milgrom makes the additional point by contrasting the verse dealing with Joseph's brothers with the special treatment he afforded to Benjamin. Benjamin had never felt malice or guilt towards Joseph and therefore reciprocated in touching. The brothers, on the other hand, thought they now saw that Joseph was sincere but did not fully accept him. If one reads the text carefully, they spoke only after there had been a sense of touch. The proof that the brothers were not completely convinced of Joseph's change of heart towards them is evidenced by the fact that no sooner did father Jacob die, than the brothers become anxiety ridden. They were sure that Joseph would take his revenge.

Any kind of bodily touch strengthens the covenant, Pedersen pointed out, because the body forms part of the entirety of the soul. The being together strengthens it. The covenant is confirmed by the shake of the hand, it is strengthened by the intimate touch of the kiss. There is a sharp contrast between the position of Maimonides, who thought that the sense of touch is shameful and disgraceful to us, and the Biblical view that emphasized the sense of touch. In reality, we need each other because we are each other. Dr. Willard Gaylin, one of our nation's leading psychoanalysts, has published an important study called *Feelings*. In a chapter on "Feeling Touched," he speaks of the commonplace expression .of how "touched you were when. . . ." Touching involves sharing. "It demands person-to-person contact." Where does the word "contact" come from? It comes from the Latin "contactus," touching, and has come to mean "coming together," communicating. What do we say as we take leave? "Keep in touch." We are touched, Gaylin writes, "by the thoughtfulness of a friend, by an unexpected courtesy . . . an unaccustomed act of kindness."

In a number of studies, it was observed that babies, as well as children, need more than physical care and medication if ill; they need physical contact. You surely remember Dr. Rene Spitz's famous study in which babies who had no real loving care, who were untouched most of the day, passed away despite the cleanliness of the nursery. It has been known that many premature infants who are handled fare much better than those who are not touched as often.

The modern day commercial of the Bell Telephone System that says "Reach out and touch someone" may have more profundity than the copywriter who fashioned these lines imagined. Hearing another's voice in dialogue is as important as physical touch. What is needed within our congregation is the ability to reach out in amity, friendship, warmth, and love.

Power

1983

Earlier this week, the President of the United States served as host at a state dinner for the visiting king of Nepal. A colleague of mine was invited to attend the function, together with some 160 other guests. He described the feeling he had at the gathering of the leaders of our nation in the President's house, which is the seat of great power. My friend said, "Now I understand how Joseph must have felt in his palace as he ruled over the land of Egypt."

The essence of power comes to mind as one thinks of the experience of Joseph and his brothers. Power is enforced by the threat and reality of punishment. Power is enforced by persuasion and an appeal to belief. A great psychoanalyst once said, "The healthy individual who gains power loves it." The leader of any group feels, through the exercise of power, an almost physical enlargement of self. Power is like a mountain-top. The air breathed there is different, and the perspectives seen there are different from those of the valley of obedience. While power at times is a social necessity, it is also a social menace. There can be suffering, indignity, and unhappiness from the improper exercise of power.

Joseph, as you remember, was the vizier of Egypt—the second person in the chain of command, immediately under the all-powerful Pharaoh. Joseph had put his brothers through a long and tortuous cross-examination. Finally, after he had boxed them in completely, after he had humiliated them to the point of total submission, the Bible relates that Judah—brave Judah—made the final plea. "And Judah went to stand before Joseph and said, please my Lord let your servant appeal to my Lord. Do not be impatient with your servant." It is a remarkable thing that something happened that caused a change in the attitude of Joseph.

From that moment forth, Joseph was prepared to be the savior of his brothers rather than their tormentor.

The question that has always concerned me has been an analysis of power. Is there a place in the armor of the powerful through which even the greatest of leaders can be reached?

Power is a popular subject. The ability of individuals or groups to control a situation, to win the submission of others to their purpose, has an established pattern. There are many books on power. I recall arriving at the old airport in Moscow in the summer of 1963. As is typical of customs inspections there, every one of the books I carried was examined. I am not sure whether or not the inspector—a burly, heavy-set man—could read English, but I remember him pulling out a paperback copy of Bertrand Russell's *Power, A New Social Analysis*, holding it in the air, looking at it and finally saying that I could bring the book into Russia, a nation where there is strict censorship. Bertrand Russell thought that power remains the highest aspiration and the greatest reward of humankind.

There are books on economic power, there are studies of political power, there are tomes on military power, there are volumes on religious power. A great American scholar, John Kenneth Galbraith, wrote a book called *The Anatomy of Power* in which he tries to analyze what power really means. Galbraith goes through the various categories of power. People submit to power because it profits them or because they feel they ought to submit. People respond to threats of punishment. Power can shift very quickly.

In our country, one must consider how the power structure suddenly changed. In 1973, a president of the United States, Richard Nixon, entered his second term after a landslide electoral victory over Senator George McGovern. He was intent upon remaking our country and its government. He possessed many of the tools for carrying out his plans. Congress was debilitated. Yet overnight the power went from the President into other hands. It came into the hands of the House Judiciary Committee, a committee which in the main does not serve as vital a role as the Senate Judiciary Committee, which has to approve all federal judges as well as the Attorney General. What happened to shift power so dramatically? Nixon hadn't changed, the presidency hadn't changed, legal authority hadn't changed. Suddenly the House realized the implications of Watergate and its power to impeach the President of the United States. There was no change in our Constitution. This power to impeach had always existed. But it had never been exercised, it was a dead letter. The people who had the new power hadn't changed. Flying on the shuttle between Newark and Washington, Chairman Congressman Peter Rodino read a book on impeachment behind a blank paper cover. He was afraid to let it be known that he might consider so high an exercise of constitutional prerogative.

The important thing we must not forget is that even a person with great power can be reached. The quality that causes one to be reachable is that little spark of compassion, humaneness, *rahmanut*, that exists in the hearts of most individuals. Not all individuals. It was not present in the heart of Hitler. It did not function in the heart of Adolph Eichmann. But Joseph, even though he had every reason to be bitter against his brothers, permitted that little spark of humaneness and kindness to be fanned and to burst into a flame of love. His total power was broken by compassion. It was an act of *zedakah*, an act of righteousness, that brought about the change in Joseph. The harsh brother who had tormented his siblings, who had played with them as a cat plays with trapped mice, rose to a new stature. He became the brother who was going to act as God's instrument of history in changing the entire future of the Jewish world.

That Joseph possessed this element of compassion and humaneness can be seen in an incident we read last week when he looked at Benjamin his full brother (they shared the same mother, Rachel) and asked, "Is this your youngest brother of whom you spoke to me?" And he went on, "May God be gracious to you, my boy." With that, Joseph hurried out, for he was overcome with feeling, and the Bible reads in Hebrew, *nechmaru rachamov*.

A great English writer, Joseph Conrad, once spoke of the importance of compassion. He said, "What humanity needs is compassion and pity in this life." To my way of thinking, this is what caused the change in Joseph—the overwhelming feeling of compassionate pity.

During the Middle Ages, there could have been little talk or thought of power. It was massively possessed only by princes, barons, and priests. For the silent masses, powerlessness was the natural order of things. Power was not discussed because only a tiny minority of the people possessed it. Rollo May, in *Freedom and Destiny,* spoke of the long relationship, interminably debated in the parliaments of the world and fought and bled over on countless battlefields, between freedom and power.

It has been widely said that a Joseph made his contribution to history and is remembered for good, while a Pharaoh was doomed to be destroyed. Pharaoh permitted his heart to be hardened, while Joseph permitted his heart to be touched and to feel compassion and pity.

Power without compassion is arrogance, which ultimately is self-destructive. The seed of compassion lay dormant within the breast of Joseph. It was Judah's plea that brought it to life and ultimate maturation.

MIKETZ

Food, A Critical Necessity

1979

There are words that cause our hearts to shudder. Such a word is *pogrom.* I remember the film "The Shop on Main Street" with its depiction of the old shopkeeper who saw the leaders of her community and the rest of the Jewish populace being rounded up in the village square prior to deportation. The elderly lady's mind was foggy. Finally it dawned on her that something terrible was about to happen, and she shouted the word *pogrom.*

Another word that causes us great anxiety is *plague.* All too often, in the face of seemingly irreconcilable conflict, we say "A plague on both your houses." The plague was a decimator of millions.

This Sabbath we think of the expression *raav* (famine). We read in the Torah section: "The famine spread over the whole world. When the famine became severe in the land of Egypt, Joseph laid open all that was within and rationed out grain to the Egyptians."

All the world came to Joseph in Egypt to buy grain, for the famine had become severe throughout the world" (Gen. 41:56-57).

Famine is frightening. I recall seeing a film version of Pearl Buck's The Good Earth. Hordes of locusts fly in; they darken the sky and destroy the grain. A shortage of food causes inflation in the land, leading to a breakdown of society. A few who lived well above the margin and hoarded are able to sustain themselves, but most people suffer bitterly. Theodore White in his In Search of History describes this process in China during World War II.

Mother Teresa, Calcutta's saint of the gutters, accepted the Nobel Peace Prize in the name of the poor and the sick. She told the Oslo audience, "Our poor people are great people, a very lovable people. They don't need our pity and sympathy. They need our understanding (and) love and they need our respect. We need to tell the poor that they are somebody to us, that they, too, have been created by the same loving hand of God, to love and be loved."

There is need for us to be concerned with the growing food shortages in our world. Human sickness and health are related to the human diet. The shortage of food in many parts of our globe must be a matter of great concern. At this season of the year when many of us, Christians and Jews alike, are engaged in our festival dinners and big parties, we ought to think a while about those who go to bed hungry at night.

In a study called Famine or Food: Sacrificing for Future or Present Generations, the author makes the point that very few people starve to death. However, the malnourished and the undernourished, especially infants and children, are highly susceptible to various diseases and frequently die from them. The diets of millions of people, especially in the underdeveloped countries, are nutritionally deficient in proteins, vitamins, and even calories.

The world is growing at an accelerated pace. The predictions for the future are dire. By the year 2000, which is only twenty years away, there are forecasts of more widespread famine than is occurring presently. There are some who argue with cogency that world population could grow many fold and the food supply would grow as well, but that the real problem lies in the distribution of food.

Harvard University Professor Robert Coles, one of the outstanding professors of psychiatry and medical humanities, was asked together with six other faculty members of Harvard: "What is the most important problem facing this nation or the world at the start of the 80's? What solutions should we be making to deal with it?" Cole responded that more than half the world lives on the brink of chronic hunger. Words such as Biafra, and now Cambodia, and the boat people, enter our minds for a moment and then are pushed aside.

In ages gone by, there was hunger too, but our century is the first that offers humankind the opportunity to win the stark battle for survival. Our generation has conquered many diseases; we have mastered the energy of the atom. Given the limits of agricultural knowledge, is there any reason why men, women, and children must suffer hunger? The heart of the issue is a moral one, Dr. Coles argued. He felt, in conclusion, that we in American will be getting closer in the next decade to the goal of solving the problem of world hunger once and for all. A striking fact is that each American depends on an acre and a half of tilled (cultivated) land and another three acres of rangeland and pasture to maintain our diet. Compare and contrast this with India and China, where each citizen depends on a third to a half acre of tilled land. In India, only a token amount of pastureland (0.07 acre per inhabitant) exists.

We must view this issue in its religious perspective. After all, this is not an exercise in agricultural economics. Several years ago, the dean of Eden Theological Seminary, Professor Walter Brueggemann, wrote on this subject in a magazine article called "A Biblical Perspective on the Problem of Hunger." He stressed the fact that just as there is not enough bread to go around, the bread we have is not equitably shared. He traced the experience of the Israelites in the desert where an effort was made to achieve equitable distribution. He cited the fact that the dominant model for distribution is the feeding by manna described in Exodus 16.

The Western world shares a responsiblity for Third World poverty. This was documented in a study on ethics and public policy published by Georgetown University. May we resolve, during this season of gift giving and gift receiving, to be concerned with the wider world about us.

Every Passover eve we extend an invitation to all: "All who are hungry, let them come and eat. All who are in need, let them come and celebrate our liberation." The true liberation of humankind will be achieved when hunger has been abolished.

Regaining Our Past

1981

This Sabbath is marked by a unique convergence: the newness of Rosh Hodesh, the promise and possibilities that lie ahead; Sabbath Hanukkah, using the oldest symbol of Jewish religious identity; and Sabbath Miketz, telling of the ascent of Joseph to greatness.

Rarely during the course of our liturgical calendar do we use three Sifrei Torah. Here we have the blend of the old and the new, the past and the future coming together in a grand moment of the sacred present. Wisely it has been pointed out that the most sacred credo of our people is to be found in our attitude towards life. Chancellor Gerson Cohen once said that we seek more than survival, we seek renewal. The Jewish people has been able to renew itself in every generation. With spiritual skillfulness, we have taken the past and translated it to the future. This process of taking from the old and giving it new meaning, taking from the new and pouring in old meanings, has produced the blend prayed for by the great master of our century, the late Chief Rabbi Kook. *Hayashan yithadesh, hahadash yitkadesh*—"The old must be renewed and the new become sacred."

Last year, I had a special experience in meeting with the president of Yale University, Dr. A. Bartlett Giamatti. Only 43 now, he was named 19th president of the University in 1977. He came to New York to help the Conservative family break ground for our new library. Recently, he published a fine work, *The University and the Public Interest*, a collection of essays on American society and education. In an insightful essay on Ralph W. Emerson, the great American thinker, Giamatti makes some unusually pertinent observations. Emerson had a great belief in self-reliance and original action. Through his approach to life, he persuaded succeeding generations that custom was a crutch, not a means of continuity. Emerson tried to reassure his readers that every person was his own pure source. The result of Emerson's thinking was that he infected American culture with a scorn for the past.

From my point of view, we need a sense of the past. Like Joseph, we must be dreamers—for the past is not merely the past of historical record, but the "great dreams of the arts." These dreams recur to trouble us with a sense of limitation. How little we know of the real dimensions of our own experience. You have many times heard the expression of Santayana that those who do not learn from history are condemned to relive it. In a striking aphorism, Christopher Fry, great student of literature, said, "Those who refuse to confront their own real past . . . are condemning themselves to die without having been born."

An appeal can be made to all Americans to absorb and not to reject the past. America will grow when we re-acquire a sense of history. America will enjoy stability when our political life reflects our heritage. I feel it is true that we must remember that the promise of a people's history is carried in each of us.

Unfortunately, history is like beauty—it is in the eyes of the beholder. History can be perverted, history can be suppressed, history can be ignored. There are those who have corrupted the past. Let me cite one extremely significant example. Art is a record of history. Michelangelo's great sculpture of Moses shows the lawgiver with horns. Rembrandt's depiction of Moses does not. With a stroke of the brush, the image of the Jew was changed from monster to human being. One art historian described it as follows: "No fuss, no fanfare heralds this momentous emancipation." The Jews had become part of the landscape of the Netherlands. They were not denizens of the deep underworld.

This day we think of Mattathias and Judah the Maccabee and of how they changed the image of the Jew. The Maccabees and their latter-day descendants showed the world that the Jew is not a coward but rather a hero. In the West Point Chapel, among the sculptures of the great military heroes of the world's past, one can find a replica of Judah the Maccabee.

As Americans and as Jews, there is much we must recall. One of the greatest thinkers of our age, Sir Isaiah Berlin, once wrote, "All Jews who are at all conscious of their identity as Jews are steeped in history. They have longer memories, they are aware of a longer continuity as a community than any other which has survived. . . . For the Jewish people, historical consciousness—the vital sense of continuity with the past—is a principal element in our being."

The Qualities of Leadership

1984

One of the great legacies of genuine masters of scholarship is that long after their passing there are echoes and reverberations of their work.

The other day I was reading a passage from the Tosefta, a work that preoccupied the great savant and my teacher, Professor Saul Lieberman. As a young scholar living in Jerusalem and serving as Dean of the Harry Fischel Institute, he helped republish the scientific edition of the Tosefta, which is a companion to the Mishnah—the authoritative code of Jewish law. Professor Saul Lieberman rose to become the Distinguished Service Research Professor in Talmud at the Jewish Theological Seminary. He was honored with six honorary degrees, including one from Harvard University. During the last decade of his life, he worked assiduously on a commentary on the Tosefta, and the passage that concerns us this Shabbat comes from that great source of Jewish wisdom. Originally oral, the Tosefta has been described as detailed rules for the application of the Bible.

The rabbis asked: Why is it that Judah, who was the fourth-born of Jacob, merited being called to kingship? They surely knew why Reuben, Simeon, and Levi had been passed over. "Reuben, you are my first-born, my might and firstfruit of my vigor, exceeding in rank and exceeding in honor. Unstable as water, you shall excel no longer." In Jacob's final blessing, which we read next week, he speaks of the disgrace Reuben brought to his father's bed. "Simeon and Levi are a pair; their tools are tools of lawlessness. Let not my person enter their council." Judah merited kingship. "You, O Judah, your brothers shall praise. . . . The scepter shall not depart from Judah, nor the ruler's staff from between his feet."

The rabbis gave their reason for the selection of Judah. His pre-eminence was merited because he saved his brother Joseph from death. Do we not read in Genesis 37:26-27, "Then Judah said to his brothers, 'What do we gain by killing our brother and covering up his blood?' " He suggested a graceful way out. "Come, let us sell him to the Ishmaelites, but let us not do away with him ourselves. After all, he is our brother, our own flesh." Among the qualities that a king must have is that of concern for the well-being of all his brothers, whether they are mighty or humble.

A second reason is advanced by our text. Judah was called to leadership because of his modesty. "When Judah and his brothers re-entered the house of Joseph, who was still there, they threw themselves on the ground before him." Still playing the merciless autocrat, perhaps repaying an old grudge, Joseph asked, "What is this deed you have done? Do you not know that a man like me practices divination?" Judah was the brave spokesman: "What can we say to my Lord? How can we plead, how can we prove our innocence?" Joseph's goblet had been found in the bag of the youngest brother, Benjamin. Joseph said, "The rest of you can go free, but he in whose possession the goblet was found shall be my slave." Judah mustered his courage, but he did it in such a way that—to use the contemporary phrase—he put his body "on the line." He had promised Jacob that he would bring Benjamin back and now Benjamin appeared to be headed for permanent slavery. Listen to the language of Judah's final plea: "Therefore, please let your servant remain as a slave to my lord instead of the boy and let the boy go back with his brothers. For how can I go back to my father unless the boy is with me? Let me not be witness to the woe that would overtake my father." The rabbis hailed Judah's modesty. He, the most powerful brother, would become the slave in place of the youngest.

This experience reminded the rabbis of how Saul, the first king of Israel, was selected. Saul was not anxious for the kingship. He hid when Samuel the judge wanted to anoint him. Samuel inquired of the Lord and was answered, "Yes, he is hiding among the baggage." So Saul was brought from there, and when he took his place among the people, he stood a head taller than all. Samuel said to the people, "Do you see the one whom the Lord has chosen? There is none like him among all the people." And the people acclaimed Saul, shouting, "Long live the king!" A king must possess the quality of modesty.

There is a third suggestion as to why Judah merited kingship: because a member of his tribe sanctified God's name when our people went out of Egypt and stood at the brink of the sea. The question was, who would have the courage to jump into the sea so that its waters would be divided? A member of the tribe of Judah went first and sanctified the name of God. About this great experience, our prayers have a daily remembrance. It was a desperate hour. Did not the Psalmist say, "Deliver me, O God, for the waters have reached my neck. I am sinking into the slimy deep and find no foothold. I have come into the watery depths and the floods sweep me away?" In our Hallel, we read, "When Israel went forth from Egypt. . . . Judah became his sanctuary, and Israel his dominion." Judah, who sanctified the name of God at the sea, merited kingship.

Judah was courageous and compassionate. Recently, an old article by Professor Reinhold Niebuhr was republished. Niebuhr was a pre-eminent Christian thinker and a great friend of the Jewish people. He wrote of a prayer he had composed that has been attributed to many other people. "God give us grace to accept serenity in the things that cannot be changed, courage to change the things that should be changed, and the wisdom to distinguish the one from the other." Judah was a man of courage and knew how to exercise that great quality.

Generational Change

1985

This Sabbath's Torah reading is a description of an era of change. It marks the end of the epoch of the patriarchs. The life of our people is no longer dominated and directed by an Abraham, Isaac, or Jacob.

The story of Joseph is over. He dies at a ripe old age, telling his brothers, "God will surely take notice of you and bring you up from this land to the land which he promised on oath to Abraham, to Isaac and to Jacob." The promise of a return to Canaan was kept. There is the period of transition as our people become the B'nai Israel to be led by Moses, the great emancipator.

In an outstanding study of events in the Soviet Union, James Billington, author of *The Icon and the Axe: An Interpretive History of Russian Culture,* makes a fundamental point. The Soviet Union, he claims, is going through a momentous and generational change as control passes from the walled-in, beleaguered generation raised under Stalin to a better educated leadership with higher expectations. Just as our ancestors went through a momentous generational change from the patriarchal age to the status of being a people, Soviet society is going through a similar critical period. "No one knows," Billington writes, "whether this new generation will move toward closer identification with the values of the rest of the civilized world community or institutionalize the increase in repression that began under Brezhnev." In sum, the old men who are ruling in the Kremlin through its Politburo, the central power apparatus, will be passing away. What will happen after they are gone?

A generational change is taking place in our country in many areas: in the realm of civil rights, in the role of women in all strata of society. Dramatic changes are taking place within each of the great religious communities. In Christianity, we witness the courageous statement of nuns, while in Judaism—at least for the Reform and Conservative movements—women rabbis and cantors are becoming the order of the day. Conservative Christianity in this country has witnessed the emergence of a new right, using the electronic media to bring its message across. A generational change is in the making in the United States Supreme Court as more and more of the justices reach their late seventies.

A great generational change is taking place in the new approach to philanthropy. As one who has been closely identified with the conventional charitable institutions, I watch with great interest the new pressures that are emerging. There is a breaking away from the familiar Red Feather, Crusade of Mercy, and Jewish Federations. Though this is not a mass phenomenon, it is interesting to observe that an heir of the IBM fortune was written about as being one of the growing number of sons and daughters of corporate America who have dug into their family fortunes to help fund alternative foundations that are concerned with social change as well as charitable deeds. As one reads the list of the scions of Fortune 500, one finds the offspring of Levi-Strauss, ALCOA, and Du Pont, who had been stirred by the protest movements of the 1960s and are now channeling their money into socially and politically conscious organizations concerned with women's rights, anti-nuclear action, and racial discrimination.

While we are in the aura of the new calendar year that gives the making of predictions legitimacy, I have the feeling that within our Jewish community vast generational changes may be felt. It is my personal feeling that the coming generations will be marked by innovations in the priorities and purpose of our philanthropies. It would be wise to alert ourselves to the implications of change and to understand what these new possibilities mean as we move towards the 21st century.

What's In a Name?

1986

This Shabbat, we come to the reading of the second of the Five Books of Moses. Shemot tells of the agony caused by Egyptian bondage. The first reference to *Am*, people, is recorded in its lines. The people are miraculously delivered; they cross the Red Sea; they hear the words of the Ten Commandments. The civil society is structured and a physical sanctuary is built.

Shemot means "names," and these are the opening words of our text: "These are the names of the sons of Israel, who came to Egypt with Jacob; each coming with his own household." Names are important because they mark a signficant development in the life of humankind.

It is interesting to note that Genesis, the first book of the Bible, also begins with the theme of names. Adam, the first person on earth, carried out his first assignment. "And the Lord God formed out of the earth all the wild beasts and all of the birds of the sky and brought them to Adam to see what he would call them. And whatever Adam called each living creature, that would be its name. And Adam gave names to all the cattle and the birds of the sky and all the wild beasts." Both Genesis and Exodus begin with the theme of names.

The giving of a name is an important experience. We give names, in love and affection, to our children when they come to this earth. Sometimes one wonders about the names that are given, but they are of importance to the giver and conjure up significant associations. There is a magnificent rabbinic passage on the opening section of Exodus which says that there are three names for each human being: the name God gives, the name the parents give, and the name the person earns. The hope is that the name the person earns and that others use when speaking of him or her may be a name that we can truly be proud of—in terms of the nameholder's achievements.

Throughout our history as a nation, Americans have pigeon-holed their fellow citizens into categories with unique names. Labels do not last forever, but while they remain they can have great impact. During the Revolutionary War period, we had those who were called Tories. In the 19th century, the "Know-Nothing" movement was fiercely anti-Catholic. In a nation of nations with so many diverse ethnic groups, Americans have labeled each other by political description, economic status, or racial and religious designation.

A new designation—the "new color" class—is coming into vogue. This group consists of people who constitute almost ten percent of the American population. They are young to middle age adults. They are computer programmers, managers of fast-food stores, and teachers of our children. They find community in the gritty, popular songs of a Bruce Springsteen. In our post-industrial economy, they are the successors to the traditional blue-collar workers. They are the new workhorses of America. Culturally, they are just a different breed. Politically, they are being cultivated by both parties.

Try to think of the names that have been given by one set of Americans to another. We had our bobby-soxers, who wore anklet socks and swooned when Frank Sinatra sang in public. There was the "silent generation" of the early 1950s. This term was used to describe the majority of Americans during Eisenhower's first administration. They were people who were content with quietly following the prevailing rules of business and society. There were "beatniks" and "hippies." Hippies who were also known as "flower children," got their name from a San Francisco political organizaton: Haight-Asbury Independent Proprietors. They preached love and peace. They led the protests against our involvement in the Vietnam War. Then there were the "yippies" or followers of Jerry Rubin and Abbie Hoffman, known for their civil disobedience and their activities during the 1968 Democratic convention in Chicago.

Richard Nixon called his backers the "silent majority," people "whose individual opinions are not colorful but different enough to make the news; whose collective opinion when crystallized makes history." There was the "me" generation, caught up in privatism and self-fulfillment. There were many, many labels given to groups, winding up with the "yuppies"—the young, upwardly mobile professionals.

Our two principal news magazines, *Time* and *Newsweek*, usually choose a person or event of the year for their final weekly cover. *Newsweek* of December 31, 1984 traced "The Year of the Yuppie." It described their style of living, what satisfies them, and what ostensibly gratifies them. The article included the following statement. After describing their physical possessions, clothing, wine, and so on, a wife says, "I guess this is a substitute for children." They are concerned with success, and one observer asked, "But are we really worse than previous generations? Has no one in America hustled for a buck before? Did we invent consumption?"

In the *American Scholar*, Winter 1985-86, a reluctant "yuppie" speaks of his life and achievements. He quotes the chapter in Tocqueville's *Democracy in America* entitled "Why There Are So Many Men of Ambition in the United States But So Few Lofty Ambitions." "Every American is eaten up with longing to rise," Tocqueville observed, "but hardly any of them seem to entertain very great hopes or to aim very high."

As the years go by, new names will be used. Let us hope that they reflect healthy attitudes on the experience of human living and what is really important in life.

ROSH HODESH SHEVAT, VAERA

Keeping the Gates Open

1986

In a survey conducted by the Roper poll for a national Jewish organization, it was reported that "4 in 10 Americans want Jews to stop reminding them of the Holocaust," in which six million of our people perished. The survey also determined that the majority of Americans who had an opinion on the subject, would like the United States to stop locating Nazi war criminals.

I read this report at a time when the American nation, particulary the Jewish community, is very involved in the showing of Claude Lanzmann's film "Shoah" (Holocaust). Many members of our congregation will be seeing the highly-acclaimed film, and a discussion of it will be conducted by our adult school.

Since 1945, there have been several important studies documenting the tragic account of the Holocaust. *While Six Million Died* by Arthur Morse, *The Politics of Rescue* by Henry Feingold, *The Abandonment of the Jews* by David Wyman. These have now been joined by Deborah Lipstadt's *Beyond Belief*. Professor Lipstadt's thorough study deals with the American press and its failure to treat the destruction of European Jews as urgent news.

If one wants to analyze the various studies of this period, from 1933 to 1945, one should deal with three elements: (1) the failure to open America's immigration doors; (2) no real intervention during the war years to prevent the movement of Hitler's captives to the death camps; and (3) the depth of involvement of Jews in the free world in the tragedy that was unfolding.

A splendid treatment of the Holocaust years in an American Jewish community is discussed in *Haven and Home, The History of Jews in America* by Professor Abraham J. Karp. There is much truth to the fact, as Hayim Greenberg wrote in 1943, that "Never before in history have we displayed such shamefully strong nerves as we do now in the days of our greatest catastrophe. We have become so dulled that we have even lost our capacity for madness."

This Shabbat I would like to focus on the issue of immigration to America. When Hitler came to power, there were people in our press who were highly skeptical regarding the accuracy of reports on the persecution of Jews. One important journal urged "a tighter curb on emotions until the facts are beyond dispute." This approach found its reflection in the opposition, reported by a Gallup poll in 1939, "to allow 10,000 refugee children from Germany to be brought into this country and be taken care of in American homes." Though the quotas for German immigration were never filled, another poll reported that 77 percent of women in Cincinnati were opposed to the entry of children. *Fortune* magazine stated that 85 percent of the non-Jews asked were adamantly against any change in immigration quotas.

I shudder as I re-read the experience of the S. S. *St. Louis* and its passengers' vain attempt to land in Cuba. One of the members of our congregation was a passenger on that ship. The *Christian Science Monitor* castigated Jewish refugees for being so selective about their destination. "Most Jews apparently have no taste for the pioneering necessary in remote and underdeveloped areas and do not take readily to some plans in their behalf. While this is understandable, they may remember that other races have carved homes out of the wilderness to escape oppression."

The 1930s were, to be sure, a difficult time for America. The administration's efforts to reduce unemployment were only partially successful. Many Americans harbored and expressed the feeling that the coming of more persons into the labor market would hurt them. Some suggested that we admit gifted immigrants like Professor Albert Einstein and Dr. Sigmund Freud. Professor Lipstadt has an interesting note that during this period, rumors circulated in American cities that some Jewish-owned department stores were firing their employees in order to hire refugees. She writes, "Despite reported denials by the stores, these rumors prevailed. They became so widespread that . . . several stores, including Bloomingdale's and Macy's, placed newspaper ads denying that they were hiring refugees." One important newspaper rejected suggestions for changing laws and counseled that the best protest was prayer.

The gates of America remained closed until the outbreak of the war, when transport became all but impossible. It is hard to read these apologetics from leading magazines: "There is no ethical principle that requires either an individual person or a nation to expose itself to a condition sure to involve a moral overstrain." "Our immigration laws . . . should be maintained and even further strengthened." "High-minded citizens have no need to feel apologetic for the limitations upon immigration into the country." There was concern that the character of America would be changed if too many newcomers were permitted to enter this land.

As one reads of America's failure to respond to this challenge, we must take Governor Richard Lamm of Colorado to task. You may recall the furor he created two years ago when he is reported to have said to the aged, "You have a duty to die and get out of the way. Let the other society, our kids, build a reasonable life." In a new book, *The Immigration Time Bomb*, Lamm and his co-author Gary Imhoff urge us to "stop fragmenting America." They write that "there is a flood of people rising right outside our door." With vehemence they deal with the subject of illegal aliens. "The alien tide must be curtailed. Illegals tend to take better jobs than we do." The governor, from his lofty perch, proclaims that "America's 'golden door' has always been open to refugees." The facts of the matter seem to be otherwise. He conjures up the dangers of an Oriental tidal wave when Hong Kong reverts to Chinese rule. He is concerned lest American Jews demand that two or three million Soviet Jews be allowed to migrate to the United States. The governor wrote that it is impossible to predict when the future will present America with painful choices that challenge our country's historic traditions. "Yet, for our children's sake we must ask, how much compassion can we afford? At some point our compassion to share what we have will destroy what we have."

I would like to remind the governor that he who saves a single life, it is as though he had saved the world.

BO

The Profundity of Simple Things

1985

This past week, I had a number of experiences relating to the struggle for freedom. I saw a motion picture based on Forster's *A Passage to India*. Beyond the extremely impressive account of India in the 1920s, one felt part of a struggle for freedom. For three nights during the same week, I watched a series on Martin Luther King's efforts from the early struggles in Montgomery, Alabama to the fateful April day when he was assassinated in Memphis, Tennessee. Many of us have seen the T.V. series "The Jewel In The Crown," which deals with the final stages of British rule in India. India became independent with the partition of the vast subcontinent into two republics, India and Pakistan.

The hunger for freedom, the struggle for liberty goes on from generation to generation. Annually, we relive this experience at our Passover Seder. Every day in our prayer service, we remember that we were freed from Egyptian bondage. The Bible tells us that one of the most important ways in which we are to remember and to relate the account of redemption from Egypt is by telling the story. "Then the Lord said to Moses, 'Go into Pharaoh's court. For I have hardened his heart and the hearts of his courtiers, in order that . . . you may recount in the hearing of your sons and of your sons' sons how I displayed My signs among them in order that you may know that I am the Lord.'" Earlier in the Book of Exodus, our people are commanded, "Thou shalt explain to your son on that day saying, It is because of what the Lord did for me when I went free from Egypt" (Exodus 13:8).

The importance of telling the story has been one of the prime methods of continuing an appreciation of the tradition from generation to generation. In every age there have been those who taught the law, but there were always those who mastered the story.

One of the greatest teller of tales of the early 19th century was a Hasidic master by the name of Nahman of Bratslav. In a splendid edition of his tales—which was published, incidentally, by the Catholic Paulist Fathers—the point is made that while other masters believed in action, Israel, the master of a good name, was always doing something: succoring the sick, helping the needy, performing miracles, engaging in dramatic situations. Nahman believed in speech, the preponderance of speech over action. One writer observed, "Our attention is focused not on what he does for he actually does very little, but upon his brief explications of reality in the light of Torah passages, his longer homilies or his stories."

We have had the great privilege in our congregation of hearing from several Nobel Prize winners, Isaac Bashevis Singer and Saul

Bellow. We have heard the words of Elie Wiesel. Think of these men. Think of Isaac Bashevis Singer. Reflect on Elie Wiesel, a master storyteller who has brought the tragedy of the Holocaust to the minds of his wide-reading public. Our congregation was one of the first to invite him in the 1960s. Saul Bellow is another great storyteller, whose child attended our day school. Bellow has taught at the University of Chicago for the last twenty years. He was once interviewed by *The New York Times*. He said, "Somewhere in the back of my mind I am putting together a novel. That germination process means thinking it out in broad terms, not trying to plot every zig and zag in the story line. I don't bother with the details," he added, "because I like to be agreeably surprised by what I write." One can reflect that the tale amplified itself.

In *Major Trends in Jewish Mysticism*, Professor Gershom Scholem ends his magisterial work by citing a story that he heard told by the great novelist and storyteller S. Y. Agnon, also a Nobel Prize winner:

When the Baal Shem had a difficult task before him, he would go to a certain place in the woods, light a fire and meditate in prayer—and what he had set out to perform was done. When a generation later the "Maggid" of Meseritz was faced with the same task, he would go to the same place in the woods and say: We can no longer light the fire, but we can still speak the prayers—and what he wanted done became reality. Again, a generation later Rabbi Moshe Leib of Sasov had to perform this task. And he too went into the woods and said: We can no longer light a fire, nor do we know the place in the woods to which it all belongs—and that must be sufficient; and sufficient it was. But when another generation had passed and Rabbi Israel of Rishin was called upon to perform the task, he sat down on this golden chair in his castle and said: We cannot light the fire, we cannot speak the prayers, we do not know the place, but we can tell the story of how it was done. And, the storyteller adds, the story which he told had the same effect as the actions of the other three.

One of the great storytellers of our generation, Eudora Welty, once said, "Writing a story . . . or a novel is one way of discovering sequence in experience, of stumbling upon cause and effect in the happenings of a writer's life."

There are many ways of teaching, but learning how to tell the story is one of the prime techniques of Jewish survival.

Escorting
1981

"Now, when Pharaoh let the people go"
Exodus 13:17

The rabbis took great liberties in translating a Biblical text in their efforts to make a moral point. Our late and distinguished teacher Professor Max Kadushin studied the ethical teachings of the rabbis. He analyzed an unusual interpretation where our teachers commented upon the character of Pharaoh. The Pharaohs were known by the collective name of "Pharaoh the Wicked One." For hundreds of years, they had enslaved our people. They had used the sword and the lash to enforce their evil ways. Yet, the rabbis interpreted the words "Let the people go" in an unexpected way. They said that "letting go," *shilluah*, meant escorting. Think of it: Pharaoh himself, according to this interpretation, escorted our people for a short distance as a means of honoring them.

The rabbis had to prove their point. They went to other sections of Scripture, to the experiences of Abraham and of Isaac. In the case of Abraham, three men came to bring him a special message. Among the words they told him were that his wife, Sarah, although advanced in years, would bear a child. The men then went on to Sodom, and the Bible tells us, "Abraham walking with them to *see them off*" (Genesis 18:16).

In the case of Isaac and Abimelech, king of the Philistines, we have similar leave-taking. "Early in the morning, they exchanged oaths. Isaac then bade them farewell and they departed from him in peace."

The rabbis were trying to convey an important value concept. This was the idea of *levayah*, to escort. A person has a responsibility of escorting other human beings. By escorting them, he or she offers a measure of protection to them. Dr. Kadushin makes the point that "Escort for the purpose of protection is one of the most important ideas in Jewish thought."

In Deuteronomy, there is reference to an unusual ritual that had to be conducted if someone was found slain in the field. As part of the special procedure, the elders of the community pronounced, "Our hands did not shed this blood, nor did our eyes see it done."

In the Mishnah, the code of Jewish law, the question is asked, "But can it enter our minds that the elders of a court of justice are shedders of blood?" They answered their own question by saying, "The man found dead did not come to us for help and we dismissed him without supplying him with food. We did not see him and let him go without escort."

In teaching that Pharaoh escorted our people so as to do them honor, the rabbis taught that escort is one of the basic premises of the moral life. What they were trying to convey to their students was that if a wicked person like Pharaoh could behave in a moral way, all decent human beings should conduct themselves in the same fashion.

Many years ago, when Naomi and I were a young honeymoon couple in Israel, we went to see an aged Rabbanit. Though well advanced in years, she insisted upon taking us to our bus stop to make sure we did not lose our way.

Escort is a great quality, which, in our age, has special meaning.

Prerequisites for Revelation

1984

On three occasions during my years of visiting Israel, I was privileged to go into the Sinai desert. The first time I was taken to the northern Sinai, as far as Rephidim. This was in July 1967, shortly after the Six-Day War. In the winter of 1969, while on a United Jewish Appeal rabbinic mission, we traveled part of the way over the Sinai by plane and then were taken by bus to the Suez Canal. These trips were on the western side of the desert. Some years ago, an army friend took Naomi and myself from Eilat down to the eastern coast of the Sinai Peninsula. One is impressed by both the barrenness and the beauty.

As one goes through the desert, one is frequently helped by finding a trail that other travelers have traversed in the past. Our people were not wandering in the bleak desert after the glorious experience of crossing the Red Sea. They were headed for Sinai, they were going to the Mountain of the Lord. There, a special and unique experience would occur.

Two important steps had to be taken before our people would be eligible to receive the gift of the Ten Commandments. This, I believe, is implicit in the Scriptural text.

The first critical step was to understand the injunction that evil must be uprooted. "Inscribe this in a document as a reminder. Read it aloud." Evil, the memory of Amalek, must be utterly blotted out. An oath must be taken on the symbolic throne of the Lord. Evil has many manifestations. It is the improper use of our tongue. It is found in any violation of business ethics. It is cruelty among fellow human beings. There is an allusion, according to the great scholar Gershom Scholem, to this passage in Exodus that the throne of God will remain incomplete as long as the power of evil, the seed of Amalek, is not abolished. The rabbis said about the verse "The Lord reigneth, let the earth rejoice" that as long as the evil kingdom abides, there will be no rejoicing in the earth, neither will the name of the Lord be whole. Only when there is no longer evil, shall the Lord be King over all the earth. That is why we conclude our *Alenu* with a majestic proclamation, "In that day shall the Lord be One and His name One."

If the first eligibility requirement is to work for the abolition of evil, there is a second stage before we can reach the Mountain of the Lord. The rabbis noticed an interesting change as they read, "On the third new moon after the Israelites had gone forth from the land of Egypt, on that very day, they entered the wilderness of Sinai and encamped in the wilderness." If one studies the text carefully, one observes that all of the movements of Israel are stated in the plural. However, when they stood before the Mountain of the Lord, the plural "many" is changed to the singular "one." Instead of *vayachanu*, the Bible reads *vayeechan*. This is the second important consideration. The many must become one. There must be unity of the people. Only then can Israel be eligible to receive the Ten Commandments.

The responsibility to remove evil from the world continues from generation to generation. Equally significant is the charge to work for oneness.

YITRO

The Great Hatred

1980

This week has been a momentous one in world history. The main focus of attention has been on the crisis in Teheran. The American embassy in Iran's capital city was seized in total violation of centuries-old international law. Some fifty American hostages are being held captive and submitted to gross indignities.

At the very same time, another event was unfolding at Mount

Sinai. Our Mount of Eternity is very much in the news. In a dramatic move towards peace, Israel returned Mount Sinai to Egyptian control, months ahead of the provisions of the Camp David agreement.

The rabbis heard a similarity in sound between the two words *Sinai* and *Sinah* (hostility or hatred). They taught that when Sinai came to the world with its message, hatred entered the world. Not that the Ten Commandments are an instrument of hatred, but from that moment forth the nations manifested a continuing intense hatred against our people (Shabbat 89a). "What is the meaning of Mount Sinai? The mountain whereon there ascended hostility, *Sinah*. The nations of the world showed their unworthiness by rejecting the moral teachings of the Torah."

No other people throughout human history has been so hated and maligned as our people, the descendants of those who stood at the foot of Mount Sinai. Wherever one goes, in every part of the world, whether it be in a monarchy or a democracy, a dictatorship of the right or a tyrannical reign of the left, there has been strong feeling, latent or manifest, against the Jew. The Jew has been compelled to live in the polluted atmosphere of anti-Semitism.

Numerous reasons have been offered for this continuous hatred of Jews. One theory says that the world hates us, not for having allegedly taken their God from them, but rather for imposing the ethics of Sinai upon them. This theory was expounded by the late Maurice Samuel, a beloved figure of American Jewish letters, first in *The Great Hatred* and later in *The Gentile and the Jew*. He came to the conclusion that anti-Semitism was not a Jewish problem. It was rather the affliction of Gentiles to which Jews had to accustom themselves. To cite the words of a biographer, "It was the great hatred in the amoral pagan soul for the jailer who had bound it with fetters of moral law."

Let us focus this Shabbat on the fact that we are living in a horrible atmosphere of world-wide hatred against the Jews and other groups. The phenomenon of terrorism is the highpoint of the Sinai-Sinah equation. A University of Chicago conference on terrorism heard from the head of our State Department Office of Combating Terrorism. "One can conceive," he said, "of situations in which terrorists will choose new weapons they previously have not used." The expert did not rule out the utilization of surface-to-air missiles and of chemical or biological agents. They may opt to focus on vulnerable points in our highly sophisticated technological society to which there is relatively easy access. They may attack power stations, computers, pipelines, and tankers.

To be sure, there were occasional incidents of terrorism in prior generations, but never to the extent and intensity we are experiencing now. In a novel about terrorism called *Black Sunday*, the author tells how a hijacked blimp hovers over a packed Super Bowl with an explosive device designed to send tens of thousands of steel darts into the crowd at the push of a button. This nightmare is a logical extension of not only the possible but the already perpetrated.

Terrorists have machine-gunned innocents. They have exploded bombs in theaters and injected oranges with poisonous mercury. They have killed non-combatants and innocent people. They have held airplane passengers and embassy personnel hostage with the threat of death. If you can hold fifty people captive, why can't you hold fifteen thousand people?

One is shocked to read that a prominent *American Church Magazine* editor wrote, "Terrorism has become the only means for public expression of outrage left to the Palestinian community." Considering the fact that the Palestinians, and even the PLO, have access to the world media and to the U.N., this outrageous statement is the ultimate expression of absurdity. (As I write this, I received a telephone call from a good friend who was in Maalot on Christmas eve, 1979. Just before midnight, the PLO broke the fragile truce and shelled Christian churches. The worshipers had to disperse, abandoning the midnight mass for the safety of shelters.)

Terrorism is abnormal because, in most instances, the terrorist chooses as a target innocent non-combatants. Frequently there is no direct connection with a cause being promoted.

Terrorism ranges from terrorism from below, where terrorists seek to topple a government, to terrorism from above, where the state itself afflicts a reign of terror on the community. In the case of Iran, fanatic religion merged with politics served to create a nationally supported terrorist act aimed at forcing another country, the United States, to concede to its demands. In this case, they demanded of our government, "Give us back the Shah." When one considers the fact that there were almost six thousand terrorist acts since 1970, with sixty percent of them having taken place in the last three years, one shudders.

What is the meaning of contemporary terrorism? Some look at it as the last stage in a trend of social and cultural disintegration. They regard it as a symptom signifying the wish of a social body for its own termination.

Terrorism affects the terrorist and changes his outlook on life. What happens to a person who commits himself to the cause of terrorism? He joins a group, and the group takes responsibility for all his actions. He no longer exists as a person. The group is responsible only for his destruction, not for his existence, since the group's leaders are not responsible for the existence of anything.

Years ago, when I was a college undergraduate, I studied the moral sources of international law. I wrote my honors thesis on it. It was a fascinating study to trace how various values from the private realm were extended into the world of public morals. There were laws of friendship and equality between nations. There were laws of war and peace.

When I came to the laws of war, I soon learned that there is a dichotomy between just and unjust wars. These theories of different types of war go back to the religious doctrine of both Judaism and Christianity. The just war was based on the right of self-defense.

From the grey dawn of time, people have been known to quarrel with one another. One need but open the first pages of the Book of Genesis. People used whatever weapons were available. With the passage of time, emphasis shifted from individual bravery to the proficiency and effectiveness of weaponry. We moved from the ax to the atom bomb.

War may be regarded as a necessary evil, but its manner and conduct should be limited. This has been incorporated into international law by the Geneva Conference. An important limit involves the security and safety of non-combatants.

In the case of terrorists, every single person of the population is their prey whether weak or strong, whether a civilian or a member of the armed forces of the so-called enemy camp.

Professor Seymour Siegal points out that what makes terrorism particularly reprehensible is the fact that in the PLO operations, the innocents have become the objectives. "The more innocent the victim, the more the success of the terrorist." We need but ring off the litany of the Lod airport, Maalot, the Munich Olympic massacres, the Jerusalem bombings, and so on. When a soldier is forced to kill in war, it is an instance of killing or being killed. But a terrorist has only one concern: to create havoc in society.

It is important to remember that the Palestine guerrilla movement has received support from various quarters ranging from the extreme right to the extreme left. Support has come from wealthy oil producers who themselves may be on the brink of a revolution. Saudi Arabia is faced with the threat of inner subversion. More than one half its armed forces are non-Saudi, coming from Yemen and from Palestine refugee camps.

The role of the Soviet Union in the Teheran embassy seizure was reflected in Persian language broadcasts by Radio Moscow shortly before and after the November 5th seizure. The broadcasts have been monitored by our Foreign Broadcast Information Service. One of them said, on November 2, "Everyone knows that it is the United States which is setting up bases in the Persian Gulf and organizing a special force nearby that, according to U.S. Senator Jackson, may be sent to Iran. . . . In regard to the Soviet Union, everyone is well aware that our country has never had military bases in other countries and has no intention of setting them up." (Note: The people of Eastern Europe, including Czechoslovakia, and the citizens of Afghanistan can furnish their own commentary on this bit of tripe.)

The day after the seizure, Radio Moscow had this to say, "In short, neither in Iran nor in other countries can anything good be expected from the U.S. imperialists. In this respect the anger of the Iranian nation and its youth, who asked that a stop be put to U.S. imperialist forces in their country's affairs, is totally understandable and logical."

All over the world there are manifestations of *Sinah*, of hostility, of hatred. Both China and the Soviet Union have direct relations with the Palestine guerrilla organizations. Ho Chi Minh, who brought terrorism to Viet Nam, was trained in Moscow. The Cubans have helped the growth of terrorism and subversion in Africa. The Soviets have given money to the Baader-Meinhof gang. Arms for the Irish Republican Army provisionals have come from Eastern Europe. The Soviets have trained PLO agents.

Since the Yom Kippur War of 1973, relations between the

U.S.S.R. and the Palestine guerrilla movement have been strengthened. The Yom Kippur War permitted the Soviet Union to demonstrate its massive support for the Arab war against Israel. They now back the Palestinians in their conflict with Israel. The aim of the Soviet Union is to create a Palestinian state in the West Bank and the Gaza Strip. This would give the Soviet Union a strong foothold in the Middle East.

The picture is not a pleasant one. Our fate has been to serve as a testimony, a touchstone, and a symbol to the world. It is essential that we understand ourselves and appreciate our destiny in life. Our lot has never been to rest on a comfortable downy bed. We have been given an uncomfortable role by history. That phase of our role will come to an end only when the message of Sinai is accepted by all of humankind. We can but hope that civilized people will appreciate that all the world is in danger. May civilized people learn to react to the threat of terrorism in a determined way and to uproot the evil from humanity's midst.

MISHPATIM

Your Life

1985

With the great advances of modern medicine, many new and perplexing questions have been raised in the ethical realm. In one day alone, I read of an innovative conference on bio-medical ethics being held at Beersheba University in Israel, and I picked up a copy of the latest issue of *Commentary* magazine (February 19, 1985) and found pages and pages of letters reacting to an article on "Infanticide and Its Apologists." In West Germany, the highest court, declaring that the constitution guarantees everybody's right to life, overturned a law authorizing abortion on demand within the first trimester of pregnancy. Again, only this morning I received a splendid paper on "A Jewish Perspective on Medical Ethics" written by Dr. Elliot N. Dorff of the University of Judaism.

Some twenty-five years ago, our late teacher, Professor Abraham Joshua Heschel, delivered an address on "The Patient as a Person." Addressing the American Medical Association, he said, "It is a grievous mistake to keep a wall of separation between medicine and religion. There is a division of labor, but a unity of spirit. The art of healing is the highest form of imitation of God, for the Talmud says, 'Just as God is seen as the healer of those who are sick, so are we to imitate Him to bring help and healing to those who suffer.' . . . To minister to the sick is to minister to God."

In our Torah reading, there is a verse that teaches, "Only he shall pay for his loss of his time, and shall cause him to be thoroughly healed" (Exodus 21:19). The Hebrew words are *rapo yerapay*. From this verse we infer that the physician is given permission to heal. But our verse in Exodus is given in a different context in Deuteronomy 22. On the basis of the Deuteronomy passage, the Talmud teaches that we also have the obligation to restore another person's body as well as his or her property. We must come to the rescue of someone who is in a life-threatening situation. We are not to stand idly by the blood of our neighbor (Leviticus 19:16). We have the responsibility of aiding, with our economic resources, any human being who is in need.

I go back to the Biblical text *rapo yerapay*, to be thoroughly healed, and ask the question that comes to mind in terminal cases. Is the physician required to continue with life support when there is no hope of restoring the patient to any type of life that has some quality to it? Rabbi Joseph Caro, the great codifier of Jewish law, believed that "The Torah gave permission to the physician to heal. It is a religious commandment and it is indeed included in the obligation to save life. If the physician refrains from healing, he is guilty of shedding blood." Why did Caro find it necessary to be so emphatic? The answer that has been given is that there are those who disagree as to the reason for illness. I, for example, do not subscribe to the famous statement in the commentary of Rabbi Moses ben Nahman. In a long comment on the Leviticus passage (26:11), "And I will set my tabernacle among you. And my soul shall not abhor you," the medieval thinker said that people became sick because they had sinned, and the degree of their sickness was a measure of their punishment. "From here," Nahman said, "permission has been given to the physician to heal." The text did not say that permission was given to the sick to be healed. The only concession that Nahman made was that the physician *might* practice his art. The normative position of Judaism, as I understand it, is that whatever improves upon nature, whatever does not interfere with nature, whatever is not inconsistent with people's dignity, may be practiced.

Humankind's right to improve nature, let us say in the case of medicine, brings to mind the famous dialogue between Rabbi Akiba and the Roman procurator Tinneius Rufus. The Roman asked Akiba whose handiwork was more beautiful, people's or God's? Rabbi Akiba showed the Roman two different types of materials, one in the raw state—that which God made—and the finished product—which people had made. Judaism assigns to people the role of partnership with God. If it is possible to heal, *rapo yerapay*, then it is the doctor's duty and responsibility to practice his or her art. The basic issue of medical ethics is the question of the improvement of life.

Much has been written and much will be written concerning the various subjects that face modern society in an era of tremendous strides in medicine. We have had Presidential commissions dealing with fetal research. Society is continually in the throes of often bitter discussions on abortion, the right to life, and other related issues. Some of the finest minds all over the world are grappling with these difficult matters. I would hope that these investigations—which must be interdisciplinary by nature and bring in the best minds in medicine, ethics, theology, and law—will become a full-time occupation in the Jewish community.

At the present, a number of my colleagues have devoted some time in their crowded schedules to treating these questions. Much more fundamental research is needed. As the parameters of medical research are being expanded daily, we who come from the background of religious knowledge and ethical teaching must make our distinctive contribution.

The Generous Heart

1984

A governor of Pennsylvania, the Honorable David Lawrence, was once invited to speak at a congregational function. He was a great raconteur and told the story of how a ship was sinking. The passengers and crew were fortunate enough to get into lifeboats. In one of them, a junior officer, feeling a sense of desperation and danger, asked, "Is there a clergyman among you?" There was no response. "Does anyone know a prayer?" No one could think of an appropriate statement. Finally, the young officer said, "Well, we have to do something religious. Let's pass the hat."

In a certain sense, many of us identify religious activity with the beautiful quality of generosity. The Jewish people have a remarkable record of being a charitable folk. Though at times we may resent the overbearing, over-structuralization of our charitable giving, the pressures that are put on recalcitrant donors, one cannot deny that from the time of Moses down to our own there has been a beautiful record of *zedakah*. If one goes through our literature, there are many recorded documents on how to give charity, how the donors ought to act, and how the recipients ought to respond. In a sense, Jewish charity started with the injunction in this morning's Torah reading, "And the Lord spoke unto Moses saying, speak unto the children of Israel, that they may take for me an offering: of every person whose heart maketh him willing you shall take my offering."

One can wonder as to why this is necessary. Does God need people's offerings? This theme was once analyzed by Rabbi Wolf Gold, who served as a powerful spokesman for American Zionism, representing the Mizrachi Movement. He participated in the Jewish delegation to the United Nations Special Assembly on Palestine. In his significant essay, Rabbi Gold asked: Is God not the great God of whom it is said, "The earth is the Lord's and the fulness thereof" and elsewhere in the Psalms, "The sea is His and He made it?" Is God in need of the gifts of flesh and blood? The answer proposed by the preacher was that God wanted His influence to grow among people, just as parents are anxious for their influence to develop among their children. Therefore, it is said, "that they may take for Me an offering." It is the offering which elevates the charitable gift that gives meaning to our existence.

In order that we do not forget, God has enjoined upon us to pray and to thank Him for the food we eat and for every legitimate pleasure we enjoy in this world. Just as a parent tries to teach a child that there is to be an expression of thanksgiving and blessing when he or she receives food to eat, beverage to drink, clothes to wear. It is not done for the parent's sake but rather for the sake of the child. The parent is moved by a desire for the child to be trained and educated, that she or he should become a worthy person and be grateful to have and enjoy all these earthly pleasures.

This is the request of Israel. People have a tendency to forget that they are but creatures and that God is the Creator. God wanted to give merit to Israel and He gave them a Torah, He gave them the Commandments and bade them serve Him. God desires the prayers of the righteous. He desires their expressions of thanksgiving and praise in order that He may bring them closer to Him and thus elevate and edify their lives. Thus, it is said by our teachers of old, "Whoever enjoys this world without saying a proper blessing, it is as if he had stolen from God Himself" (Berachot 35b). In the Psalm that I cited before, it is written, "The earth is the Lord's and the fulness thereof," and it is also written, "The heavens are the heavens of the Lord, but the earth hath He given to the children of men!" There is no contradiction: in the one case it is before a blessing has been said, in the other after a blessing has been recited, that people can enjoy the fruits of the earth. Therefore we have a blessing for all we enjoy. We must even recite a blessing for the gift of life itself. A person must thank God for the miracle of existence. How remarkable it is when we have been unable to catch our breath for a moment that we are able to breathe again. The essence of the message of the book of gratitude, the Book of Psalms, the book of praise, lies in its concluding phrase, "every living thing shall praise the Lord." A person must thank God for every breath of life.

In order that people, who have learned the art of giving, can be saved from descending into the depths of despair, they were given an additional instrument to elevate their lives and to uplift their souls. God commanded that it was not enough just to give, but that we give for a purpose. One of the central purposes of Jewish existence was, "And they shall make me a Sanctuary and I shall dwell therein." From time to time the people of Israel will come to the sanctuary of the Lord, they will draw of the Holy Spirit from it. The well in which our people can purify themselves from the dust of our secular life and the impurities of our daily activity is, of course, the sanctuary of the spirit, God's dwelling place. That is why, when Moses was commanded to build a sanctuary, he was afraid and said to God, "Master of the Universe, behold the heaven and heaven of heavens cannot contain You and You say to me, make a Sanctuary unto me that I may dwell therein." Moses had to be reassured. Moses had to learn that just as it is impossible for the world to exist without a moral law so, too, it is impossible for the Jewish people to continue without a sanctuary.

The sanctuary helps us to receive a blessing. It acts as the central point for our participation in the spiritual life. The erection of the sanctuary causes the Jew to be able to observe the spirit of the Torah. The main center of the Torah's influence in Biblical times was to be in the land of Israel. But even in the desert the Jews could participate in a rich, meaningful spiritual life. The Torah was given in the desert, in a land belonging to all. This was to teach that the moral law of the Torah was intended not only for our people, but was to be a guide for all humankind. The Torah was to be shared with all the nations of the world. Given in the desert, in an open place, it belongs to all.

The sanctuary in the desert, its uniqueness and holiness belongs to our people. We are to accept the responsibility commanded in Exodus 19:6, "You shall be unto me a kingdom of priests and a holy people." We are to be the priests of all humankind, not to lord over it but rather to be able to help it ascend to a higher level of sanctity. The lower rungs are the rungs of generosity; the upper rungs are the building of the sanctuary.

Ambassador Sol Linowitz wrote wisely, "The real challenge of our prosperity is not just how to keep it, but how to use it."

Inside, Outside

1981

Several years ago, I translated *Sefer Hayashar, The Book of the Righteous*. There is an interesting passage which tells that "We see that the work of the Tabernacle proceeds rationally." There is sense and order to the way it is built.

The Tabernacle is a picture of the whole world. Professor Louis Ginzberg, my great master, observed that "The separate parts of the Tabernacle had each a symbolic significance, for to all that is above there is something corresponding below." The Sanctuary and its furnishings mirror the cosmos.

Many of the elements of the ancient Tabernacle are still to be found in the modern synagogue. The Menorah, for example, which is a symbol for wisdom, had seven branches that reminded one of some of the principal stars of heaven. The Ark, too, was interesting. It was to be overlaid with gold, both within and without. The rabbis were puzzled by this command to gild the inside of the Ark. They could understand the desire to put gold on the outside, but why put it on the inside where no one could see it? They developed an answer to their own query. They said that a scholar whose inner manner and outer expression were not equal was not to be considered a true scholar. There has to be a single mindedness in one's outer expression that mirrors one's truest inner feelings. Inside and outside there should be the same honorable character. A great writer once said, "Our belief is what our actions show we believe."

I was very moved by an analysis of the writings and personality of Czeslaw Milosz, the 1980 Nobel Prize Winner in Literature. He was born in Lithuania some 70 years ago. After World War I, his family returned to newly independent Poland from Siberia. He grew up in Wilno. He has had a very interesting career as a writer and a diplomat, and is now Professor of Slavic Literatures at the University of California at Berkeley.

He deals with many themes, among them the subject of honesty. There are times when we want to be honest, but circumstances and conditions hold us back. Milosz, in his remarkable book called *Native Realm*, deals with the search for self-definition. In a beautifully composed work, he grapples with the chaos of life, trying to find glimmerings of meaning.

When *Native Realm* first appeared in 1968, it attracted little attention. The book is an exercise in consciousness. How can a person be honest with oneself, one's time? We have mentioned the rabbinic statement that one's outer words must match one's inner conviction. Hear these words of Milosz: "My feeling of living a lie and of wasting my life reached a peak then." He writes of his work with the Polish radio: "Beyond satisfying the need to earn a living, my job . . . gave me an alibi. It took me away from the literary milieu, where, uncertain myself, I found only more uncertainty. When one loses one's sense of direction and all activity seems futile, writing becomes sheer rhetoric under which falsehood . . .is all too detectable." Hear another citation: "Only that double life could have earned me the right to breathe and to walk the earth like everyone else."

That one's outer statements should match one's inner convictions is a wonderful ideal. In a study group prior to today's service, I raised a question as to what we should do in the case of a parent whose condition we know to be very grave. Should our outer statement match our inner knowledge? One of the students was a physician, and his answer was that you have to tell the truth. The others debated with him on this sensitive ethical question.

This sermon has been heady. Perhaps we ought to conclude on a lighter note. There was a grand debate between the School of Hillel and the School of Shammai. How do you describe a bride who is not the comeliest? Kind Hillel said, "Every bride is beautiful." Shammai, a little starker, said, "Tell it as it is. If she is beautiful, say so. If she is not, say she is not." I am sure that from your personal life you can draw many other examples. What holds us back from being completely honest and frank is our desire to win acceptance from our fellow beings.

The gold lining of the Ark ought to be a constant beacon to us.

Without and Within

1979

"They shall make an ark of acacia wood. . . .
Overlay it with pure gold—overlay it inside
and out."

Exodus 25:10-11

This is an unusual text. We can understand why the ark was to be overlaid with gold from without; the people seeing it would be impressed by its beauty. But why gild it on the inside, which no one sees?

A great master, Rabba, taught the principle that "Any scholar whose inside is not like his outside is no scholar." Inside and outside, one must have the same golden qualities. True, we don't see the inside, but from a moral point of view, a person's inner feelings and outer reactions must match one another.

Some fifteen years ago, a young Israeli scholar visited our congregation. His name was Amitai Etzioni. He had had an interesting career as a journalist in Israel but had decided that his future lay in the field of sociology. Since that visit to Anshe Emet, the name and reputation of Amitai Etzioni has grown. He is now a professor of sociology at Columbia University in New York and director of the Center for Policy Research.

Etzioni believes that America suffers from a split personality. Despite all the problems that face our nation, Americans are far more hopeful about their own personal future than about the future of America. Etzioni makes the point that the private self and public self of the American persona have split from each other. Privately, most of us feel self-confident. We think we will be able to cope with whatever the future brings. On the other hand, when it comes to the exterior view, we are quite pessimistic.

There is dissatisfaction, a feeling of inability to deal with the global problems of our time. The future is no longer in our nation's control.

This split between the inner and the outer American is important. The private realm of family, of work, is more or less satisfactory. When it comes to the public self, Etzioni believes that the community is out of kilter. The Gallup Poll revealed that 42 percent of Americans feel very happy. This number has grown in recent years. By 1977, those who were fairly happy numbered about 48 percent. How do we compare to other people? We are twice as happy as West Germans, who have one of the most prosperous economies in the world.

There are real questions that must be raised about this sunny disposition. But on the whole, investigation after investigation seems to show that Americans feel they are better off than they were years ago. The discontent is not a personal one. The discontent is with our President, Congress, and the Supreme Court. Our major institutions—like the armed forces, organized labor, and corporations—have a low confidence rating.

People think that, as far as the nation is concerned, "what I think doesn't count anymore." The outer and the inner do not match each other. Think of our exercise of responsibility at the polls in the last twenty years. The proportion of Americans who bother to vote has shrunk. In 1960, 63 percent of the eligible voters cast their ballot for either Kennedy or Nixon. By 1976, the percentage had dropped to 54 percent. In Congressional elections last year (1978), the percentage of eligible voters hovered at the 50 percent mark. People don't want to carry out their nominal role as voters for a number of reasons: (1) They can't stand politics. (2) They don't care for the candidates. (3) They feel that their vote doesn't really count. Here we have the dichotomy between the inner personal feeling and our outer public activity. What would happen if we were to remove ourselves from society? The future of our country would be dimmer than the most pessimistic view we could possibly have.

If we involve ourselves in the community, if we help to better our society, if we are less concerned with our individual kicks, then we can mold a community that will be truly golden and to our liking. If people think, as so many do, that their personal outlook is promising but that the collective outlook is dragging along, they are disinclined to invest themselves in public affairs and give of their money, their time, and their effort.

The growing tax rebellion, which started with California's Proposition 13, is not merely a reflection of resentment of increased taxes. It also reflects the sentiment that the nation makes no sense, that our country is going nowhere. Why spend hard-earned cash on the political process?

It is to be hoped that if our future is to be golden, our outer concerns and our inner feelings will match one another.

TETZAVEH

The Right to Privacy

1984

The garments of the priests are described in this week's Torah reading. On the hem there were to be pomegranates of blue, purple, and crimson yarn, with bells of gold between them all around. There is a beautiful lilting sound to the Hebrew: "A golden bell and a pomegranate, a golden bell and a pomegranate, all around the hem of the robe. Aaron the high priest shall wear it while officiating, so that the sound of it is heard when he comes into the Sanctuary before the Lord" (Exodus 28:34).

Many reasons are given for these bells. Anthropologically-minded scholars say that bells of this type were widely used in Europe, Asia, and Africa to ward off evil spirits. As a matter of fact, in the new and outstanding Reform commentary on the Bible there is a quote from John Milton calling the priest "the bell man." "The bell man's drowsy charm to bless the doors from nightly harm." I would rather interpret this verse to say that the sound of the bells was to teach us that one should not break into another individual's home, not physically, but visually. One should not invade the privacy of another.

Modern law has been greatly concerned with protecting the right of an individual to privacy. A little while ago, a great professor of political science at the Massachusetts Institution of Philosophy, Dr. Ithiel de Sola Pool, passed away. His father was the distinguished spiritual leader of the Spanish and Portuguese synagogue, and his mother was an outstanding president of Hadassah. Dr. Pool was one of the world's greatest authorities on the social impact of computers. He was deeply concerned about the use of computer-stored material and the violation of the privacy of those whose records were stored in this great memory device.

In our tradition, this concern over the right of an individual to privacy goes back for a long period of time. At the very beginning of this morning's Shabbat service, we recited the words: "How goodly are your tents, O Jacob, your dwelling places, O Israel." A Biblical account tells how Balaam the soothsayer went out to curse the Israelites, but when he saw their encampment he blessed them. The scholars' interpretation of this change of attitude is described in the Talmud (*Baba Batra* 60a): When Balaam looked at the camp of the Israelites, he saw that the opening of the Israelite tents were not directly opposite one another. He blessed them for respecting one another's privacy and intimacy. Jewish law legislates this high regard for privacy and established many prohibitions against even the most subtle forms of prying. There are times when one should not pry into the affairs of another nor enter into another's private domain. When a person is in deep mourning, one must know how to speak to that person. One should not enter another person's home without warning. In this regard, we learned good manners from God Himself who remained outside of the Garden of Eden and called to Adam before entering. Does not the Bible say, "The Lord God called out to man and said, Where are you?" When you make a loan to someone, you must not enter that person's house to seize the pledge. You must remain outside while the person to whom you made the loan brings the pledge to you.

In the Talmud, we learn that if a man's roof overlooks a neighbor's courtyard he must build a parapet or railing around his roof that is four cubits high. There is a special reason for this rule. The owner of the courtyard cannot say to the owner of the roof, "I use my courtyard only at fixed times, but you have no fixed times for using your roof. I have no way of knowing when you might go on your roof so I can keep out of your sight and maintain my privacy."

In our American way of life, the key passage guarding the privacy of the individual is found in the Fourth Amendment, which was adopted in 1791 as part of the first ten amendments to our Constitution that we proudly call the Bill of Rights. It reads in part: "The right of the people to be secure in their persons, houses, papers and effects against unreasonable searches and seizures shall not be violated and no warrants shall issue but upon probable cause, supported by oath or affirmation, and particularly describing the place to be searched and the persons or things to be seized."

One of the most outstanding articles on the right to privacy, entitled "The Right to Privacy," appeared in the *Harvard Law Review* (December 15, 1890). A law professor who teaches at Northwestern University Law School and attends our daily minyan was kind enough to get me the full text. It is interesting to note that Louis D. Brandeis, who later became one of the preeminent judges of the United States Supreme Court, is listed after Samuel D. Warren. The two men wrote the article together.

Among the points made is the following: "That the individual shall have full protection in person and in property is a principle as old as the common law; but it has been found necessary from time to time to define anew the exact nature and extent of such protection." The authors spoke of the development of the law. They recognized that the intense intellectual and emotional life that came with the advance of civilization "made it clear to men that only a part of the pain, pleasure and profit of life lay in physical things. Thoughts, emotions, and sensations demanded legal recognition." They cited Judge Cooley, who spoke of the fact that recent inventions and business methods called attention to the next step that must be taken for the protection of persons. Cooley insisted on guarding the right of people "to be let alone."

The chips from the axe that cuts down the portals to our privacy fall in many places. In 1825, a distinguished surgeon sought to restrain the publication in the British medical magazine *Lancet* of unpublished lectures he had delivered in a London hospital to people who had been admitted as students. These "students" wrote down the lectures in shorthand and hoped to sell what was the private expression of a great physician.

In the Warren-Brandeis article, the point is made that "If the invasion of privacy constitutes a legal *injuria*, the elements for demanding redress exist since already the value of mental suffering, caused by an act wrongful in itself, is recognized as a basis for compensation." In the British House of Lords, there was recently a vote to insert a clause on telephone-tapping in the telecommunications bill. The struggle to prevent the invasion of privacy by wire-tapping has gone on in England for a long time (*The Economist,* February 25, 1984). The new proposal is to make it clear that it is illegal for anybody to listen in to telephone calls without a warrant.

Telephone-tapping is only one way to pry. An English observer said there is no good reason why the privacy of data kept on computers, which are frequently sent along telephone lines, should be dealt with under a different law from information picked up by bugging devices. A recent U.S. Supreme Court decision held that jurors are entitled to privacy and protection from harassment even after completing their service. A lower-court judge had ruled that individuals and the press were banned from making repeated requests for interviews with jurors who might not wish to be interviewed.

Much is heard about "the invasion of privacy." Children are asked personal questions about their parents' life together. The telephone breaks into the serenity of our homes with polltakers and verbal questioning. Joseph Wood Krutch once wrote, "When an interviewer calls me on the telephone to ask what make of refrigerator I have in the kitchen I tell him it is none of his business." Krutch remembers from the early days of movies when the business card of a private detective read: "Other people's business promptly attended to." Some argue that we will have to learn to live with these invasions of privacy. To which one can answer: Who says that we have to give up this precious right?

Almost a thousand years ago a great master of Jewish tradition, Rabbenu Gershom, wrote that one cannot read another person's mail. Jewish law has sought to protect people's privacy against the eyes and ears, against visual and aural surveillance and other forms of non-physical trespass. The privacy of persons is a sacred element in our way of life. In an age where national data banks are spoken about, in an age where people buy information from various sources so that the various government revenue services, both federal and state, can judge the lifestyle of a person to find out whether or not the person is paying too much or too little in taxes, there should be concern on our part.

It is frightening to realize that chronic eavesdropping has been practiced even in our democracy. I was rereading sections of a fine study on the life of Henry Kissinger, who played a critical role as secretary of state in the Nixon administration and recently headed a special study group on the Caribbean nations. It was almost revolting to learn in this study that there were tape-recordings fighting tape-recordings during various administrations. The head of the United States Information Agency invaded the privacy of people who conversed with him by using electronic eavesdropping.

We are aware of many instances reflecting invasion of the privacy of public personalities and private individuals. We must be alert to defend the privacy of our individual lives lest it be tampered with "for the good of society."

The desire to protect people's privacy and well-being is well grounded in Jewish law. The last two presidents of the Yeshiva University have written on this theme. Respect for the privacy of individuals is a bulwark that maintains the structure of our democracy. Every possible effort ought to be made to preserve and protect this basic freedom.

Little bells adorned the hem of the robe of the high priest. The lesson learned from this manner of coming into the presence of God should be emulated by human beings. We should knock before entering into the privacy of others.

Radical Evil

1980

This morning we took out two Torah scrolls, one for the regular reading of Tetzaveh and the second for the special Sabbath of Remembrance, Shabbat Zachor. Tonight will be Purim, and the Sabbath before is always the Sabbath of Remembrance.

The Torah reading deals wth the commandment, "And thou shalt command the children of Israel, that they bring unto thee pure olive oil beaten for the light, to cause a lamp to burn continually."

The important point is made that we deal with light—the light is to be brought unto you rather than unto God. It is humanity who needs the light. God is not in need of light—people are in need of light. As one of the great masters, Rabbi Samuel Ben Nahmani, expressed it, "Unto thee, but not unto Me, for I am not in need of light." The rabbis stressed the importance of light. The light was a symbol of joy. A person's mind is only clear when it is light. The rabbis continually associated light with joy.

In a few hours we will hear the Megillah of Esther. "The Jews had light and gladness and joy and honor." These words are always included in the home service at the end of Shabbat, and we add the words to the Scriptural text: "So be it with us."

The first Torah reading is, in a sense, a joyous, bright one, while the second section deals with Amalek. Amalek was the manifestation of what theologians call "radical evil." This evil must be removed from the earth for if it is not, God's world is incomplete. As Rabbi Berachiah said, "As long as the seed of Amalek is alive, the full presence of God is not felt in this world. There is no delight before the heavenly throne." Another teacher explained that as long as the seed of Amalek exists, God is incomplete. He based his comment on the text in the Midrash on Psalm 97: "The

Lord reigns, let the earth rejoice." There is no rejoicing in this world when the enemy continues to survive. That is why we read a very difficult passage on this Sabbath of Remembrance: "Remember what Amalek did to you on your journey, after you left Egypt—How, undeterred by fear of God, he surprised you on the march, when you were famished and weary, and cut down all the stragglers in your rear. Therefore, when the Lord your God grants you safety from all your enemies around you, in the land that the Lord your God is giving you as a hereditary portion, you shall blot out the memory of Amalek from under heaven. *Do not forget!*" This passage causes us great difficulty, for it commands the rooting out of a complete people.

Some years ago, Rabbi Emanuel Rackman dealt with this issue in an essay entitled *Violence and the Value of Life: Of The Halakhic View.* He offered the position that "Violence is at one and the same time an important way both to destroy and to conserve . . . human life. Violent action usually endangers the life of the aggressor as well as the lives of those against whom the violence is directed. . . . One's own life is regarded as having the highest priority, but if one is to engage in violence, it must be in accord with Jewish law and in behalf of the value of life or a value even higher than the value of life. Never is one to lose sight of the ultimate value to be achieved." He then stressed that "War for war's sake," which in Judaism is represented by Amalek, "is the essence of evil." There can be no compromise in opposition to such policy.

Perhaps a different position can be taken in dealing with the Biblical section on Amalek. We must realize that this demand was expressed some thousands of years ago. Just as we modified the earlier requirements of Scripture of "an eye for an eye," saying that one replaces the loss of the eye with its monetary value, so, too, in dealing with one's enemy, we must develop a more humane ethic of war.

Just a few days ago, I lectured on this very difficult subject before the faculty and students of the Leo Baeck College in London, England. This institution trains rabbis and teachers for the non-Orthodox congregations of Western Europe. While preparing for my talk, I came across a study of a valuable new book on the ethics of war by two Christian thinkers. The reviewer observed that one of the background facts drawn attention to in

this important book is that the professionals—soldiers, strategists, political policy makers—seldom have time to consider the
ethical implications of what they do. Hence, the ethics of war has
been a preserve of amateurs—people of strong moral conviction,
but not in any way able to challenge the military on the level of
professional expertise.

In trying to deal with the ethics of war from the Jewish point of
view, one has to cull from various sources the Jewish ethical
impulse on this vital area. It is only since the reestablishment of
Jewish sovereignty in 1948 that Jewish thinkers had to deal with
the problems of the ethics of war and peace as faced by an
independent state. However, there were some guidelines laid
down prior to 1948: the experience of the Haganah, the pre-state
defense force of Israel. They developed a number of important
moral principles. One of them was *Havlagah*—to abstain from
war or any form of violence for as long as possible. Particularly
during the years from 1936 to 1939, when there were horrible
Arab riots in all of Palestine, the tradition of *Havlagah* was
maintained.

A second important doctrine evolved from the *Havlagah* experience. This was called *Tohar Hanechek*, which means "the purity
of arms." This was to be pursued with much determination and
was followed with a great measure of success despite the difficulty
of imposing inner moral discipline in very difficult situations.
Purity of arms implied far more than the internationally recognized code dealing with the treatment of prisoners. *Tohar Hane-
check* was a Jewish rule of moral guidance as to what may be
done in fighting and what must be ruled out.

Some years ago, the chief rabbi of the Israel defense forces,
Rabbi Mordecai Piron, published an essay on "War According to
the View of Judaism." He deals with many troublesome situations
and tries to bring the message of Jewish morality to bear upon
the ethics of war.

It is difficult to follow the impulse of Jewish ethics when one is
an occupying power. There is a great debate raging in Israel today
about proper military conduct in the administered territories. It
is one thing to speak in vague terms about the grandeur and
splendor of our ethical system. It is another thing to be able to
carry out the moral dictates of Jewish thought in this practical
area.

How does one conduct security measures against terrorists in a heavily populated area? Mistakes have happened over the years. To the credit of the Israel defense forces and the civilian administration, in most instances Israel has had the courage and the moral fortitude to attempt to right the wrong and to acknowledge shortcomings when they have taken place.

So we read today that which is a reflection of light and darkness, the light of hope and the darkness of hate. May it be our privilege to be among those who bring light and joy to this world. And if life compels us to be engaged in acts of defense, may it always be done in an atmosphere of purity.

ZAKHOR

A Need to Remember

1984

This day is Shabbat Zakhor, Remembrance Sabbath. The Jew is called upon to remember the events of the past, the fateful days that one historian called "Jewish History and Jewish Memory."

In a remarkable study, small in size but great in historical insights, Professor Yosef Hayim Yerushalmi traces the fortunes of Jewish history. He begins with the Biblical and rabbinic origins of our people, goes through the glories and distresses of the Middle Ages, recounts the events that followed in the wake of the expulsion from Spain, and concludes with modern times.

In dealing with the period of the Spanish Expulsion, which is his particular area of specialization, Yerushalmi traces how the tragedy of 1492 raised the perennial problem of Jewish exile and suffering to a new level of urgency. Jews in the 16th century groped for a new understanding of ancient enigmas, and they responded by taking new paths. During that period, there was the development of Jewish mysticism and the longing for a messianic deliverer. There was the spread of the revolt of Sabbatai Zevi, who tried to tear down the entire framework of the Halachah, our distinctive way of life.

Yerushalmi has beautiful insights in his book *Zakhor.* He is noted for another great work called *Haggadah and History.* He denies that the celebration of Passover is merely a study of Jewish nostalgia, and affirms a union between the events we recall and Jewish history. Jewish memory and Jewish history are intertwined. All of our festivals are occasions for memory. The most magnificent of our festivals is Pesah. The Haggadah is its book of remembrance and redemption. Annually at our seder tables, we renew the memory of our people and we sustain our hope for the future.

There are times when Jews, who are a history-minded people, were not overly concerned with history. This may seem to be out of sorts, but during the Middle Ages some Jews turned their backs on historical reflection. Maimonides, the great savant of the 12th century, called it a "waste of time." Jewish memory moved instead through ritual and liturgy, through the practice of rabbinic custom and through the observance of Jewish law.

Yerushalmi shows how our people used different vehicles in the medieval period as instruments for memory. New penitential prayers were introduced into the liturgy. Individual communities had memorial books. An interesting practice was to introduce a second Purim. We will observe the re-enactment of the first Purim tonight. We will remember the deliverance of Jews in Persia in ancient times. There were almost miraculous deliverances of our people in every part of the settled Jewish world. They were remembered by these special Purims. It would be good to read about them in the Jewish encyclopedia. There were the recollection of catastrophes. The beginning of the Crusades, from which there had been no deliverance, were remembered in these memorial volumes. In the Middle Ages, the law, philosophy, and Kabbalah (mysticism) were more important than historical reflection.

In the 16th century, in the aftermath of the Spanish Expulsion, a new phenomenon took place. As the Jews of the Iberian Peninsula spread through the Mediterranean basin, they found that Jewish spiritual life was not enough. They needed Jewish history for added strength. They wanted to remember. They had to have the additional power that comes from remembering. Memory was needed for Jews to survive the catastrophe of the Spanish Expulsion.

In the modern period, there has been an attempt by some to say that the past is past. In the age of tradition it was not so; the past was ever-present. It was one of the prime purposes of Jewish ritual to abolish time, to make Jews who were divided by history into contemporaries. In this way, many communities were united into a single folk and the experience of many Jews into a single tale.

I spoke of Passover a moment ago. Let me add another reflection on this particular theme. No one who has been present at a seder table can deny the pull of participation that this reliving of the Exodus gives us. But as the past becomes more immediate, it loses its sharpness and preciseness. The similarity with the present matters more than the differences.

Memory is a many-faceted experience, if we can bring a term from the physical world into the psychological world. Yerushalmi speaks of memory as being problematic, deceptive, at times a treacherous thing. Memory is the most fragile of our faculties. In the Bible, the word for memory is found no less than a hundred and sixty-nine times, usually with God or Israel as the subject. There are two sides to the coin of memory. The obverse of "to remember" is to forget. As Israel is commanded to remember, so it is sworn not to forget.

The great historian Herodotus once said that we must preserve from decay the remembrance of what people have done. He asked, in his time, that the wonderful actions of his fellow Greeks not be erased, not be lost. A beautiful point has been made that Herodotus was the "father of history." But the Jewish people were the fathers of the *meaning* of history.

Memory has become crucial for us. Outside the Holocaust memorial, the Yad Vashem in Jerusalem, there is the declaration of Israel, the master of a good name, telling us how important it is to remember and how memory is related to the length of the exile. Our Ten Commandments speak of God as the God of history. Memory is crucial to our faith and ultimately to our very existence. "Remember the days of old, consider the years of ages past." A little while ago we read: "Remember what Amalek did to you."

Memory flows through two channels, ritual and recital. The ritual of the Sabbath, the ritual of our daily experiences. The ritual of the Passover has to be spoken of, proclaimed, as well as being recalled in the mind.

Memory can be a taxing thing. But it is healthier for us to remember and recall rather than to repress and obliterate.

KI TISSA

The Mask of Moses

1980

The Bible relates how Moses returned from his second ascent to Mt. Sinai's peak. As he came down from the mountain bearing the two tablets, he was not aware that the skin of his face was radiant. Aaron, Moses' brother, and all the Israelites saw that Moses' face was radiant because he had spoken with God. They hesitated to come near him. Then an interesting thing took place. Moses put a veil over his face. The Bible gives these details: "Whenever Moses went in before the Lord to speak with Him, he would take the veil off . . .; and when he came out and told the Israelites what he had been commanded, Moses would put the veil back over his face until he returned once again to speak with God."

Some years ago, I interpreted the word "veil" in a different fashion. I made the point that some Bible scholars think *masveh* meant a type of mask. The English word we use for "person" comes from the Latin *persona*, which means a mask. This was the practice of the ancient theater. Roles were normally played by men, but they put on different types of masks: a red mask meant a slave, a white mask meant an old man, and so on.

There is a lesson in the thought that all too frequently we put on a mask when we stand in the presence of other persons. We strip ourselves of our masks, as Moses did, when we stand before God.

Recently my attention was drawn to an article in *Psychology Today*. The question was raised, "Is there a true self, apart from the social roles we play?" People play so many differing roles and wear so many masks that there is a confusion between their true selves and the roles they play.

A great student of the human mind, Dr. Carl Jung, once stressed that there is the persona, a mask that is the conscious. Behind that persona is the shadow, the unconscious. W. H. Auden, the English writer, once observed that "The image of myself which I try to create in my own mind in order that I may love myself, is very different than the image which I try to create in the mind of others in order that they may love me." Each one of us wears a mask. Some of us have interchangeable masks as we stand in the presence of a different set of persons.

Historically, we Jews, when faced with implacable foes and trying to win them over or at least pacify them and reduce their hatred, were compelled to put on a mask. We were forced to become dissemblers, to hide our true feelings because of our enemy's bitterness. Our outer personality differed from our inner feeling, and this was a mode of self-defense. When the Renaissance, the great rebirth of learning and culture, came to the Western world, there were groups of Jews—the Sabbatians, the followers of Sabbatai Zevi—who made a religion out of dissemblance. It was impossible to tell their real feelings from their outer behavior.

There was once a great rabbi by the name of Rabbi Jonathan Eybeschuetz who was involved in a controversy with Rabbi Jacob Emden. Eybeschuetz was one of the great Talmudic scholars of the 18th-century. He had served as a rabbi in Metz and eventually led the communities of Altona, Hamburg, and Wandsbek. Rabbi Jacob Emden, who was the scion of a family that had fought against the Sabbatian movement, claimed that Eybeschuetz had distributed Sabbatian amulets to the community. Eybeschuetz, who had studied Kabbalah and apparently had some connections with Sabbatian groups in his youth, denied the accusation. The fight went on, and Emden pursued the issue for a number of years.

Discussing this controversy, Professor Gershom Scholem, the

world's most famous student of Jewish mysticism, was asked about his views on Eybeschuetz and his supposed Sabbatian leanings. Scholem responded that nothing in history surprises one. The duty of a historian is to peel away every mask that people wear.

A few weeks ago, the March 3rd issue of *Time* magazine featured an article on Peter Sellers. The cover read, "Who Is This Man? The Many Faces of Peter Sellers." The article touched on many aspects of this very fine actor, a man who is blessed with skills of comedy, timing, disguise, charm, and wit. One of the world's most famous actors, he is an elusive personality. To use the words of *Time* magazine, he is "a man who prefers to wear a mask." Now what does this do to him and to his self image? It is worthwhile reading or re-reading some of the article's copy. He was asked, "Is it possible for you to just relax and be yourself?" "No," he replied, "I could never be myself." "Never yourself?" "No, you see, there is no me, I do not exist." Sellers has played so many parts, so many roles have been poured into him, that he has been poured out of himself. "An actor has no personality of his own," it has been said by another player. "He has been emptied out."

A number of years ago, I read an interview about one of the great actresses of the English theater and the Hollywood cinema, Glenda Jackson. The point was made that, strictly speaking, "no actor or actress is normal." The reporter wrote the feature article on "The Magic of Glenda" and said that "Actors spend their lives pretending to be someone else. It's why they often disappoint in real life. The roles they play tend to be more interesting. Actors are mediums, transformed and made by someone else's personality." Players are compelled to wear masks; they are not attuned to a strict sense of reality. Most of their time is spent living and working in fantasy, and many of them prefer it there. Actors and actresses have a tremendous need to be loved and adored. "Within the actor," it has been said, "can be found the child and the child's love of make-believe: play."

The theme of the make-believe masks we wear is an exciting one. There are striking gaps and contradictions between a person's public appearances and his or her private realities of self. William Jones, one of America's greatest psychologists, once observed that the man has as many social selves as there are individuals who recognize him and carry an image of him in their mind. People put on masks; they show a different side of themselves to different groups. Youngsters who are well behaved in one set of relationships become completely different persons when they are among their peers. As parents, we show ourselves to our children in one light; we show ourselves to ourselves in another light. We talk one way to those whose favor we must curry, and we talk in another way to those who are lower than ourselves in the pecking order.

The theme of Moses wearing a mask for people and removing his mask before God is a pregnant one. There are times when we have to wear masks. But even if necessity tells us to wear a mask when we face others, let us never forget that when we stand in the presence of God we must strip ourselves of all pretense, for God is the great examiner of hearts, who understands our innermost thoughts.

VAYIKRA

The Little Aleph
1982

The Torah scroll must always be handwritten. We have special instructions as to how the Torah text is to be spaced. In addition, there are several instances where unusual elements are added to the Torah text. In a number of verses, there are dots above the letters. Just before the great passage we chanted as the Torah was taken forth from the Holy Ark, "And it came to pass when the Ark moved forward," there is an inverted *nun*. Just after, at the completion of the text we chant when we return to the Torah, "When the Ark rested," there is another *nun*. These unusual elements have been commented upon by great teachers.

In the case of the opening of today's Torah reading, regarding the first word, *Vayikra*, the instruction is given that the word is to be spelled with a small aleph. This reflected the modesty of Moses, the greatest man ever to live on the face of this earth.

Moses waited to be called. The Bible speaks of his modesty. "Now Moses was a very humble man, more so than any man on earth." The rabbis stressed the quality of humility. They suggested that a person should have a proper estimation of his or her role as a human being. Commenting upon the verse in Proverbs, they said, "Far better is it that it be said to you, 'come up here' than you should be put lower in the presence of the Prince." Rabbi Akiba taught, "Go down two or three rungs lower in the Academy and take your place until they say to you, 'come up' rather than you should go up and they should say to you, 'go down.' "

Our generation can learn from this quality of Moses. Our contemporaries, in the main, reject the notion that modesty is the ladder by which one ascends to God.

Daniel Yankelovich, one of America's most distinguished analysts of changing social values, writes of this phenomenon in his new study *New Rules*. This generation has been frequently referred to as the "me generation." In a search for self-fulfillment, in satisfying the urge to express one's potential, the "me generation" reflects a privatist ethic. The idea of recognizing yourself as a real person finds expression in language borrowed from pop psychology. A religious sociologist, Donald Miller, spoke of the celebration of individualism as one of the outstanding trends of our time. He said, "Judging by the number of psychology self-help books that inundate our drugstore and supermarket shelves, one would think that the greatest moral failure of our time is to be bound by another person's wishes or desires."

The "me generation" has passed its zenith. As we go into the 80's, Yankelovich reports that me-ism, narcissism, privatism, are losing their grip. You may ask, why? The answer is found in the hunger for deeper personal relations. Research findings demonstrate that a "me-first" attitude leads to unsatisfactory relationships, relationships that are superficial and transitory. People want to link themselves with other people. They want to develop more satisfying connections with other human beings. A recent study revealed that 70 percent of Americans now realize that while they have many acquaintances, they have few close friends.

Moses, the greatest of men, was modest. The prince of the prophets taught our people and reached out to God, but remained a humble man.

There is a lovely statement by Simhah Bunem of Pshiskhah who once said, "A little bird, even when it stands on top of a mountain, remains as small as it was." Though Moses had ascended Mount Sinai twice, he still remained the man Moses. This, I think, is at the heart of the lesson of the small aleph.

SHEMINI

"Are You Prepared?"
PROFESSOR SAUL LIEBERMAN
1983

We have the expression "darash" (Leviticus 10), which means that Moses diligently inquired. The Bible text has a footnote below: The word *darash* marks the halfway point in the Torah. In life, one has to examine carefully and study well. My subject is the study of a giant who examined carefully and studied well.

My teacher, Professor Saul Lieberman, had a favorite expression. Calling a student by name, he would ask, "So-and-so, are you prepared?" How can one really be prepared to bid farewell to so great a spirit and so profound an influence on our lives? Our Seminary is now like Paris without the Eiffel Tower—the giant is now gone.

The rabbis speak of "death by a kiss." Professor Saul Lieberman, one of the greatest savants of all time, passed away while on an El-Al plane, sleeping in his seat. He was going to Israel to spend the Passover with his family. His wife, Dr. Judith Lieberman, had predeceased him. She was the daughter of one of the great leaders of the religious Zionist movement, Rabbi Meir

Berlin. When the Jewish state was established, he changed his name to Bar-Ilan.

Professor Lieberman had a way of addressing his students. His method was that of being hard in class and extremely pleasant in his home. I must tell you something about this man, for his death is a loss to the entire Jewish world.

To understand Professor Lieberman, we must appreciate his background and the world from which he came. Lithuania was the heart and head of Russian Jewry. The Lithuanian yeshivot served not only their local communties but also attracted students from afar. The hundreds of students came from Poland, the Ukraine, from Russia and the far corners of Greater Russia, including the Caucasus and Siberia. Some students, even years before World War II, came from across the Atlantic.

After spending several years in the yeshiva, they returned to their own communities. They carried the "very fragrance and spirit" of their yeshivot with them. That widespread attraction found everywhere—attraction to the love of Torah and a yearning for the spirit of ancient Israel—that very attraction caused the young scholars who returned to their birthplaces to have great influence and to build a community founded on extreme devotion to the tradition. The students were gifted in intellect and in spirit. Some were sent by their parents. Some came voluntarily out of personal longing against the very wishes of their parents. Many came when they were mature people. Some had studied at smaller schools and had moved to the more famous ones. A great number of our distinguished people came from there: scientists, administrators, writers, poets, revolutionaries, politicans. Some remained loyal to Torah and others abandoned it. Needless to say, many rabbis and Jewish scholars were also graduates of these yeshivot.

The students of the yeshivot were involved in a close reading of the text. They absorbed its very words. It was more than study; it was doing God's work. "The words of the wise are as goads" (Ecc. 12:1). As a goad directs the beast along the furrows, so the words of the Torah direct humankind along the paths of life.

Professor Lieberman was born in the small city of Motol, the birthplace of Chaim Weizmann, the first president of Israel. He was ordained to the rabbinate as a very young man at Slabodka.

After the Russian Revolution, he studied at Kiev University and in France. Finally, he took up residence in Palestine. The interesting thing is that when the Slabodka Yeshiva moved to Hebron in 1925, Professor Lieberman moved intellectually into the Hebrew University. There, he chose to train himself in a scientific study of rabbinic sources while at the same time mastering Greek and Latin because he felt they were critical for the understanding of the world of the rabbis. Professor Lieberman did not go to Hebron in 1925 with his masters; he chose Jerusalem. Just before World War II, he was invited to our Seminary.

Several months ago, a decision of the New York State Court of Appeals ruled that a *ketubah*, the Jewish wedding contract, is a binding legal instrument under civil law. It is not only a religious covenant but a civil instrument. Speaking for the majority opinion, the judge of the court held that "The ketubah should ordinarily be entitled to no less dignity than any other civil contract." It is a tragedy of Jewish life that the husband is the active partner in executing a divorce. At times, a recalcitrant husband refuses to issue a divorce. Some scoundrels even indulge in using the *get*, the Jewish divorce, as an instrument for blackmail. Professor Lieberman came up with a proposal. He resolved that a clause be added to the ketubah to the effect that should the marriage have difficulties and it was impossible to get the husband to deal properly, that the ketubah will be enforced by the court and that the court could force the husband to issue the *get*.

It was exciting to reread the Proceedings of the Rabbinical Assembly from thirty years ago. The professor said, in passing, "I saw that some of you were accused of being frightened by the Orthodox rabbis. I want to tell you that I am not frightened by them at all." He explained to the Assembly the import of his ketubah amendment.

His addition to the 2,000-year-old text read: "Husband and wife, look forward to living with each other in peace, harmony and mutual consideration, each loving the other as himself and herself and honoring each other beyond oneself. If serious difficulty should arise between husband and wife, they should seek the counsel of their rabbi." Then he said, "In the event either party obtains a civil divorce from the other, which is valid under the laws of the state in which they reside, each party to the marriage consents to the preparation and delivery of the *get* at the request of the other party. If they do not wish so, then it shall pass on to a national Bet Din for arbitration and the Bet Din shall have the power to fix and determine the amount of money to be paid to insure that a divorce be prepared." This freeing of the woman and protecting her rights marked a great advance in Jewish life.

Professor Lieberman's contributions to Jewish scholarship were reviewed by an older colleague on the occasion of his 50th birthday in 1948. Dr. Alexander Marx spoke of the vast impact Professor Lieberman had. His main fields were the Talmud, our books of Jewish law, and the Midrash, commentaries on the Bible. As he worked in each field, his own knowledge expanded. One could see the brilliance of the man. Sometimes he brought a reference from an out-of-the-way source from far-flung fields. He was an expert on philology, the meaning of words. He mastered Greek and the Roman law. He was blessed with a prodigious memory, with instant recall of all that he had read. He was blessed with a total mastery of all of rabbinic literature, and at times he showed how a scholar in the 10th, 12th or 14th century may have quoted a source that is no longer available to us.

From the very beginning, he was interested in the correct reading of ancient texts. One of his earliest writings came out some 54 years ago. When he was a young man of 31, he found parts of the Palestinian Talmud, the Jerusalem Talmud, in a Vatican manuscript. These readings corrected the text that had been current for centuries.

His great work was in the study of the Tosefta. Tosefta is an additional text similar to the Mishna, the code of Jewish law. Here he corrected an edition that had come out years before. His corrections would help us understand how different traditions had sprung up among the Jews of Babylon and among the Jews of Palestine.

In one of his early books called *Shkiin*, published in Jerusalem just prior to the outbreak of the war in 1939, we see one of the truly magnificent examples of his scholarship. Professor Lieberman collected legends, customs, and literary sources that were preserved in Karaite and Christian works. The Karaites were a sect that had broken off from Judaism because it did not believe in anything that had developed in Jewish practice after the closing of the Bible. As we believe in the rabbinic interpretation, the Karaites rejected it. A simple example of a Karaite position is when the Bible says, "You shall not kindle fire in any of your dwellings on the Sabbath day." The Karaites said this meant that there should be no fire whatsoever, no illumination, no Shabbat candles—the home had to be dark.

Of great importance is the analysis of one Raymund Martini. As a member of a 13th-century Spanish board of censors of Hebrew books, Martini had access to many current texts. Martini gives copious extracts from these manuscripts in the form in which he found them, even though he did not always understand and translate them correctly. His excerpts of the different books are of great value to us as they often help the reader in determining which texts on the rabbinic works offer the version then current in Spain. The charge that Martini forged some of the quotations he used for polemic reasons is proven to be unfounded.

Professor Lieberman was able to find materials heretofore unknown to us. "After full examination and comparison of his quotations with Midrashic literature in old editions and manuscripts . . . almost all the passages he quoted have been proved to be accurate and his translations are faithful."

Raymund Martini has been suspected of being a rabbi who converted to Christianity, but Professor Lieberman makes the point that the mistakes he sometimes made in either reading or in the translation are of such a crude nature that a Jew who had studied Talmud since childhood could never have made them. Still, we must ask how a non-Jew who did not devote all his time to Jewish learning could have mastered Jewish literature to such a degree as to quote it so frequently and so accurately. It can be presumed *a priori* that the appropriate quotations were compiled for him from the Jewish books submitted to the investigation of the board of censors.

In his Tosefta, Professor Lieberman deals with a classic Jewish passage. Caravans of men are walking down a road. They are accosted by non-Jews, who say to them, "Give us one from among you that we may kill it, otherwise we shall kill you all." Though all may be killed, you may not hand over a single soul of Israel. Better for the whole group to perish than to become accessory to murder by handing over one individual to extradition and death. However, if the demand is for a specified individual who is guilty of a capital crime and has been convicted by a legitimate court, they should surrender that individual rather than all being killed. The

Tosefta states that human life is not measured by the number of individuals any more than by the number of years. The worst fate that can befall a person is not to be murdered but to murder.

Ezekiel Landau, a decisor of several centuries ago, was asked a question as to what happens when it is demanded of a Jewish community that they turn over some young people. Is it permitted to just turn them over when you know that they would lose their faith or perhaps their lives? Even if some are dullards or delinquents, one is not permitted to turn them over. Professor Lieberman's publication of his Tosefta in 1955 was regarded as one of the great milestones in Jewish history.

Professor Lieberman lectured in many languages on many different occasions. One great address delivered at Brandeis University was on the theme of "How Much Greek in Jewish Palestine?" He was an expert on these cultures. In his address, he brings out the point that from the time of Alexander the Great in the 4th century (approximately 330 BCE) until about 400 CE, the Jews of Palestine lived amongst nations with a more or less developed Hellenistic culture. At the same time, the Palestinian rabbis shaped Rabbinic Judaism, which has influenced the life of our people up to modern times. Rabbinic literature has been studied by the Jews for two thousand years and has left deep imprints on their minds and hearts. Ancient rabbinic works reflect certain attitudes toward the behavior of the non-Jewish world. It is good to know how much Greek there was in Jewish Palestine, how much knowledge of the world surrounding them the builders of Rabbinic Judaism possessed.

Professor Lieberman discusses a famous text. Two people are walking in a waterless desert. One has in his possession a canteen of water. Were he alone to drink from it, he would survive and reach an inhabited place; but were he to share the water with his companion, both would perish. Ben Petura says let them both drink and die. But Akiba objected: "Your life comes before the life of your brother."

This is a very difficult passage, and it is remarkable to see how Professor Lieberman deals with it. Should a man give away the property upon which his life depends? Normally a man is master over his property, but he is never a master of his life. Nobody has the right to decide that his own life is less important than the life of another single individual. In the case that his life depends upon his property, he actually gives his life away when he surrenders his property. This is the reason for Rabbi Akiba thinking your life comes before the life of your brother. You're not supposed to give away your life by your own hands in order to save the life of another person. It is the factor of ownership that determines the ruling in the rabbinic case.

Professor Lieberman traces this passage and notes a similar type of experience in the *De officiis* of Cicero, the Roman writer. Lieberman refers to a recent discovery by Solomon Pines of a familiar passage in the writings of Al-razi, a philosopher and physician who lived in the first half of the 10th century. Two people are in a waterless desert. One has in his possession an amount of water sufficient to sustain himself but not enough for both of them. Under such conditions, it is proper that the water be assigned to the one more useful to humankind.

The rabbis drew their information from personal conversations with philosophers and other intelligent men. The Talmud of Babylon and Palestine, the Midrashim, frequently mentioned such discussions between rabbis and philosophers. It is reasonable to assume that there were many learned Jews among the upper classes of Jewish Palestine who communicated some of the Greek doctrines. We should bear in mind that in the 3rd century there was at least one synagogue in Palestine, in Caesarea, where the Shema was recited in Greek. This indicates that Greek was spoken by Jews in that locality. We know, likewise, that some rabbis visited Greek-speaking communities outside of Palestine and engaged in learned discussions there.

At the service for Professor Lieberman, this passage was read from the Tosefta: "Hillel the Wise said, 'At a time when people hold close, spread. At a time when people spread, pull in. At a time when you see the Torah and all rejoice therein, you be among those who spread, among those who scatter, as it is said, There is that scatters and yet increases and there is that withholds more than is meet, but it tendeth to only want.' "

What is the meaning of the time when people are scattering? Professor Lieberman adds the note that there are times when the students are scattering the Torah but are not gathering it. You have to bring your words together, be cautious, making certain that you are among the preservers. When you see that the Torah is being forgotten amongst our people and no one cares to guard over it, you be among those who gather in, as it is said in the Psalms, "It is time to work for the Lord. They have made void your Torah."

With great devotion, Professor Lieberman mentions in his Tosefta that those who preceded him did not have the benefit of newly discovered sources. "Let us never forget the reality that these earlier scholars were pioneers who made possible the preparation of a larger and a more complete commentary. They had no one upon whom to depend. Not we, for we stand on their shoulders and we drink of their waters." That is the spirit of this tribute. We stand upon their shoulders and we refresh ourselves with the living waters of the Torah they preserved for us.

TAZRIA METZORA

On Children in America

1979

Our Torah reading this week deals with the birth of a child. It is good to re-read the Book of Leviticus and try to appreciate its values and message for our time—particularly in the area of the life of a child. The Book of Leviticus has important messages for us. Many of us ask the question that Manoah and his wife, the parents of Samson, posed. They had received word from God that they would be blessed with a child. Manoah pleaded with the Lord. "Oh my Lord!" he said, "please let the man of God that You sent come to us again, and let him instruct us how to act with the child that is to be born" (Judges 13:8). How to act with a child that is born, a child that is growing up, is critical.

I read an unusual interview given by Dr. Kenneth Keniston, one of America's greatest students of young people. Keniston, who teaches at MIT, has written extensively of youngsters in American society. His books—*The Uncommitted, Young Radicals, Youth and Dissent*, and others—are classics. The background of the interview was the fact that this is the "International Year of the Child." Twenty years ago, the United Nations issued a Declaration of the Rights of the Child, using as a theme the epigram, "Mankind owes the child the best it has to give."

Keniston was interviewed by a Catholic publication and the title of the interview was called, "Is America Anti-Child?" As individuals, Americans love their own children, but in public policy we often give the welfare of children low priority. Until recently, our society was labeled as child-centered. We were condemned for being child-indulgent. Now, if we examine motion picture films—which are the world's most popular art form—we have evidence that an alarming transition has taken place. They reveal a deep level of cultural discomfort with children. *The Exorcist*, which has been recently revived and is being shown in downtown moviehouses, and *Rosemary's Baby* are cases in point. One reviewer tabbed *The Omen* the strongest anti-child movie in history.

Children are being taken for granted. There is a higher level of child abuse than in decades past. Too many of our children grow up in poverty. America's children spend more time watching television—which is sated with nonsense—than attending school. More significantly, in many homes there is no adult present and children have the all-too-familiar key-with-chain necklace.

Ann Landers, who is featured in the *Sun-Times*, ran a survey two years ago. Seventy percent of the ten thousand respondents said that if they had to do it over again, they would not have children—children were too much bother, caused too many worries, and were ultimately ungrateful to their parents.

The problem in our system is not with the schools, it's with the parents. Too many parents have nothing to tell their children. Remember the words that we heard just a few weeks ago during our Passover seder: "In every generation each Jew should regard himself as though he personally went forth from Egypt. That is what the Bible means when it says: 'And you shall tell your son on that day' " (Exodus 13:8).

Dr. Keniston, whom I mentioned earlier, is the chairman of the Carnegie Council on Children. He said, "Parents, however, need the spirit of the community."

If one compares our culture to Israeli society, there are vast differences. Today, we have as our guest The Honorable Moshe Kol, a former minister of the Israeli government. For two decades prior to joining the government, Kol was head of Youth Aliyah— that successful effort to save our children and bring them to Israel, where they were cared for in a most beautiful fashion.

Many Americans, on visiting Italy, note the obvious love the Italians have for their children. In northern Europe, in Denmark, the American visitor saw the following scene. There was a crying child left outside a shop in a stroller. All sorts of people came and tried to console the youngster. When the mother came out of the shop, the bystanders chewed her out for leaving the child alone. Americans have taken on the unfortunate attitude of being non-involved bystanders. We follow the line of non-interference. We think of children as belonging solely to their families. Even if we have the impulse to pick up a crying child, we say, "It's none of my business."

We come from a grand tradition. When the Torah was offered at Sinai, the question was asked by God, "If I give you the Ten Commandments, who will be your surety?" "Shall I," the Holy One said, "give you the Torah without some bondsmen?" Israel offered the ancestors. God said, "Your fathers are My debtors and therefore not good bondsmen." They offered the prophets who were to speak forth in centuries to come and electrify the world. God rejected them, for the prophets had labeled themselves "foxes in the desert." "Bring me good bondsmen and I will give you the Torah." Israel answered, "We will give you our children."

Children were our surety then and our hope now. In every possible way, we must strengthen the family and encourage the child.

Senator Sam J. Ervin, Jr.

1985

This week's Torah reading speaks of the *metzorah*, "the leper." This has been interpreted as alluding to the "moral leper," a person who uses God's great gift of language and abuses it.

Words give us the ability to communicate with one another. In the entire kingdom of God's creation, only humans can speak. Speech can be, to be sure, a blessing or a curse; it can be used for benediction or malediction. Words can be used to tell the truth or to spread lies.

Against that background, let us think of the passing of Senator Sam J. Ervin, a great hero of our country. His great concern was with the use of words. In his calling as an attorney, later as a judge, and finally as a senator, he was constantly involved with the Constitution, the Bill of Rights, and the interpretation of constitutional law.

He had three great passions in his life. Professor Philip Kurland called them "major commitments." One was his love of family. The second concern was with the Bible. The third was his intense devotion to the Constitution.

Though concerned with his own family, his one important shortcoming was his inability to be able to come to grips with the human family. Senator Ervin was a Southern gentleman in the fullest sense of the word. He was, unfortunately, blind to the problems of blacks in our country. The father of our country, General George Washington, was a slave holder. President Thomas Jefferson, the archangel of American liberalism, was also myopic in this area.

Senator Ervin's love of the Bible was reflected in many of his addresses. Known to his friends and colleagues as "Mr. Sam" and "the Judge," he would regale his colleagues in the upper house of Congress with Biblical verses, with snatches of poetry, and with the wisdom of an old uncle, Ephraim, whom he described as an "arthritic mountaineer."

Regarding the Constitution of the United States, his strict interpretation of our fundamental statute defied easy political classification. He was one of the Senate's most respected authorities on constitutional law. He was both a critic of civil rights legislation and a champion of civil liberties. He fought affirmative action proposals and battled efforts to establish prayer in the public schools. He exposed military surveillance of anti-war protestors and other dissenters during the Vietnam War. He was thoroughly independent. He was not "a member of the club." He fought a mighty battle against Senator Joseph McCarthy of Wisconsin in the 1950s. He was concerned that McCarthy, whose idol was Adolf Hitler, wanted to establish an imperial presidency. He was a devoted member of the Presbyterian Church and stood firm on his interpretation of the First Amendment.

Sam J. Ervin, Jr. wrote on his religious faith. His prose takes on the wings of song. It is good to hear his words, to read them again:

> I look at the universe and behold with wonder the life-giving sun, which rises in the east at morn, travels across the sky by day, and sets in the west at eventide; the galaxies of stars, which twinkle in the infinite heavens; the clouds, which bring the soil-refreshing rain; the majestic mountains with hills at their knees; the rivers, which water pleasant valleys and fertile plains and run endlessly to the sea; the tall trees, which lift leafy arms heavenward to pray; the arbutus and dogwood, which brighten springtime, and the marigolds and roses, which ornament summer; the glory of the leaves and ripened crops of autumn; the crystal snowflakes, which descend so gently in winter; and the other beautiful things past remembering, which adorn the earth.
>
> Religion adds hope to man's desire for immortality. This desire is not to be attributed simply to the egotism of men, or their fear of the unknown beyond the grave, or their repugnance to the thought of their nothingness after death.
>
> I revere religion. I revere religion because it gives us these promises and this hope. I would preserve and protect the right of freedom of religion for all men.

Personally, I recall with gratitude the opportunity to testify before the Committee on the Judiciary in 1966, explaining the position of the Jewish community on the crucial issue of prayer in the schools.

Sam Ervin's finest hour was during the Senate Watergate hearings. He took much of the heat and looked in our Constitution for guidance on the rationale of the separation of powers between President and Congress. He turned to two distinguished law professors, the late Alexander Bickel of Yale and Philip Kurland of the University of Chicago.

Kurland was called upon to eulogize Sam Ervin at the National Presbyterian Church in June of this year. Kurland's first contact with Senator Ervin was in the Senator's request that the professor become a consultant to his newly formed committee on the separation of powers. One can subscribe most heartily to Kurland's beautiful statement, "Honorable was, for Sam Ervin, not a title but a description." Kurland's estimation of Sam Ervin rings out, speaking of his unique contributions to American life: "Ervin's voice was the voice out of the Age of Reason. It was the voice . . . of one fervently dedicated to democracy and liberty. For him, the document [the U.S. Constitution] . . . was not an artifact of history. It was the essence of the hopes for uniqueness for the United States of America, where government could not oppress, where religion would be personal, where speech would be unconfined . . . where judicial trials would not mock justice, where the rule of law would govern and not the whim of man."

We are grateful for this assessment, which spoke so idyllically and lovingly about a giant of the human spirit. Our nation was blessed by the presence of this dedicated leader who was at once a political leader and a prince of principles.

Give Honor to the Aged

1985

We reach a lofty point in Judaism's moral teachings in today's
Torah reading. The imperative is stated simply and clearly: "The
Lord spoke to Moses, saying: Speak to the whole community and
say to them: You shall be holy, for I, the Lord your God, am holy."
Shifting from the many to the one, from the plural to the singular,
our Kedoshim reading contains some of the most magnificent
expressions in the Bible. "Love your neighbor as yourself" is the
Golden Rule of Judaism.

In an age where there should be an increased concern for the
elderly, where there is a graying of the community, we are taught,
"You shall rise before the aged and give honor to the old."

Monday I was in New York and met with my mother, who will be
eighty-nine in June. Later I called on my great teacher, Professor
Louis Finkelstein. A profound human being, Dr. Finkelstein has
made, and is still making, many great contributions to the world
of thought. One of his principal gifts was in helping to make a
180-degree turn in the realm of Jewish-Christian relations. He
engendered an attitude of respect for the Jewish tradition. In one
of his works, he describes the limited knowledge that even distinguished Christian professors had of our faith. "Tragically, we
must report that there are false notions about Judaism and
Jews." So distinguished a philosopher as Bertrand Russell
thought that the source of "Love your neighbor as yourself" was
the Book of Mark in the New Testament. So great a Bible scholar
as Rudolph Kittel, whose study of Bible variants is used in most
Christian seminaries, had startling misconceptions of Judaism
today. The story is related by another of my teachers that when he
was about to leave Leipzig, Germany, to go to his native Romania
to celebrate Passover, he went to say goodbye to Kittel, who
wondered about the reason for the trip. The then-student ex-

plained that Passover is a Jewish family festival, much as Christmas is for Christians. At that point Kittel remarked, "By the way, there is a question about Passover I always meant to ask you. Now that the Temple is destroyed, where do you Jews sacrifice the Paschal lamb?" Kittel should have known that Jews have no sacrificial system. We have not had one for almost two thousand years, since the Temple was destroyed. Our worship service consists of prayer and study. We adhere to the moral and ritual commandments. But the information was fixed in his "effective consciousness" that Passover had no meaning without a Paschal lamb.

Dr. Finkelstein established the Conference on Science, Religion and Philosophy. He called the Institute for Religious and Social Studies into being. Some of our senior rabbinical colleagues, including a number of the most prominent among them, railed against Dr. Finkelstein. A distinguished editor wrote that Dr. Finkelstein was leading us to conversion.

Dr. Finkelstein's work was aided by Professor George Foot Moore, whose classic study of Judaism, published by Harvard, meant the shifting of the intellectual tides. In the 1930s, it was difficult for us to open America's doors to German refugees. For example, when two Jewish seminaries invited a young scholar to come to this country and be saved from the Nazi beasts, the American consul in Amsterdam asked the prospective immigrant, "Do you know any English?" The young scholar said, "No, but I will learn." The consul glowered, "How can you teach Americans who know only English?" The young scholar was sent back to Hitler's Germany and was among the six million who perished.

Dr. Finkelstein's efforts were strengthened by the unusual contributions made by the late Dr. Abraham Joshua Heschel. In a famous lecture entitled "No Religion is an Island," Dr. Heschel spoke of the fact that "a world without the people of Israel would be a world without the God of Israel." Dr. Heschel was the visiting Harry Emerson Fosdick professor at the prestigious Christian seminary, the Union Theological Seminary. He told the story of how a Protestant pastor was asked by Frederick the Great, "Herr Professor, give me proof of the Bible, but briefly, for I have little time." The pastor respectfully answered, "Your Majesty, the Jews."

Dr. Heschel played a prominent role at the Second Vatican Council. Working against the ancient notion of deicide, of Jews being Christ killers, he graciously urged the Church to give up its missionary activities. He told Pope Paul VI, the successor of Pope John XXIII, that he would rather go to Auschwitz than convert. As one rereads the documents of Vatican Council II, one can feel the great acts of Dr. Heschel. When he met with Cardinal Bea, the two discussed the Song of Songs and how it was interpreted as an allegory by Christians and Jews. It is easier for many Christians to understand the Judaism of the 1st century than it is for our contemporaries to grasp the importance of 20th-century Judaism.

Here a third presonality has played a pre-eminent role. I am speaking of Elie Wiesel, who has had so much prominence in recent days because of the Bitburg controversy. When he opposed publicly, in the White House, the visit of President Reagan to a cemetery where there were graves of Nazi soldiers, Elie Wiesel wrestled with two irreconcilable realities—the reality of God and the reality of Auschwitz. The Holocaust confronts Christianity with challenging theological questions: How can we believe in God in a world where the Holocaust has taken place? How can we muster the strength to look squarely at the Holocaust and realize that it would never have taken place without being fueled by centuries of anti-Semitism? Robert McAfee Brown has written about Elie Wiesel's unique contribution to this difficult issue. Christianity must have the courage to face both the Judaism of the ancient world and of the 20th-century.

This is the twentieth anniversary of the Declaration on the Relations of the Church to Non-Christian Religions. In 1974, this declaration was updated. The initial statement speaks of the fact that "In this age of ours when men are joined more closely together and the bonds of friendship . . . are being strengthened, the Church examines with greater care the relations which she has to non-Christian religions." A leading churchman said that "Only by bringing this new mood of enhanced and improved relations, only by speaking more about love will it be possible to bridge the gap between Christians and Jews."

Dr. Finkelstein, Dr. Heschel, and Elie Wiesel each made a special and unique contribution. In this epochal era, one is reminded of the statement I found in a pamphlet distributed at the World Council of Churches Conference Center near Geneva, Switzerland: "How can we sit down at father's table without the oldest son?" Surely the Biblical teaching, "You shall rise before the aged and give honor to the old" can refer to our faith. May the daughter be respectful of the mother, and may the mother treat her offspring with understanding.

Do Not Forsake Me

1984

If all of the Bible is holy, this Sabbath's Sidra is the holiest of the holy. The Lord spoke to Moses, saying, "Speak to the whole Israelite community and say to them, 'You shall be holy for I the Lord your God am holy.' "

Martin Buber, when translating the Bible from Hebrew into German, rendered the Hebrew *kadosh* not as "holy" but as "hallowing." If people are called to be holy, this means they are called to hallow the world.

The sector of the world that concerns me this Sabbath is the universe of the aged. In the Sidra, we have cryptic phrases but powerful demands: "Love your neighbor as yourself." "You shall rise before the aged and show deference to the old." "When a stranger resides with you in your land, you shall not wrong him."

Our concern this Shabbat is with the aged of our nation and of the world. The thought of dealing with this issue came to mind after reading the words of the governor of Colorado, Richard Lamm. When he was elected governor at the age of 38, a correspondent for the *New York Times* observed that "Sometimes his fast-moving tongue becomes tied up by his faster-moving mind." The Colorado governor created a furor about a month ago when he spoke before the Colorado Health Lawyers Association. He was reported to have said to the aged, "You've got a duty to die and get out of the way. Let the other society, our kids, build a reasonable life." This strong, abrasive statement was understood to be an invitation for the aged to leave by the nearest exit.

To be fair to the governor, what he was speaking about was the use of the modern techniques of medicine, machines, and artificial hearts that keep life going. He was speaking of the terminally ill, of an extraordinarily expensive medical technology that has developed faster than a corresponding ethical code, and of the resulting heavy financial burden that our nation must bear. There was a certain callousness in the governor's statement when he spoke of the duty to die. It is always very hard for a physician to reach a decision, for a family to come to the point of no return and to say this is as far as we want our aged to go. But the fact of the matter is that every year brings new techniques for the prolongation of life, and society is called upon to make decisions that as yet it is not prepared to make.

All of us are involved in the process of helping to make the decision as to whether or not to discontinue life-sustaining treatment. It is a moral challenge for the patient, if he or she is strong enough and alert enough, to realize that additional medical care will be of little avail. It is a challenge to the family who stand by a bedside and watch a loved one slowly disappearing before their very eyes. It is a torment for physicians and administrators. The community at large is likewise involved in the process.

Several years ago, a great article appeared in *The American Scholar*. Dr. Leon Kass of the University of Chicago had this to say: "We must see ourselves as species-directed, and not merely self-directed. We are built with leanings toward and capacities for perpetuation. Is it not possible that aging and mortality are part of this construction, and that life span and the rate of aging have been selected for their usefulness to the task of perpetuation?" This is a profound question, and Dr. Kass goes on to write, "Why should we die? Why should we, the flower of the living kingdom, lose our youthful bloom and go to seed? Why should we grow old in body and in mind, losing our various powers—first gradually, then altogether in death? Until now, the answer has been simple: We should because we must. Aging, decay, and death have been inevitable, as necessary for us as for other animals and plants, from whom we are distinguished in this matter only by our awareness of this necessity. We know that we are, as the poet says, like the leaves, the leaves that the wind scatters to the ground." The words the governor borrowed from Dr. Kass's citation come from "The Iliad," in which the Greek poet Homer wrote, "As is the generation of leaves so is that of humanity. The wind scatters the leaves to the ground, but the live timber burgeons with leaves again in the season of spring returning. So one generation of man will grow while another dies."

The Colorado governor, taking up this idea, said, "Like leaves which fall off a tree forming the humus in which other plants can grow, we've got a duty to die and get out of the way with all of our machines and artificial hearts, so that our kids can build a reasonable life." There was a tremendous uproar concerning the address of the governor. But, in a sense, his address served a purpose. It drew our attention to the elderly of our community. Aging, the process and the people involved, merits our attention. What happens to our older citizens first affects us when we see our parents and older relatives aging and we witness what happens to them. But, ultimately, aging is a personal issue for, unlike other conditions of life, old age comes to each of us. Everyone has heard the familiar little dialogue. "I'm getting older." "Yes, but think of the alternative."

At the beginning of the 20th century, there were about 3 million American citizens over the age of sixty-five. By 1975, the number had grown to 22 million. It is projected that in the next half century, over 50 million Americans will be over the age of sixty-five. There are all kinds of myths being spread in our nation, among them that Social Security is going down the drain because of the over-abundance of retirees—most of whom made financial contribution to the Social Security system. There are millions of aged who are clearly below the official poverty threshold. There are many older people who live alone without the companionship of a mate or a friend. Many of our elderly are living in deprived conditions. They are unable to purchase new clothes and, more desperately, cannot afford medication. I saw one estimate that there are at least 5 million elderly who cannot afford a telephone.

Many elderly have grown poor as they have grown old. Pension funds have shrunk due to inflation. In some cases, widows have suffered the dual loss of a husband and a pension. Other difficulties afflict our aged: lack of good public transportation, crime in our cities, victimization, and the difficulty of maintaining old and deteriorating homes even if the mortgage is paid. Many of these issues were raised earlier this week in a touching telecast, a two-hour movie called "A Doctor's Story." An old man sitting on a park bench overlooking the East River and staring at the magnificent Manhattan skyline, sums up life's greatest final challenge: "You get used to people looking right through you," he says. "They look at you like you don't exist anymore." We can think of the alienating experience of the aged, of the dehumanization of the industrial workplace, but, for me, this particular T.V. film summed up the concern we must have for the aged.

In a biting indictment, Simone de Beauvoir, in *The Coming of Age*, said, "Society cares about the individual only insofar as he is profitable. The young know this. Their anxiety as they enter into social life matches the anguish of the old as they are excluded from it." Jonathan Swift once wrote, "Every man desires to live long, but no man would be old."

As we think of our older citizens whom we have, in the main, neglected, let us remind ourselves of the divine imperative to hallow our existence. We ought never to forget, "You shall rise before the aged and show deference to the old."

BEHAALOTEKHA

Light and Warmth

1979

Our Torah reading this Sabbath contains the instructions given to Aaron, the high priest, through Moses, "Speak to Aaron and say unto him, 'when you mount the lamps, do it in such a way as to throw the light forward.'" The rabbis sought a connection between last week's reading, which dealt with the final actions connected with the setting up of the tabernacle, and today's portion. At the first occasion all the tribes were represented save for one, the tribe of Levi. They were saddened by this seeming slight. Aaron was concerned that his tribe, which had given so much service and had been designated for future responsibilities, had not been called upon. In a classic comment, the rabbis asked, "Why is this section dealing with the Menorah put in juxtaposition with the section telling of the offerings of the princes?" They answered their own query by saying, "When Aaron saw the dedication offerings of the heads of the other tribes, he became uneasy because neither he nor his tribe was with the others at the great occasion of dedication." The Holy One, as it were, reassured him, "By your life, your role is greater than theirs."

The mood of discomfort and the uneasiness of Aaron because he felt he had been slighted, are typical. Many of us feel uneasy when we are left out, when we fail to get an invitation to a grand occasion. We are troubled when we are unrecognized. Even Aaron, the great first High Priest, had to be reassured.

In Hebrew, the opening word of the Sidra is *Behaalotekha.* This easily could be understood as "*Behithaalotkha*—when you cause yourself to grow." Within each one of us are latent talents waiting for us to use them. The use of these faculties will be a source of much reassurance as to our personal worth.

Aaron was told, "Your role is greater than theirs. It is greater than theirs because your role in life, in the long run, is a more significant one." The other princes gave once, but Aaron and his descendants gave or are giving continuous service. He taught our people that lights, as a mode of Jewish religious expression, must be kindled throughout the generations. We kindle lights on the eve of the Sabbath. We kindle the Havdalah candle at the end of the Sabbath. We kindle the Menorah lights at Hanukkah time. I have been at wedding services where the bride and groom were led in by escorts who had burning candles in their hands. This is still a custom among some Orthodox Jews and is practiced both here and in Israel.

The other day, I read a magnificent tribute to a woman who was the wife of a distinguished professor. Her husband offered a special word of tribute to her. He wrote of his gratitude and thankfulness for the many sacrifices she had made throughout the years. She helped him to help others. During one of the professor's lecture tours, a colleague inscribed a book to her, "To the warmth that accompanies the light." The husband added his own words of gratitude, "May the warmth long persist when the light has dimmed away." Aaron caused the lights to grow, but together with the illumination there was warmth. Aaron was the warmest of men. Aaron sought peace and pursued it.

The kind Hillel said to Aaron's descendants, "Be like the disciples of Aaron, love peace, pursue peace, love mankind and draw them to the Torah." Where there was misunderstanding, Aaron brought harmony. Where there was cantankerous debate, he brought understanding and unity. He would sit down with two adversaries and serve as a good mediator. He would remain with them until he had removed all rancor and hate from their hearts.

Like Aaron, let us kindle the Menorah and pray to be blessed by its light and warmth.

BEHAALOTEKHA

The Blessing of Light

1980

"When you light the lamps . . ."
(Numbers 8:2)

"Behold a Menorah all of gold . . ."
(Zechariah 4:2)

Our Torah portion and our Haftarah reading deal with the kindling of the Menorah. This reminded the great medieval scholar Rabbenu Bahya ben Asher of the verse, "Light is sown for the righteous and gladness for the upright in heart." He went on to say that the Bible's use of the word "light" refers to all blessings in this world. It means more than physical light; it refers to peace, honor, and gladness. Light is compared to the sowing of a single seed. From the little seed, there can be an abundant crop *(Kad Hakemach)*.

You remember the account of the Purim story. It ends with, "The Jews had light and gladness." Evil is referred to as darkness. Job, in his saddest moments, cried bitterly, "Let that day be darkness." "Who is this that darkeneth counsel by words?"

The Menorah with which we are concerned this Sabbath had seven cups. The Menorah stood in the temple, near the Holy of Holies. The first lamp did not have a special name, but the second lamp was called "the western lamp," the *Ner Maravi*. The western lamp contained no more oil than the other lamps. While the other lamps burned only until the morning, the western lamp continued to burn throughout the night and the entire next day until it was refilled by a Kohen. During the kindling ritual that took place at dusk, the priest would kindle the other lights from it. This miraculous occurrence attested to the fact that God's glory rested among His people.

Now, the legends concerning the *Ner Maravi*, the western lamp, burning continually should be of significance to us. As long as we have one light that still continues to burn, we ought not to be pessimistic about the Jewish future. If, on the other hand, all of the lights are out and there isn't a flickering bit of light here or there, we would find ourselves in a most difficult situation. Even if our numbers grow statistically smaller, even if the various indicators of Jewish loyalty point downward, as long as there are sparks of light we must be strengthened by their presence and encouraged by hopeful expectation.

There is a very sad legend which reports that forty years before the destruction of the second Temple, the *Ner Maravi*, this western lamp, was found extinguished in the morning. It did not burn for the 24-hour period any longer. Our sages felt that this was a sign of imminent destruction and impending catastrophe.

It is good to read about the kindling of the Menorah. May it enhearten us to place ourselves among those who are kindlers of the light. Wherever we find in our community a bit of light still burning, it is our duty to add to its strength and to increase its intensity.

As long as there is a western light that still burns, there is hope. We should be among the lamp lighters, who bring strength and a renewed sense of purpose to our people.

A Positive Response

1980

Just a few moments ago, following our prayer for universal peace, we recited a personal prayer, "O Lord, guard my tongue from evil and my lips from speaking guile."

This Sabbath's Torah reading deals with such an experience. The Lord spoke to Moses saying, "Send men to scout the land of Canaan. Send one man from each of their ancestral tribes" (Numbers 13:2). The men were distinguished personalities; each one was a leader. Moses gave instructions how to study the land. "See what kind of country it is. Are the people who dwell in it strong or weak, few or many? Are the cities open or fortified? What is the nature of the terrain? What is its soil like, is it wooded or not? Take pains to bring back some of the fruit of the land." It happened to be the season of the first ripe grapes.

All of us remember from our religious school days how they brought back the fruits of the land; a large cluster of grapes, pomegranates, and figs. They went for forty days. Forty is perhaps a symbolic number. Moses had been on Mount Sinai's peak for forty days, and when he came down from the heights, he found the camp below in disarray. Ten of the twelve began their report on a favorable note. Then they changed course and blurted out, "We cannot attack that people for it is stronger than we." The camp was thrown into panic. However, Caleb and Joshua gave a positive report. Caleb said, "Let us by all means go up and we shall gain possession of it for we shall surely overcome it" (Numbers 13:30). Here we have two sets of perceptions of the same experience. The big majority saying, "No, we cannot succeed" and the minority declaring, "Yes, we will go up." We ourselves have experienced the same set of facts being given varying interpretations.

In California, a computer-based study came out with a most negative analysis. They used certain indices measuring the durability of civilization. What factors make for the continuation of life? What will happen to Israel in the next decade or the next score of years? The answer was one that we do not want to hear. The study predicted that the beautiful undertaking of which we dreamed for two thousand years and labored for so mightily for the last one hundred years cannot survive.

We are now in the midst of observing the 13th anniversary of the Six Day War, which began on June 5, 1967. In that very year, a French sociologist, Georges Friedmann, published a work in this country that had originally appeared in French. The question he posed was, "Does the establishment of a Jewish state in Israel demonstrate the eternity of the Jewish people?"

We can but respond in the spirit of Caleb and Joshua, "Let us by all means go up and we shall gain possession of it, for we shall surely overcome it."

In two years, we will observe the one hundredth anniversary of the BILU Movement. Taking as their call the phrase, *"Beit Yaakov Lekhu Ve'nelkhah*—House of Jacob, come ye and let us go up," a handful of pioneers went up to the land in 1882. They set the foundation for the state of Israel. On their first stamp, they noted the words of Isaiah, "The smallest shall become a thousand and the least a mighty nation." Who would have dreamt that the decimated Jewish people, who had lost one-third of its numbers during the Holocaust, would succeed in establishing a land that now has three million residents? With all of its problems, the state is here and it will remain. The key words are, "We shall go up."

We face many immediate problems. There is no peace for the city of peace.

The U.N. Security Council voted 14 to 0 to condemn Israel's posture on the occupied territories, including Jerusalem. The U.S. abstained. Later in the General Assembly, there was another negative vote against Israel. This time the U.S. voted "No."

Jerusalem is our city of cities. It has been our capital for centuries, the spiritual and physical center of all our aspirations. We pray that we will never have to weep over Jerusalem again, that we will never have to be comforted over the loss of our holy city. The statement of the prophet is strong and demanding. "For the sake of Zion, I will not keep silent, for the sake of Jerusalem, I will not be still until her victory emerges splendid and her triumph like a flaming torch."

When the Bible was to be completed with 11 Chronicles as its last book, the editor selected a statement from another Biblical book, the Book of Ezra. The last parts of Chronicles were sad: they were an account of national disaster. As we are a hopeful people, the editor looked back. He found the words of the decree of King Cyrus of Persia, who permitted those who were in exile to return to the land. This was the king's edict: "All the kingdoms of the earth hath the Lord, the God of heaven, given me; and He hath charged me to build Him a house in Jerusalem, which is in Judah. Whosoever there is among you of all His people—the Lord his God be with him—let him go up to the land of his fathers." The last word in Holy Scriptures is "v'yaal—let him go up."

This is the mood of Caleb and Joshua. "Let us by all means go up." May their spirit strengthen us in our resolve to speak positively concerning our commitment and our hope for the future.

KORAH

Freedom of Speech

1978

In our Torah readings these weeks, there are a number of verbal attacks on the leadership of Moses. In one, the Bible records how two men, Eldad and Medad, prophesied in the camp. A youth ran out and told Moses of the incident. Joshua, Moses' attendant, spoke up and said: "My lord Moses, restrain them!" Moses responded: "Are you wrought up on my account? Would that all the Lord's people were prophets, that the Lord put His spirit upon them!"

This same attitude is found in Moses' response to the children of Korah. Korah was engaged in the art of free speech, but he used demogogic techniques in questions he asked of Moses. Moses was uncomfortable with the words of his protagonist, Korah. He was disturbed when he heard: "You have gone too far, for all the community are holy, all of them, and the Lord is in their midst." Korah was using Moses' own argument to downgrade his leadership. Moses let Korah speak, and then said: "Let God give the answer."

I raise this issue because we are now involved in our community in trying to understand the meaning of free speech guaranteed by our First Amendment. A few days ago the United States Supreme Court, by a narrow vote of 5-4, decided what was called the "seven dirty words case" and ruled that the government could bar radio broadcasts of words that are "patently offensive" but fall short of the constitutional definition of obscenity. The Federal Communications Commission had warned a New York station that a twelve-minute selection from a comedy album containing indecent language could not be played at times of the day when children are in the audience.

The court rested on what Associate Justice John Paul Stevens, in writing for the narrow majority, described as the broadcast media's "uniquely pervasive presence in the lives of all Americans." The justice drew an analogy between an offensive broadcast and an indecent phone call. The right of an individual to be let alone outweighs the First Amendment rights of an intruder into a home.

What is most important is that the Supreme Court has backed the FCC on the use of offensive words. What concerns me is that the use of dirty words is wrong. However, when a Nazi says "Gas the Jews," the ultimate obscenity of genocide, he has the permission of the courts to parade and shout.

At the Nazi rally in Marquette Park, some of the obscene words heard included the phrase "Kill the Jews." A few days later, a columnist reported that the American Civil Liberties Union lawyer, David Goldberger, had once been asked if the Nazis should be allowed to demonstrate if they carried signs saying "Kill a Jew Today." Goldberger answered that they should be. "That sign is not likely to cause imminent violence," he responded. The *New York Times* quotes a St. Louis Nazi leader as saying to a crowd: "Do you want us to put you in the ovens? We will. We say one more time, all you Jews are going to get it."

The right to free speech is a priceless possession. We can but hope that the great Supreme Court that upheld the Nazis' right to freedom of speech and maintained a diverse opinion in the "seven dirty words case" will clarify its thinking.

Moses, who was tongue-tied, knew the difference between the proper and improper use of words.

BALAK

"Who Can Count the Dust of Jacob?"

1985

The *New York Times* has for many years carried the caption, "All the news that's fit to print." With this slogan as our background, I would like to share an experience I had in New York this week.

Leaving the office of the United Synagogue of America, I went into a Russian bookstore to browse. I bought a few music tapes, and then my eye caught a copy of a publication called *Soviet Life*, published by the U.S.S.R. Embassy in Washington. There was a most interesting article on Pinsk in Byelorussia (White Russia).

The name Pinsk brings back many recollections. My father's family came from a small community not too far from Pinsk. Such communities as Minsk and Brest-Litovsk, which our ancestors called Brisk, are not too far away. Pinsk was in the heartland of the Pale, the restricted area where most Jews were compelled to live.

The article had many wonderful elements in it. However, despite an occasional mention of Jews in the lengthy feature, the author obliterated one critical factor: Pinsk, prior to the Holocaust, was a community in which three out of every four residents were Jewish. In 1871, the Jewish population was 77.4 percent, and there was no perceptible drop during the next 70 years. Mention is made of the almost 60,000 "local residents who were shot, hanged or burned alive." The next sentence states that the Nazis set up concentration camps and ghettos for Jews in the town.

Pinsk was a Jewish town. Its fate was like the fate of so many villages, towns, and cities in Europe during World War II. Just prior to the war, a Yiddish poet, Mordecai Gebirtik, who worked as a carpenter all his life, wrote a moving poem: "Unzer Shtetl Brent—Our Town Is Burning." The bard who composed both words and melody had a prescience that Eastern Europe was doomed. The first words of his poem have been sung at many a memorial meeting. Together with his wife and daughters, he was murdered by the Nazis in June, 1942. "Our town, brothers, burns."

Pinsk was important in terms of Jewish history. Its most distinguished child was Chaim Weizmann, the first president of the state of Israel. Born in Motol, near Pinsk, Weizmann spent most of his youth in Pinsk. There he received his education and showed the beginning of his talents in science. Pinsk sent the first immigrants to settle in Palestine. Some of the founders of the BILU movement came from there. They included Yaakov Shertok, the father of Prime Minister Moshe Sharett. Pinsk contributed to the rebirth of Jewish nationalism. Chaim Weizmann was one of the first students of the modern schools founded by the early Hovevei Zion Movement.

The religious life of Pinsk was rich and meaningful. There were grand debates as to which direction Judaism ought to take. Hasidism spread to Pinsk during the 1760s and found many willing adherents. The Gaon of Vilna, Rabbi Elijah, issued a ban against the Hasidim. In the great debate as to whether study or prayer is more important, the followers of the Gaon said study, the Hasidim said prayer. No less significant a personality than Rabbi Levi Isaac of Berdichev had to leave his post as rabbi of Pinsk. The streets of Pinsk resounded with Jewish words and melodies. There are very few Jews left in Pinsk. The many synagogues are no more. The last Bet Hamidrash was shut down by Soviet police in 1966. The old cemetery has been converted to a park.

"All the news that's fit to print" has been changed by the Soviets to "All the news that the Soviets think fit to print." A great teacher of mine once said, "There is a good answer and a true answer to a question." There is a good article and there is a true article. I miss truth in this account of Pinsk.

What can one say in summation of how I feel? A long time ago in our Torah reading, this text was heard: "Who can count the dust of Jacob, or, by number, the ashes of Israel?" (Numbers 23:10). Jewish Pinsk is gone, but our remembrance of it will be constant.

MATTOT

A Lesson of Summer

1981

The Bible describes how the tribes of Reuben and Gad owned cattle in great numbers. Feeling that the eastern side of the Jordan was good for their flocks, they turned to Moses and made a special request of him. They said, "We will build here sheepfolds for our flocks and towns for our children. And we will hasten as shock-troops in the forefront of the Israelites" (Numbers 32:16). They did not plan to shirk their duty to the rest of the people, but were concerned for two things: to build adequate sheepfolds for their flocks and housing for their children.

Moses listened very carefully to their request. He charged them with the duty of helping to conquer the land of Canaan, but then there is a most interesting change in language. Moses said, "You may go ahead, but remember, build towns for your children and sheepfolds for your flocks." In simple language, Moses reversed the order of the request and stressed how important it is to provide for the children. Their spiritual and emotional growth should be a paramount concern for us.

I had the opportunity of being in Camp Ramah in Conover, Wisconsin, where I taught staff and the oldest campers. It was a beautiful thing to see the more than 400 young people, together with their counsellors and specialists, involved in the holy experience of total immersion in Jewish life.

Ramah, which was started as an act of faith by Chicagoans together with the Jewish Theological Seminary and the United Synagogue region, has truly been one of the greatest achievements of the Conservative Movement. Now spread to other camps in Massachusetts, New York, Pennsylvania, California, Canada, and Israel, Camp Ramah has provided us with two generations of young people who are at home in Jewish life and are dedicated to our people.

As I walked along the paths of Ramah to a Friday evening service, the campus was still but I could hear in the distance the collective voices of the total camp, seated on the lakeside, preparing for the welcome to the Sabbath. It was a stirring occasion, but through my mind I heard, too, the words of lament that are in the spirit of this time of the year. "Thus saith the Lord: A voice is heard in Ramah, lamentation and bitter weeping. Rachel weeping for her children. She refuses to be comforted for her children because they are not." Yes, there were times when we could weep with Rachel of old, but in modern day Ramah, (the high places) instead of the voice of sadness, there was truly the voice of gladness.

Ben Aronin, of blessed memory, who knew camping quite well, once spoke of Camp Ramah and said that "Ramah is the Holy of the Holies." He understood the impact of the camp upon our children. I met with our youngsters casually every day, and we had an Oneg Shabbat in our quarters on a Sabbath afternoon.

In Ramah, campers feel a sense of pride in being Jews. They feel a sense of identity and of kinship through the interaction of camper students and the faculty. There is a total involvement in a community of people who are celebrating life in the Conservative Jewish tradition. Bonds of friendship are formed, bonds of affection that will remain constant long after the camping experience has been over.

I had the pleasure of meeting parents of campers who were campers themselves years ago. Some of the parents occupy distinguished places in the community. Many of our rabbis, cantors, and educators have been through the process of Camp Ramah. Camp Ramah has expanded its facilities, it has added the Tikvah (hope) program for youngsters with learning disabilities. It is a program that is to be commended.

As one walks through Ramah campus, one finds that there is not a stilted, artificial atmosphere but a genuine reaching out, in the best sense of the word.

Our congregation has been involved with Camp Ramah since it was called into being. Title to the campsite was cleared by a past president of Anshe Emet. There are numerous buildings that contain inscriptions recalling the generosity of people—some already gone, some still with us—who helped make Camp Ramah what it is today.

One can gingerly say "first things first," but in Jewish life the first thing has always been the spiritual health and educational growth of our children. Mourning can be changed into joy if one works with the next generation and nurtures their innate feelings of loyalty to the Jewish community.

EKEV

On Words

1984

Speech is a great blessing. In the entire kingdom of God's creation, only humans can speak. Speech can be for blessing or for cursing. It can be used for benediction or malediction.

A recent play quoted these words, "An ambassador is an honest man sent abroad to lie for his country." There are some who make a great cult of silence. Among the pietists of the Eastern European yeshivot, there were the *Schweig Bachurim* who, save for the vocal expression of prayer, did not speak from the beginning of the last month, Elul, until the tenth day of the next month, the Day of Atonement. In Christian tradition, there are orders like the Trappists who do not speak. James Boswell quotes Samuel Johnson as being opposed to an important monastic order that did not speak. The great literary figure said, "Their silence is absurd." We read in the Bible of those who were sent to preach "but not to hold their tongues." The advice was given in Scripture: "For God is in heaven and you upon the earth, therefore let your words be few."

In an outstanding essay on the life of Queen Elizabeth I, Yale University's president, A. Bartlett Giamatti, makes this observation: "She learned patience and delay . . . she learned how to keep silent. When she was twenty years old . . . she scratched in the window-pane during confinement at Woodstock: Much suspected by me, nothing proved can be. At court, by watching and waiting, she developed the instincts, the habits and the style that later became her motto: *I see and am silent.* . . . She learned how to give . . . "an answer answerless." All this is in the spirit, "Unto you silence is praise" (Psalm 65:2).

There are times when we must speak and there are times when we should remain silent. In the Mishneh Torah, we are instructed, "When a man sins against his fellow, the injured party should not hate the offender and keep silent." Maimonides recalls in his commentary on the Mishnah, "O wise ones, be careful with your words."

A great study of Judaism recalls R. Johanan citing the saying of R. Simeon ben Yohai that injurious words "are a greater wrong than a monetary injury. One affects his fellow personally, the other only in his property." The Biblical teaching made the demand, "You shall not wrong one another, but you shall fear your God" (Lev. 25:17). To put another human being to open shame is one of the greatest sins that can be committed. The rabbis were very careful to spell out the meaning of "the evil tongue," slander and calumny based upon the word for wrong, *tonu.* Over and over again, the rabbis stressed that wrong in words is more grievous than wrong in monetary matters. The former is the greater wrong since, as one authority points out, the verse prohibiting it adds "but you shall fear your God," whereas the verse prohibiting wrong in money does not do so.

Maimonides stressed the cultivation of the habit of silence. A person should speak on topics of wisdom or on matters of moment to one's existence. Of a great rav, it was reported that throughout his life he never indulged in the idle conversation of which most people's talk consists. A person should not speak much, even of material needs. In the *Ethics of the Fathers* there is the suggestion, "He who multiplies words causes sin." Maimonides recommended that a person's words should be few but full of meaning. When one's words are many and their meaning is minute, there is foolishness, "for the dream comes with much discussion and a fool's voice with abundance of words" (Eccles. 5:2).

In their own style, the rabbis told the story of a peddler who was making the rounds of the area of Sephoris (an ancient city in Galilee). "Who wants to purchase the elixir of life?" Everyone came to him, and finally he revealed what the elixir of life is. It is the verse of Psalms 34:13, "Who is the man that desires life," and the verse that follows, "Guard thine tongue from evil." This, incidentally, is part of the closing prayer of the Amidah, the silent and spoken devotion that is at the heart of the daily prayer system. The rabbis were anxious that we do not misuse words, that we do not pollute our mouths with foul language. "Whoever pollutes his mouth with foul language even though it had been decreed in heaven that he should live for seventy good years, causes the decree to be reversed." An individual person who tells tales about someone in secret has no share in the world to come.

A classic passage in the Midrash on Psalms states that an evil tongue is more destructive than murder, for one who commits murder kills only one individual, but a person who speaks *lashon ha-ra*, evil tongue, kills three (the one who speaks, the one who hears it, and the one about whom it is being said). One of the sages gave his son this general advice: "If you cannot bear to hear one word of insult, you end up hearing many more words of insult; but if you remain silent to the insult you will also silence the one bent on insulting you. If you wish to avenge an evil act, there is no better vengeance than remaining silent and not replying."

The improper use of words is not only in the spoken word but also in the written word.

In a highly significant study of Western culture in the computer age, *Turing's Man*, the author writes, "But for an instant, the spoken word lives in a way that the printed word does not," and again, "Poets of any age remind us that their words are meant to be heard as well as seen."

I read the moving words of Rabbi Joseph B. Soloveitchik: "Halakhic man (a man of law) is not a man of words." He uses language, "taking particular care not to multiply needlessly words or phrases. Too much is as bad as too little." He goes on to write: "He does not fling about terms and phrases as a substitute for thought and reflection." The great masters of our past "strictly limited themselves in their use of words but soared to the furthest expanses on the wings of thought."

During this season of the year, many words issue from our lips. May they come from contrite hearts that use words to reflect our turning towards God. There is a popular expression, "From your mouth to God's ears," but what is more important is: from your heart and soul to God's heart. May our words be meaningful, reflective of a desire to live a fine life in a world in which men and women will enjoy the true blessing of peace.

An Ingathering of
Ideas

The Modern Theatre As a Preaching Resource

RABBINICAL ASSEMBLY PROCEEDINGS, 1968

The modern theatre is a fountain flowing with ideas and illustrations for the preacher. Reading the lines of this sensitive art form helps to trigger our own thoughts about crucial issues of our time.

The people who write for the modern theatre (and I am not now referring to those gifted writers who are devout religionists) are writing in an atmosphere of abandonment and dereliction. But one can sense that these writers are possessed, in what ever sense you want to interpret the word, with an infinite longing, one that has been described as an almost negative transcendence. These writers, looking at the disorders of modern life, often try to come up with answers to the perplexities of our difficult age.

Recently I came across Leo W. Schwarz's lecture on "Mutations of Jewish Values in American Fiction." He notes that "A number of writers are attempting to correlate theology and contemporary literature. The attempts thus far appear to overlook the fact that if a writer treats religion it is simply because it is an ingredient of life, and not because he attempts to theologize." I feel that there is much more involved in probing the relationship between modern literature and the theological gropings of its writers.

A number of years ago I had the privilege of meeting a most stimulating theologian, Nathan Scott Jr., a professor at the University of Chicago in both the Divinity and the Graduate Schools. His latest book, *The Broken Center, Studies in the Theological Horizons of Modern Literature*, is filled with dozens of splendid ideas. Whenever I go through it, I find it a wonderful source of seminal thoughts. His writings are filled with splendid insight, bursting with intellectual energy and brilliance. An article in *Time* magazine (December 22, 1967, page 51) describes what

233

Scott is trying to do, and what a man like Tom Driver at Union Theological Seminary is attempting. In a number of schools throughout the country there are classes in theology and literature, joint seminars on the highest academic level. What these men are researching in terms of the relationship between theology and literature can be helpful to pulpit practitioners like ourselves. These efforts of scholars might be compared to a description once given me by a distinguished research scientist, speaking of the difference between a research scientist and a practicing physician. The scientist, the inventor, is like the person who made the railroad possible. The practicing physician is the conductor who keeps the train moving on the tracks. Theologians like Scott, Driver, and others, develop ideas; they have the soaring concepts. It is for us who are practitioners to bring to our people what the theologians are saying.

Theology is being written not only by theologians. Theology is being written also by creative artists. These men and women are trying to pierce the cultural fog of our time, trying to alert us to the dangers that lie ahead.

Drama is one of the oldest forms of religious expression. Drama touches the critical question of our profession concerning communication. How are we going to articulate our thoughts? One observer has commented, "We come into the theatre to hear what we cannot express for ourselves." This is the experience all of us surely have when we read a remarkable book. The literature of the modern theatre is in that category. The literature of the modern theatre not only gives us ideas. It also offers us what is so important when one has the practical problem of having to speak publicly almost every day. The modern theatre is a great source of illustrative material.

All of us face the problem of how to articulate our thoughts. How shall we make our approach to life clear? It is important to remember that there are very few new ideas. Ours is the constant challenge of presenting an eternal message that the contemporary ear will appreciate, that the modern mind will understand.

Permit me to give you one quotation as an example of illustrative material. It is taken from Robert Bolt's *A Man For All Seasons.* "The law is a causeway, on which so long as he keeps to it, a citizen may walk safely." How vivid and apt is this phrase. How many of our sermons dealing with the theme of law could be enriched with a statement such as this as to the role of law in our life.

This quotation is taken from a wonderful anthology, *The New Theatre of Europe*. The first two volumes of this series were published several years ago, and a third volume will appear shortly. The editor is Robert Corrigan, formerly of Carnegie Tech in Pittsburgh, who is now teaching at New York University. His introduction to the first volume of the series is a marvelous essay, "Five Dramas of Selfhood." He deals with the question of identity, of knowing who we are, where we are, and where we are going. His introduction to the second volume is an essay called "The Disavowal of Identity in the Contemporary Theatre." We are surely familiar with the fact that there are many people who do not want to be what they are. They don't want to participate. They don't want to have a specific identity. They want to hide. They want to cover up their identity and, as far as I am concerned, their responsibility. The introduction to the third volume is called "The Drama of the Disengaged Man."

Let me add another illustration, taken from Jean Paul Sartre's *No Exit*. "Hell is other people." Why is hell other people? "Hell is other people because none has the courage to be his own judge." We always measure ourselves in terms of other individuals and their opinion of us. David Riesman wrote about it in *The Lonely Crowd*. We are always concerned with what other people will say about us, how they will judge us and our activities. Some years ago our teacher, Dr. Simon Greenberg, preached a Rosh Hashanah sermon. He said in essence that God judges us, we judge others, and we must learn to judge ourselves.

Let's take the opposite point of view. It has been expressed that hell is being alone. There is a tremendous satisfaction in being in the company and presence of other human beings. Brecht, one of the greatest writers of the modern theatre, extended this thought by saying, "The proper study of mankind is not man; the proper study of mankind is man's relationships." Man does not have to be examined; rather we must study his relationship to other human beings. For Brecht, the smallest social unit is not an individual but two people.

Let us return to our basic theme again. Paul Tillich, the great Protestant theologian of our age, developed what might be called a theory of correlation. He tried to connect theology, modern life, and cultural forms. He understood that theology is an answer to the questions that culture poses. In drama, we see the questions that bother people. It is important for us to learn what disturbs people, what concerns them. Aristotle spoke of drama as catharsis, but drama is more than that. Drama is our whole culture speaking powerfully to us.

Martin Esslin, in *The Theatre of the Absurd*, wrote that "Ultimately a phenomenon like the theatre of the absurd does not reflect despair or turn to dark, irrational forces, but expresses modern man's endeavor to come to terms with the world in which he lives. It attempts to make him face up to the human condition as it really is, to free him from illusions that are bound to cause constant maladjustment and disappointment . . . for the dignity of man lies in his ability to face reality in all its senselessness, to accept it freely without fear, without illusion and to laugh at it."

There are a number of obvious dramas that are worthy of public discussion. One that comes to mind, of course, is Hochhuth's *The Deputy*. There are other plays of Jewish interest. There is, for example, a play by the Swiss writer Max Frisch that is a complete allegory of the rise of the Nazi mentality in terms of the Biblical story of Esther, Mordecai, and Haman. Frisch has another play, *Andorra*, which is an examination of anti-Semitism.

Let me give you another example of an illustration. Thornton Wilder's play *The Skin of Our Teeth* reminded us that Cain never dies. He only slumbers by the hearth from time to time. If man does escape, it is only by the skin of his teeth. This phrase can be used in many ways. Genesis 4:7 deals with the whole question of destructive forces in the world and our relationship to them.

Perhaps the most important modern play, one that has become the focal point for many discussions, is Samuel Beckett's *Waiting for Godot*. According to experts, this particular play, first seen in 1952, changed the character of modern theatre. This play is regarded as one of religious significance, but it brings to mind the whole question of waiting.

There are different types of waiting. Two tramps, the central figures of this play, are waiting for Godot who will not come. They are wasting their lives. There is another type of waiting. Opportunities are all around us; yet we keep pushing them off. We are like Scarlett in *Gone With the Wind*: we are always thinking of tomorrow. You remember the phrase in the *Ethics of the Fathers:* "When I have time, I will study."

There is a third form of waiting, a virtuous form of patient endurance. Zionism was such an instance. A people waited. The Hebrew word for waiting is related to the Hebrew word for hope.

Maimonides wrote: "I believe with perfect faith in the coming of the Messiah, and even though he may tarry I daily wait for his coming." We are able to wait when we have perfect faith.

Some years ago, Edmund Steimle preached a splendid sermon at the Union Theological Seminary on the importance of waiting. The sermon, based upon Psalm 130, was later published in the *Union Seminary Quarterly Review* (January, 1967). Psalm 130 contains the wonderful verse, "I wait for the Lord, my soul doth wait, and in His word do I hope. My soul waiteth for the Lord, more than watchmen for the morning; yea, more than watchmen for the morning." The Hebrew root *kvh* can mean many things. It means "to wait," it means "to hope," and it also can mean "to pray." (I am grateful to Rabbi Seymour Siegel for bringing this to my attention. Those who want to check the scientific apparatus ought to turn to *Psalms 1-50*, edited by Mitchell Dahood in the Anchor Bible Series.)

Humanity must look towards redemption, in repudiation of despair. Professor Abraham Joshua Heschel declared that "waiting for wonder is not in vain." Eli Wiesel once wrote, "Most men exclude waiting from their lives, and that's their misfortune. In their hurry to set out, to arrive, to succeed, they run too fast, reach their destination too soon, and either abandon their dream or are abandoned by it. In the East they will tell you that the man who can control his breathing and his will forges a key to the kingdom. Immortality is the prize of those who are long-winded."

Without endangering my credentials in the civil rights movement, I should like to suggest that it would be well to think of this theme in terms of the possibilities of the more gradual approach to the resolution of some of the conflicts of our nation.

Another theme with which the modern theatre deals is silence. Of course, we are familiar with the great text of the Bible on the passing of Aaron's sons. In my volume of essays, *A Time to Speak*, I develop this theme in "The Eloquence of Silence" (page 223). Words can sting like anything, but silence breaks the heart.

In Kafka's writings, silence can be destructive. In *The Castle*, the hero can't express himself. In *The Trial*, no one listens. In Menotti's *Consul*, there is an attempt to get a visa, and no one is ready to listen.

Ionesco states that man is an island unto himself. Each of us speaks a language no one else quite understands. The inspired person is both blessed and condemned to live on an island that, like Robinson Crusoe's, is especially distant. On this island all the stars are dead, except one: his own. Whether we agree or disagree with this view of Ionesco, it is one that has to be treated.

Kay Baxter, in an article entitled "Being and Faith in the Theatre," points out that Ionesco's influence probably will be felt increasingly in religious dramatic writing since he makes things speak. In a play such as *The Chairs*, nothing is said about the supernatural, and everything that happens is real, but all is imbued with an interior reality. People exist; they talk because silence frightens them. Language is, for them, an escape from reality. Ionesco holds that it is in the depths which underlie our ripples of conscious communication that we shall discover our oneness. Each of us is, deep down, everyone else. Ionesco feels that the theatre is the most compelling medium with which to state this view of the human condition. This idea of Ionesco, that people talk because silence frightens them, is also mentioned in Eli Wiesel's *The Gates of the Forest*. "Already in the cave, he became used to silence and loved it. Gavriel told him that men talk because they are afraid. They're trying to convince themselves that they're still alive. It's the silence after the storm in which God reveals himself to man. God is silence" (page 63). In *Waiting for Godot*, the two tramps speak of their inability to keep silent. "It's so we won't hear . . . all the dead voices." For an incisive study of this see Tom F. Driver's "Beckett by the Madeleine" (*Columbia University Forum*, Volume IV, Summer, 1961).

This theme of silence is extremely suggestive. One can deal with it in terms of the devaluation of language. George Steiner has treated this theme in "The Retreat from the Word," which is reprinted in his *Language and Silence*. "It is no paradox to assert that much of reality now begins outside of language."

In *The Theatre of the Absurd*, Martin Esslin mentions the radical devaluation of language. Language still plays an important though subordinate part in this conception. But the action on the stage transcends the words spoken by the characters.

"The Sounds of Silence" is a song in the motion picture "The Graduate."

And in the naked light I saw
Ten thousand people, maybe more.
People talking without speaking;
People hearing without listening;
People writing songs that voices never shared;
No one dared
Disturb the sounds of silence.

"Fool," said I, "You do not know,
Silence like a cancer grows.
Hear my words and I might teach you;
Take my arms and I might reach you."
But my words like silent raindrops fell,
And cut the sounds of silence.

And the people bowed and prayed
To the neon god they made.
And the sun burst out its warning,
And the words that it was forming
And the sun said,
"The words of the prophets are written
    on the subway walls
And tenement halls."
Echoed in the sounds of silence.

In Beckett's *The Unnameable,* the necessity to speak, the desire to be silent, and the awareness of the emptiness of language are combined in a feverish intensity. For Beckett, language is seen as both too much and too little.

I have been translating *Orchot Tzadikim, The Paths of the Righteous,* which has a splendid chapter on silence. This particular chapter has its counterpart in other ethical texts. In *Pirke Avot,* Rabbi Akiva states, "The safeguard of wisdom is silence." Again in *Pirke Avot,* a great teacher states that he grew up among the wise and found nothing better than silence. Solomon Freehof once developed a sermon dealing with the silence of listening. Silence is not a negative factor. It is not doing nothing. There is an active type of silence that can teach us wisdom.

In an analysis of Samuel Beckett, Richard Ellmann observed that Beckett was addicted to silences, as was Joyce. These men engaged in conversations that consisted of "silences directed toward each other." This reminds me of the story of the Hasid who went to see his Rebbe. Upon his return to the village other followers of the Rebbe who did not have the opportunity to go to the hof inquired as to what the Rebbe did. The answer came back, swift as a rapier's thrust, "The Rebbe was silent, and we all listened to him very carefully."

Further, we might speak of the silence of those who were involved with the *Schweig Bachurim*, followers of Rabbi Israel Salanter of the Musar movement. In Agnon's story, "Tehilla," reference is made to the view that each person has a definite allotment of words in his or her lifetime. When Tehilla was young, she was warned that she would use up her quota of words if she talked too much. This concept comes, I believe, from the *Sefer Hasidim*. Here are Tehilla's thoughts:

How shall I begin? Let me start with my childhood. When I was a little girl, I was a great chatterbox. Really, from the time I stood up in the morning till the time I lay down at night, words never ceased pouring from my lips. There was an old man in my neighborhood who said to those delighting in my chatter: "A pity it is for this little girl. If she wastes all her words in childhood, what will be left for her old age?" I became terribly frightened, thinking this meant that I might die the very next day. But in time I came to fathom the old man's meaning, which was that a person must not use up in a short while what is allotted him for a whole lifetime. I made a habit of testing each word to see if there was real need for it to be said, and practiced a strict economy of speech. Through this economy, I saved up a gret store of words, and my life has been prolonged until they are used up. Now that only a few words remain, you ask me to speak them. If I do, it will hasten my end.

The use of masks is a very interesting technique of modern theatre, recalling one of the essential and original elements of the theatre. Anouilh's Becket can play his part well only when he wears the costume symbolic of the part. By putting on the habit of the monk, or the sumptuous robes of the archbishop, he succeeds in identifying himself with the honor of God: a serious masquerade, but a masquerade none the less.

I developed a sermon called "Mask to Mask" (*A Time to Speak*, page 199). A congregant of mine visited the famous statue of Moses in Rome's St. Pietro in Vincoli, which has always been a great tourist attraction. After the appearance of Irving Stone's *The Agony and the Ecstasy*, there was a heightened public interest in the artist. The Torah reports that when Moses came down from Mt. Sinai with the second set of tablets, he was not aware that the skin of his face was radiant, *ki karan or panav.* The word *karan* can mean either "radiate light" or "horn." The Hebrew word was understood by the Latin translators to mean "horn." When Michelangelo, who knew the Bible only in Latin translation, executed his magnificent statue of a seated Moses, he portrayed the great emancipator with horns coming out of his forehead. The Biblical account states that when the people saw Moses descending from Mt. Sinai, they were afraid to approach him. Moses at first did not realize what had happened. When he became aware of the radiance, he put a veil over his face. Thereafter, whenever he faced the people he put a veil over his face; whenever he went in before the Lord, he would take the veil off.

Biblical scholars are not certain what *masveh*, the word translated as veil, means. Some think that *masveh* was a type of mask. The English word "person" comes from the Latin *persona*, which means a mask. In the ancient Greek and Roman theatres, each character wore a distinctive mask.

We put on a mask when we stand in the presence of other people. We must strip ourselves of the mask when we stand before God.

Attending a social gathering often means being set adrift in a sea of conversation. Discussion is not possible. It is not an encounter between people; rather it is mask speaking to mask. The speakers are stereotypes of noncommunication engaged in conversation. Ask yourself candidly: "When I speak to other peo-

ple do I really confront them or do I talk from behind a mask?"
Shakespeare said, "All the world's a stage, and all the men and
women merely players." Too many of us are content to play out our
lives. We hide behind the mask. We shield our real identity. We
camouflage our real intentions.

At times, a mask is necessary. There are times when we cannot
allow our faces to reveal the concern of our hearts. After Pearl
Harbor, President Franklin D. Roosevelt had to don a mask lest
the American people become terrified. In his speech to Congress
on December 8, 1941, Roosevelt could not reveal the full extent of
the damage at Pearl Harbor. If we had known then, we would have
been completely traumatized.

A physician must put on a mask when speaking to a person
afflicted with a terminal illness. But even if necessity compels us
to wear a mask when we face other people, let us not forget that
when we stand in the presence of God we must strip ourselves of
all pretense. He is the great examiner of hearts. He understands
our innermost thoughts.

At times, we are content to wear masks because we ourselves do
not know who we are. In Arthur Miller's *Death of a Salesman,*
Willy Loman wore one mask when he was at home, and another
mask when he was on the road. He was a good father at home, but
on the road he was a lecher. When his son discovered this, he was
shattered.

How shall we treat the reality that we wear different masks at
different times? It has been observed, "We live too diversely to live
at one."

Why do we put on masks? Masks identify with an aspect of our
being. Why do we adopt certain guises? We do this, perhaps,
because at times an identity is forced upon us. Our profession
forces a certain identity upon us. There are things we are compelled to do because of our position in society. Perhaps, as one of
my colleagues has expressed it, "This is our modern idolatry." We
lack the courage to be what we really are. There is a tension
between our public mask and our private face.

Dr. Arnold Band, in his book on S. Y. Agnon, writes:

Agnon is so protean, displaying several masks at once while
concealing others, it is also understandable that critics have
fallen into the trap of homily and personal confession: each

critic finds in Agnon what he was looking for. . . . Agnon is a man of many masks, but that very fact that he does wear a series of masks or that he intuitively chooses one mask over another, is significant. Indeed the complexity of the man is reflected in the complexity of the writing, which often uses personal experience as the raw material for fiction (*Nostalgia and Nightmare*, pp. viii-ix).

There is a great need for a single unifying identity that would serve as an integrative factor in our lives.

There are good masks. When we recite the Haggadah, we are putting on the mask of assuming that we ourselves were redeemed. On Passover, Oriental Jews put on old clothes and make believe that they are leaving Egypt. There is a community in which Jews pour some water in front of their homes on Passover eve and try to re-enact the crossing of the Red Sea. This is a good mask. We pretend to be what we are not, in order to be what we should be.

T. S. Eliot, in his "Love Song of Alfred J. Prufrock," wrote, "We put on a face to meet the faces we meet." At times, we distort the truth. Picasso has said, "I have to tell a lie, to tell the truth."

I would like to offer to you one last illustration, from *Becket*. A cardinal is speaking to the Pope in Rome. His words are a mask. "Sincerity is a form of strategy like any other. In certain matters of negotiation, when matters are not going ahead, and usual tactics cease to work, I have been known to use it myself." This phrase seems to suggest possibilities of a sermon dealing with "Smokescreens of Sincerity." People say that they are the best friends you have. Sometimes friendship can be more dangerous to integrity than open opposition. On the topic of "Smokescreens of Sincerity," one illustration that comes to mind is Esau asking his nearly blind father what sort of tithe he had to give upon salt.

There is no end to the number of themes and illustrations from the modern theatre that we could list and discuss. Let us remember in addition that our tradition has the power to make judgments upon the modern theatre, just as the theatre makes judgments upon life. I commend the texts of the modern theatre to you as a great source of sermonic material.

Judaism and the Worlds of Business and Labor

RABBINICAL ASSEMBLY
PROCEEDINGS, 1961

A Crisis in Conscience

There is mounting evidence of a growing concern by the American business community for its ethical standards. Following the recent conviction of leading electrical companies on charges of price-fixing and bid-rigging, hard questions were being asked in our nation's schools of business administration.[1] What are the responsibilities of business people? How can they best be equipped to handle the ethical dilemmas they face in their day to day affairs? For some time our business administration schools have been concerned with their role in American society. Their courses of study are undergoing constant revision in the hope of making their graduates more effective business executives and better citizens. In trying to understand itself, industry has been advised to hire professional philosophers. Dr. R. S. Rudner suggested that business people need help in the field of ethics in trying to identify goals and values.[2]

The current business mood concerning ethical practices is less sanguine than the euphoric attitude expressed by one outstanding administrator: "Business begins to stand in awe of its complexities, its power, its responsibilities. Business begins to wonder about its own destiny and the destiny of the outer world. There will be no holding back by business when the business schools assert intellectual and spiritual leadership."[3]

The business community was recently challenged by the attorney general of the United States to prepare a code of ethics.[4] Only this morning the *New York Times* reported that the Secretary of Commerce expressed his concern over "the revelation of more business scandals."[5] He said he feared that a handful of business people who deserved public censure might impair the good standing of all business.

This concern by the American business community for its ethical standards is mirrored overseas by the anxiety of Jewish leaders regarding Jews in business. A leading British rabbi, Dr. Chaim Pearl, speaking in London in February 1961, expressed his concern for the business practices of the Anglo-Jewish community.[6] The Annual Conference of Anglo-Jewish Preachers last year devoted considerable time to our subject.[7]

There is a genuine search for values in present-day America. The atmosphere is saturated with the desire to find the way to a more rewarding life. Walter Lippmann, in describing America, has spoken of our generation as being a "self-indulgent one . . . in large part an unhappy one. We are very rich but we are not having a good time, for our life that is full of things is empty of the kind of purpose and effort that gives to life its flavor and its meaning."

Americans want "a clear definition of life." Though our physical and spiritual needs have been fulfilled, there is a mood of emptiness in the land. "There is no doubt," one observer has said, "that the average American is far from being happy."[8]

John Steinbeck, coming back to America after a long stay overseas, wrote to Adlai Stevenson that he had two great impressions of contemporary American society. He detected "a creeping, all-pervading nerve-gas of immorality which starts in the nursery and does not stop before it reaches the highest offices both corporate and governmental." He also observed "a nervous restlessness, a hunger, a thirst, a yearning for something unknown—perhaps morality." Steinbeck went on to say, "I am troubled by the cynical immorality of my country. I do not think it can survive on this basis and unless some kind of catastrophe strikes us, we are lost, but by our very nature we are drawing catastrophe to ourselves. What we have beaten in nature, we cannot conquer in ourselves."

America as a whole is searching for national purpose[9] and for a system of values. Columbia University recently devoted an extensive faculty seminar to the contents and methods of the social sciences. This group attempted to describe the basic values of Western culture. Out of this enterprise there was published an eloquently written book by Shepard B. Clough, *Basic Values of*

Western Civilization. The author maintained that we in the West have been far too inarticulate about our fundamental values. He thought it was high time that we studied them and made them more explicit.

The quest for values is a reflection of the growing moral deterioration of our times. This hunger for high purpose often sets in after intervals of decadence and periods of corruption. The issues that troubled us in the thirties and the forties concerning the economic structure of our society are no longer the vital ones.

The minds of people are no longer preoccupied with the choice between the relative merits of a socialist society and a capitalist one. Both Russia and America have demonstrated that they are materialistic lands, consecrated to the machine and to the notion of the biggest and the best. In both economies success is gauged by material standards. George Thomas in *The Christian Heritage in Politics* has said, "Both Communism and Capitalism are secular in nature . . . the same bondage to material motives and physical fear unites both East and West" (page 117).

We are troubled with the fact that materialistic societies have stuffed people's stomachs without satisfying their souls. We must contribute our share in satisfying humanity's quest for values.

Jewish Contributions to Business Ethics

In surveying the literature of religious values in general and business ethics in particular, one observes that there have been limited efforts in this field in the Jewish community. One can list a host of writings in the general community and in the religiously-oriented Christian community. To be sure, we have had occasional writings by our own Professor Louis Finkelstein and Rabbi Leo Jung. Some splendid papers by Gerson Cohen, Samuel Dresner, Seymour Siegel, Dr. Simon Federbush, and David Aronson have appeared. Yet, on the whole, we have not been too successful in relating our underlying religious thinking and applying our principles to the everyday problems of life.

What ought to be the general considerations underlying our thinking about the business community? Our point of departure in approaching this entire area should be an attempt to express ourselves *in terms of the values of our tradition.* We need not follow the will-of-the-wisp of every liberal thinker. We ought rather to speak clearly and coherently in classic Jewish terms.

That there is a relationship between people's religious values and their economic life has been adequately demonstrated by Max Weber, R. H. Tawney, and our own teacher, Professor Louis Ginzberg. Benjamin Nelson, in his *Idea of Usury*, has traced the relationship between an individual's religious position and the manner in which he or she earns a livelihood. The problem of the biblical prohibition of usury has troubled Jewish authorities down to our own day. The floating of the Israel Bond issue, for example, has brought this question to the fore.[10]

Professor Marx, in his *Studies in Jewish History and Book Lore* (page 167), dealt with the account of Rabbi Jehiel Nissim, a banker who functioned in the city of Pisa as a rabbi. Nissim was disturbed at the possibility that certain types of bills of exchange violated the law against usury.

"Public fasts should not be decreed on Thursdays in order not to cause a sudden rise in market prices."[11] On Thursday people began to buy food for the Sabbath. If a fast were held on the same day, the consumers would have to buy also for the breaking of the fast in the evening. In the unexpected rush for larger quantities of food, sellers might be induced to raise the prices.

Paul Tillich has reminded religionists that "There is no vacuum in spiritual life as there is no vacuum in nature." "An ultimate concern must express itself socially. It cannot leave out any sphere of human existence."[12] We must concern ourselves with the ethical issues faced by our people.

Much of our thinking and preaching is irrelevant. (This is true of both Christian and Jewish teachers.) The sages of yesteryear were familiar with the business community. They knew it because they were engaged in the work-a-day world. We need not repeat the names of the sages who were laborers or merchants. Let us but call to mind that most of the Tannaim and Amoraim had occupations. During the Middle Ages, Rashi was a vintner and Maimonides a physician. Abraham Danzig, author of *Ḥayye Adam,* was a merchant. In *The Living Talmud,* Judah Goldin presents an interesting series of comments on the concept of Rabbi Zadok, "Do not make then the Study of the Words of Torah a Crown for Self-Exaltation nor a Spade to Dig With."[13]

Problems of An Age of Specialization

We live in an age of specialization, one in which it is hard for us to understand the efforts and activities of others. Our ethics and moral values come from biblical and post-biblical sources that are examples of "face-to-face" ethics. Even the moralistic teachings of the Hasidic masters come from a society that was far less complex than our own. When Rabban Simon ben Gamaliel required that "The shopkeeper must clean out his measures twice a week and rub up his weights once a week and polish up his scales before each and every weighing," he was dealing with circumstances far different than our own.[14]

His was a simple economy. How different is that shopkeeper and his relationship to the consumer from the highly impersonal role of a consumer and producer in our complex age. Our colleague Max Kadushin in a recently published study dealt with the problem of how "abstract ethical theories oversimplified the moral life. . . . One of the problems of moral life is its complexity and this complexity is due to the variety and sheer number of the value concepts."[15]

The difficulty with applying concrete ancient principles to modern situations can be seen in two instances cited by Aron Barth, who during his lifetime was head of the Bank of Israel.[16]

In the course of my work in Germany I heard the following story. The two largest metal firms were founded at the beginning of the nineteenth century by two observant Jews, one at Halberstadt, and the other at Frankfurt. These two industrialists would meet occasionally on their commercial journeys in the provinces, stay in the same hotel, pray and study a daily portion of the Talmud together in the morning, and then each would call on his respective clients. Never would one go to the firms approached by his rival. They scrupulously observed the injunction of Deuteronomy: "Thou shalt not encroach on thy neighbor's boundary."

I myself witnessed a similar incident. In a small village in Southern Germany where my late father was born, there were about thirty Jewish families, all engaged in the cattle trade. They knew that everyone had his own region and none dared to enter that of his neighbor. When I visited the village I found one member almost ostracized by the community. He was pointed out as having *encroached on his neighbor's boundary*—he had entered the region of his neighbor.

The question which we can ask ourselves is, "How far can one go in applying this principle of encroachment in the modern economic world?"

How Shall We Establish Relevancy?

Another dilemma that faces us in the realm of business ethics is that we operate with *several ethical standards*, each claiming our loyalty. A Jewish businessman comes to his decisions with different and, at times, conflicting moral values—yet he must make his determination. In addition, there is no clear-cut way of making a decision between right and wrong. Obviously, to steal is immoral and to cheat is improper. Business decisions are made in the great grey areas of life.

Lord Moulton in his essay on *Law and Manners* spoke of the fact that all human action falls into three great domains.[17] In the domain of positive law, the definite laws determine what may or may not be done. The second domain is one of free choice. In this area people have complete freedom to do as they please. Between the two, the domain of positive law and the domain of free choice, there lies a third. In terms of moral decision-making, it is the most fallow. This is the domain of *obedience to the unenforceable*. The rabbis were familiar with this type of thinking. They stressed that the law was a minimum, that "one could be a scoundrel within the letter of the law." Moral considerations go beyond the letter of the law into the inherent ethical spirit. Living only within the letter of the law can be destructive of society. The rabbis spoke of the Flood as resulting from the improper moral conduct of the generation of the Flood. "*The end (ketz) of all flesh (basar) is come before Me:* The time has come for them to be cut down *(hikkatzetz);* the time has come for them to be treated as unripe grapes *(boser);* the time of their indictments has come. Why all this? Because the earth is filled with violence *(ḥamas)* through them. What is *ḥamas* (violence) and what is *gezel* (robbery)? Said Rabbi Hanina: *ḥamas* (violence) refers to what is worth a *perutah; gezel* (robbery), to what is of less value than a *perutah*. And this is what the people of the age of the Flood used to do: When a man brought out a basket full of lupines (for sale), one would come and seize less than a perutah's worth, so that he had no redress at law. Whereupon the Holy One, blessed be He, said: "Ye have acted improperly, so will I too deal with you improperly."[18] The common-law theory that the law does not concern itself with trifles *(de minimis non curat lex)* is not acceptable to Jewish ethics. Any violation of the moral law can be destructive to humankind.

We must try to develop a clearly-expressed statement of our ethical teachings for the modern business community. There are at least two approaches that could aid us in this task.

One approach has been utilized by some of us in teaching groups of business people. We have taken texts from the Bible, the Talmud, later rabbinic sources, sermons, and ethical wills, and we have tried to give them contemporaneity, to make them applicable to modern conditions.

An alternate approach is found in the problem method, in which a concrete problem in the business community is analyzed against the background of our moral heritage. The problem method is the mode of teaching used in the Harvard Business School, and the problems raised can be real or fictional. We are familiar with the fact that many talmudic cases are in reality fictional cases. The classic example of a fictional case would be the one of "two men travelling on a journey far from civilization and one has a pitcher of water. If both drink, they will both die, but if only one drinks he will be able to reach civilization."[19]

A fictional problem upon which Jewish thinking could be brought to bear might deal with the moral questions revolving around the issue of relocation. A factory located in New England, in an old multi-storied plant, finds that its cost of production is no longer competitive. Management suggests that the firm relocate in a newer plant, perhaps in the South where labor costs might be less. To whom does the firm have a moral responsibility? To the employees who spent their life working for the corporation? To the older community that had an entire social framework developed about this plant as the principal employer? To be sure, our first reaction is to worry about them. However, the question will be raised: "What about the stockholders, the people who live hundreds of miles away and for whom this is an investment?" To complicate your thinking, the stockholders are mainly widows and orphans.

The present problem of automation has contributed to chronic unemployment in this country. This, too, would be worthy of our thinking. To begin with the problem of automation in a discussion, one might bring to mind the interesting fact that a little over a hundred years ago (1856) there was a shift in production from hand-baked *matzot* to machine-made *matzot.* Aside from the Halakhic questions involved, the rabbis of Austria were concerned with the fact that there would be a loss of income for the people who had formerly made them by hand.[20]

Business as a Vocation

In the general community, the older idea that a commercial career is somehow inferior to a career in one of the learned professions has all but disappeared.[21] The sages have taught that "When a person enters business he is engaged in a matter of religious consequence."[22]

Our tradition has recognized the importance of every calling. A frequent expression in the mouth of the rabbis was: "I am a creature of God and my neighbor is also a creature of God. My work is in the city and his work is in the field. I rise in the morning to go to my work and he rises in the morning to go to his work. As he cannot excel in my work, so I cannot excel in his work. Perhaps you will say that I do great things and he does small things. We have learned that it matters not whether one does much or little, if only he directs his heart to heaven."[23]

We cannot accept the attitude that there is a dichotomy between business values and spiritual values.

Let us think together on some issues that affect business in the United States. What does our tradition have to say in positive terms concerning the dilemmas of the business person? How can we enrich the value system of America?

The Dilemma of the Split Personality

A big problem that we face is that we somehow split our personalities. "How can we preserve the wholeness of the personality if we are expected to worship God on Sundays and Holidays and maim Him on Mondays through Fridays?"[24]

Some ten years ago Dr. Theodore M. Green of Yale University testified before the Senate Committee on Labor and Public Welfare. He drew distinctions between what he called the dominant motivations of people and the basic moral and religious convictions that they professed. "I am not accusing them of hypocrisy. They are quite sincere when they talk about their deep moral convictons on a Sunday in church, but which, in fact, do not operate through their lives very effectively. They are not dominant motivations. I think we have found a national schizophrenia that expresses itself in all sorts of normal people."[25] According to O. A. Ohmann,[26] the business community hungers for meaning and value in life. Consider these expressions of sensitive leaders of the business community:

"We have come to worship production as an end in itself, which, of course, it is not. It is precisely there that the honest critic of our way of life makes his attack and finds us vulnerable. Surely, there must be for each person some ultimate value—some purpose, some motive, some expression, that makes the experience we call life richer and deeper.

"To produce more and more with less and less effort is merely treading water unless we thereby release time and energy for the cultivation of the mind and the spirit and for the achievement of those ends for which Providence placed us on this earth."[27]

Of course business deals with material goods. But surely business is the response to all satisfactions, not material ones alone. A publisher selling books on poetry or an art dealer selling paintings is surely meeting spiritual needs. Economic activity is the exchange and flow through the body politic of all goods, whether physical or cultural. Everything has a price and can be bought. The catch is that it cannot be bought unless it exists; that is, unless it has been produced. On the other hand, cultural goods cannot be produced by business; only the artist can create the painting; only the scientist can yield the scientific discovery. In this sense, then, it is a fact that business is confined to the area of material goods.

Even so, there is no reason for believing that secular values are hostile to spiritual values. The earth can provide a ladder to heaven, though many people trip and fall in the process of climbing. My car enables me to get to the place where I can hear a lecture which improves my mind. Our various domestic appliances make for health, which is good for the soul; also for cleanliness, which is next to godliness. We hear much about the depersonalizing impact of machinery; yet machinery, by diminishing arduous physical labor, makes man less of a beast of burden.

Industrial civilization, to the extent that it eliminates squalor, contributes to the spiritual dignity of man. Man cannot live by bread alone; nor can he live without it. To condemn material things because they are material is to exhibit a snobbishness of the spirit which is as bad as social snobbishness.

Martin Buber has made the distinction in life between that which is holy and that which is not yet hallowed. Industrial society, if it wishes, can eliminate poverty and contribute to the spiritual enrichment of humankind's life here on earth.

Commerce is a civilizing influence in that "it promotes intercourse by persuasion instead of force," as Whitehead observed.[28]

The same note was struck in the following talmudic passage comparing the values of a developed society with the days of the first human being: "What labours Adam had to carry out before he obtained bread to eat! He ploughed, he sowed, he reaped, he bound the sheaves; he threshed and winnowed and selected the ears, he ground them, and sifted the flour, he kneaded and baked, and then at last he ate. Whereas I get up, and find all these things done for me. And how many labours Adam had to carry out before he obtained a garment to wear! He had to shear, wash the wool, comb it, spin it and weave it, and then at last he obtained a garment to wear. Whereas I get up and find all these things done for me. All kinds of craftsmen come early to the door of my house, and I rise in the morning and find all these things before me."[29]

The business person has an opportunity to carry out his or her work at the highest possible spiritual level, as Ignatz Maybaum has stated: "Nobody is so dependent on the validity of moral agreement as is the merchant, the businessman."[30]

Spiritual Responsibility of Business

Business has a spiritual responsibility in terms of sanctifying the name of Heaven. There are many rabbinic texts that speak of the integrity of others, of guarding against taking advantage of the error of the non-Jew.

Maybaum made this striking observation: "The opportunity of honoring a contract occurs nowhere more often than in business life, where everything depends on the possibility of trusting and of being trusted. The German theologian Ernst Troeltsch, who travelled and studied some years in England and America, . . . told of a stock exchange . . . he saw somewhere in New England and where he found the inscription: 'The businessman is the most honest man.' Indeed a businessman more than anyone else has the opportunity to prove his mettle as a honest man."[31]

That business people through their manner of conducting their affairs can bring people closer to God is illustrated in a number of texts. " 'And thou shalt love thy God.' This means that one should act so that the name of God shall be beloved by others, that one's business should be conducted honestly, that one's relations with people should be proper and commendable, so that people might say: 'Happy is his father who taught him Torah. Happy is his teacher who taught him Torah, for the conduct of this one who has studied is exemplary.' "[32]

One must guard oneself not only against over-reaching in buying and selling, but also against wronging another. One is not to inquire as to the price of an object if one does not intend to buy it.[33]

High ethical standards, maintaining the integrity of words, and telling the whole truth are, for the Jew, acts that sanctify God's name. If a person returns lost property in order to sanctify God's name, causing persons to praise the Israelites and to realize that they are honest, it is praiseworthy.[34] The rabbis were concerned with the integrity of others. They were troubled by those who "stole the heart." "There are seven kinds of thieves. First there are those who steal the hearts of other people."[35]

A fraud in words is greater than a fraud in money matters, for in the latter case the money can be returned but in the former case there can be no return. The latter involves money and the former involves one's very being.[36] The verse "And thou shalt fear thy God" (Lev. 25:17) is appended to the amendment against oral deception because it is a matter of the heart.

A classic story of the sanctification of the name of God is told concerning Rabbi Simeon ben Shetah. "He once bought an ass from an Ishmaelite. His disciples found a precious stone suspended from its neck. They said to him: 'Master, the blessing of the Lord, it maketh rich' (Prov. 10:22). Rabbi Simeon ben Shetah replied: 'I have purchased an ass, but I have not purchased a precious stone.' He then returned it to the Ishmaelite. And the latter exclaimed to him: 'Blessed be the Lord God of Simeon ben Shetah.' "[37]

The advertising industry is taking a hard look at its methods from the perspective of integrity.[38] The rabbis understood some of the problems of the merchandiser. They recognized the distinction between fraudulent and honest persuasion. It is forbidden to paint items in order to make them appear new. It is forbidden to clandestinely introduce one product into another although what is introduced is as fresh as the rest and even worth more.

But, in the course of bargaining, how can we avoid trying to convince our neighbor that the article we want to sell is worth the price we are asking? It is perfectly proper to point out to the buyer the good qualities the article possesses. Fraudulence consists in hiding the defects in one's ware, and is forbidden.[39]

Representative Jewish teachers have repeatedly urged our people to preserve the finest standards of business ethics. "Even practices not in themselves unlawful should be rejected as they give the impression of dishonesty and lack of integrity."[40]

Jewish law does not recognize absolute ownership; our wealth is not our absolute possession. This is derived from the biblical verse which states, "The land is not to be sold in perpetuity, for the land is Mine and ye are strangers and sojourners with Me."

God's claim is first. The sages have compared human beings in this world to sojourning visitors. Their 'ownership' is limited. God is compared to an innkeeper who permits the use of his facilities for the limited time the guest is staying. "Give to Him of His own, for thou and thine are His," reads one rabbinic statement. King David is quoted as having said, "Everything is from Thee, and of Thine own we have given to Thee."[41] This is the concept of stewardship.

People are stewards not only of their wealth but also of their health. Rabbi Jonah, interpreting the idea of limited ownership, said that "This statement refers both to a man's body and his wealth."[42] We are commanded to guard our well-being: "and keep thy soul diligently" (Deut. 4:9).[43] This surely could be expanded into a concern for the physical well-being of business people.

A later sage, the Rabbi of Berditchev, once saw a man hurrying along the street, looking neither right nor left. "Why are you rushing so?" he asked. "I am after my livelihood." The rabbi responded: "And how do you know that your livelihood is running on before you so that you have to rush after it? Perhaps it is behind you and all you need to do to encounter it is to stand still."

The question of guarding one's health was recently emphasized by the fact that business managers and proprietors generally work the longest work week reported by the Bureau of Census. "Managers and proprietors today generally work a fifty-three-hour week. . . . The seventy-hour-week is nothing strange in top management circles. The same machinery and industrial planning that substituted mineral power sources for the labors of men, thus freeing some of them from the long work week, have kept the nose of the executive firmly to the grindstone. This may be why the businessman may know a great deal about the sources of modern leisure, and yet know all too little about the consequences of it."[44]

Business people are also responsible for being the stewards of those who are in their employ. Howard Bowen in *The Social Responsibilities of the Businessman* points out that "Commensurate with the dignity of human personality is included the element of the personal growth of those who work for him." In terms of our religious tradition, the responsibility an employer has to an employee, or a senior executive to a junior, is an extension of the principle of the teacher-student relationship or the relationship of two friends. We must help to develop the relationship. Other people ought not to be thought of merely as things.

Daniel Bell discusses how our Protestant industrial economy cannot adopt the system of family wage to be found in Italy and other countries where Catholic social doctrine applies "whereby a man with many children receives more wages than the man who has none, though both do the same work."[45]

In India, executives often refrain from putting in a new machine that might throw three out of four workers out of their jobs. A recent visitor brought back the following account. "One of them said: 'That would send those men home, and they need the work.' One obstacle, of course, to 'sacking' (discharging) is that when an employee is kept on for three months his employer is virtually obligated to guarantee that man's livelihood for the rest of his life. And in line with all of India, one never hears a harsh word spoken, nor a blow thrown in an argument."[46]

In Japan, there is much evidence of old-time Japanese paternalism in business. The company is very concerned for the welfare of its employees. There is little job turnover.[47]

The Needs of the Community

It was pointed out earlier this year that "According to the Chicago Association of Commerce and Industry, thousands of workers must be imported in the next few years to meet Chicago's industrial needs. As these unskilled and semi-skilled workers (mostly Southern Negroes) come flooding into the city, they will move into the already overcrowded, deteriorated areas of the city, sections in which social disorganization is highest. They will be living where seventeen out of every 100 adolescents have court records. Thus, in their quest for new opportunities, they can expect new kinds of troubles. Those who now live in the ghettos of our cities will seek to move out; and unless the pattern changes decidedly in the years ahead, they will meet with resistance, hostility, and even violence."[48]

The business community has to concern itself not only with providing work. What happens to its employees after the work day is of vital importance.

It is still a moot point in law as to whether or not a corporation may give a charitable donation. Though it is the current practice for corporations to participate in all manner of drives, there are those who challenge the right of a corporation, an artificial person, to do an act of charity, since it is not the stated reason for the incorporation. The business person cannot say, "What concern do I have for the need of the community?" When the community is in distress, one should not say, "I will go home, eat and drink, and peace be upon my soul."[49]

The following text is concerned with the social responsibilities of the business person:

> Joseph used to eat so little during the years of famine that he was always hungry. The people said to him: 'O thou, on whom God has conferred wisdom, why art thou hungry, while storehouses filled with grain are at our disposal?' He answered: 'I fear that, if I am satisfied, I might forget the hungry.'

The business person was to be in partnership with learning. "Rabbi Dimi related that Hillel and Shebna were brothers. Hillel engaged in the (study of) Torah and Shebna was engaged in business."[50] This partnership between the student and the businessman had its earlier counterpart in the legendary account of the tribes of Issachar and Zebulun. Zebulun went to sea with his wares, while Issachar studied. Both were in "partnership," to cite the Midrash, "in this world and the world to come."[51]

A second important factor is the matter of vocational selection. Parents, trying to relive their own lives, frequently discourage youngsters from going into manual crafts. One of the key problems of America today is to encourage people to go into what are called "the blue-collar occupations." The rabbis believed in the importance of work. It was important, they taught, for a man to teach his son a craft. The rabbis extolled the institution of work in sharp contrast to Greek thought, which considered physical work to be unworthy of a free man. Labor is highly regarded throughout Tannaitic literature, sometimes even in exaggerated terms.[52] We are taught that Adam was commanded to work so that his descendants should know the value of work.[53]

The rabbinic attitude to work can be seen in the classic story of Rabbi Simeon ben Yohai and his son. Having been confined to a cave for twelve years in order to escape the wrath of the Romans, the father and son spent their lives involved in mystic speculation. During this period of time they were divorced from the normal pursuits of life. When they left their cave, they came upon a group of farmers working the land. The rabbi and his son grew angry. "They forsake eternal life and busy themselves with the life

of the moment." The account goes on to tell that so great was the
anger of Rabbi Simeon and his son that "wherever they cast their
eyes the fields withered under their gaze." The legend ends with a
bat kol telling them "Have ye emerged to destroy my world? . . .
Return to your cave."[54] This story is an obvious protest against
super-piety. It affirms the fact that practical work is necessary for
the world.

The rabbis extolled work in interpreting Exodus 18:20 "And
thou shalt teach them the statutes and the laws and shall show
them the way in which they must walk, and the work that they
must do." A medieval commentator explained that this means
"Teach them a craft so that they shall be able to sustain themselves."[55]

In *Abot of Rabbi Nathan*, Rabbi Simeon ben Eleazar is quoted
as saying: "Even Adam tasted nothing before he worked, as it is
said, 'And He put him into the Garden of Eden to till it and to keep
it.' Only then is it written, 'Of every tree of the garden thou mayest
freely eat.' "

The *Ethics of the Fathers* contains the statement of Shemaiah:
"Love work." The comments included in Judah Goldin's edition
speak for themselves.

> Love Work: What is that? This teaches that a man should love
> work and that no man should hate work. For even as the
> Torah was given as a covenant, so was work given as a
> covenant; as it is said, 'Six days shalt thou labor, and do all
> thy work; but the seventh day is a Sabbath unto the Lord thy
> God.'

> Rabbi says: How important is work! For whoever does not
> engage in work is the subject of everybody's conversation:
> 'How does so-and-so get food, how does he get drink?' A
> parable is told: To what may this be likened? To a woman who
> has no husband but struts about in the marketplace in all her
> finery, and men talk about her.[56]

The medieval commentator did not believe in having idle or free
time. Listen to the comments of Rabbi Jonah and the *Meiri*.

> Let no man neglect to work, for idleness will throw a man into
> depression.

Even the rich must love work, that is to say, must engage in some worthwhile occupation, and not remain idle—for idleness is the cause of terrible things.

The literature of our tradition is replete with great concern for the worker. Some typical examples reflective of this concern are found in the following accounts:

Rabbi Levi Yitzhak discovered that the girls who knead the dough for the unleavened bread drudged from early morning until late at night. He cried aloud to the congregation gathered in the House of Prayer: "Those who hate Israel accuse us of baking the unleavened bread with the blood of Christians. But no, we bake them with the blood of Jews."

Once Rabbi Israel Salanter was staying at an inn with two of his colleagues. It was during the coldest days of winter and Rabbi Israel, keen-eyed observer that he was, noticed through the window the maid fetching water in two buckets suspended on a yoke over her shoulders. He observed how difficult it was for the poor girl to carry the buckets. When supper time came and the three guests went to perform the rite of washing the hands before a meal, the friends noticed that Rabbi Israel took only one glass of water, enough to wash his finger tips, though they each used a quart of water for their lavation. When they inquired of him why he used the water so sparingly, he answered: "One should not be over strict in his observance of the law at the expense of someone else."[57]

The same Rabbi Israel, while staying over the Sabbath at the home of a student, refused to sing the *Zmirot*. He rushed through the meal in order to give the cook, who had been working hard all day, an opportunity to retire to her well-earned rest.[58]

The rabbis, in their great affirmation of labor, were anxious to protect the laborer's rights, and yet they pointed out that the *working man has obligations to his employer*. At the present time, there is considerable discussion about moonlighting, a condition in which one person holds two jobs. The practice is undoubtedly motivated by the need to maintain a standard of living. Yet heed this ancient text: "The worker must not do his own work at night and hire himself out during the day . . . all because he steals labor from the employer."[59]

The Talmud relates the story of Abba Hilkiah, who was a wonder worker. Whenever there was need of rain, the rabbis sent a message to him. He would pray and rain would fall. Once there was an urgent need for rain and the rabbis sent a pair of scholars to ask him to pray for rain. First they went to his house and did not find him there. Afterwards they went to the field and found him plowing the ground. They greeted him, but he took no notice of them. His action was a flagrant breach of good manners. "Why," they asked him later, "did you not take notice of us?" He answered: "I hired myself out for the day, so I thought I had no right to interrupt my work."[60]

Rabbi Jacob Emden advised one who has hired himself out to an employer, to work with him in faithfulness. As people say, "If you have hired yourself out to someone, pull his wool."[61] Even if the work is unpleasant, you nevertheless have an obligation you must fulfill.

Modern laborers have all but lost the sense of commitment or vocation. It has been observed that there is a higher incidence of mental disease among the lower income brackets. A series of case studies have indicated the direct relationship between the strains imposed in a competitive society and emotional illness. According to one account, "Patients commonly report as one of their deepest sources of neurotic guilt that they have not been able to provide more fully for their families." The British Trade Union Congress understood this need for a sense of vocation and tried to attach a higher meaning to the work process when they said: "Work is not an end in itself. It is the means to the enjoyment of a higher standard of living and more leisure for rest, recreation and personal development, leading to a fuller and more satisfying life."[62]

The problem of finding joy in one's lot was appreciated by the rabbis a long time ago when they answered the query "Who is rich?" with "He who is happy in his lot." Karl Jaspers, in *Man in the Modern Age*, has stated that "The maintenance of joy in work has become one of the fundamental problems in the world of technology."[63] Employers have to advertise: "Varied, interesting work." To be sure, one of the problems of our highly specialized economy is the fact that workers are deprived of the satisfaction that once was the artisan's in making a finished object.

Another recent study has pointed out that there is a higher incidence of heart disease among lower-salaried employees than among the top-salaried group. Persons occupying higher managerial positions, it appeared, derive a great deal of satisfaction from the demands of their jobs, while those at lower levels with a minimum of responsibility may suffer from feelings of resentment and frustration due to the lack of personal fulfillment and their relatively low position on the economic scale.[64] Recapturing a sense of vocation is one of the great tasks of religious teaching.

Labor and Leisure

Another area in which we can make a vital contribution is that of leisure.

Much of modern people's attitude towards leisure is conditioned by their approach to labor. As Americans, we share in the cultural tradition inherited from both ancient Greece and early Christian society. In both systems of thought, labor was regarded as punishment. Hesiod, for example, in *Works and Days*, speaks of the golden past when people were free from work. The Greek word for labor had the double meaning of work and sorrow. Work was meted out by Zeus because Prometheus had deceived him. In Christian thought, the pain of labor was the penalty for what Christians call "original sin." "In the sweat of thy face shalt thou eat bread." In Jewish tradition this was rarely conceived of as punishment for humankind. The text was re-interpreted to mean that if people lived by the sweat of their brow, it would be good for them, both in this world and in the world to come.

The consuming interest that Americans have in leisure can only be appreciated when seen against this background. Television's Mike Wallace asked Eric Fromm, an outstanding student of the mind, "How do you regard man in relationship to his work?" Fromm answered, "I think if you ask most people whether they like their work, they will say 'Yes' consciously, but if you probe into their dreams and how they feel in the evening or when they come home from work, I think you will find many millions of Americans who really hate their work."

The question as to whether or not people like their work has often been raised. One school of thought has it that while people grumble about having to work and daydream idly about a life of

AN INGATHERING OF IDEAS

leisure, most of them carry on with their jobs when there is no longer any financial necessity for them to do so.[65]

The *New York Times* of August 8, 1960 carried a most interesting account of a remarkable research project. The report told of how one thousand men were tested. They were given illustrations of six people in differing dress—a jet pilot, a doctor, a laborer, a business man, a socialite, and a sportsman. Those who were questioned were asked which of the men illustrated they would like to be. According to the account, the most popular choice was that of the sportsman, dressed in a sport shirt and casual jacket, leaning on a fishing pole.

Upon being questioned as to the selection of the sportsman, it was determined that his image represented a carefree life "a life of leisure, a life that represented no work." The jet pilot calling was "too dangerous," the socialite's life "too fussy," too confining and demanding. Even the social prestige of the doctor in white dress and the business man in a grey flannel suit were unappealing. These categories smacked too much of the work element. As for the laborer, the *New York Times* story went on to tell that one of the men studied responded, "Who wants to work?"

The director of the research project commented, "Our results strongly indicate that men are in conflict with everyday working life with its pressures and uncertainties. There is a very great appeal to the idea of a carefree existence symbolized by the sportsman.

"Time to relax, freedom from constraint, the interest and excitement of sport are the goals men seek today. The status and material success open to professional and business men are valued, but not nearly so highly as what men perceive as the happiness and easy life of the sportsman."

Many people today retain an ancient notion regarding the place of work in their lives. They look to it as something unpleasant. "Work easy and play hard" is a reflection of this attitude.

In Jewish tradition, labor and leisure are regarded as being part of a divinely ordained plan for the world. We read in Exodus concerning the Sabbath, "It is a sign between Me and the children of Israel forever, for in six days the Lord made the heavens and the earth and on the seventh day ceased His work and rested." This rhythmic pattern of work and rest, of labor and leisure, is part of God's design for our living.

Jewish thought stresses the fact that when Adam was created,

"The Lord God took Adam and placed him in the Garden of Eden to till it and to keep it, and the Lord God commanded Adam saying, 'From every tree of the garden you are free to eat.' "[66] Man is told to *till* the garden, to *keep* it, and as a reward for his efforts he will enjoy the fruits of his labor.

The laborer was extolled by our teachers. Our sages said, "Great is work for it honors the workman. See what a great thing is work! The first man was not to taste of anything until he had done some work. Only after God told him to keep the garden did He give him permission to eat of its fruit."

This desirability of work runs through the thought pattern of our people. Prime Minister David Ben-Gurion, speaking to the Anglo-American Committee on Inquiry in 1946, said, "We do not consider work as a curse, or as a bitter necessity, nor even as a means of making a living. We consider it as a high human function, as the basis of human life."

We can contribute this unique Jewish approach to labor to American society. Leisure should not be regarded as an escape from work but rather as an opportunity to refresh our souls and to renew our spirits.[67]

It was wisely observed that leisure is to labor what air is to life. The more air you breathe out the more air you must breathe in. In a tense age like our own, when people expend so much energy in their work, our leisure should be purposeful, our periods of rest must be creative.

It is obvious from this dicussion that we are merely on the threshold of trying to develop our thinking. Much more has to be done in the areas of basic research, publications, and public information.

I would respectfully suggest the establishment at our seminaries and Jewish universities of chairs in Jewish social ethics. Our scholars could be most helpful in doing basic research and probing into the texts for the many nuggets of inspiration that wait to be uncovered.

Some years ago James Parkes suggested the establishment of an Institute of Jewish Ethics. The Herbert H. Lehman Institute of Ethics established in 1958 may rightly be regarded as a start in this direction. In terms of publications, it is lamentable that there has been no fully systematic treatment of the subject of Jewish ethics since the time of M. Lazarus.[68] I am certain that the business world would greatly appreciate tracts and fuller studies dealing with their moral dilemmas.

In the area of public interpretation, one might draw attention to the fact that since 1952 a group of clergy and laypersons have been meeting three times a year at Downside Abbey to discuss the problems involved in communicating Christian doctrine to the men and women of our century. Once every two years the meeting is enlarged by inviting other men and women, highly qualified in their own spheres, to a symposium lasting a week. The Seminary has had one such gathering in the past. However, there is need for a continued process of study between business-people and theologians. It would be good if clinics of business-people, economists, and teachers of religion could be established to deal with the real day-to-day problems.

The ethical standards we will offer to the business community will be the ideal. Though this ideal is often in conflict with the real, this fact should not deter us from our efforts. When we see inequity, our moral fibre must be firm and we must understand how to act. "It is required of a man that he shall share the action and passion of his time at peril of being judged not to have lived," Justice Holmes once said.[69] Certainly our moral dilemma in making decisions between the ideal and the real is ever present. Life does not always permit us to choose between clearly and sharply defined cases of right and wrong, between virtue and vice. All too frequently our choice is between two nearly-right courses of action. Our function is to narrow the gap, to annihilate the distance between the ideal and the real.

Notes

[1]*New York Times*, March 12, 1961.

[2]*Business Week*, September 7, 1957, p. 86, "Philosophers Descend from Ivory Tower . . ."

[3]"Business and the Good Society," Leland Hazard, *The Saturday Review*.

[4]*New York Times*, April 5, 1961, p. 1, col. 1.

[5]*New York Times*, April 25, 1961.

[6]*Jewish Chronicle*, February 10, 1961.

[7]Addresses Given at the 13th Conference of Anglo-Jewish Preachers, "Jewish Ethics and Their Application to Modern Commerce and Industry," S. Goldman.

[8]*Business and Religion*, Ernst Dichter. Edited by Edward C. Bursk, p. 204.

[9]*The National Purpose*, N. Y. 1960. Holt, Rinehart and Winston.

[10]*Noam*, Vol. II, 5719, pp. 33-37 "Im yesh khashash ribit bemilvah memshalti?"

[11]*Taanit* 10a.

[12]*The Churches and the Public*, p. 58. *The Presence of the Church*, by William Clancy.

[13]For a similar study, see M. Waxman, *Sefer Hadoar*, 1957, pp. 103 ff.

[14]*Mishnah Baba Batra* 5:10.

[15]Kadushin, Max, *Introduction to Rabbinic Ethics*, Yehezkel Kaufmann Jubilee Volume, p. 97.

[16]Aron Barth, *The Modern Jew Faces Eternal Problems*, Pub. The Religious Section of the Youth and Hechalutz Dept. of the Zionist Organization, Jerusalem 1956.

[17]Boaz Cohen, *Law and Tradition in Judaism*, p. 219.

[18]*Bereshit Rabbah*, p. 240, Soncino translation.

[19]*Baba Metzia*, 62a. For differences on the Catholic and Protestant approaches to moral and ethical questions, see *Life, Death and the Law* by Norman St. John Stevas, pp. 13-34.

[20]J. D. Eisenstein, *Ozar Dinim ve-Minhagim*, p. 248.

[21]H. Bowen, *Social Responsibilities of the Businessman*, p. 92.

[22]*Torah Shelemah*, Vol. 15, p. 33, Item 125.

[23]*Berakhot* 17a.

[24]*Harvard Business Review*, Vol. 33, No. 3, May-June, 1955.

[25]*New York Times*, June 16, 1958, *More Blessed to Give*, James Reston.

[26]*Harvard Business Review*, Vol. 33, No. 33, May-June, 1955.

[27]Clarence B. Randall, *A Creed for Free Enterprise*, p. 16.

[28]Herbert Muller, *Issues of Freedom*, p. 81 f.

[29]*Berakhot* 58a.

[30]Maybaum, *Jewish Existence*, p. 34.

[31]*Ibid.*, p. 36.

[32]*Yoma* 86a.

[33]*Baba Metzia* 58b.

[34]Maimonides, *Book of Torts*, Treatise III, Chapter XI, 3.

[35]*Mekhilta*, Vol. III, p. 105.

[36]Maimonides, *Book of Acquisitions*, Chapter XIV.

[37]Rabbi Simon preferred that praise to all of the riches of the world.

[38]*New York Times*, November 8, 1959, "Advertising. When Will Other Shoe Drop?"

[39]*Baba Metzia* 60a.

[40]Louis Jacobs, *Jewish Values*, p. 85.

[41]1 Chronicles 29:14.

[42]*The Living Talmud*, p. 126.

[43]Deuteronomy 4:15. "Take ye therefore good heed of yourselves." (See interesting application *Berakhot* 32b.)

[44]Reuel Denney, *The Leisure Society*, *Harvard Business Review*, May-June, 1959, p. 47.

[45]Bell, *Work and its Discontents*, p. 7.
[46]*Pittsburgh Press*, December 9, 1960.
[47]*Wall Street Journal*, January 9, 1959, p. 1, col. 1.
[48]Alvin Pitcher, *The Importance of Being Human*, Harvard Business Review, January-February 1961, p. 42.
[49]*Taanit* 11a.
[50]*Sotah* 21a.
[51]*Yalkut Shimoni*, part I, 161.
[52]For an excellent description of this, see Federbush, *The Jewish Concept of Labor*, particularly the chapter "Labor—Blessing or a Curse." Also the "Jewish Conception of Work," C. H. W. Reines, *Judaism*, Vol. VIII, No. 4, 1959, pp. 329 ff. Also *"Work"—Christian Thought and Practice*, edited by John M. Todd, London, 1960.
[53]*The Legends of the Jews*, Vol. V, p. 92.
[54]*Shabbat* 33b.
[55]*Torah Shelemah*, Vol. XV, p. 33.
[56]*The Living Talmud*, p. 62.
[57]Menahem G. Glenn, *Israel Salanter*, p. 96.
[58]*Jewish Values*, p. 48.
[59]*Tosefta Baba Metzia* 8:2.
[60]*Taanit* 23a-23b.
[61]*Yoma* 20b.
[62]*New York Times*, December 29, 1959, p. 1, col. 7.
[63]Karl Jaspers, *Man in The Modern Age*, p. 64.
[64]*Journal of the American Medical Association*, Vol. 175, No. 6, p. 465.
[65]*Work and Its Discontents*, p. 36.

A report on *Neurosis in Industry* brought out by the Medical Research Council discovered that of 3,000 workers (a random sample from about 30,000 workers in the light and medium engineering industries), fifty-eight per cent reported that they liked their job and only thirteen to fourteen per cent that they disliked it or were bored with it (Edward Rogers, *God's Business*, p. 63). On the other hand, Erich Fromm approaches the problem differently. He writes that "Is there any empirical evidence that most people today are not satisfied with their work? In an attempt to answer this question we must differentiate between what people *consciously think* about their satisfaction, and what they *feel unconsciously*. It is evident from psychoanalytic experience that the sense of unhappiness and dissatisfaction can be deeply repressed; a person may consciously feel satisfied and only his dreams, psychosomatic illness, insomnia, and many other symptoms may be expressive of the underlying unhappiness. The tendency to repress dissatisfaction and unhappiness is strongly supported by the widespread feeling that not to be satisfied means to be 'a failure,' queer, unsuccessful, etc. (Thus, for instance, the number of people who consciously think they are happily married and express this belief sincerely in answer to a questionnaire is by far greater than the number of those who are really happy in their marriage.)" *The Sane Society*, p. 296.

[66]Genesis 2:15-16.

[67]"Work as a Public Issue," *Saturday Review*, December 12, 1959, by Harvey Swados. See "Alienation and the Decline of Utopia," Kenneth Kenniston, *The American Scholar*, Spring, 1960.

Ernest Barker, *Church, State & Education*, p. 211. "It is not only that we work so hard; it is also that we play so hard. Perhaps the monotony and uniformity of work sends us in reaction to the hazards of games, or the excitement of watching them, or the still greater excitement of betting upon them; perhaps the urban aggregations in which men now live make them unhappy unless they are crowding together to some common game or spectacle. Whatever the reason, poor leisure is far too often out in the cold, while reaction is romping about all the rooms in the house. One need be no kill-joy or Puritan to think or talk in this strain. Life is something more than a series of alternate layers of lean work and fat hearty play. It is meant for the growth and development of the human spirit. And that growth needs its growing time, which is leisure."

Edward Rogers, *God's Business*, p. 60. "We strive to construct a wholeness of life in our hours of leisure, and can never wholly succeed—for we drive too hard in our flight from work and we lack in the substitute whole a requisite ingredient supplied only by satisfaction in labor. The problem is increasing in intensity. When the agricultural laborer toiled from dawn to dusk, and when the industrial artisan put in a twelve-hour day six days a week, his work was his life. It was grim and tough and in many ways stultifying, but it was a unity. It is a sad fact that in those still comparatively few countries where the burden of excessive drudgery has been to some degree lifted the new and serious problem of social life is the 'problem of leisure.' It would have seemed incredible a century ago that leisure could ever be a problem."

[68]*Ethics of Judaism*, Philadelphia, 1900.

[69]*The Mind and Faith of Justice Holmes*, edited by Max Lerner.

The Negro-Jewish Dialogue

SYNAGOGUE COUNCIL OF AMERICA, 1962

By Way of Introduction

The Bible, in describing the ninth plague, relates: "And Moses stretched forth his hand towards heaven; and there was a thick darkness in all of the land of Egypt . . . they saw not one another" (Exodus 10:22, 23).

The sages commented at length on the meaning of the words "thick darkness." One simple yet profound interpretation explained the meaning of the Egyptian experience in this manner: "The words 'they saw not one another' meant literally, in the original Hebrew, that man did not see his brother." Darkness was more than a physical phenomenon. The affliction was not in people's eyes but, more significantly, in their hearts.

In analyzing our contemporary American scene we must, regretfully, report that in the area of race relations we still are beset by thick darkness. When we do not regard our fellow human beings as our brothers and sisters, our society is plagued.

This essay on Negro-Jewish relations is an attempt to pierce those barriers that prevent a better understanding between Negroes and Jews. It is to be hoped that there will not be a permanent blackout in intergroup relations. Let us see one another as brothers and sisters and, in that splendid vision, attain a more peaceful society.

The Wider Problem

One of our country's most vexing problems with the widest of ramifications revolves around the role of the Negro in American society. The strained Negro-white relations in our country affect us not only within the bounds of this land but flow out into our conduct of international affairs. One need but recall the riots at the United Nations headquarters following the death of Patrice Lumumba, the pointed questions asked of American spokesmen overseas concerning the treatment of our Negro minority, or the incidents revolving about the small number of Negroes in our Peace Corps. Tom Mboya, general secretary of the Kenya Federation of Labor, speaking in Chicago, said in passing: "Unless the colored people resort to gaining their own freedom and self respect, no one else is going to give it to them. . . . I cannot be free in Kenya when Negroes are suffering elsewhere. . . . It would be terrible to think that once I left the shores of Africa and came to Mississippi I would be denied service in a bar. . . . This cannot be."[1]

It would be well, in a complicated subject such as Negro-white relations, to narrow down the areas of consideration to those that affect the Jewish community directly, not in the sense of avoiding the larger implications of the problem but for the sake of clarity in dealing with this matter.

Moving to the Northern City

The urbanization of the Negro has a direct impact upon American Jews who are primarily resident in the cities and the adjacent suburbs of our nation. The population facts speak for themselves and need little commentary. In 1910, 90 percent of American Negroes lived in the states of the Confederate South. By 1960 only 52 percent remained in that area.[2] This vast internal immigration has brought the primarily rural Negro to the cities of the North with all the problems of adjustment attendant upon relocation. The impact of the population shift can be seen from these figures: in Washington, D.C. Negroes are now 53.9 percent of the population; in Baltimore they account for 34.8 percent; in Detroit 28.9 percent; in Cleveland 28.6 percent; in St. Louis 28.6 percent; in Philadelphia 26.4 percent; in Chicago 22.9 percent; in Pittsburgh 16.7 percent; in New York 14.0 percent; in Boston 9.1 percent.[3]

Negroes and Jews Meet

Perhaps the heart of the problem that most directly concerns the Jewish community is the confrontation of Jews and Negroes in these and other Northern cities. Arnold Rose observed that "The American minority group with which the Negroes have had the closest contact has been the Jews." He felt that "Negroes have always been mildly anti-Semitic because it was part of Christian American culture to be so. As anti-Semitism increased generally in America, it increased among Negroes."[4]

Obvious areas of encounter and of tension are the relations between Jewish employers and their employees, particularly domestic workers; the Jewish businessman in Negro areas; and the Jewish landlord in Negro neighborhoods.

During the war years, a weekly magazine, written for high school age youngsters but widely circulated to the general Negro public through the corner newsstands, frequently carried editorials attacking Jewish merchants. Jewish civil rights organizations tried to counteract this trend of thinking. The editor of the magazine then published the following editorial in the Spring of 1944:

LOVE THY NEIGHBOR

Jewish leaders pleading for tolerance and an abatement of anti-Semitism among Negroes should look at the score! Such apparent hatred as may be held by Negroes against Jews is a direct outgrowth of abuses practiced by the children of Israel on their Black brethren. While calling upon the world to sow good will toward the Jew, these people do nothing themselves to restrain the greed of Jewish merchants, realtors and money-lenders.

Here in Bronzeville an organization of Jewish businessmen arbitrarily holds down competition. No Colored merchant is permitted to operate a competing establishment in a good location except under conditions which make bankruptcy inevitable.

Let the Jewish church and civic leaders, who ask our help in the world fight on Jews, bring the social criminals of their race to task. Stop over-charges, let down residential barriers, and elevate business ethics. Day-to-day fair play will drive our hate away.[5]

Leslie A. Fiedler has commented on the confrontation of the two groups in America's Northern cities:

It is in the big cities of the industrial North . . . that the Negro and the Jew confront each other and that their inner relationship is translated into a spatial one. The 'emancipated' Negro fleeing poverty and the South, and the 'emancipated' Jew fleeing exclusion and Europe, become neighbors, and their proximity serves to remind both that neither is quite 'emancipated' after all. In America, to be sure, the ultimate ghetto . . . is reserved for the Negroes, except for the marginal Jewish merchant who finds himself inside the Negro quarter, forced to squeeze his colored customers for his precarious livelihood and to bear the immediate brunt of their hatred for all white men.

It doesn't matter how much newer and richer are the homes which the Jews attain in their flight toward the tonier suburbs and how shabby the dwellings they leave to the Negroes who follow them; they feel the pressure of those Negroes always behind them, five years away or twenty or thirty; and they can never lose the sense of being merely a buffer between the blacks and the 'real' whites. Insofar as they are aware of their undeniable economic superiority to the Negroes, middle-class Jews are likely to despise them for lagging behind at the same time that they resent them for pressing so close. It is not an easy relationship.[6]

For many there is a genuine lack of understanding of these basic elements that create tensions in our cities, specifically between Jews and Negroes and in a broader sense, between Negroes and whites,[7] and there is need to increase our information about Negro life.[8] But first of all, there is a basic problem of the Negro that ought to be discussed.

The Two Ways

The Negro community has many solutions for changing the status of the Negro in American society. These proposals range from total integration to total separation. A prominent Negro professional man, in a recent conversation, indicated that one of the goals that he regarded as imperative was the full integration of all Americans. In contrast to the Brandeis doctrine that America is a nation of nationalities, he hoped for the day when America would become a single, monolithic community. Some day America would no longer need 'Nationality Days' in which each national group, wearing its distinctive costume, performed its ethnic dances and songs, with the Negro singing spirituals.

At the opposite pole there are men like Elijah Muhammad, and his Black Muslim movement, who seek complete separation for the Negro and ultimately, perhaps, even a separate state. "The Muslims demand an entirely separate black economy, arguing that not until the Negro is economically independent will he be, in any real sense, free."⁹ Elijah Muhammad's appearance in Chicago in February, 1962 was graced with the presence of George Lincoln Rockwell and a handful of his swastika-wearing followers.

Gunnar Myrdal, the Swedish economist and famed author of *An American Dilemma*, pointed out the significance of the Negro's acceptance of complete integration in America: "The integration of the Negroes in American society has already proceeded so far that without any hesitation you can feel that what is good for America is good for the Negroes—and equally you can feel that what is good for the Negroes is good for America."¹⁰

Education—The Key to the Better Life

Many of the Negro tensions emanate from a social syndrome of economics-education-environment. The Civil War gave the Negro emancipation but not equality. The Negro community, in analyzing its status, senses that full equality is possible only when Negroes can improve their standard of living, take unqualified advantage of America's educational opportunities, and enhance their environment. The key to the door to a better life bears the label 'education.' Eli Ginzberg, one of America's finest experts on manpower problems, mentions that "Not only do Negroes complete fewer years of schooling than whites; the education they do receive is, for the most part, far inferior."¹¹ Current efforts of the Negro leadership reflect the stress placed upon improvement of education, accompanied by fully integrated housing and completely open employment opportunities.¹²

Economically the American Negro is still among the lower income-producing segments of the population. The wages of the average Negro worker are now only 60 percent of the wages of the average white worker. This compares to 41 percent in 1939. Income is tied to education. Better trained people are better income producers than those with less academic or technical training. The failure to receive proper education limits the employment opportunities open to the Negro, even when direct discrimination against hiring is not present. Limited to lower paying jobs, even with both husband and wife working, the Negro family must maintain a lower scale of living, in inadequate slum quarters that inflict damaging effects upon family life.

The Negro community feels that many of the social ills suffered by their group are the result of a failure to receive adequate educational opportunities. For every one white student, two Negro students drop out of high school. What happens to these dropouts? They suffer from a higher unemployment rate than high school graduates. Although Chicago is only 26 percent Negro, 40 percent of the unemployed and 65 percent of the jail population, according to the Chicago Urban League, are Negro.

Strengthening the Family

The Negro child's educational experience is directly affected by family life. Negro children, on the whole, suffer from the fact that there is no real stimulus to study because of a lack of intellectual tradition within the family. Lower scholastic aptitude readings are recorded in the neighborhoods of low socioeconomic status. James B. Conant, in his *Slums and Suburbs*, has pointed out that there is a correlation between the child's ability to read and the socioeconomic, cultural level of the home.[13]

A University of Pittsburgh educator once told of a striking experience concerning Negro children in a slum school of Pittsburgh's Hill district. They were asked to color in some outlines of bananas. Inevitably, the crayon that was used was brown. Although yellow crayons were available, these youngsters have never seen a banana that was not overripe. This is the type of merchandise that often comes from the slum stores.

Struggle in the Schools

The Negro community wants an educational system that will not confine Negro students to schools whose population is largely Negro. This is behind the drive for open enrollment, which would permit youngsters enrolled in schools with large Negro populations to transfer to other areas. Day by day, this issue is raised in school districts throughout the country.

Dr. James Conant, former president of Harvard, who has been studying American schools, discussed this issue in his recent volume. He argues against the open enrollment system, which would break down the *de facto* segregation that exists in most of our northern cities. He argues that "Little or nothing can be done for or with the parents of the children who face such serious problems in their homes. These problems directly affect the child's health, attendance, emotional and personal adjustment, his learning and his progress (or lack of it) in every respect. In all probability at least one-half of our children will be school dropouts. In our opinion, the children need, desperately, for desirable development, in addition to good schools—good homes, churches and communities."[14] The Negro community is greatly concerned about Dr. Conant's study. They regard segregated schools as a blight on America.

One cannot easily argue away the position of Dr. Conant. Open enrollment does not solve all the problems of the Negro child. In New York City, it was estimated that only 7,500 children out of a school population of a million took advantage of the right to open transfer. Moving a child by bus, as is proposed, from his neighborhood school to another neighborhood where he can have the experience of studying with white children, creates a new set of circumstances. There is a dichotomy in the lives of these children between the school in which they study and the play environment to which they must return after school hours. The enriched experience of the school is not reflected in the home. This problem is now being felt by Negro children who attend white private schools on scholarships.

One of the great problems is that in city after city the tide is running back toward segregation in the public schools. Keeping the whites in integrated schools is almost as difficult as getting the Negroes out of segregated schools. All-Negro schools tend to stay that way. All-white schools, after integration, become all-Negro schools as the whites move out. This was most evident in a recent survey in Washington, D.C. Although Washington has a population of 54 percent Negro and 46 percent white, there are 81.5 percent Negroes and 18.5 percent whites in the Washington D.C. public schools.[15] (It might be noted that part of the increase in nonpublic school attendance is due to parents enrolling their children in institutions that cater primarily to white children.)

However, the Negro believes that there is a symbolic value to open enrollment. Just as the right to live anywhere is as important as actually residing there, the right to attend a white school is as significant as actually going.

Perhaps one of the greatest boons in allowing Negro children a fuller educational experience can be seen in the remarks of one of the nine Negro children who were involved in the Little Rock integration fight in 1958. When asked about her experience, she related:

> When I used to go to Horace Mann School I thought that white people were different. When I saw the colored kids at Horace Mann acting silly or doing something that I didn't think they should do, I guessed they used to do this because they were colored. Now that I am at Central High School I see the white children do silly things, too. Just like there are some dumb colored children there are some dumb whites, and there are some smart whites and some smart colored. I guess what I have learned is that they are not so different and we aren't so different.[16]

We must realize not only the academic but the social factors involved in integrated schools. The realization of the Negro girl of the sameness of the two races could as easily have come, in reverse, to a white child. The social education provided by integrated schools is needed not only for the Negro but also for the white child.

Negroes are trying to find and to identify themselves. James Baldwin, the author of *Nobody Knows My Name*, said recently: "You have to decide who you are and force the world to deal with you, not with its idea of you."[17]

Our Role in Better Education

The issues of school attendance will ultimately be decided by the courts and the communities of the nation. The courts will set the legal pattern. School boards throughout the country will react, each in its own way, in setting up the administration that we hope will promote effective full desegregation. School boards will need the support of local communities to carry through any complete desegregation effort.

The struggle to improve America's schools will be a long and difficult one. American public schools face a host of almost insoluble problems, compounded by the need for true desegregation. The American Jewish community will have to do its share in the general campaign to improve public schools. On all possible levels of community action, our voice ought to be clear, speaking affirmatively for the progressive improvement of this basic institution of American democracy.

Enhancing the Family

The Jewish community can be most helpful by exerting a teaching role in strengthening the fabric of Negro family life. The Negro community realizes that it has to buttress family life. To use the words of Martin Luther King, Jr., they must "push programs to raise the moral, cultural climate in Negro neighborhoods." The Negro family needs much reinforcement. Casual standards of sexual behavior sap the strength of family life. It is Conant's finding that "The women, on the whole, work and earn fairly good wages, but the male Negro often earns less than the woman and would rather not work at all than be in this situation. . . . The women are the centers of the family and, as a rule, are extremely loyal to the children. The men, on the other hand, are floaters, and many children have no idea who their father is."[18] The effect of this upon the Negro male is to prevent him from playing the masculine role.[19]

The instability of the Negro family is a source of personal disorder. America will have to pay for the social ills that come from these circumstances. Carl Sandburg once spoke of the fact that the "slums always seek their revenge." James Baldwin has reflected upon the "anguish of a Negro man, who, in the first place, is forced to accept all kinds of humiliation in his workday, whose power in the world is so slight that he cannot really protect his home, his wife, his children, and he finds himself out of work. And he watches his children grow up, menaced in the same way he has been menaced."[20]

The Jewish community has an abundance of resources—the experience and basic know-how in the field of family life. Would it be too much to ask that some of our skill be used to help the Negro family? In analyzing the problems of the expanding metropolis, Nathan Glazer pointed out that if one takes the five subcommuni-

ties of our cities—Catholic, white, Protestant, Jewish, and Negro—"the Negro, has great needs; . . . in another, the Catholic,
needs and resources are in balance; two others, the Jewish and
the white Protestant have greater resources than needs. In some
way, the greater resources of these communities must be allo-
cated to those who need them, and the tradition of Protestant
charity and social welfare which is still alive offers models as to
how Jews can develop a better relation to Negroes."[21]

Jewish community agencies in many cases have had their
facilities turned over to the Negro community. This was the case,
for example, with the establishment of the Anna B. Waldman
Center, which became the successor to the famed Irene Kaufman
Settlement House in Pittsburgh.

The Negro community must not only be helped but must learn
to help itself. It has been reported that "Well-to-do Negroes, while
they contribute generously of their time and effort, seldom contribute their money to Negro protest organizations or to the relief
of impoverished Negroes. There is no traditions of philanthropy
on their parts as there is on the part of Jews, Japanese, immigrants from Europe, and other minority groups in America. Most
of the financial support for the Negro protest, Negro private
education, and Negro improvement organizations comes from
whites. There is no private charity organized by Negroes for
Negroes."[22] Gunnar Mydral's appeal was that "Every Negro intellectual must feel called upon to supplement his work in his
chosen vocation by being a 'race man.' "[23]

The Negro has had great difficulty in climbing the economic
ladder. Part of this is due to cultural traits that, as Oscar Handlin
pointed out, handicap the Negro businessperson. "The recollection of long periods of deprivation encourage 'mad spending
sprees' when funds become available."[24] A study of the Negro
market revealed that Negro families tend to spend more than
white families in the same income group. It was reported that
"The average Negro man during his lifetime buys 80 percent more
shoes than the average white man. Moreover, Negroes, account-
ing for 11 percent of the adult male population, purchase 20
percent of all men's dress shoes sold."[25] It was recently reported in
Business Week that "Food, drink, the elements that make up
home entertainment, still absorbs a lot of the Negroes' dollar,
partly because of the taboos that close the doors on outside
festivities."[26]

It was reported that Negroes have difficulty in developing practices of saving or of holding on to a surplus that can be used as equity capital or to transmit to the young the nest-egg that will allow them to make a better start in life.

Negro Middle Class

The Negroes also have had great difficulty in developing a middle class. Though the rise of the Negro middle class is treated by E. Franklin Frazier in his *Black Bourgeoisie*, and though he regards their business to be insignificant from the standpoint of the American economy, there are evidences of a breakthrough by Negro professional and middle-class groups that will bring conflict in the area of Negro-Jewish relations. "Professionals and white-collar workers, on the whole, voiced greater feelings of resentment against Jews than any other segment of the Negro population. There are probably two reasons for this: at this level, there is the greatest competition between the two groups; and each not only feels threatened by the other but Negroes believe that Jews, as a cohesive group, are against them."[27]

An Area of Conflict

Some 15 years ago, a study was made by Harold L. Sheppard of the Negro merchant. It revealed that Negro anti-Semitism was related to the changes in the class structure of Negro society and to the accompanying social movements, such as the rise of a Negro business spirit and business chauvinism. Business associations within the Negro community among Negro and white merchants reflect these movements and the tensions that ensue from the struggle of Negro merchants to win customer patronage from white merchants in competitive positions. Because of the ethnic character of these white merchants, the antagonism has taken the form of anti-Semitism.

The Negro business community has, at times, used phrases like "Patronize Your Own" and "Sustain Negro Enterprise." "To the small, struggling Negro merchant, faced with the superior competition of white merchants, there is no alternative to the policy of appealing to racial solidarity in bidding for Negro patronage."[28]

Unlike the ordinary business association, these ethnic groups sought to reach the potential consumer by relying upon what Sheppard has labeled "self-assumed role of race-protector." Here is a typical attitude, quoting the Association's president defending his policy: "This situation boils down to the law of nature known as the struggle for the survival of the fittest. And our slogans, our programs, are a weapon in that struggle. . . . The Jew's weapons are reputation, business contracts, control of the best districts, and a good training in business. The Negro doesn't have those weapons and if he is going to survive and get ahead, then he has got to insist that his people patronize his store, and not the Jew's. After all, the Jew can open a store outside of the Black Belt, but can the Negro?"[29]

Another source speaks of the strained relations existing in this area: "There is no doubt about it. They (the Jews) get together and put into business anybody they want. And most of the time it's another Jew. . . . They get together to throw out of business anybody they don't want—Negroes, of course. That's what happened to me. I opened a laundry . . . and was doing O.K. for about a month, and then the Board of Health forced me out. . . . I know the Board was urged on by Jews who don't want colored business, even in our own community."[30]

"Discrimination in Reverse"

In 1960, many Jewish liquor stores in Harlem were threatened with picketing on the grounds that they refused to buy their wares from Negro salesmen.[31] At that time, the *New York Times* commented in an editorial, "Discrimination in Reverse":

The store owners have justification for fearing that Mr. (Representative Adam Clayton) Powell's efforts are, in reality, designed to force them to close shop. Should they reject the recommended salesmen's list, their trade would suffer. Should they accept Mr. Powell's dictate, they could face prosecution under the State's anti-discrimination laws.

The laws were written to protect Negroes and other minority groups from discrimination in employment and other fields.

That a Negro leader should flout the laws and threaten repris-
als against those who might uphold them certainly smacks of
demagoguery.[32]

During the depression and the war years that followed, when
the Negro community was poorer and more harassed than today,
anti-Semitism was common, particularly among the Negro business community, which felt competition from white businesses,
in many cases Jewish, that were operating in the Negro areas.[33]
Gunnar Mydral, speaking at Howard University, stressed the fact
that with the integration of the Negroes in the wider American
society, "The Negro professional middle and upper class will have
to surrender economic monopolies which they have held, and are
still holding, on the basis of prejudice. The future society of
equality is a society of free competition, and you will have to face it
and prepare yourselves to deal with it successfully. You cannot cry
for the breaking down of the walls of segregation and discrimination while, at the same time, hoping to retain petty monopoly
preserves among a Negro clientele to give you a comfortable and
uncontested economic safety."[34]
Another area of conflict will be the expression of Negroes in the
field of politics. Even after the bulk of the Jewish population has
left an older neighborhood, Jewish leaders often remain in power.
Struggles for succession to the leadership positions arise.

Negroes and Israel

There are also tension and bad feelings in the Negro community
concerning the Jewish concern for Israel. During the fight for the
establishment of Israel, many prominent Negroes sided with the
'colored' Arabs in the fight against the 'white' Jews. An extremist
view of the Black Muslims on this subject may be seen from the
following statement of a Black Muslim leader:

We make no distinction between Jews and non-Jews so long
as they are all white. To do so would be to imply that we like
some whites better than others. This would be discrimination, and we do not believe in discrimination. However, the
Jews, with the help of Christians in America and Europe,

drove our Muslim brothers (i.e., the Arabs) out of their homeland, where they had been settled for centuries and took over
the land for themselves. This every Muslim resents.

In America, the Jews sap the very life-blood of the so-called
Negroes to maintain the state of Israel, its armies and its
continued aggression against our brothers in the East. This
every Black Man resents.

The European and American Christians helped to establish
Israel in order to get rid of the Jews so that they could take
over their businesses as they did the American Japanese
during the war. The scheme failed, and the joke is on the
white man. The American Jews aren't going anywhere. Israel
is just an international poor house which is maintained by
money sucked from the poor suckers in America.[35]

It would be good for the Jewish community to inform American
Negroes, who maintain a significant press, regarding the help
that Israel has been giving to the new Negro states in Africa in
assisting their governments to establish themselves.[36]

Negro Anti-Semitism

That there is Negro anti-Semitism has been studied by many
observers. It is a social phenomenon that cannot be wished
away.[37] Negro anti-Semitism may be among the permanent resid-
ual elements present in the historic religious conflict between
Christian and Jew.[38] James Baldwin has observed, "All over
Harlem, Negro boys and girls are growing into stunted maturity,
trying desperately to find a place to stand; and the wonder is not
that so many are ruined but that so many survive. The Negro's
outlets are desperately constricted. In his dilemma he turns first
upon himself and then upon whatever most represents to him his
own emasculation. Here, the Jew is caught in the American
crossfire. The Negro, facing a Jew, hates, at bottom, not his
Jewishness, but the color of his skin. It is not the Jewish tradition by which he has been betrayed but the tradition of his native
land. But just as society must have a scapegoat, so hatred must
have a symbol. Georgia has the Negro and Harlem has the Jew."[39]

Richard Wright has said, "All of us black people who lived in the neighborhood hated Jews, not because they exploited us, but because we had been taught at home and in Sunday school that Jews were Christ killers. . . . To hold an attitude of antagonism towards Jews was bred in us from childhood; it was not merely racial prejudice; it was part of our cultural heritage."[40]

Our Involvement in Negro Affairs

The Jewish community has had a long role of involvement in Negro affairs. Individuals such as Julius Rosenwald made possible many of the advances in Negro education through his generosity. Jewish community relations organizations have been in the forefront of the struggle for civil liberties and fair employment practices. Many of the great cases that have won Negroes their rights have been participated in by Jewish organizations like the Amerian Jewish Congress, who are expert in the field of legislation and have developed special talents in court proceedings. Jews and Negroes have had good working relations between their respective defense organizations. They have cooperated in attacking various forms of racial prejudice and discrimination.

Jews in the labor movement have been in the vanguard for reducing discrimination in Negro employment opportunities. Though the American labor movement has had a blemished record and has permitted discriminatory practices in union membership, the so-called Jewish unions in the needle trades, like the I.L.G.W.U., the Amalgamated, and others, have stood their ground in eliminating bigotry in the trade union movement. "As members of the ethnic group with the longest record of persecution and adverse discrimination, they (the Jews) cannot but feel pride in their own clear record on the minorities issue when judged by the test of deed. It is doubtful that there is another union milieu where a Negro feels as much at home."[41]

In housing, the Negro has found that Jewish areas are easiest to permeate. Not that Jewish home-owners and landlords have put out big welcome-mats. But in Chicago, when the Negroes moved into the Trumbull Park and Back of the Yards area, there were riots and disturbances. When they moved into the Hyde Park area and other predominantly Jewish neighborhoods, there were no demonstrations.

The Negro community has enjoyed a partial amelioration of their acute housing situation through the various low-rent, public housing projects. The Negro community is in desperate need of higher income housing for those elements of the Negro community that can afford better housing. Oddly enough, many Negro civic leaders and housing officials say privately that "one of the biggest and greatest roadblocks to middle-income housing . . . is what they call 'the professional Negro politician.' " One Negro leader summed it up this way: "These politicians have a stake in low-rent housing. They know people who live in better housing wouldn't be as easily led."[42]

An important role must be played by our religious community, and it is potentially able to make very distinctive contributions. Negro leadership is largely religious. Men like the Reverend Martin Luther King, Jr., of the Southern Christian Leadership Conference, and the Reverend Mr. James Robinson are religious personalities. The church plays a very significant role in the life of the Negro. Let us rememeber that Negroes lived for a long period of time in the Bible Belt of America. Although some observers believe that the Negro church will ultimately lose some of its power with the development of the new leadership elements among the Negro middle class, the Negro religious leader will continue to play a distinctive role with his people.

Bridges of Understanding

In establishing any real bond of communication, the religious elements of the American Jewish community must begin to function. We ought to build bridges of understanding between Negroes and Jews. In these days of general Christian-Jewish dialogue, we ought to make certain that Negroes are incorporated in the discussion, as well as in specifically Jewish-Negro conversations. It was reported last year that in Cleveland such a dialogue was taking place between leaders in the Jewish and Negro community relations organizations.[43] A similar discussion group has been established in Milwaukee. This group, which deals with Jewish-Christian as well as Negro-white relationships, was established through the joint efforts of the Milwaukee Board of the Urban League and the American Jewish Committee. One of the reported questions asked by the Negro participants was, "What is the motivation of the Jews?"

Our Religious Concern

Our concern for the Negro is not part of a selfish strategy for Jewish survival. Our concern is a religious one. This is a fundamental principle of our creed. Like all people, we are created in the image of God.

The Jewish religious community might well serve to stress the significance of respect for law in society. The Negro community is bound to lose its respect for law when it watches the mixed morality of Southern courts. What respect can one have for courts when one witnesses manifestations of the attitude once expressed by Senator Carter Glass: "The people of the original thirteen Southern states curse and spit upon the Fifteenth Amendment—and have no intention of letting the Negro vote. We obey the letter of the amendments and the Federal Statutes, but we frankly evade the spirit thereof."[44] Constant frustration before the bar of justice helps to aggravate one's contempt for law.

James Baldwin once said, "There is much that remains to be done by people of good will. . . . The country does not know what it has done to Negroes. And the country has no notion whatever— and this is disastrous—of what it has done to itself. North and South have yet to assess the price they pay for keeping the Negro in his place."[45] Let us hope that the hour is not too late, nor the price of prejudice too high, and that we still have time to prevent America's moral bankruptcy.

We need more than our community relations people working on this. Our national congregational organizations ought to seek out their counterparts in the Negro religious community; the rabbinic organizations, their colleagues and brothers in the ministry. A body like the Synagogue Council of America, which coordinates the efforts of our six national, congregational, and rabbinic organizations, could well serve in a coordinating capacity in working with Negro religious leadership. As this article was being prepared for publication, an announcement was made that a

National Conference On Religion and Race will be held in Chicago in January, 1963. The Conference is being sponsored by the National Council of Churches, the National Catholic Welfare Conference, and the Synagogue Council of America.[46]

References

[1]Chicago *Daily Defender*, February 27, 1962, p. 2.

[2]Theodore H. White, *The Making of the President 1960*, Atheneum, New York, 1961, p. 231.

[3]"The Negro's Force in Marketplace," *Business Week*, March 26, 1962, p. 80. The general problems faced by the Negroes in our Northern cities are treated in *The Negro in American Civilization*, by Nathaniel Weyl, Public Affairs Press, Washington, D.C., 1960.

[4]Arnold M. Rose, *The Negro's Morale*, University of Minnesota Press, Minneapolis, 1949, pp. 128-129.

[5]Harold L. Sheppard, "The Negro Merchant: A Study of Negro Anti-Semitism," *American Journal of Sociology*, September, 1947, pp. 96-99.

[6]Leslie A. Fiedler, "Negro and Jew-Encounter in America," *Midstream*, Volume II, Number 3, p. 11.

[7]C. Eric Lincoln, *The Black Muslims in America*, Beacon Press, Boston, 1961, p. 40: "Hurt and angry, yet too frightened to act against his powerful tormentor, the Negro sometimes thrashes about, seeking a target for his hostility. Often unconsciously, he displaces his aggression onto other minority groups—Jews, for example—which cannot retaliate so effectively. All too often, the aggression is simply inverted: Negroes turn their rage against other Negroes or against themselves."

[8]In *The Negro's Morale*, (pp. 129), Rose amplifies his findings on the tensions between Negroes and Jews with the following observation: "There were special areas of friction with Jews—a large proportion of the white merchants who solicited Negro trade and set up shop in Negro slums were Jews; many of the housewives who hired Negro servants in the Northern cities were Jews; and many of the property owners who were willing to sell or rent to Negroes were Jews.

"Negro hatred for the merchants was based partly on the relatively high prices a small merchant—a large part of whose business is credit—must charge; partly on the inferior quality of the goods sold to a customer who demands 'the cheapest'; and partly on the failure of the merchants—who often staffed their small stores with members of their families—to hire Negro clerks. Since the Jewish storekeepers were located in Negro areas, they were subjected to strong retaliation in the Northern cities, especially in the 'don't buy where you can't work' campaigns and on the part of the nationalist racketeers who required storekeepers to pay for 'protection'."

In his *Notes of A Native Son*, Beacon Press, Boston, 1955, James Baldwin says, "Negroes of the professional class (as distinct from professional Negroes) compete actively with the Jew in daily contact; and they wear anti-Semitism as a defiant proof of their citizenship; their positions are too shaky to allow them any real ease or any faith in anyone. They do not trust whites or each other or themselves; and, particularly and vocally, they do not trust Jews" (p. 70).

[9]Lincoln, p. 20.

[10]From an address delivered by Dr. Gunnar Myrdal on the occasion of the 94th Annual Commencement at Howard University, Washington, D.C., June 8, 1962; reprinted in part in the Chicago Sun Times, June 10, 1962, p. 6.

[11]Eli Ginzberg, The Negro Potential, Columbia University Press, New York, 1956, p. 53.

[12]On the influence of family, see Ginzberg, The Negro Potential, p. 97 ff. He quotes the distinguished student of Negro life, E. Franklin Frazier, p. 99.

[13]James B. Conant, Slums & Suburbs, McGraw-Hill, New York, 1961, p. 13.

[14]Conant, pp. 16-17.

[15]U.S. News and World Report, "How Mixed Schools Get Unmixed," December 4, 1961, p. 86.

[16]Eli Ginzberg, ed., The Nation's Children, 1: The Family and Social Change, White House Conference on Children and Youth, Columbia University Press, New York, 1960, p. 112.

[17]James Baldwin and Studs Turkel, "Black Man in America," WFMT Perspective, December, 1961, p. 30.

[18]Conant, p. 19.

[19]E. Franklin Frazier, Black Bourgeoisie, The Free Press, Glencoe, Illinois, 1957, p. 221.

[20]Baldwin and Turkel, p. 31.

[21]Nathan Glazer, "The Exploding Metropolis and Intergroup Relations," National Community Relations Advisory Council Plenary Session, June 22-25, 1961, p. 69.

[22]Rose, p. 71.

[23]Gunnar Myrdal address, p. 4.

[24]Oscar Handlin, The Newcomers, Anchor Books, Garden City, 1962, p. 74.

[25]New York Times, September 24, 1961.

[26]Business Week, p. 80.

[27]James H. Robinson, "Some Apprehension, Much Hope," The ADL Bulletin, December, 1957.

[28]Sheppard, p. 96. Lincoln reports in The Black Muslims in America: pp. 140-141: "Negro big-businessmen, like Negro politicians, are very much aware of the Muslims—and especially of their economic potential. They do not like Muhammad's religious and racial extremism, but they welcome his continued stress upon economic self-sufficiency and upon racial solidarity in protecting and strengthening Negro financial interests. Those who do business with the Muslims have found them reliable and businesslike. The Muslims do not buy beyond their means, but they tend to buy merchandise of good quality, usually for cash.

"Negro businesses were well represented at the 1960 Muslim Convention in Chicago. Banks, insurance companies, retail stores and service enterprises accepted Muhammad's invitation to display their wares and advertise their services at special 'bazaars' in the giant Chicago Coliseum, where the convention was held."

Of interest too, are some of the expressions quoted by Lincoln of the Negroes' reactions to the Muslims: p. 162: "One Chicago businessman said, 'When Mr. Muhammad urges Negroes to build up solid economic holdings in the community, I agree with him 100 per cent. But I can't go along with some of his other ideas.' A Philadelphia lawyer's comment was, 'He's merely trying to give the Negro the education and an understanding strictly from an economic point of view, that the Jew has been getting and using for centuries. It would be a tough job, but organizing the Negro's financial intelligence into one solid buying power would be a good thing. We don't stick together and pool our capital as other groups do.' In Los Angeles, a real estate broker's comment was, 'I don't know too much about the other things they want, but if they can get colored people to support colored business 100 per cent, I wouldn't be able to count all the money I'd make selling houses.' A Hartford, Conn., man said, 'If . . . (Negroes) want better schools, good jobs and homes they should follow the leadership of Elijah Muhammad, for he is telling the Negro to unite because unity is the key to their freedom.' "

[29]Sheppard, p. 97.

[30]James Q. Wilson, *Negro Politics*, The Free Press, Glencoe, Illinois, 1960, p. 325.

[31]*New York Times*, March 6, 1960, 43:5.

[32]*New York Times*, March 28, 1960, 28:1-2.

[33]Wilson, p. 155.

[34]Gunnar Myrdal address, p. 5.

[35]Lincoln, p. 166.

[36]An example of the attitude of the Negro intellectual community can be seen in "East Meets West in Israel," by Samuel Koenig, *Phylon*, Vol. XVII, No. 2, p. 167 ff.

[37]James Baldwin, in his *Notes of a Native Son*, (p. 68), speaks of the Jews in Harlem. He describes them as "small tradesmen, rent collectors, real estate agents and pawnbrokers; they operate in accordance with the American business tradition of exploiting Negroes, and they are therefore identified with oppression and are hated for it. I remember meeting no Negro in the years of my growing up, in my family or out of it, who would really ever trust a Jew, and few who did not, indeed, exhibit for them the blackest contempt. On the other hand, this did not prevent their working for Jews, being utterly civil and pleasant to them, and, in most cases, contriving to delude their employers into believing that, far from harboring any dislike for Jews, they would rather work for a Jew than for anyone else."

[38]Several years ago, Reverend James H. Robinson, writing on participating in a symposium on "What Negroes Think About Jews," (*ADL Bulletin*, September, 1957), observed that "There is, at least, one major difference between the hostilities of some Negroes to Jews and hostilities

of majority whites to either Negroes or Jews: anti-Semitism among Negroes is based upon suspicion rather than hate. There are Negroes with anti-Semitic attitudes born from unhappy experiences with Jewish property-owners and storekeepers operating in communities to which Negroes are restricted, experiences with housewives who have exploited domestics. . . . Somewhat more negative attitudes were encountered among workers and domestics and among the housewives in segregated residential areas where there are many small shops owned by Jewish merchants."

[39]Baldwin, pp. 71-72.

[40]Richard Wright, *Black Boy*, World Publishing Company, Cleveland, 1950, p. 53.

[41]"Jewish Unionism and American Labor," *Publications of the American Jewish Historical Society*, Vol. XLI, p. 337.

James H. Robinson said, "Laborers, who were members of the trade unions had more positive attitudes than unorganized laborers—an indication that the former have constructive and mutually supporting contracts with Jews in the labor movement while the latter do not."

On the history of discrimination by organized labor against the admission of Negro members, see: Harry H. Millis and Royal E. Montgomery, *Organized Labor*, McGraw Hill, New York, 1945, p. 262; Herman D. Block, "Craft Unions: A Link in the Circle of Negro Discrimination," *Phylon*, Vol. XVIII, No. 4, pp. 361 ff and 372.

[42]*New York Times*, June 8, 1962, 33:8.

[43]Glazer, p. 72.

[44]Chicago *Sun Times*, "Racial Parley Here to Make History," March 21, 1962, 1:4-6.

[45]Arnold Rose, *The Negro in America*, Beacon Press, Boston, 1948, p. 144, footnote 1.

[46]Baldwin and Turkel, p. 34.

A Plea to God and Man

(ADDRESS GIVEN AT NEW YORK CITY RALLY OF ALL JEWISH ORGANIZATIONS, MAY 28, 1967.)

We come today before God and man to give witness concerning our deep anxiety for Israel. We come today to bestir ourselves and to arouse the conscience of all who cherish peace.

We are a small people whose ranks have been cruelly decimated during this generation. We are a people who have lived through the agonies of Auschwitz and the terrors of Treblinka. We shall not stand idly by remembering our six million martyrs and permit, Heaven forbid, another two and a half million to live continually under the threat of annihilation. We are told that we talk too much about the past. But for us, talking about the past means being concerned about the future.

The urgency of Israel's need, the grave threat to world peace, the grimness of this maddening hour, bids us cry aloud. We are urged to be calm. We are asked to be cautious. Israel is warned not to be precipitous. Are we made of stone? How can we remain silent? How can any decent human being be mute in the sight of the Damascus sword of death that hangs over the people of Israel?

On behalf of the united religious community, we welcome the statement of leading Christian clergymen—Catholic and Protestant, Negro and white—who urged that as an act of conscience, America support the independence, integrity, and freedom of Israel. "Men of conscience must not remain silent at this time," they declared. If religious cooperation, which is a hallmark of our times, has any meaning, now is the time for our Christian neighbors to speak forth! Now is the time to speak. There is a time to be silent and there is a time to speak.

Decent people know the pains of war. Decent people yearn for the security of peace. That peace must be a peace of justice. That peace must be a peace of righteousness. No more Munichs in our time! We need no more white bandages covering moral gangrene. Commitments have been made to Israel: solemn declarations by the great powers, including our own government, that Israel's sea lanes, her vital life lines, would be kept open.

When a nation, or the U.N., gives its promise, it must keep its word. Our generation has witnessed the degradation of the Jews and their return to dignity. Our generation will not be silent at this real danger of destruction.

The coming days will be trying. The depth of our commitment will be plumbed. In this hour, we remain men and women of faith. We lift up our hearts to the guardian of Israel. "Guardian of Israel, guard the remnant, let not disaster overcome Israel. Father of mercies, be merciful. Remember the covenant with the patriarchs. Deliver us from evil times. Answer our plea, grant us mercy and help. Fulfill, we plead, Thy promise: 'I will grant peace in the land and no one shall make you afraid!' " The firmness of our bond will be tested.

To Israel and to ourselves we proclaim: The road to freedom is demanding and heartbreaking. Be strong, be strong. Let us strengthen each other. To the world we proclaim: If there is righteousness, if there is morality, let it appear!

Acceptance Address

(UPON TAKING OFFICE AS PRESIDENT OF THE RABBINICAL ASSEMBLY, 1980—EXCERPTS.)

People sometimes seek to escape obligation. . . . There is something I learned from Egyptian history—the Egyptians devalued human history. They sought to escape human history. They had a cyclical approach—they go back over and over again. In the Temple of Luxor are repetitive statues of the sheep-god. In Egyptian history, battles are reported a thousand years after they took place, and the report is similar to the initial report. We as Jews have a different conception of time. It is not straight up; there are zigzag movements. But there is always a recognition of the past, as well as future responsibilities. . . .

Dr. Salo Baron, one of the pre-eminent historians, wrote an article many years ago in which he said that the prevailing mood in American life is that of pessimism and he could not understand this mood because he is a person who is always on the upbeat. If we look at the American scene, however, many of the reasons for optimism are gone. The frontier is gone, the second chance. Opportunities are gone for so many and there is pessimism because of Vietnam, because of a deterioration of our political life, beginning with the very White House office.

But this pessimism will, in time, be dissipated. There will be room for optimism and there will be room for what one great writer predicted, "There will be one last river to cross." We will, in our own way, help to restore that which the early dreamers of America dreamt of—this land becoming a Garden of Eden. . . .

There is another thing which is part of our age—and some of you saw this on television some years ago. It was an in-depth study on Marion County and the key line was, "I want it all and I want it all now." I was talking with one of our parents who was describing with trepidation the manner in which her children are buying a home that is very, very expensive. Our spirit now is the spirit of "I want it all and I want it all now." I heard a brilliant analysis by one of our colleagues at the Cantors Convention who spoke of the fact that ours is an age of psychological fulfillment. People think they are entitled to a certain standard of living. There is a television commercial for Sony, the Japanese firm that produces television sets, about a twelve-year-old who wants a portable Sony—and the commercial says, "She's entitled to it."

The synagogue as an organization is affected by the fact that so much of our emphasis, and properly so, is placed upon the participation of children. Our birthrate is decreasing, many families are childless, conception is delayed until the time when the number of children of the union is limited to one or two. We face a disaster area in marriage. Many marriages end in divorce. The rate of this legal separation rises each year. In 1976, one out of seven marriages broke up; now the rate is two out of five. The high rate of divorce may be due to many factors. It may be due to a narcissistic self, to a privatization of self. But we must be concerned with the fact that the synagogue in America has always been linked to the family and the family is breaking down.

We live in an age where the rate of change is accelerating, as Alvin Toffler pointed out in his book *Future Shock*. The closing in of the world around us, as a result of population expansion, makes prompt change more necessary than ever. Whitehead once said, "We give credit, not to the first man to have an idea, but to the first man who takes it seriously." Anyone can prepare position papers and policy changes. Implementing a change is a more difficult task. Bureaucracies have vested interests and it is our duty to keep moving ahead, towards a better functioning Jewish community.

We can speak proudly of the fact that in the last few years, more emphasis has been focused upon the internal life of the R.A. Surely we are concerned with the world without, but we must also be involved with the world within.

I will not trouble you with trying to document my gut feelings on the changes of the synagogue. My instinctive feeling is that the synagogue of the next decade or two will be much smaller physically, but more intense in activity. The large congregations, the dinosaur-type of institutions that we cherished in the '20s and '30s, some of which have remained to this day, may become a thing of the past. I feel this intuitively. There are some who like to have statistics, who like to have the bare facts. I am reminded of a story about Sir Isaac Newton, who once met Halley of Halley's Comet fame. Halley said, "How do you know that? You haven't proven it." Taken aback for a moment, Newton replied, "Well, I've known it for years. If you will give me a few days, I will certainly find the proof for you."

There are other critical issues that face us. What should be done about the immigration from the Soviet Union? We have had very little impact with our Federations in trying to make fundamental decisions about the religious and cultural integration of this group. In ever-increasing numbers, Jews are coming from Israel. I do not like to call these individuals *yordim;* they are Jews who have decided that they want to live here in the United States. But they, too, have to be the subject of our special concern.

In all of this picture, you must understand that Judaism has a basic and fundamental lesson to teach. Harvey Cox wrote a remarkable book called *Journey East.* He played around, as some of our theologians like to play around, with Asian religions. Then he decided that this new Orientalism is full not only of promise but also of peril. Spending some time with some Buddhists in Boulder, Colorado, he accepted an invitation to spend a Shabbat with a small Jewish community. In a magnificent chapter on meditation and Shabbat, he deals with that theme, with the great contribution that Judaism can make to the Western World in bringing in the element of tranquility, of *menuḥah,* of *shalvah* to each one of us.

Jerusalem now has the Damoclean sword hanging over it. It may be whetted by an advisor to the President, it may be whetted by other members of our State Department, by the European Economic Community, by the Japanese and others. Jerusalem, we pledge, will remain Jewish, united and under the sovereignty of Israel only if we struggle for it. The fact of the matter is, if we will ever permit Jerusalem to be divided, the barbed wire to go up again, the concrete walls to be erected, this will be the greatest *ḥillul hashem* in two thousand years, and we won't be able to reverse history once again.

"Jerusalem, my friends, is a cradle city rocking me. I am a Jerusalemite, the dust is my conscience, the stone is my subconscience," Yehuda Amihai once wrote.

There is much that can be added. There is the great statement of Cyrus, in II Chronicles 36:23, who gave our people a positive charge. "Whosoever there is among you of all His people, the Lord his God be with him, let him go up." We must have an *aliyah* in our personal expectations. We must have an *aliyah* in our spiritual dimensions. We must have an *aliyah* in our love and friendship for one another.

We have been through a difficult ritual of passage which had to be performed. The Bible tells us, in II Kings 10:15. "And we find Jehonadab coming to greet the King. Jehonadab greeted him and said to him, 'Is your heart right, as my heart is with your heart? And Jehonadab answered, 'It is.' 'If it be,' said Jehu, 'give me your hand.' " When you meet another Jew, you wish him well, you give him a greeting of peace. "Is your heart at one with mine? Is your heart right as my heart is with your heart? And the answer was, yes, yes. And he said, "If that be so, lend me your hand."

Presidential Address

(RABBINICAL ASSEMBLY, 1982—ABSTRACT)

We are living in an era of great moral and religious uncertainty. We have been through similar periods in the past, particularly during the great depression, but never have religionists felt so direct a challenge to our moral system. The notion that religion will fade away in a secular age is disappearing. The myth of the death of religion has, in a sense, been dissipated by the reappearance in great force of fundamentalism. We have our share of fundamentalists in the Jewish community. The main-line churches are on the wane, fundamentalism and the cults are growing. Cults have grown because of the dilemma of a technological society. There is also a variety, ever-growing, of non-Western religious cults. If you have a car and want to travel three miles from this hotel, you will find there an Oriental cult filled mainly by Jewish young people.

There are new ideologies that are competing with religion, ideologies that direct modern technological society in the same manner as traditional religions unified older societies. In the West, scientific progress is the new religion, while in Communist societies it is the faith of the Marxist. We must ask ourselves in all candor how is it that traditional religion, which has the power of history or of historical experience and the continuity of the millennia behind it, no longer seems able to serve as the cohesive binding factor in our society?

For forty years I have been identified with Conservative Judaism. I have seen the tremendous growth of our common venture. Forty years means a long time. When the Bible says the land was quiet for forty years, it means it was peaceful for a goodly period of time. Most of my teachers were advanced in age when I entered the Seminary. Men like Professor Marx and Professor Ginzberg were men up in the seventies when I came to Morningside Heights. We are still privileged to have others of my teachers with us, though they are no longer on the active teaching roster. They are engaged in scholarship. I was thrilled to learn that the *aryeh sheb'havurah*, the lion of the group, Dr. Louis Finkelstein, will be issuing two volumes of his Sifra on Leviticus. This will be followed by two other additional volumes in about another year's time. May God bless him with *arikhut yamim.*

During this last year, three of my teachers retired: Professors H. L. Ginsberg, Robert Gordis, and Moses Zucker. We note that Dr. Gordis will celebrate the fiftieth anniversary of his ordination at our Seminary this coming June.

In the forties, when we were students, most of us were concerned with the fate of our people. The tremendous tragedy of the war years and the Holocaust unfolded before our eyes. I remember the announcement of D-Day on June 6, 1944. We asked ourselves the question: Would there be a Jewish people to serve? In 1946, after the war, some of us went to Europe to do our duty on behalf of our people. Mayer Abramowitz wrote a magnificent article in *Moment* dealing with the chaplaincy and the *Bricha.* I went to Palestine with my bride in 1946 to work there on different matters, but we were all concerned as to what would happen with the remnant that had to be saved. The state, which we hoped for, would arise.

The last forty years have been truly eventful years, marked by the emergence of the state of Israel, the dramatic changes in the United States, both racial and demographic, the entry of the Conservative movement into the World Zionist Organization. It was in this very hotel that the issue of Conservative Judaism and the World Zionist Organization was debated. Several of the debaters are present with us this morning.

Vast structural changes took place in American Jewish life. We have had changes of leadership. We have demonstrated over and over again that we are blessed with regeneration. We remember the words of the prophet Zechariah who said, "From your midst will come the cornerstone." The luminous administration of Dr. Finkelstein came to a close when he was succeeded in 1972 by Dr. Gerson Cohen. This year's convention marks the end of a full and fruitful decade of his dynamic leadership.

We are grateful for the continuing educational program, which took on formal structure during the last two years.

There has, unfortunately, been a tragic movement to the right in American political life. The world's economic problems have grown more difficult. At the same time, it is estimated that in our nation forty billion dollars will be cut from the voluntary government programs for the needy. You need but think of the psychological, physical, and social damage that is being done in depriving the weakest element of our community. We have been asked that the burden be maintained by our voluntary agencies, but this is nigh unto impossible.

These last forty years have marked a dramatic change in mood. We are concerned with *how to do* rather than *why to do. How to do* is important. Techniques have replaced the theological *why to do.* There are things that I miss in these last forty years. Yes, a lot of the ferment and the tension is gone. We have difficulties, but I miss the dynamic atmosphere of the intellectual controversy we had in prior years. The great debates have petered out. I recall with fond affection such personalities as Solomon Goldman, Billy Greenfield and, to differentiate between those who have gone on to their eternal reward, men like Aaron Blumenthal, David Aaronson, Israel Levinthal, and Professor Mordecai Kaplan. I recall how they stood toe-to-toe with Chancellor Finkelstein debating the program of the Seminary and the various directions that his administration had taken.

In our own country, the United States Supreme Court's jurisdiction is being threatened in three areas: school prayer, busing, and abortion. Right-wing elements want to get these three types of cases away from the jurisdiction of the U.S. Supreme Court and the federal court system. They are trying to move the jurisdiction of cases dealing with these issues from the federal courts to the state courts. If they work through the state courts, where there are local pressures upon them, the right wing hopes to get more favorable decisions. If they do not succeed in that approach, they hope to have the entire Constitution amended by a three-quarter vote of the states or special constitutional convention. Under their reading of Article 3, Section 2, there is the possibility of moving this country many degrees to the right.

The issue of prayer in the public schools was dealt with by our Supreme Court in 1962: "The constitutional prohibition against laws respecting an establishment of religion must at least mean that in this country it is no part of the business of government to compose official prayers for any group of the American people to recite as part of a religious program carried on by government. . . . Neither the fact that the prayer may be non-denominationally neutral or the fact that its observance on the part of the students is voluntary can serve to free it from the limitations of the Establishment Clause."

It is expected that President Reagan will propose a constitutional amendment permitting voluntary prayer in public schools. I regard this to be a dangerous infringement upon the First Amendment rights of all Americans.

In the last few decades, there have been impressive changes in the life of the Jewish family and in the activity of women.

Let us try to briefly flesh out the dramatic character of the changes. Last fall, more than half of our nation's college freshmen were women. In law school, they are about forty percent and in America's medical schools they number about one-third.

There is an increased number of women in our labor force. Plainly speaking, women may be divided into two groups: those who want to work and those who have to work. In recent years, a majority of America's women have joined the labor force. It is expected that within three years more than sixty-five percent of U.S. women will be engaged in gainful occupations. Debate rages as to whether or not it is possible to draw a balance between jobs and normal family life. Despite the strain that seems to exist, there is little evidence that women will return to home full time.

The reaction of women at work is varied. Some are delighted by the ability to express their personalities without being tied down to their homes. Others resent it. A recent study reported this dialogue: "Women like me go to work because we have to, there is no alternative but living poorer lives."

The impact upon the children of working mothers was capsulized in the dream of a little boy whose mother goes to work each day with her briefcase in hand. In his dream his mother had gone to work and had forgotten to take her briefcase. She had to come back home. He was later heard saying, "I hope that mommy will lose her briefcase." To him, the loss of the carrying case meant mother's return to the household.

In a nation where there are millions of working mothers, new health situations are developing. Being a working mother means that there has to be a coping with time pressures. Time pressures may mean reduced sleep. Reports have it that some childhood illnesses are on the rise, apparently because some parents do not have the time to take their youngsters for regular checkups. Doctors in emergency wards are seeing more children in the evening.

There has been a fantastic increase of women with young children under the age of six re-entering the labor market. America was accustomed to mothers of teenagers, college students, and empty nesters returning to work. The fact that there are tender children at home means that the community has to have proper day care centers. While some of them exist in our nation, most of them have to be upgraded. There are not enough child care centers doing a truly creative job with their young wards. We must concern ourselves with the psychological needs of young children whose mothers are absent during most of their waking hours.

Things are changing in America. A professor told me of a pregnant medical resident who had her affairs so arranged that she had induced labor on Friday so that she could return to rounds on Monday. This reminds me of Pearl S. Buck's heroine in *The Good Earth* who returned to the rice paddies a few hours after delivery.

Some women want to work, others have to work. Educated women, on the whole, are career-oriented. The more educated, the greater the desire to remain in purposeful work. Highly trained and greatly motivated, many women do not want to lose their skills during the early years of their youngster's childhood. If they do not return to full time work, they try to be satisfied with part-time jobs.

Women are not only re-entering the labor market, but more and more are returning to school. Many who had deferred career preparation to fulfill roles as mothers now outnumber men in their corresponding age groups. The desire to improve one's skills, the correlation between a good education and a good job has not gone unnoticed by women. As the average woman, whether single or married, has many years remaining of productive work, the desire to obtain a sound education looms larger and larger. As more women aspire to move up the career ladder, more are returning to college and additional education.

The economic factor is a critical one. An ad, widely reprinted by an insurance company, touched on the economic element: "Two of us . . . in a new age. The two-income family. Prices up. Interest down. That's why, as responsible parents, protection of our family income has become a major concern. Both of us count. What if something happened to either of us? Have we provided for each other? For our children?"

Many working women are the heads of a single-parent family. This situation may be due to divorce, death of a mate or the failure to marry. Statistics reveal that single-parent families are growing year by year. In 1964, one college student out of ten came from a one-parent family. Today, the ratio is one in five. The odds are not getting better. There seems to be a general increase in marital hypochondria. Summed up, there is the feeling that one's marriage should be re-evaluated like a car. If the marriage is not measuring up, trade it in. A demographer predicted that the divorce rate will eventually rise to one out of every two marriages.

Much more has to be done by the community for the single-parent family, both for the parent as well as for the children. The growth of the single-parent family is but a symptom. It is the tip of the iceberg, a reflection of the declining value placed upon the marriage and family life in American society.

How will these factors of more women at work, more single-parent families impact our way of life? Women at work affect not only their own well-being but also that of the community. The American way of life has been largely dependent upon volunteerism. Think of the den mother, the church worker, the political campaigner. The prestige of voluntary work has decreased. There has been a major revolution in the voluntary element of human experience. Why give hours and hours to a cause without pay if you can be working at a desk and earning added income for your family?

Volunteering was once an activity women did instead of real work. It was unpaid, often menial, and certainly undervalued. In political campaigns, women stuffed envelopes. In hospitals, they sometimes were allowed to perform minor nursing duties. With the advent of the women's movement and the heavy influx of women into the work force, there has been a change in the appreciation of voluntary work.

We must begin an in-depth examination of the changing character of our society and plan intelligently for its future. Much depends upon what we will do for the women and children of our community. There is a desperate need for a proliferation of child care centers. There is hardly a synagogue in the land that could not use a good child care center. We are delighted that our colleague, Rabbi Shlomo Levine, has published an impressive study on this subject and a guide for future activity. We must hear the cry of those who turn to us for help. Frequently they are victims of circumstances beyond control.

The R.A. is not a matter of dollars and cents, it is a high cause. The R.A. is a religious community. The feeling of community is one that we must strengthen. We are a professional organization, but we are more than that, we are an association of deep and abiding friendship. We must learn to stop fighting merely to score a few political points. We must have the ability to call to each other, to reach out both in times of sickness and adversity, in times of good health and prosperity, in times of difficulties and problems.

You all remember the retelling by Elie Wiesel of the story of the Gerrer Rebbe and the Chasid. When the rebbe asked the Chasid how Moshe was getting along, he answered, "I don't know." The rebbe responded, "You pray under the same roof, you study the same text, you serve the same God, and yet you do not know whether Moshe is in good health, whether he needs help or advice or comforting." The R.A. will truly be an assembly banded together for the sake of Heaven when we learn to share and to really care. Not to talk about our concern, but really be involved.

These are not limp phrases, these are cries of the heart. I have before me a number of past presidents of our assembly, who, during their administration, knew what it meant to receive calls during the night and early in the morning, who heard the sighs and the anguish expressed verbally or by mail. The idea of community is vital. The breakdown of community has occurred throughout our society. While there are those who hail the secular city, others are concerned that with the release from the linkage of family, faith, and friends we face destructive times. Our cities are in shambles, people dread to walk the streets at night. As one observer expressed it, and he took the phrase from Hobbes, "Fragmentation of community produces a war of all against all."

In the course of my rabbinate, I experienced loneliness. I saw what happens when every element of community is weakened. There is a sense of isolation in every human heart when there is no community to give us strength. The paradox is that the more unbound individuals there are, the greater are the pangs of loneliness. We live in a terribly lonely society. A pollster once told the story that the greatest act of loving kindness that you can do is to walk up to someone's door, ring the bell, and ask some questions and say, "Talk, we want to hear you out." No person is alone when he seeks and wins and receives the fellowship of other human beings.

Yankelovitch, in his *New Rules*, talks of the high cost of what happens when we destroy the resting places of the human spirit. Gone are the symbols of community yesteryear. It was heartbreaking to see the emotionally charged response to the demolition of some old theaters in Times Square in New York. In our highly technological society, we purchase our economic well-being at a great human cost, a chief symptom of which is the destruction of the community.

Yankelovitch writes about the meaning of community. I think each one of us can fit into his words: "The idea of community is precious to people, the idea of community invokes in the individual a feeling that here is where I belong, these are my people. I care for them, they care for me, I am part of them. I know what they expect from me and I from them. They are my concerns. I know this place, I am on familiar ground, I am at home."

When the R.A. will be able to think and to act in this spirit as a religious community, we will be carrying out our historic cause, we will become a true community, unselfishly concerned with each other's tasks and needs, and rejoicing and friendship will be freely expressed.

Just two weeks ago, we read in the Torah portion of *Shemini* concerning the dedication of the Sanctuary (Leviticus 9:5). When the community learns to become closer to one another, then you stand before the Lord. But when you act otherwise, a revocalization of the text can mean, "when you sacrifice one another." A decision has to be made as to whether we are going to sacrifice one another or draw closer to one another, to throw barbs at one another or be a true *havruta*. Remember the dictum: either fellowship or death.

Before we conclude our service with the *Aleinu* on shabbat, we read a text from Psalms. As I went through the last few months, the text became more vivid and stronger; its letters seemed to jump out at me from the printed page. "For the sake of my brothers and my friends, I will seek peace concerning you." Only when we have peace between brothers can we experience *malkhut shamayim*.

On September 1, 1939, the Second World War broke out. W. H. Auden wrote words which he included in some editions and deleted in others: "We must love one another or die." The Rabbinical Assembly will have to learn to live with one another, live in harmony and peace.

Religious Freedom and the Constitution

(*CONSERVATIVE JUDAISM,* SPRING–SUMMER, 1963)

The American Constitution is one of the greatest products of the human mind. When William Gladstone, the prime minister of Great Britain, reflected on its one hundredth anniversary, he wrote: "I have always regarded that Constitution as the most remarkable work known to me in modern times to have been produced by the human intellect . . . in its application to political affairs."

The American Constitution was a revolutionary document. As Jews and as members of a minority people, we are grateful for what it has meant to all minorities. Together with all Americans, we are beneficiaries of the American doctrine of non-interference of the state in religious matters.

The incorporation of Article Six into the Constitution, providing that no religious test should be required of "the holder of any office or public trust in the United States," represented a radical change in the status of the Jew. At the time of the Constitutional Convention, Jonas Phillips, a Philadelphia Jew, wrote to that body, concerned that the document might not provide for religious equality. He pointed out that the Pennsylvania Constitution, which had been adopted in 1776, required a person to take an oath that "I believe in one God . . . and I do acknowledge the Scripture of the Old and New Testament to be given by Divine inspiration."[1] Phillips did not know that, two weeks earlier, at a closed meeting of the Constitutional Convention, a no-religious-oath article had been incorporated. Incidentally, the new Pennsylvania Constitution, adopted in 1796, removed this disability against Jews.[2]

It must be observed that in the mother country, Great Britain, a democratic land, the requirement of a religious oath for those holding public office was not abolished until 1858. At that time, after a long battle, a Jew was permitted to sit in the House of Commons. In Britain, the entire body of medieval legislation that reduced the Jew to the position of a yellow-badged outcast remained on the statute books, though remembered only by antiquarians. As late as 1818 it was possible to suggest in the courts Lord Coke's bias that "Jews were, in law, perpetual enemies; for between them, as with the devil, whose subjects they are, and the Christians, there can be no peace."

Universities were also closed to Jews (though the University of Edinburgh graduated a Jewish physician as early as 1779). At Oxford, well into the nineteenth century, Jews had to take a Christian oath upon matriculation, and thus were excluded at the outset. In Cambridge, Jews could not graduate unless they would make a similar statutory declaration. It was only in 1871 that the University Test Act opened the universities to all people, including Jews, on equal terms.[3]

Although the parliamentary act of 1740 allowed Jews to become citizens in the British colonies after seven years of residence, Rhode Island refused to naturalize Aaron Lopez in 1762. Ezra Stiles, the president of Yale College and a great lover of the Hebrew language, recorded his belief that Jews would never become citizens.[4] Lopez went to Massachusetts, where he was accepted. All of the colonies, with the exception of Rhode Island, maintained restrictions against Catholics as well as Jews.

Even after the Constitution was adopted, Jews labored under disabilities in those several states whose constitutions antedated the Federal Constitution. In 1809, Jacob Henry was elected to the House of Commons in North Carolina. Since, for religious reasons, he could not affirm the "Divine authority of the New Testament," his right to his seat was challenged by a fellow legislator who claimed that "Henry denied the Divine authority of the New Testament and refused to take the oath prescribed by law for his qualification."[4] Henry spoke briefly to the legislature, delivering one of the great gems of American oratory. He was seated.[5]

Connecticut and Massachusetts maintained forms of establishment into the nineteenth century. In Connecticut, religious liberty did not win out until 1818. New Hampshire maintained the word "Christian" in the state bill of rights until 1902. The expression was dropped only in 1912.[6] A similar struggle went on in

Maryland, where a debate raged until Jewish disabilities were removed in 1828. North Carolina removed them in 1868.

The First Amendment of our Constitution states that "Congress shall make no law respecting the establishment of religion or prohibiting the free exercise thereof, or abridging the freedom of speech or of the press; or of the right of the people peaceably to assemble and to petition the government for a redress of grievances." On this amendment, Anson Phelps Stokes has commented, "These rights are interrelated. They are all of importance from the standpoint of the Churches. Freedom of speech is related to preaching; freedom of the press to religious journalism; freedom of assembly and petition to Church meetings."[7]

Even after the amendment's ratification, established churches remained as such in the South. Some interpreters claim that the amendment was intended to limit the powers of Congress and to protect the local established churches from Congressional interference. The courts have held that the First Amendment binds the states no less than the Federal Government.[8]

Jews welcomed the First Amendment as a broad, creative American invention. They had suffered an unhappy history with established churches in Europe. The American Constitution was permitting religion to function as the free choice of free people. The prophetic insistence that religion is the constant critic of humanity's efforts could operate most freely in American society. The church was not to be wedded to the state, indebted to the government for its support, or dependent upon the sufferance of political authorities. (To this very day, the Anglican Church must use a prayerbook that is approved by the English Parliament, members of which include Catholics and Jews as well as nonbelievers.)

Justice Black, writing the majority opinion in the New York State Prayer Case, spoke of the maintenance of the integrity of religion:

> The Establishment Clause, unlike the Free Exercise Clause, does not depend upon any showing of direct governmental compulsion and is violated by the enactment of laws which establish an official religion whether those laws operate directly to coerce non-observing individuals or not. This is not to say, of course, that laws officially prescribing a particular

form of religious worship do not involve coercion of such individuals. When the power, prestige and financial support of government is placed behind a particular religious belief, the indirect coercive pressure upon religious minorities to conform to the prevailing officially approved religion is plain. But the purposes underlying the Establishment Clause go much further than that.

Its first and most immediate purpose rested on the belief that a union of government and religion tends to destroy government and to degrade religion. . . . The Establishment Clause thus stands as an expression of principle on the part of the Founders of our Constitution that religion is too personal, too sacred, too holy, to permit its 'unhallowed perversion' by a civil magistrate.[9]

The roots of Justice Black's sentiments may well be traced back to the first confession of faith of the English Baptist Church (1611), organized not in its mother country but in Dutch exile: "The magistrate is not to meddle with religion, or matters of conscience, nor to compel men to this or that form of religion."[10]

During the Pennsylvania Bible Case hearing before the United States Supreme Court, Justice Black is reported to have said that the most creative and fruitful periods of Christianity were in eras when religion had not received the support of the state and, conversely, the worst, most corrupt periods of Christianity were those in which religion had become enmeshed with politics and politicians.

From the lives, letters, and pronouncements of the Founding Fathers it is clear that the United States was conceived of as a secular state, which is not to be confused with a secular society. In a democratic community there is a fundamental difference between the state and society; a society can be religious even though the state itself is nonreligious. Only in a totalitarian community are state and society identical; all activities, therefore, including religious ones, are within the province of the totalitarian state.[11]

J. Coert Rylaarsdam, an eminent Protestant Bible scholar, made the following perceptive observation at a recent Protestant-Jewish dialogue at the University of Chicago: "Ever since the era of Napoleon there have been meetings such as this, meetings in which Jewish citizens and Christian citizens met for the common good on a platform provided by neither Judaism nor Christianity but by an emancipated or secular cultural order that claimed the attention of both on its own terms. Jew and Christian were, in effect, asked to leave their respective platforms and work together on this third so-called 'neutral' platform provided by neither."

We cannot subscribe to the notion advanced by Dean Erwin Griswold in a recent address:

> Is it not clear, as a matter of historic fact, that this was a Christian nation? . . . It is true that we were a rather remarkable Christian nation, having, for various historical and philosophical reasons, developed a tolerance in matters of religion, which was at once virtually unique and a tribute to the men of the 17th and 18th centuries who helped develop the type of thought which came to prevail here . . . but to say that they required that all trace of religion be kept out of public activity is sheer invention.[12]

Griswold went on to speak of America as being a "community of religious tolerance." His position is based on the assumption that the Christian majority should be able to maintain the Christian character of the culture, and that minorities ought to learn tolerance.[13] The Bill of Rights, however, is a document bespeaking, not tolerance, but equal freedom for all, including minorities.

Is America a Christian country? This question has been a source of discussion since 1892, when Justice David J. Brewer, in rendering a decision of the Supreme Court in the case of the Church of the Holy Trinity against the United States, indulged in the remark that "This is a Christian nation."[14] Louis Marshall, who was the president of Temple Emanuel in New York City and chairman of the board of the Jewish Theological Seminary of America, writing on this issue at that time, traced the struggle for religious freedom in this country. He pointed out that, "In the convention which framed the Federal Constitution, although its deliberations lasted for months, no prayer was uttered."[15] Our great national instrument, the Constitution, has no reference to God. When our first president negotiated a treaty with Tripoli, the 11th article of that instrument stated, "As the Government of the

United States of America is not in any sense founded on the Christian religion, as it has in itself no character of enmity against the laws, religion or tranquility of Mussulman . . . it is declared by the parties that no pretext arising from the religious opinions shall ever produce an interruption of harmony existing between the two nations."[15a]

Dr. Franklin H. Littell of the Chicago Theological Seminary has recently written:

There is a wide-spread misapprehension that America has been, and still is, a Christian nation. . . . Contrary to the reactionary legend of the Nativists, the generation of the Founding Fathers was not the heyday of true religion and simple virtue—from which high level degenerate sons and daughters have been steadily falling away. The legend is a white Protestant construct, and it is heart and core of the vicious assault of the Radical Right upon our present national leadership and—more fundamentally—upon our Constitution and upon those agencies entrusted with interpreting it and enforcing it.[15b]

Jews are zealous for the maintenance of the principle of separation of church and state—but not because we have placed ourselves on the side of the secularist or in the camp of the atheists.[16] We do not completely appreciate the tenor and character of the editorial in *America*, "To Our Jewish Friends," September, 1962, pp. 665 f. That the publication *America* seems bound to identify Jews with secularists can be seen in a recent issue.[17] William B. Ball, Executive Director and General Counsel of the Pennsylvania Catholic Welfare Committee, writing on "Religion in Education: A Basis for Consensus," stated: "In the courts, major Jewish and secularist groups are waging an ardent battle to remove religious practices from public school life." To be sure, we must record and accept at face value the Catholic position on church-state relations most recently articulated by Archbishop Egidio Vagnozzi, Apostolic Delegate to the United States, in an address at Loyola University, Chicago, on March 18, 1960:

In practice, the Church will not interfere, and has not interfered, in local situations where the separation between

Church and State may be considered the greater and more general good.

In considering freedom as applied to religious belief and worship, it is well to remind ourselves that the very concept of complete separation between Church and State is a relatively modern idea. Even some of the largest Protestant denominations were born out of a stricter and more nationalistic interpretation of a close relationship between religion and the civil power.

In the practical field of relations with civil powers, the Catholic Church shows, with reciprocal international agreements called Concordats, a considerable variety of provisions in particular questions, depending on local traditions, customs and practices. In fact, it is extremely difficult to define the neat line of demarcation between the domain of the Church and of the State. Actually, even in some traditionally and predominantly Catholic countries, no preferential juridicial recognition is granted to the Catholic Church.

As far as the United States is concerned, I feel that it is a true interpretation of the feelings of the Hierarchy and of American Catholics in general to say that they are well satisfied with their Constitution and pleased with the fundamental freedom enjoyed by their Church; in fact, they believe that this freedom is to a large extent responsible for the expansion and consolidation of the Church in this great country.

Whether they remain a minority or become a majority, I am sure that American Catholics will not jeopardize their cherished religious freedom in exchange for a privileged position.[18]

The first Catholic Bishop in this land, John Carroll, accepted the emerging pattern of a pluralistic society.[18a]

We are a deeply religious people; yet we feel that the integrity of religion, the maintenance of the prophetic voice, is best realized when it is not tied to the state. William E. Hocking once said, "Religion is never political in its nature." Have you ever considered how it is that the Hasmoneans, who were so greatly beloved by our people and so highly regarded for their bravery, ended their careers in so dreadful a fashion? They grew to be hated by their people and were glossed over by our tradition. Most of the references that we have to the Hanukkah story and the activity of the Hasmoneans are contained in works that are outside the Bible. Only a few centuries after the events leading to Hanukkah, a rabbi asked, "What is Hanukkah?"

Perhaps the answer to these questions can be found in the very nature of the structure of ancient Jewish society. Since the establishment of the monarchy in the days of Saul, David, and Solomon, there had existed a clear and sharply defined division of responsibility between the religious leaders of the people—the priests who conducted the Temple worship—and the kings who possessed political power.

Dr. Abraham J. Heschel, in his recent study *The Prophets*, has a passage dealing with "The Separation of Powers." He points out that the kings of Egypt, Assyria, and Phoenicia, Israel's closest neighbors, possessed priestly authority and functioned as priests. This combination of the royal and priestly functions in one person was common to early society. Even in advanced Rome, the ruler was both king and priest. Among our people, the king was not a priest. To be sure, some kings did attempt to take unto themselves priestly prerogatives. For this they were condemned by people and prophet.

After the Davidic line lost its political power, the priests never arrogated to themselves the dual crown of kingship and priesthood. The early Hasmoneans, who were of priestly stock, at first sought only to win back Israel's religious freedom. They struggled primarily to establish the right of the Jew to worship God.

Upon ascent to power, some Hasmoneans hailed and applauded for their military triumphs felt that they could take unto themselves the title of king. This fusion of political and religious power in one individual was disastrous, for it became a temptation to convert others by force rather than by example.

Writing on the nature of prayer and the results of prayer in a coerced routine, a prominent Protestant averred:

The formulators of the First Amendment were not indifferent to religion. The principle of separation of church and state was not worked out solely to keep denominations out of each other's hair, as present critics of the Supreme Court seem to imply. Basically, the First Amendment was adopted because the Founding Fathers believed that religion flourished best when it is the responsibility of the church and the home—when it is voluntary rather than dependent on the coercive power of the state. At the time the U.S. Constitution was being formulated delegates to several church assemblies—Baptist conventions in Rhode Island and New Jersey, for example—went on record to declare that only voluntary religious activity is really significant in the sight of God.[19]

In terms of the general welfare, Lord Bryce, an observer of American life said:

It is accepted as an axiom by all Americans that the civil powers ought to be not only neutral and impartial as between different forms of faith, but ought to leave these matters entirely on one side, regarding them no more than it regards the artistic or literary pursuits of the citizen.[20]

Two diverse stands of rationalization are present in developing the doctrine of separation of church and state. For Roger Williams it was needed to keep the state from imposing on religion. For Thomas Jefferson it was justified because of the necessity to prevent religion from imposing on the state.[21]

Some religionists are concerned with the superficial character of religion in this country. The would-be religiosity of some of our nation is sharply criticized in Peter L. Berger's *The Noise of Solemn Assemblies.* He observes that "Swedish democracy has not suffered from the prevalence of secularism, and Portuguese democracy has not derived much from the prevailing religiosity."[22] Let us not confuse religious forms with the spirit of religion. If religion in America is faced with the peril of secularism, will it be saved by a "recitation religion"?

Those who are anxious to establish a more formal religious tone in our nation ought to be mindful of the introduction of the following measure to the 87th Congress by Representative Eugene Siler, 8th District, Kentucky:

Section 1. This Nation devoutly recognizes the authority and law of Jesus Christ, Saviour and Ruler of Nations, through whom are bestowed the blessings of Almighty God.
Section 2. This amendment shall not be interpreted so as to

result in the establishment of any particular ecclesiastical organization or in the abridgment of the rights of religious freedom, or freedom of speech or press or of peaceful assemblage.

Section 3. Congress shall have power in such cases as it may deem proper to provide a suitable oath or affirmation for citizens whose religious scruples prevent them from giving unqualified allegiance to the Constitution as herein amended.[23]

Such a provision, added to our Constitution, would make our Supreme Court the ultimate decider of Christian doctrine. Those who are motivated by personal religious reasons and theological insights to change the interpretation of the Constitution of the United States ought to recognize what Justice Brandeis once observed: "We must ever be on guard lest we erect our prejudices into legal principles." His observation was in the spirit of Justice Frankfurter in the 2nd Flag Salute Case:

One who belongs to the most vilified and persecuted minority in history is not likely to be insensible to the freedoms guaranteed by our Constitution. Were my purely personal attitude relevant, I should wholeheartedly associate myself with the general libertarian view in the Court's opinion, representing as they do the thought and action of a lifetime. But as judges we are neither Jew nor Gentile, neither Catholic nor agnostic. We owe equal attachment to the Constitution and are equally bound by our judicial obligations whether we derive our citizenship from the earliest or the latest immigrants to these shores. As a member of the Court I am not justified in writing my private notions of policy into the Constitution, no matter how deeply I may cherish them or how mischievous I may deem their disregard. . . . It can never be emphasized too much that one's own opinion about the wisdom or evil of a law should be excluded altogether when one is doing one's duty on the bench.

Since the New York State Prayer Case last June, the atmosphere in the area of religion in the public schools has been supercharged. The United States Supreme Court has two cases dealing with religion in the schools under consideration (as of June,

1936).[23a] One is a case from Baltimore, Maryland, involving the requirement to read from the Bible and to recite the Lord's Prayer. The second is a Pennsylvania case concerning the requirement to read the Bible every morning at the beginning of class sessions.

The public schools have a difficult task. One distinguished observer wrote a decade ago:

> As to public schools, the problem of neutrality may be stated as a problem of keeping the schools secular (*i.e.*, ruling out any attempt to inculcate religious belief) and yet avoiding inculcation of secularism (*i.e., a philosophy of life which leaves no place for religion*). Such neutrality is not easy to achieve.
>
> Except in the released time and flag salute cases, the Supreme Court has not yet been required to decide questions concerning public school programs. The problem of Bible reading was recently before the Court, but the case was dismissed without decision. *Devotional exercises in public schools, however, simple and nonsectarian, are difficult to reconcile with a rule of neutrality.* Such exercises present a problem quite different from that presented by incidental inclusion of religious material in literary and social studies. Occasionally, advocates of strict church-state separation demand careful exclusion of all references to religion. Handling of such material on a basis of neutrality may not always be easy, but consistently to exclude it is to abandon neutrality at the outset.[24]

"Nonsectarian prayers," composed by state authorities, have generally been regarded by the Supreme Court as "establishment." In November of 1961, the New York State Board of Regents adopted the prayer, "Almighty God, we acknowledge our dependence upon Thee, and we beg Thy blessings upon us, our parents, our teachers and our country." It was opposed by most Jews and some Protestants.

It should be remembered that much of the pressure against the recitation of prayers in the public schools historically comes from Catholic sources.

The issue of prayer in the public schools focuses now about the recitation of the Lord's Prayer. Dean Pike, who was upset after the

New York Prayer Case decision, declared that the Supreme Court had "deconsecrated the Nation" and that this decision led to the "secularization of public life." Testifying before a congressional committee, he said:

> Now something broader, like the Lord's Prayer which is used in many schools now, and which, by the way, is a very Jewish prayer in its concepts—as well as Christian—presents nothing sectarian in the sense that you can call Christianity a sect. The policy again is another matter. I would not think it would be the establishment of a church any more than the reading from the Bible because none of us have a monopoly on the Bible and the Lord's Prayer.[25]

During the hearing of the Baltimore, Maryland, Prayer Case at the United States Supreme Court, the city solicitor of Baltimore, Francis Burch, argued that the use of the Lord's Prayer does not constitute religious establishment, that its purpose is to have a disciplinary, moral, and ethical impact. He felt that its religious connotations are incidental and secondary. It is reported that he said, "The dominant purpose and effect of these exercises is not to aid or foster a religion, or religiousness in general, but rather to utilize these works which have transcended their religious origins, so as to inculcate moral and ethical precepts of a sobering and inspirational nature. The public school does not aid religion here." Justice Stewart queried, "If the purpose of the Lord's Prayer is to quiet the children down at the beginning of the day, why not give them tranquilizers?"

This is an old argument. In an earlier case, the assertion was made that the prayer's purpose is "to prepare the children for their work to quiet them from the outside."[26] One suggestion that has been advanced is "to have each school day commence with a quiet moment that would still the tumult of the playground and start a day of study.[27]

A spokesman for Reform Judaism declared before a Congressional hearing:

> We, therefore, feel constrained to state that under no circumstances would Jews ever consider the Lord's Prayer to be any but a Christian prayer. Whereas it is true that the ideas and the words are taken from Jewish tradition, nevertheless the

form in which it is recited, the status attached to it and the associations it recalls are part of the Christian and not the Jewish tradition. The very title is Christian, "the Lord's" referring to Jesus and not to God as Jews conceive Him.[28]

The Lord's Prayer ought not to be recited by Jewish children. The latest statement of the Synagogue Council of America, I believe, represents the normative Jewish position:

It has come to the attention of the Synagogue Council of America that recitation in the public schools of the prayer known as the "Lord's Prayer" is frequently justified on the grounds that this prayer is nonsectarian.

The Synagogue Council of America believes that it does not rest with any public official to determine what is in consonance with the theology of Judaism or any other religion by determining whether a prayer is sectarian or non-sectarian. The First Amendment to the Constitution of the United States leaves to the individual and religious associations the right to determine the nature of religious beliefs and practices.

The prayer is taken from the New Testament, the basic source of Christianity. The designation "Lord" used in the title refers to Jesus, whom Christians regard as "Lord." Eminent Christian authorities, both Catholics and Protestant, insist on the distinctively and uniquely Christian character of this prayer.

Accordingly, this prayer is of a sectarian nature and should not be recited by Jews. Requiring students in the public schools to recite this prayer is an infringement on freedom of religion and conscience.[29]

In 1910, the high courts of Illinois had to decide on a Catholic objection to the recitation of the Lord's Prayer in the public schools of that state. In its context, the prayer represents Jews in a most unfavorable light. In the Illinois prayer case, the court had this to say:

It is true that this is a Christian State. The great majority of its people adhere to the Christian religion. No doubt this is a

Protestant State. The majority of its people adhere to one or another of the Protestant denominations. But the law knows no distinction between the Christian and the Pagan, the Protestant and the Catholic. All are citizens. Their civil rights are precisely equal. The law cannot see religious differences, because the constitution has definitely and completely excluded religion from the law's contemplation in considering man's rights. There can be no distinction based on religion. The State is not, and under our constitution cannot be, a teacher of religion. All sects, religious or even anti-religious, stand on equal footing. They have the same rights of citizenship, without discrimination. The public school is supported by the taxes, which each citizen, regardless of his religion or his lack of it, is compelled to pay. The school, like the government, is simply a civil institution. It is secular and not religious in its purposes. . . . The truths of religions . . . do not come within the province of the public school. No one denies their importance. No one denies that they should be taught to the youth of the State. The constitution and the law do not interfere with such teaching, but they do banish theological polemics from the schools and the school districts. This is done not from any hostility to religion, but because it is no part of the duty of the State to teach religion. . . . The exclusion of a pupil from this part of the school exercises in which the rest of the school joins, separates him from his fellows, puts him in a class by himself, deprives him of his equity with other pupils, subjects him to a religious stigma and places him at a disadvantage in the school, which the law never contemplated. All this because of his religious belief. If the instruction of exercise is such that certain pupils must be excused from it because it is hostile to their parents' religious belief, then such instruction or exercise is sectarian and forbidden by the constitution.[30]

In a public school, the principle of nonparticipation is illusory and creates a feeling of being apart. Voluntariness, Jesse Choper explains, is a concept, not merely a word, "Compulsion which comes from circumstances can be as real as compulsion which comes from a command."[31] Let us consider the situation of a Jewish child, when he is excused from attendance. It would be best to listen to the impressions of a British mother.

"Tell them that Jesus was a Jew," I said to my young daughter.

"Oh, I couldn't do that; it would be rude," she replied. "And besides they wouldn't believe me!"

I felt too emotionally involved to deal with the situation adequately—to restore the confidence of a seven-year-old whose faith in human nature had been rudely shaken. I remember my first realization that I was different—and the punishment meted out to me because of this.

At my first day at a girls' high school I went into prayers. Everybody went into the main hall and I followed. I read the unaccustomed passages, listened to the hymns I did not know, and knelt to pray with the others.

Later, a nice little girl with long pigtails returned to the form room with me and bagged the desk next to mine. "We'll be friends forever," she said solemnly and I, feeling strange and lost amid new surroundings, thankfully agreed and thought perhaps this new school wasn't going to be so bad after all.

"I've got a friend and I went into Christian prayers," I told my mother that evening. She told me that Jewish girls were excused from school Prayers and were allowed to sit in the classroom and read the Old Testament. As I had been feeling rather worried (I had always realized we prayed to God but not to Christ) about partaking in Christian prayer, I was relieved.

Immediately after prayers, Angela dashed into the form room, slid into her desk and gasped: "I looked for you all over at Prayers and couldn't find you—where on earth have you been?" Quite uninhibited then, I replied, "Oh, I shan't be going into Prayers—I am Jewish—you see we—" Without a word she rose, moved her books and sachel and went to set elsewhere. No one else came to sit at the empty desk.

Now 30 years later, my young daughter is telling me: "They've been saying things to me" and although the "things" were irrelevant and stupid, they hurt.

Many of my friends who live away from Jewish communities prefer their children to attend Christian prayers. As one of them put it to me: "I suffered so much in my own youth, I am determined my daughter won't have the same experiences."

As one would expect, I am strongly against Prayers in State

schools. They do not instill tolerance and kindness to one's neighbour, surely the essence of Christianity. They are just a formula for some and a punishment for others who happen to worship differently.[32]

Choper relates that "Religious educators have warned 'that so-called voluntary exemption (from religious observances) does not overcome the compulsion exerted by majority behavior.' "[33]

At the time of the prayer case, it should be observed, no religious group was in complete unanimity as to the wisdom of the decision. The preponderance of Catholics were opposed to it; the Protestant group was divided; the Jewish leaders, on the whole, accepted the decision, though there were some isolated voices that regretted it.

In terms of other religious observances in the public schools, there has been a continuous struggle within the framework of the schools to eliminate practices that are offensive to any segment. This has been true of all groups. The Catholic community has reacted to the fact that "The public school system, as it first developed and as it has continued in some parts of the country to this day was essentially a Protestant school system, and it is not surprising that despite the Protestant emphasis on separation of church and state, the reading of the King James version of the Bible as a devotional exercise was not uncommonly an accepted part of the public school program. And the idea that no public fund should go to support competing schools, notably parochial or religious schools, has revealed another distinctive aspect of Protestant thinking."[34]

The American parochial school is indigenous to the United States.[35] It was a reaction to the Protestant-dominated public schools.

As early as 1831, Bishop John Hughes attacked the public school system as using public money for sectarian education that forced Catholic students into compulsory Protestant Bible reading, services, and textbooks. Public school texts at that time contained anti-Catholic legends and catch-phrases.[35a]

In 1843, Jews whose children attended the public schools got together with Catholics and Universalists in New York to protest the sectarian nature of the textbooks. The city authorities pointed out that the "Christian religion is in fact the prevailing religion of this State," and consequently the attempt to bring about the exclusion "from our Common Schools all books which inculcate the principles of the Christian religions, or else deprive such Schools of all participation in public money . . . (is) a most extraordinary and untenable position." Moreover, "The Jews have not . . . and . . . cannot have the same privileges as those who embrace the Christian content in the textbooks used in the public schools." Nor was the Board impressed by the argument that Jews should not be taxed for the support of schools in which the Christian religion is taught, since "these institutions were established before they came," the majority of people having insisted on them, and "it would therefore be absurd and unreasonable that they should be changed to suit the peculiar views of a sect" that is a minority.[36]

How, then, shall we deal with religion and religious values in the public school curriculum? How may public schools cooperate with religious groups in religious education? Various proposals have been made. Thirteen years ago, I reviewed in a more complete fashion the approaches toward the question of how the public schools may cooperate with historical religions in bringing religious education to its pupils.[36a]

One of the suggestions is released time, in which the public school is a cooperating or joint agency in religious education. This approach was first developed in Gary, Indiana, in 1914. Our Supreme Court has dealt with released time in both the McCollum and Zorach cases. The court has ruled the public schools can allow released time arrangements only if the instruction is given outside the school. Although this has been ruled to be constitutional, there are many in the Jewish community who are deeply concerned that released time is divisive.[36b] In the McCollum decision, Justice Frankfurter wrote:

The fact that this power has not been used to discriminate is beside the point. Separation is a requirement to abstain from fusing functions of Government and religious sects, not merely to treat them all equally. That a child is offered an alternative may reduce the constraint; it does not eliminate the operation of influence by the school in matters sacred to the conscience and outside the school's domain. The law of limitation operates, and non-conformity is not an outstanding characteristic of children. The result is an obvious pressure upon the children to attend. . . . The children belonging to these non-participating sects will thus have inculcated in them a feeling of separatism when the school should be the training ground for habits of community, or they will have religious instruction in a faith which is not that of their parents. As a result, the public school system of Champaign actively furthers inculcation of the religious tenets of some faiths, and in the process sharpens the consciousness of religious differences at least among some of the children committed to its care. These are consequences not amenable to statistics. But they are precisely the consequences against which the Constitution was directed when it prohibited the Government common to all from becoming embroiled, however innocently, in the destructive religious conflicts of which the history of even this country reports some dark pages.[36c]

There are those who believe that religion should be taught directly in the schools, arguing that the separation of church and state does not imply a separation of religion and state. Some have suggested the direct teaching of the Bible revered by all followers of the Judeo-Christian tradition.

We know that in some states the Bible can be read without comment, but in most states this action is unconstitutional. It is interesting to note that in the Kentucky courts it was ruled that the King James edition or any other edition of the Bible is not a sectarian book.[37] The argument as to whether or not the Bible is nonsectarian was involved in the original hearing of the Schempp case before the Federal Court (Eastern District) of Pennsylvania. Dean Weigle stated that the Bible was nonsectarian. Dr. Solomon Grayzel, the Jewish expert witness, contrasted the Jewish Holy Scriptures and the Christian Holy Bible. I cannot subscribe to Weigle's point of view, knowing only too well that each translation is deeply rooted in the theology of the translators. The last verse of the second Psalm which, in the light of Jewish opinion, states "Do homage in purity," has been translated by Christian commentators as "Kiss the Son."

The reading of the Bible without comment has often been suggested. This argument ignores the fact that to some sects, "the reading in public of any portion of the Scriptures unaccompanied by authoritative comment or explanation, or the reading of it, privately by persons not commissioned by the church to do so, is objectionable, and an offense to the religious feelings."[38]

The introduction of Bible study into the public school systems may well turn the present educational unity into a sectarian divisiveness.

There are those who have proposed a common core, which would be agreed upon by the interpreters of different faiths. One of the difficulties of the common core is that religion in general is nothing if it is not embodied in some specific tradition or body of practices.[39] Seymour Siegel has said, "Religion in general is like love in general; you can sing about it, write about it, but never be satisfied with it."

The American Council on Education noted some time ago:

The notion of a "common core" suggests a watering down of the several faiths to the point where common essentials appear. This might easily lead to a new sect—a public school sect—which would take its place alongside the existing faiths and compete with them.

The Bible is precious to us. Yet we regard distribution of Bibles by proselytizing organizations like the Gideon Society as, unfortunately, intrusion into the public school system.

It would appear the channels of cooperation between the public school systems and organized religion can be retained without violating the principle of the separation of church and state. Justice Douglas wrote in the Zorach case:

We are a religious people whose institutions presuppose a Supreme Being. . . . When the state encourages religious instruction or cooperates with religious authorities by adjusting the schedule of public events to sectarian needs, it follows the best of our traditions. For it then respects the religious nature of our people and accommodates the public service to their spiritual needs.[40]

The freedom to run nonpublic schools has been established by the courts since the well-known Pierce case in Oregon. Oregon had enacted a statute that would have outlawed parochial and private schools. This was declared unconstitutional. It is well to recall the role of the American Jewish Committee, through its counsel Louis Marshall, in becoming an *amicus curiae* on behalf of the appellees in *Pierce v. Society of Sisters* (1925).

The question of state aid to parochial schools has gone beyond fringe benefits. Free transportation, secular textbooks, and school lunches have been accepted as being "constitutional."[40a] The substance of the argument of those who want direct aid for nonpublic schools rests upon a difference in interpretation of the First Amendment. Does it mean that the state can support no religion? Or that it may support all religions if there is no discrimination and each religion is treated equally?

Current literature is filled with articles interpreting the First Amendment. Some maintain that the First Amendment, as composed by the Founding Fathers, intended only that there be a bar to the establishment of a national church of any single denomination. This would be the limit of the First Amendment and would permit the government to be free to aid and cooperate with all religious groups, provided it treated all religious groups equally.

Philip Kurland advanced the position that aid to parochial education is not unconstitutional. However, he went on to explain that he accepts the thesis of Justices Brandeis and Frankfurter that "The standard of what is desirable is different from what is Constitutional." Speaking at Anshe Emet Synagogue (March, 1962), he said, "As a legislator, I should vote against aid for parochial schools, for I think parochial schools an unmitigated evil." Despite his personal values, if called to rule on this matter, he would have to "sustain the validity of a non-discriminatory grant of aid to religious schools."

Kurland's position, which was given wide publicity when first published in the University of Chicago Law Review, is based upon his analysis that there is a single, unifying doctrine for the meaning of the religious clauses of the First Amendment. These provisions of the Constitution—the separation and toleration clauses—he reads together. It is his interpretation that the government cannot utilize religion as a standard for action or inaction; together they prohibit classifications in terms of religion either to confer or deny a benefit or to impose or relax a burden.[41]

On some differing views on the First Amendment, one must refer to the writings of Wilbur Katz, who delivered the 1963 Julius

Rosenthal Lectures on "Religion and the American Constitution" at Northwestern University Law School. His interpretation is that the First Amendment, which prohibits laws "respecting the establishment of religion," states "a rule of full government neutrality, including neutrality between believers and non-believers." He said:

> The neutrality position has been under current attack from two opposite directions. It is attacked by those like Bishop James A. Pike . . . who urge that government may properly aid religion so long as it does not favor a particular church. But it is attacked also by those who demand strict separation, not mere neutrality. Strict separation is required, they argue, as a means of insulating the government from all demands for aid, an insulation deemed necessary for the protection of both civil and religious liberty and to reduce occasions for religious controversy in civic life. . . .
> The neutrality interpretation which I have been defending is based on the assumption that American religious pluralism is not so charged with hostilities that religious issues must be avoided by enforcing a rigid principle of separation. We cannot of course expect perfect brotherhood in these matters. . . . But in words attributed to Henry Sloan Coffin perhaps 'A certain measure of divisiveness in the community is not too high a price to pay for the maintenance of religious convictions.'[42]

Does the Constitution prohibit aid or does it not prohibit aid? The Jewish position is not monolithic. William W. Brickman of New York University, who has come out for public aid to Jewish day schools, mentions in one of his essays that early in 1960,

> The proposal by the delegation of the Merkos L'Inyonei Chinuch of the Lubavitcher Movement to the Golden Anniversary White House Conference on Education and Youth in behalf of governmental grants for secular studies in religious schools was unprecedented in American Jewish history. . . . Unless sufficient support is made available, the Yeshivot and Jewish day schools might not be able to reach the lower economic groups. . . . While there is a case for full Federal and

state aid to the religious school, without control, this is not the occasion to prove it. At the present time, it is clear that it is the proper province of the government to subsidize the secular work of the religious school, inasmuch as such a school offers a parallel program to that of the public school, thereby relieving the public of a great tax burden and contributes to the furtherance of the national interest.[42a]

The argument of those who believe that the Constitution permits aid is based on their interpretation of the First Amendment. Their reading of history says that the separation of church and state meant that there should be no established church; it did not mean that there was a restriction against any future system of nonpreferential aid. The parochial schools are entitled to aid on the grounds that they are doing a public service. What value in the freedom of religion if the material needs to exercise this freedom are given to some schools and not to others? This position is held by sponsors of public schools within the various religious camps.

Let us examine what was meant when the First Amendment was added. It would be good to remember that the First Amendment followed in the wake of the battle in Virginia on the question of an assessment for the support of religion. The proposal to make all churches in effect state churches and to sustain them through taxation was supported by Patrick Henry and George Washington. Thomas Jefferson had introduced a bill for religious freedom into the Virginia Assembly in June, 1779. It was not adopted until 1785. Although Jefferson was almost entirely responsible for its composition, James Madison was the most potent force in securing its adoption.[42b] Jefferson considered this bill so important that on his tomb at Monticello he included it among the three achievements of his life that he most wanted commemorated. At the time of the debate, James Madison delivered his famous Memorial and Remonstrance.

Jefferson developed the phrase "a wall of separation between church and state" in a letter to the Danbury Baptist Association, January 1, 1802:

Believing with you that religion is a matter which lies solely between man, and his God, that he owes account to none other for his faith or his worship, that the legislative powers of government reach actions only, and not opinions, I contemplate with sovereign reverence that act of the whole American people which declared that their legislature should "make no law respecting an establishment of religion, or prohibiting the free exercise thereof," thus building a wall of separation between church and state.[43]

The "establishment of religion" clause in the First Amendment, the Court declared, meant at least this:

Neither a state nor the federal government can set up a church. Neither can pass laws which aid one religion, aid all religions, or prefer one religion over another. Neither can force nor influence a person to go to or remain away from church against his will or force him to profess a belief or disbelief in any religion. No person can be punished for entertaining or professing religious beliefs or disbeliefs, for church attendance or non-attendance. No tax in any amount, large or small, can be levied to support any religious activities or institutions, whatever they may be called, or whatever form they may adopt to teach or practice religion. Neither a state nor the federal government can, openly or secretly, participate in the affairs of any religious organization or groups, and vice versa. In the words of Jefferson, the clause against the establishment of religion by law was intended to erect "a wall of separation between church and state."[44]

The position of those who believe that non-state schools should be aided, a position held by most Catholics and some Jews, rests on the theoretical assumption that no one but the parent has a natural right regarding the education of children and that this right has priority over all other claims in this area.[44a] The state, in the field of education, merely acts as a surrogate for parents making it possible for them to exercise their right: the government school and the religious school are thus equally public and equally deserving of tax support. What value is there in religious freedom if the material needs to exercise this freedom are given to some schools and not to others?[44b]

Clearly expressive of the Roman Catholic position are the observations of John Courtney Murray:

> With regard to religious schools, the "underlying issue," as a writer in the Harvard Law Review put it, "is brutally simple: are parochial schools to be encouraged or not? Until American society has reached an equilibrium, the judicial decisions will continue to reflect uncertainty." I must put the issue with even more brutal simplicity: the problem of "encouragement" here is not a financial one but a juridical one: it is not a question primarily of "aid" by money but of "aid" by legal recognition.
>
> Is there to be cooperation between parents and public schools toward the religious schools to remain a sheer immunity or to become a genuine freedom, endowed with the full juridical status that only a just measure of government aid can give it?
>
> . . . How free do we want religion to be? The Court has given one answer. I think it is unreasoned and unreasonable.[45]

It is interesting to read Edmond Cahn's statement, "The people who have always said that parents have a 'natural right' to control their children's education and have cited Pierce v. Society of Sisters, 268 US 519 (1925), to prove it, are the very ones who now affront the parents by insisting on collective prayers in the public schools."[46]

The argument that the public schools and the religiously sponsored schools are equally public must be examined. What is a public school? I believe that a public school assumes not only maintenance and support by a governmental unit, but also public control. In education, the role of the state is more basic and embracing than serving merely as the channel through which tax monies are collected and disbursed for public education. We are grateful to Professor Robert Gordis for his thinking in *The Root and the Branch*. He points out that an individual is not only a biological creature but is also a citizen of society. The school is more than a surrogate delegated by the parents. There are simultaneous, parallel relationships, both to the parents and to society. Parents have the right to transmit to their young the values by which one's family lives and continues its distinctiveness. Society has a responsibility to transmit the standards needed for the civic good. Parents have the right to maintain separate schools when they are not satisfied with the community schools, but they have no right to claim the help of the state in maintaining their separate systems.[46a]

Government aid is not always an unmixed blessing. Justice Jackson said, "If the state may aid these religious schools, it may therefore regulate them. Many groups have sought aid from tax funds only to find that it carried political controls with it."[47]

There is another interesting paradox. On one hand, there is the claim that there is no such thing as a separation of religion and culture; that religion infuses all of life; that it is impossible for even a secular school to be nonreligious; that the schools cannot be neutral about religion. Yet, when it comes to the question of the support of the parochial schools, the argument is offered that there is a division between secular studies and the religious studies. If you are supporting secular studies, what difference is it where these studies are taught? This type of argumentation is reflected in the statement of Robert M. Hutchins, when asked, "Do you feel there is any danger of thought control or political control in our schools if federal aid to education is increased?" He responded:

The answer to this question is no. I am for federal aid to education. I am for federal aid to parochial schools. I am for federal aid to anybody who will do a sound educational job. The demand for education is such that all who offer it are now tax-exempt. The next step will be to recognize that since they are assisting in the performance of a public task, they may receive public help.[48]

A prominent Protestant layman, Paul G. Kauper, has said:

This writer is not advocating federal aid for parochial schools, but it is his opinion that consistent with the non-establishment principle of the first amendment and the separation limitation derived from it, and in view of the interpretations given to this language and the practices that have been sanctioned, Congress may grant some assistance to these schools as part of a program of spending for the general welfare so long as the funds are so limited and their expenditure so directed as not to be a direct subsidy for religious teaching. . . . But it should also be stressed that the issue of constitutional power should not be confused with the question whether it is desirable or wise as a matter of policy for the government to give support to parochial schools. . . . But these are questions of policy to be debated and argued in the public forum and in the legislative halls. Debate on these issues should not be foreclosed or obscured by indiscriminate invocation of the separation principle derived from the First Amendment.[48a]

To my way of thinking, if secular studies are not different, how is it that publishing houses like Scott Foresman publish different editions for sectarian groups? Why do some Jewish day schools want to have special English primers? Significant too for our discussion is a case in Vermont. A taxpayer, C. Raymond Swart, asked for a declaratory judgment in equity of his rights with respect to the payment of tuition for attendance of students of religious denominational high schools.[48b] The town of South Burlington, Vermont, had no public high school. The practice was that if there was no public high school, payment was made for students to attend schools, both public and parochial, in nearby towns. The Vermont Constitution does not specifically deal with education in church-state matters. The court made its findings based upon the First Amendment of the Federal Constitution and ruled that payment for parochial school students was unconstitutional.[48c] The court asked and ruled in the affirmative on the question, "Does the payment of tuition to a religious, denominational school by a public entity finance religious instruction, work to fusion of secular and sectarian education?" The court went on to say, "But the same fundamental law which protects the liberty of a parent to reject the public system in the interests of his children's spiritual welfare enjoins the state from participating in the religious education he has selected."

The danger in accepting public support is that the support brings a measure of administrative and curricular control that will endanger the freedom of the religious schools. In moving toward partial establishment, there is a threat of ultimately leading to complete establishment. "Wherever the state buttresses the church, the results have been an external, soulless conformity at best, and a violent antagonism at worst."[49]

Shared time—which is a newer development, has now received many supporters, and is in operation in this very area—has been hailed by some Protestant and Catholic clergymen as a long-range solution to aiding the parochial schools without going beyond the constitutional separation of church and state. This program was first given its name by Dr. Harry L. Stearns, former director of education of the United Presbyterian Church, and later superintendent of schools in Englewood, New Jersey.[50]

In Pittsburgh, some 5,000 parochial school children have been involved in a program that is 50 years old, in which classes in industrial arts for boys and home economics for girls of parochial schools are conducted in nearby public schools. A similar program has been in operation in Kansas City, Hartford, New Haven, and other communities. In Monroeville, Pa., the children of St. Thomas School in the 11th grade take such subjects as English, social studies, and mathematics there, and take scientific work at the Forbes Train Area Technical School. Though students of the constitutional law believe that this approach is legal under the federal constitution, in some states there would have to be an amendment of the constitution to make it permissible. Shared time ought to be considered carefully in terms of its possible effect upon the public schools as well as the possible effect to and the impact on Catholic children who would feel "segregated" in public schools, coming and leaving as a group. The matter of administration of this program is not germane to our discussion.[51]

Respect for our court system is essential. The United States Supreme Court has been sharply attacked by those who outwardly speak for more religion in the schools as a mask for their resentment against the Court's decision on segregation. Stated in the baldest terms is the unfortunate comment of a Southern congressman, who said, "They put the Negroes into the schools and now they have taken God out of them." Proponents of states' rights and opponents of civil rights have used the New York prayer case decision to whip the courts. The courts merit our respect. In Jewish tradition, included in the seven basic laws of human morality that Noah was required to observe was the positive commandment to establish courts of law. The courts need our support. The court of law is a bulwark of freedom. In thinking of our courts of law, we ought to remember the wise statement of our President following the New York prayer case decision:

> The Supreme Court has made its judgment, and a good many people obviously will disagree with it. Others will agree with it. But I think it is important for us if we are going to maintain our constitutional principle that we support the Supreme Court decisions even when we may not agree with them. . . . I would hope that (the people) will support the Constitution and the responsibility of the Supreme Court in interpreting it, which is theirs, and given to them by the Constitution.

Note:
This essay was completed shortly before the landmark decision of Abington Township versus Schempp, 374 U.S. 203, 1963 which held that the establishment clause prohibits state laws "requiring the selection and reading at the opening of the school day of verses from the Holy Bible and the recitation of the Lord's Prayer by the students in unison." In this landmark decision a new era began.

With God's help, I hope to update the study of church-state relations. The 200th anniversary of our U.S. Constitution, to be observed in 1987, will be the catalyst for this study.

References

[1]Schappes, *Documentary History of the Jews in the United States 1645–1875.*

[2]Marcus, *Early American Jewry,* p. 132 ff, p. 161.

[3]Roth, *History of the Jews in England,* p. 239 ff.

[4]Marcus, *The Jew in the Medieval World,* p. 80.

[5]Blau, Joseph, *Cornerstones of Religious Freedom in America,* Beacon, Boston, 1949, p. 72 ff.

[6]Littell, Franklin Hamlin, *From State Church to Pluralism,* Anchor Books, New York, 1962, p. 28.

[7]Stokes, Anson Phelps, *Church and State in the United States,* New York, 1950, p. 539.

[8]Cantwell v. Connecticut, 310 U.S. 296 (1940). In the April, 1963, issue of the American Bar Association *Journal,* Detroit attorney, Irvin Long, asks, "Is the First Amendment made applicable to the states by the 14th?" Mr. Long denies that it does. He finishes his observations with this final argument: "The contention here made is briefly this: (1) A State can go the whole way and establish a religion, subject always to the

condition that no forced adherence to the same is exerted. (2) It can, therefore, go part way on the path, subject to the same conditions, and direct and authorize practices which tend to favor or increase the prestige of one form of religious belief over another. (3) The only question which would then be left to the federal courts, as cases similar to *Engel* come to them, would be whether the complaining party has been deprived of freedom in the exercise of religion." See views of Senator A. Willis Robertson, *Prayers in Public Schools and Other Matters*, Washington, 1963, p. 38.

[9]*Engel v. Vitale*, 370 U.S. 430–431, quoted in *Prayers in Public Schools and Other Matters*, pp. 6, 7.

[10]Cited by Edmond Cahn, New York University *Law Review*, Vol. 36, November 1961, p. 1289.

[11]La Noue, George R., *Public Funds for Parochial Schools*, p. 11, f.n. 29. There is some religious ritual and symbolism in our public life. There are occasions at which religion is present at the initiative of, and for the personal benefit of, someone who also happens to be a public official. In these instances, the religion present might be considered an exercise of religious freedom by the individual office holder. The official may choose to take his oath of office on a Bible, but he cannot be required to do so. See the opinions in *Engel v. Vitale*, at 421. Compulsory religious practices are probably in all cases unconstitutional. *Torcaso v. Watkins*, 367 U.S. 488.

[12]Griswold, Dean Erwin, "Absolute Is In The Dark," *America*, March 16, 1963, p. 374.

[13]Griswold, p. 375.

[14]143 U.S. 457.

[15]Marshall, Louis, *Champion of Liberty*, Vol. 2, p. 941. An interesting account is reported of the Constitutional Convention. When the proceedings of the Convention reached a most difficult point, Benjamin Franklin, the presiding officer, moved that "Henceforth prayers imploring the assistance of heaven and its blessings on our deliberations be held in this assembly every morning before we proceed to business." *The motion was never adopted.* [Boles, Donald E., *The Bible, Religion and The Public Schools*, Iowa State University Press, Ames, Iowa, p. 17.]

[15a]Marshall, p. 942.

[15b]Littell, Dr. Franklin H., "Religion and Race: The Historical Perspective," delivered at the National Conference of Religion and Race, Chicago, January 15, 1963.

[16]10 N.Y. App. Div. 2d 189/90

"The inculcation of religion is a matter for the family and the church. In sponsoring a religious program, the State enters a field which it has been thought best to leave to the church alone. However salutary the underlying purpose of the requirement may be, it nonetheless gives to the State a direct supervision and influence that overstep the line marking the division between Church and State and cannot help but lead to a gradual erosion of the mighty bulwark erected by the First Amendment. This does not mean that the State is or should be hostile to religion—merely that the State should not invade an area where the constitutionally protected freedom is absolute and not open to the vicissitudes of legislative or judicial balancing."

[17]April 20, 1963, p. 528.

[18]Kerwin, Jerome G., *Catholic Viewpoint on Church and State*, p. 92.

[18a]*An address to the Roman Catholics of the United States of America by a Catholic Clergyman* (John Carroll), Annapolis, 1784, p. 115. A recent statement by one of the nation's leading Catholic prelates, Cardinal MacIntyre, on the subject of the separation of Church and State, said, "The Constitution does not say anything about separation of church and state, but it does state that this is a nation that believes in God. There cannot be any separation of church and state unless you want to be communists or materialists—and if you want to, that is your privilege." (*New York Times*, May 21, 1963, p. 23). It is interesting that the *Times* of the next day contained the following report: "Des Moines, May 21—The United Presbyterian Church, meeting here in General Assembly, approved today a statement on church-state relations.

"Denominational leaders regard the statement as the most comprehensive document on the subject ever prepared by a Christian body. It takes issue with such acts as Bible reading and prayer in public schools, religious observances and displays on public property and Sunday closing laws . . .

"In an introductory comment, the statement said, 'We Presbyterians wish to live, teach and evangelize within a political order in which no church will dominate the civil authorities or be dominated by them." [*New York Times*, "Presbyterians Bid Churches Cut Ties to Civic Authority." May 22, 1963, p. 1.] Included in the document was the United Presbyterian opposition to devotional Bible reading and prayer recitation in the public schools. The Massachusetts Council of Churches issued a special message to the churches, urging a calm approach "if the Supreme Court rules against compulsory Bible reading and prayer in the public schools." (Jewish Telegraphic Agency *Bulletin*, May 8, 1963, p. 3.)

[19]Miller, Edward O., "True Piety and the Regents' Prayer," *Christian Century*, August, 1963.

[20]Bryce, James, *The American Commonwealth*, 3rd Ed., New York, Vol. 2, p. 766.

[21]Jefferson's views on religion and education have been studied by Robert M. Healey, *Jefferson on Religion in Public Education*, Yale University Press, New Haven, 1962. One of the most incisive statements on the meaning of "establishment" was made by Edmond Cahn:

The Court and the individual Justices have been working with two different understandings of the scope of "religion" in the "establishment of religion" clause. The narrower understanding may be called the Jeffersonian or Enlightenment view; the broader may be called the Madisonian or Dissenter view. If one adopts the Jeffersonian or Enlightenment view, one treats the "establishment" clause as an adjunct or auxiliary to the clause guaranteeing the "free exercise of religion"; if one adopts the Madisonian or Dissenter view, one treats the "establishment" clause not only as an implement of other guarantees, but also as a self-sufficient and independent imperative, meriting the most scrupulous obedience because it safeguards the purity of organized religion itself. Though the difference between the two views is merely one of degree and emphasis, it is quite important enough to determine how a judge will cast his vote in a close case. Consequently, any judge who does not distinguish one view of "religion" from the other is quite likely to oscillate between them in a series of "establishment of religion" litigations. New York University *Law Review*, Vol. 36, Nov., 1961, pp. 1281–2.

[22]Berger, Peter L., *The Noise of Solemn Assemblies*, p. 138.

[23]*Prayer in the Public School and Other Matters.*

[23a]This material was completed a month prior to the United States Supreme Court decision on religious practices in our schools. To be brought up to date on this subject, I recommend reading the full texts of the Supreme Court decision, including the majority opinion, concurring opinions (particularly that of Justice Brennan), and the minority opinion of Justice Stewart.

[24]Katz, Wilbur, "Freedom and Religion and State," University of Chicago *Law Review*, Vol. 20, pp. 246, 438.

[25]*Prayer in the Public Schools and Other Matters*, p. 58.

[26]*Billard v. Board of Education*, 69 Kan. 53, 58, 76 Pac. 442, 423 (1904).

[27]Editorial, Washington *Post*, June 28, 1962, Sec. A., p. 22, col. 2, cited in Choper, p. 371.

[28]*Prayer in the Public Schools and Other Matters*, p. 137.

[29]Mathew 4:9–13; Hastings' *Dictionary of the Bible* (1952), p. 141; Luke 11:2–4; *Our Father*, Becker & Peters, Editors (1956) p. 46, p. 77; *The Lord's Prayer*, E. F. Scott (1952) p. 48, p. 63, p. 124; *The Catholic Encyclopedia*, Vol. 14, pp. 597–600, p. 530—Volume 9, p. 356—Volume 11, p. 312—Volume 13, p. 121; *20th Century Encyclopedia of Religious Knowledge* (1955) Volume 2—Article "The Lord's Prayer"; *The Lord's Prayer—An Interpretation*, Dr. Emmett Fox (1934), p. 9; *The Lord's Prayer—An Interpretation*, Dr. Ralph W. Sockman (1947) p. 1.

[30]245 Ill. 334 (1910) p. 351.

[31]Choper, Jesse H., "Religion in the Public Schools: A Proposed Constitutional Standard," Minnesota *Law Review*, Vol. 47, No. 3, Jan. 1963, p. 416, f.n. 570. He quotes Emerson's aphorism, "You sent your child to the schoolmaster . . . 'tis the school boys who educate him."

[32]Horton, Dora, "Children Who Are Excused Prayers," *London Observer*, August 12, 1962.

[33]Committee on Religion and Public Education of the National Council of Churches of Christ, "Relation of Religion to Public Education—A Study Document," *International Journal of Religious Education*, April, 1960, pp. 21, 29.

[34]Kauper, *Civil Liberties and the Constitution*, 1962, Note 70.

[35]*Prayer in the Public Schools and Other Matters*, p. 142. Statement of the attorney for the Roman Catholic Archdiocese of New York:

It is a fact of American history that a motivating factor in the establishment of the Catholic parochial school system in this country was objection to the indoctrination in public schools of Catholic children in the religious tenets and practices of other denominations. Catholics would make the same objection today to denominational teaching or services in our public school system.

35aAn example: "Huss, John, a zealous reformer from popery, who lived in Bohemia toward the close of the fourteenth, and the beginning of the fifteenth centuries. He was bold and persevering; but at length, trusting to the *deceitful Catholics,* he was by them brought to trial, condemned as heretic, and burnt at the stake." [Bourne, William O., *History of the Public School Society of the City of New York,* 1963, pp. 192–193, quoted in Stokes, p. 574.]

36Brickman, William W., "Public Aid to Jewish Day Schools," *Tradition,* Vol. 3, No. 2, Spring, 1962.

36aCohen, Seymour J., "Religion in the Public School," *Reconstructionist,* Vol. 16, No. 4, pp. 15 ff.

36bOn the other hand, Seymour Siegel argues: "I feel it unfortunate that the Jewish community by and large has not cooperated with the released time plan. It seems to me that it would be most advantageous to integrate released time with the programs of religious education in our various congregations." [Siegel, Seymour, *Conservative Judaism,* "Some Reflections on Religion and the Schools" XV; No. 3, pp. 27–31, Spring, 1961.

36c333 U.S. 203 (1948) pp. 227–228.

37The consistency of holding, on the one hand, that the Bible is nonsectarian and then holding, on the other hand, that it is saved from religious liberty objection because of the right of nonparticipation has long been questioned. See People ex rel. *Ring v. Board of Educ.* 245 Ill. 334, 351, 92 N.E. 251, 256 (1910); Note, 3 Rutgers L. *Review,* 115, 125, (1949).

38Choper, p. 376.

39Johnson, F. Ernst, *Religion in the Public Schools,* pp. 74–75, opposes its introduction.

40*Zorach V. Clauson,* 343 U.S. 306.

40aIn an Alaskan case, the State Court held that bus transportation for parochial school students "violated the Constitutional prohibition against direct benefits to non-public schools." [Pacific Reporter 362 P. 2d 932.] Courts in Washington, Missouri, Delaware, Wisconsin and Oklahoma have made similar rulings. (at 943). Obviously, the state constitutions may be amended.

41University of Chicago *Law Review,* Vol. 29, No. 1, Autumn, 1961, p. 96. Also in "Religion and the Law." Professor Kurland was most gracious to me in clarifying the intricacies of these constitutional issues. He gave freely of his wide learning and profound wisdom.

42*The Reporter,* Northwestern University School of Law, April, 1963, p. 3. Another significant interpretation has been Choper, p. 330, p. 334.

"The proposed constitutional standard is that for problems concerning religious intrusion in the public schools, the establishment clause of the first amendment is violated when the state engages in what may be fairly characterized as *solely religious activity* that is likely to result in (1) *compromising* the student's religious or conscientious beliefs or (2) *influencing* the student's religious freedom or conscientious choice. . . . It prohibits certain governmental action that is likely to result in (1) a student's doing something that is forbidden by his conscientious beliefs, thus *compromising* his scruples, or (2) a student's engaging in religious activities that, although not contrary to his religion's beliefs, he would not otherwise undertake, thus *influencing* his freedom of religious participation or choice. The results the proposed standard produces seems to me to be, for the most part, favorable; those that are not are nonetheless acceptable."

Also see Cahn, Edmond, New York University *Law Review*, Vol. 36, No. 7, November 1961, and Vol. 37, No. 6, December, 1962; Pfeffer, Leo, "Court, Constitution and Prayer," Rutgers *Law Review*, Summer, 1962.

42aBrickman, pp. 174, 177; also, "Hebrew Day School Society asks for Federal Aid to Religious Schools," Jewish Telegraphic Agency *Bulletin*, April 4, 1961.

42bCousins, *Living Ideas in America*, p. 508.

43Cousins, *In God We Trust*, p. 135.

44Justice Black in *Everson*, 330 U.S. (1947) 15–16.

44aThis position cites the court's statement in *Pierce v. Society of Sisters*, (1925), 265 U.S. 510.

"The fundamental theory of liberty, upon which all governments in this Union repose, excludes any general power of the state to standardize its children by forcing them to accept instruction from public teachers only. The child is not the mere creature of the state; those who nurture him to direct his destiny have the right, coupled with the high duty, to recognize and prepare him for additional obligations." This was quoted in the dissent in *Mathews v. Quinton*, Pacific Reporter 362 P 2d 959.

44bPR 362 P 2d 959. In the dissent in the Alaska case, Justice J. Dimond said, "This liberty to choose the kind of education for their children . . . has lost most of its effectiveness and meaning by the majority decision in this case. . . . Those persons who exercise their inherent right to direct the destiny of their children must now pay the price of being denied the equal rights to which the Constitution says they are entitled."

45Murray, John Courtney, *Separation of Church and State*, p. 331, pp. 341, 342.

46Cahn, p. 992, note 29.

46aGordis, Robert, *The Root and the Branch*, pp, 98–101.

47330 U.S. (1947) pp. 27–8. See also 366 P 2d 544 which raises the point that aid might result in state control of religious instruction. Reference was made to the *Catholic Encyclopedia*, Vol. 13, 1912, p. 560.

48Hutchins, Robert M., *A Conversation on Education*. In *Cochran v. Board of Education*, 28 U.S. 370, 1930, the court declared as constitutional a Louisiana statute which supplied secular textbooks to non-public schools.

[48a]Kauper, Paul G., "Church and State Cooperative Separatism," Michigan *Law Review*, Vol. 60, No. 1, Nov. 1961, pp. 39–40.

See 366 R 2d 533. Oregon had had a so-called free textbook statute since 1931. The state would purchase the texts and lend them to both public and private schools. The text books were for "secular" studies. Among the significant statements in the case was, "The evidence establishes, and the trial judge finds, that the purpose of the Catholic Church, in operating the St. Johns school and other similar schools under its supervision, is to permeate the entire educational process with the precepts of the Catholic religion." (At 536) Study guides were prepared by the superintendent of schools for the Archdiocese of Portland. The decision continued, "The study guides used by the teachers in St. Johns School indicate that, to some extent at least, the use of the text books furnished by the district is inextricably connected with the teaching of religious concepts." The court dismissed as specious the argument that "since the public schools are performing a task which the school itself must perform through the use of public schools, the expenditures made are not 'aid' but 'remuneration,' and therefore, not prohibited by the Constitutional principle of the separation of church and state." (At 542)

[48b]*Swart v. S. Burlington Town School District,* 167A 2d at 514.
[48c]*Swart* at 520.
[49]Gordis, Robert, *Religion and the Schools,* p. 24.

In the Oregon case, the court accepted the observation made in *Judd v. Board of Education* 278 New York at 209, 15 NE 2d at 581, that aid would "open the door for a dangerous and vicious controversy among the different denominations as to who should get the largest share of public funds."

[50]*Religious Education,* "Shared Time—A Symposium," Jan., Feb., 1962.
[51]New York *Herald Tribune,* Dec. 3, 1961.

Kaddish in Many Places

Thursday was a landmark date for me. It was the fifteenth day of Shevat, an easy day to remember, for it was the new year of the trees. Yesterday was the first day in eleven months that I was not required to recite the Kaddish—to join the row of mourners in remembering their sacred dead. Yesterday was the beginning of a new year in Israel and of a new stage in my life. In Israel little saplings were planted on this day. They will grow into beautiful trees, gracing the landscape of our Holy Land. In my life many memories were planted during this year that has now ended. Let me name some of them:

At times during this year I have said Kaddish in unusual places. A few weeks ago, waiting in the El Al terminal for the plane to Israel, I noticed a family in a corner of the waiting room who were quite bereft, and whose garments had been torn with the traditional *keriah*. I was asked, "Would you like to *daven* Minḥah with us?" I joined them in Minḥah, and then, after the service, I asked discreetly about the family. I learned that they were to fly on the same plane. They were like the family of our ancestors, Jacob and Joseph, who pleaded that they not be buried in Egypt, but that their remains be brought back to the land of their birth. They were bringing back the remains of a member of their family, born somewhere in Europe, but in the spiritual sense, born in the land of Israel three thousand years ago.

On the plane, we had another minyan in the morning. The sun was rising over the Mediterranean, or perhaps we were over the Italian peninsula, and we read from a small Torah scroll that was going to be presented by some congregation to Zahal, the Israeli defense forces. We had no table, so the Torah was held up by two men. A Bar Mitzvah boy read from the scroll, *"Bo el Pharaoh"*— "Go to Pharaoh and tell him to let my people go." I was deeply touched by this. The Bar Mitzvah boy's grandfather had been my teacher in high school days and taught me Talmud years ago. It was so symbolic. In the hold of the plane were the remains of a Jew who had passed on, and above, in the passenger compartment, a vibrant dynamic minyan was reaffirming its continuity and its faith in God.

During the course of this last year I recited Kaddish many times in our synagogue chapel. Day after day the minyan starts while it is still pitch-dark. It is an experience to come to this *bet hamidrash* and see how a handful of men make up this daily service and keep up the continuum of praise to God. The individual members of the minyan come and go but the minyan continues every single day of the year, every single year of the synagogue's life. It is touching to see how the members encourage each other, how their friendships develop, how concerned they become if one does not show up for a few days. They are truly a *ḥavurah*, a fellowship, and they care for their *ḥaverim*. In recent weeks, a fine woman has joined the minyan. She comes to pray for the well-being of her grown family and to recall the sacred memory of her mother. At first she seemed an outsider; now she is a part of the group.

During the course of the year I recited Kaddish at the *Kotel Maaravi*, the Western Wall. There the tears of Israel have been shed since the destruction of the Temple. I felt priviledged saying the ancient words there, and I felt that in a sense I was saying them there as my father's representative, since he never had the privilege of being there.

But there were happier settings in which I said the Kaddish. There were the Hasidic *shtiblach* to which I had been introduced by my friend Rabbi Abraham Karp. I had been to Meah Shearim many times, but I never knew that just a few yards away from the din of the Meah Shearim marketplace there was another din, not of peddlers and housewives debating the price of fish, but of men raising their voices in prayer. I had been to Jerusalem many times. I didn't know about this particular little set of miniature synagogues, these little spiritual diamonds in the rough. What a charming atmosphere pervades them, "Minḥah, Minḥah, Minḥah," was the cry as I walked in, "we need a tenth man for the minyan." I needed them for my Kaddish, and they needed me for their minyan, and so we felt connected, these Hasidim and I, even though we had never met before. The service was the service of the Sephardic ritual. I noticed that the prayer books that they used were very torn. My book dealer, Mr. Schreiber, was there, and so I said, "Perhaps you ought to get them some new prayer books. Order them for the synagogue, will you please, and inscribe my father's name." I had never been there before, and I do not know when or whether I will be back there again, but meantime something of me and something of my father's memory is there in those books.

Once a week, on Thursdays, the eve of the eve of the Sabbath, the little people of Jerusalem, the humble beggars, come in to that synagogue. With great dignity they receive their offerings. I noticed one beggar giving a bit of charity to another. This is the custom among these people—even the poorest has to help others.

One day, after leaving the "Minḥah, Minḥah, Minḥah" setting, I saw people running. They were loading on lorries, small trucks. "Where are you going?" I asked. "Why, it's the Yahrzeit of the Or Hahayim," the answer came.

The Or Hahayim is the famous mystical commentator on the Bible whose works are beloved and revered by both the Ashkenazic and Sephardic Jewish communities. (I once met a cab driver in Jerusalem who goes up to the grave of the Or Hahayim every morning at 4:00 a.m. to light an oil lamp.) The old Yiddish expression has it that if the whole world runs, you should run too. So I went to my Hertz car and followed them up to the Mount of Olives. There, in one of the oldest burial grounds of Jewish history, I came to the grave of the Or Hahayim, where I found the Jews of my little synagogue praying and reciting the words of the Psalms. In one corner there was a Minhah service. A little while later, as twilight came to Jerusalem, which is a glorious experience in itself, as the blue skies turned gradually to purple and finally to black, there was an Ashkenazic service. For the first time in my life I did not worship in an easterly direction, toward Jerusalem. Instead I prayed toward the west, for the Mount of Olives is east of the Temple site. There I could see the massive walls of Herodian stone that have stood as silent witnesses for thousands of years, testifying to the love of the Jewish people for the city of Jerusalem. I was praying for the first time in a westerly direction, for I was on the other side of the wall, but I could see the Jews at the Wall in mind from where I stood, and in my mind I could join my prayers to theirs.

On the way home from Jerusalem last summer, I stopped off in London. One morning I went to a small synagogue near my hotel for services and for Kaddish. I noticed that the leader of the service prayed with the tallit draped over his head. The voice sounded vaguely familiar, but it was not until the service was over and he doffed his tallit and turned around that I realized who it was. It was the Chief Rabbi of England, in mourning for his mother, who was leading us that day in the Kaddish. But until the service was over and he turned around, I did not know that. It could have been any ordinary Jew leading the prayers or mourning for his parent. The words were the same and the service was the same and the grief was the same, no matter who happened to be leading the prayers.

Yes, there were many places and many occasions when I said

Kaddish during these eleven months. Of all of them, however, this is the one that means the most to me. A week ago I visited the soldiers at Hadassah Hospital. Those who are still there are the ones who are most difficult to treat. They have been there since the Yom Kippur War, and as I went from bed to bed shaking hands and mumbling a few inadequate words of encouragement to them, I felt so feeble, so helpless, so unable to say what I wanted to to them. Finally, after I had spent some time with them, I broke away from the group and went to the synagogue of the hospital to get some emotional relief. I went in there and sat down to look at the Chagall windows that are so lovely and to be by myself for a few minutes just to think. As I sat studying the windows, I noticed a *mohel*, a circumcisor, come in. I asked him, "When will the brit be?" "In a little while," he replied. Then a modest Sephardic family and their guests came in. Soon they were joined by the proud father, who was one of the soldiers from the ward upstairs, still in his bandages and still in his cast. Then they brought the little child in, and the brit began.

At the end of the service, they recited the Kaddish. I don't know for whom but I was delighted to join their quorum. As I did, I sensed the whole cycle of life revolving before me. I had said the Kaddish once on a plane carrying a man to his last resting place. Now I was saying it again as a new life entered the Covenant of Abraham. I was reciting Kaddish for my father, surrounded by the majestic beauty of the Chagall windows, but more than the creation by man was the creation of God. I was thinking of my father, who lay many thousands of miles away, but I was in the company of new kinsmen with whose path mine had now crossed. Somehow, I had the feeling that there is a wondrous continuity, a never-ending flow of life, to death and through death, and that therefore, despite all its aches and all its pains, there is great beauty and great meaning in our lives.

I have said Kaddish in many places and with many different people during these eleven months. The Kaddish has brought me into contact with many Jews, and with my father, and with myself. I think that he would be pleased.

From Words of Comfort

SPOKEN AT THE FUNERAL SERVICE FOR BEN ARONIN, 1980

Uncle Ben's favorite prayer was *Hashkiveynu*, asking that God cause us to lie down in peace and awaken us to life. Surcease has come to his sorrow, relief has come to our tribulation and he will awaken to the life eternal.

"To every thing there is a season and a time to every purpose under God's heaven. There is a time to be born and, alas, a time to die; a time to mourn and a time to rejoice; a time to keep silence and a time to speak." All of us speak by our presence and our comfort.

Ben Aronin's passing marks the physical end of one of the most unusual human beings any of us has ever met—a beautiful person, a majestic blend of mind and heart, a loyal kinsman, a devoted and trusted colleague, a dedicated teacher, an understanding confidante, a fighter for justice. His long career, his 55 years of service to this congregation and to this community, has left an indelible impact on each of us. We are all mourners today—the family, the friends, those who have gathered from near and far. I am deeply touched by the fact that some of his younger students, who are just establishing themselves in their professional careers, tore themselves away in the midst of the day to pay tribute to the man who, in a spiritual sense, gave them life. The rabbis speak of the difference between a parent and a teacher. A parent brings us into this world, but a teacher brings us into the life everlasting by teaching us the permanent values of faith and civilization.

The lamentable report of his death has spread far and near. Just yesterday at the Seminary, colleague after colleague asked me to express condolences to his family. Ben Aronin is survived by Frieda darling. I remember many a conversation from his study as he spoke to her. Frieda would say, "Come home, it's time enough. The boys and girls will study tomorrow." And he would respond,

"But Frieda darling, another minute, another ten minutes," which meant another hour or two. The loving father of Gerard and his Marlene, Rachel and her Norton. Devoted grandfather and fond brother of Blanche, of Cele and Aaron and the late Janice. A wonderful, wonderful family, knit together by bonds that can never be drawn asunder.

We are grateful today and we express our thanks to the physicians who labored over these last fifteen years during which Ben suffered from a difficult illness. We thank the nurses, the hospitals. We thank this congregation. We thank all of the friends who buoyed one another up during the time of his growing disability.

Ben Aronin was a unique person. At once a master of his folk, he was a servant of his people. His concern for all was expressed by the Great Emancipator, "with malice towards none." I never, never heard Ben say a harsh word about any individual. I assure you that there were one or two here and there who deserved some chastisement. He was an inspiration to all of us by his gentle way. A Jew is embarrassed but does not embarrass others. He was an exemplar of the love of Jewish life, of high dedication to Jewish values. His overbrimming love for young and old has been a lesson for each of us.

"The Lord, your God," the Torah tells us this week, "commands you to observe these laws. Observe them faithfully with all your heart and soul." Did you ever meet a man with more heart? Did you ever meet a person with more soul? A man who understood the sacred charge of Jewish people to be "a kingdom of priests." Ben was a *Kohen* and a Holy people. "You shall be as God promised, a Holy people to the Lord, your God."

Ben was a bookman, the writer of many works. I was touched when a young person came in and said to Frieda before this service, "If you have another book or two at home, I'd like to have it for my personal library as a permanent memorial of my teacher." This is what Ben did in this institution. I do not think anyone in this synagogue—I speak of its great rabbis who preceded me, spiritual forces, the masters and teachers who were assembled here over these last 105 years—touched the hearts, minds and spirits of people as did our Ben Aronin. He wrote not only for his immediate pupils; he wrote for the world.

The other day I read this description. "The words of the poet outlive the events they narrate and make the poet immortal." Today is just the first exercise in the immortality of Ben Aronin.

"Time cannot gnaw good words to dust. If my book is truth and beauty, enough of it will endure." John Keats once said, "If poetry comes not as naturally as leaves to a tree, it had better not come at all."

During the summer, I was seated in the library at Harvard. While waiting for some material, I picked up a copy of *Moment* magazine and read a review of new children's books. How touching it was to come across this description of Ben's latest effort (I do not say last, for there are still other manuscripts): "The author is filled with faith and fortitude." Somehow the reviewer used words that captured the essence of Ben Aronin: *faith* and *fortitude.* Here was a man who went through some very difficult times. All of us who were witnesses to his illness were deeply concerned, moved, and at times tormented. But he was buoyed up by the rabbinic teaching he loved: "All that God does, He does for the good."

The nature of a man can be seen in the little expressions he uses. We speak of a son-in-law, we speak of a daughter-in-law. Ben spoke of Norton as a son-in-love, of Marlene as a daughter-in-love. He loved his grandchildren with a passion. I remember how he would gather everyone together for a Passover Seder. Once I said, "Ben, you know with fifty guests there's money involved." "But," he replied, "this is my family. This is the time when we must get together."

He was a great human being. He was concerned with his fellow human beings but, overall and above all, he was a Hasid, a Lubavitcher Hasid. This meant, on the one hand, that he loved the teachings of *Habad,* of wisdom, of understanding and knowledge. It meant, on the other hand, that he also loved those Hasidic teachings which are related to joy. What a pleasure it was to see him, just a few years ago, dancing on Simchat Torah on this very pulpit. He tried to drag me into the dance but, being a dignified Litvak, I stood aside.

Ben would have enjoyed your laughing today. How important it is for a man to be joyful in his inner spirit and in his outer ways.

Ben was a good poet, a good writer, a fine translator. The United Nations Education and Social Council selected several of his translations for their publication program. He was a man who had physical strength. And, above all, he was a man of the spirit. He had that strength which is granted to but a few.

Charles Reznikoff, the great poet, once wrote, "Not for victory, but for the day's work done as well as I was able. Not for a seat upon the dais, but at the common table." Ben never pursued honors as so many of us pursue honors. He did not want a seat on the dais; he wanted to sit with *amcha* at the common table. "Give us the flowering of a new heart and the fruit of it. Light a candle of understanding in our hearts, Lord—that everyone—may live."

This morning, I had a chance to look through my library and my children's library. There I found some of Ben's works: *The Lost Tribe, The Moor's Gold, Cavern of Destiny* and *The Abramiad*, which has been described as one of the three great epics since the Bible. Ben's interpretations were touching and illuminating. He was an encourager. You know, in life there are discouragers and encouragers. He was an encourager who was a shepherd to those who were lost. I remember the trek of people who came to his office to seek his counsel. When I arrived, it was on the third floor, and then he had an aliyah by being moved down to the second floor. The little and the great alike came to be strengthened by him. He was a man of the spirit. He loved James Joyce enormously. On one of his last long trips in the 1960s, he went to Dublin, for he said he could not lay his head to rest without seeing James Joyce's locale.

Our faith understands the importance of speech, and Ben was as articulate as an attorney before the bar of justice. A man of gifted words, he was gifted both when he spoke with you and when he spoke with you without uttering a word. Genuine speech is distinct from noise. As a great writer once said, "when the silences turn." There is a time when you can say more by being silent than by speaking forth.

Ben was, to be sure, a master teacher of his physical children. He was a master teacher of his spiritual children, and they were a thousand in number. "For I have singled him out, that he may instruct his children and his posterity to keep the way of the Lord by doing what is righteous and good, by doing what is just and right, in order that the Lord may bring about for Abraham what He has promised him."

Yes, he taught his children, he taught our children, he taught them what is just and what is right. One must be generous to be just, that is our way of life.

We are in the concluding days before Rosh Hashanah. Week after week we read from the comfort section of Isaiah: "I, even I, will comfort you." But, more important, in this week's Haftarah, we will read our great credo of faith and immortality: "Thy people shall be all righteous, they shall inherit the land forever; they are the branch of My planting, the work of My hands, wherein I glory." As Dr. Louis Finkelstein translated, "All Israel has a destiny in the future eternity."

Uncle Ben, you have been blessed in your coming and we know that you will be blessed in your going. Last week we read "and when you go out," but this week we will read "when you come to the land of promise" where there is no pain, where there is no grief and no sorrow. You leave this terrestrial life, but you go to the land that God has promised to the righteous. "I send an angel before you to guard you on the way."

As the western sky is still aglow with the glory of his presence, and that afterglow will remain for many a decade to come, we speak the words of comfort of Isaiah: "Never again shall your sun set, nor your moon withdraw your light, but the Lord shall be your everlasting light and the days of your mourning shall be ended" (60:20). *Zecher Zaddik Livracha*, may the memory of this Zaddik, of this righteous man—may the memory of this Hasid, this man of high moral standards—remain always for a blessing. God rest his soul, God rest his pure and precious soul. Amen.

A Plea for Soviet Jewry

CONGRESSIONAL RECORD, VOL. III, WASHINGTON, MONDAY, SEPT. 20, 1965, NO. 173

We come today before God and man to give witness concerning the fate of our brothers and sisters in the Soviet Union. We come today to bestir ourselves and to arouse the conscience of all humankind.

We come today to consecrate ourselves anew to the solemn task of securing and assuring the religious and cultural continuity of our brothers and sisters in Russia.

It is fitting that we should do this. It is proper that we should do this here and now. We are one short week before the new year.

Now is the time when people must search their hearts. Now is the time when people must reflect on their responsibilities. Now is the time when we must concern ourselves with the welfare of others. Now is the time for prayers to God and for action by people.

We plead with the God of the covenant, remember them and help us.

What is the tragedy of Soviet Jewry? The tragedy can be stated simply. They are subjected to a process of spiritual and cultural attrition. They are losing their identity as a distinct group. Unless this process is stopped, a great and historic Jewish community will disappear.

Before God and man we ask: Can we allow the disappearance of any Jewish community as a result of external pressure?

Before God and man we ask: Can we be silent as they are prevented from teaching their children the faith of our fathers?

Before God and man we ask: Dare we stand by as they are intimidated from free association with Jews at home and abroad?

Before God and man we ask: Can we be the silent witnesses as they are being condemned to a lingering spiritual death?

Place yourself in the position of a Soviet Jew and ask: Is that type of life tolerable?

Soviet Jews stand utterly alone. They have been isolated from their religious heritage. They have been cut off from cultural tradition. They are cut off from their past. Their present is severely restricted. Their future is bleak.

What is life without the strength of roots? What is life without the pride of history? What is life without the warmth of memory? What is life without the ennoblement of culture? What is life without the fellowship of community? What is life without a link to eternity?

The Soviet Jew as Jew is in limbo. His is not life. It is rather spiritual death.

It is hard to believe that a great government aims consciously at the forceable assimilation of a minority of its population. Can we be silent as a link is torn from the millennial chain of Jewish life? Our fate is intertwined with theirs.

They are bone of our bone, flesh of our flesh. We are bound to them by the cords of memory. We are all part of a covenant people who share a common history, faith, culture, language, and tradition. They are precious to us. Dare we stand with folded hands? The bar of history would not forgive our inaction. We are a small people with a great heritage, a heritage which teaches that when anyone is fallen—you, you must help him stand.

We are a small people whose ranks have been cruelly diminished during this past generation. Can we afford to stand idly by when a quarter of our remaining family is denied the liberating air of spiritual and cultural equality? Will we stand by as this denial of their rights leads to their spiritual asphyxiation?

Conscience demands the elementary right of every people to group life. Conscience demands the elementary right of each individual to worship God as he or she sees fit.

We plead for those for whom the synagogue and its schools stand at the very heart of their Jewishness. We implore for those who cherish Hebrew and Yiddish, love their language, and see it at the very core of their cultural being. There are those Soviet Jews who saw their dearest perish in the Holocaust. Shall they be denied the fundamental right to be reunited with their remaining families? The Soviet Union has affixed its signature to the Universal Declaration of Human Rights. Religious liberty, cultural fulfillment, family reunification—all are basic human rights.

In this hour, we welcome the condemnations of anti-Semitism that have appeared in the Soviet press. The remarks of Premier Kosygin and the recent *Pravda* editorial are first steps. We hope that they are the beginning of a process of the rectification of lingering wrongs. The Soviet Union is not insensitive to world public opinion. We must continue our labors until there is a fundamental change in the situation of Soviet Jews, a fundamental change that will enable them to live their lives as Jews in dignity, honor, and pride.

Before God and man, we declare that we make our demands in the cause of peace. Together with all persons of good will, we hope for the improvement of relations between all nations. Fervently in our daily prayers, we ask for world peace. We pray that there be a rapprochement between our beloved nation and the U.S.S.R. Let us never forget, however, that the elimination of a moral grievance that causes tension will surely remove an obstacle to understanding. We know the pains of war. We yearn for the serenity of peace. It must be a peace of justice. It must be a peace of equality for the Jews, for all peoples of the Soviet Union.

Our demands are just. We ask for our brothers and sisters that which is promised to all Soviet citizens.

In this solemn hour, our hands are uplifted in solemn oath. We will not rest until justice is done for our people in the Soviet Union.

We pray to the All Merciful, who answers the broken hearted, that He will answer us, that He will save, and that He will have mercy upon our loved ones. Together with our prayers go forth our continued commitment to our labor. We shall struggle to enable our brothers and sisters to maintain their religious loyalty and cultural identity. We shall not rest until we secure their right to associate with fellow Jews within and without the Soviet Union. We hope for the day when severed families will be reunited again. Their cause is dear and precious to us. The urgency of their need, the lateness of the hour, bids us to cry aloud, to proclaim before all humanity that we have come to seek justice for our people.

Message To Our Graduates

1979

This is a great occasion in your personal history. Your graduation from our Religious School or from the Academy is set within the beautiful framework of Shavuot.

The great Maimonides, in the twelfth century, wrote a letter of comfort to the Jews of Southern Arabia. This famous message is called "Iggeret Teiman—A Letter to the South" or "Petah Tikvah—Gate of Hope." The Jews of Yemen were under great pressure. They had to choose between apostasy (leaving the faith) or martyrdom (death). There were great tensions within the community. The desire to survive was overwhelming.

Maimonides, the great teacher, wrote to encourage them. He turned to the book of Isaiah and found this helpful expression: "Strengthen hands that are weak, make firm the tottering knees" (Isaiah 35:3). Maimonides tried to strengthen their hands by writing these words: "My brothers, it behooves us to keep ever present before our mind, the great day of Sinai, for the Lord has forbidden us ever to forget it. Rear your children in a thorough understanding of that all-important event. Explain before large assemblies the principle it involves, know you the truth of which is testified by the most trusted witnesses. A whole people heard the word of God and saw the glory of divinity. From this lasting memory, we must draw our power to strengthen our faith, even in a period of persecution and affliction such as the present one."

From the letter of Maimonides, we move across the generations. A very scholarly member of our congregation, Edmund Berg, was kind enough to share with me some thoughts after reading my description of post-Holocaust Prague. He cited an important statement of the modern master Professor Martin Buber. One must place his words in their historic context. They were written in Germany in 1933. Adolph Hitler and his ilk forced their way to power on January 30th. Months after, in September 1933, Professor Buber published these words (my translation is adapted from Berg's).

"I live not far from the town of Worms, on the Rhine. Worms is close to my heart because generations of my family lived there. From time to time, I travel to this town. When I arrive there, I go first to the Cathedral. It is a visible harmony of construction. I walk slowly around the Cathedral in total joy. Afterwards, I go to the Jewish cemetery (the German word for cemetery, *friedhof*, means "haven of peace"). The cemetery consists of crooked withered, formless tombstones. I stand in the midst of the cemetery, look up from this disarray to the magnificent harmony of the Cathedral. Below, there is no trace of harmony, one has only withered stones and the ashes beneath them. One has the ashes, even if they are not visible anymore. One has an idea of those human beings who are now the ashes. One has this thought, these human beings are not physically close to me on this planet, but they are alive within me, in my memory, far back into our history until the time of Sinai. I had this inner connection with the ashes and through it, my connection with the patriarchs. This is the remembrance given to all Jews: what God did to them at Sinai. The harmony and completeness of the Cathedral cannot change my feelings, nothing can make my mind deviate from the time when Israel was so close to God. I stood there and something happened to me. Surrounded by death, the ashes, the withered stones, the quiet misery; but, God's nearness to me remains firm. I lie prostrate on the ground. I am fallen like one of those stones, but I have not been forsaken by God. The Cathedral is as it is, the cemetery is as it is, but we are not forsaken by God."

Two towering spiritual giants—one in the Middle Ages, the other in our own time—are examples of how our masters and teachers gave strength to our oppressed people by drawing upon the spiritual power of Sinai.

To this year's class of our elementary and high school departments, all of us extend best wishes. We are grateful to those who taught you, to those who transmitted the spirit of Sinai to you. To the members of our faculty, to our lay leadership who are so concerned about your education, we extend our best wishes and our congratulations.

Like all the generations of our people in the past, your generation, too, stands at the foot of the mount of revelation. I am reminded of an incident in early American history. The ancestor of one of America's most important families was about to leave his native France for America with his two sons. Their mother had died some time before. He took his sons to their mother's grave and made them swear to remain united forever. Then he blessed them: "May each generation of your descendants strive unceasingly to make the next generation better than its own."

May you, my friends, help make your generation and the next generation better than our own.

Forty-Six Glorious Years

A TRIBUTE TO A COLLEAGUE, 1986

"Though your beginning was small, amply He will enrich you in the end" (Job 8:7). This verse comes to mind as one reflects on the trepidation that any person has upon accepting new and awesome responsibilities. When Hazzan Moses J. Silverman came to Anshe Emet with his young bride from Connecticut, many concerns confronted him. Only 24 at the time, he would be standing in the pulpit which was then presided over by one of the great personalities of 20th-century Jewry, Rabbi Solomon Goldman. Thank God, our community took Hazzan Silverman, together with his beloved Roselyn, to their very hearts and made him one of their most beloved.

A Hazzan is a *Sheliah Tzibur*, the messenger of the congregation. The congregation is most important in Jewish worship. Public worship is certainly people's most socializing instrument. When people pray together with their families, they strengthen the bond of family unity. When they pray together with the community, they buttress the cornerstone of our communal life. When we pray in the company of others, we do not step out of the world; rather, we see the world in a different setting. Our tradition permits private prayer but it prefers public worship. The prayers of a *tzibur*, of a community, give us a deepened sense of mutuality and inter-dependence. We are no longer isolated individuals, but rather a community standing in unity before God. When our Hazzan leads us in prayer, we pray together with the generations of an eternal people.

The rabbis commented on the verse, "Then sang Moses and the children of Israel," that from the day when God created the world until our ancestors stood near the Red Sea, no one save Israel sang to God. Adam, at the time of his creation, could have sung. Abraham, in the hour of his deliverance, could have chanted. Isaac, rescued from the knife, and Jacob, preserved from Esau, could have raised voices to God. Only when Israel as a people was saved, were they able to sing songs before Him. Therefore the Bible reads, "Then sang Moses and the children of Israel."

The beauty of our public worship can never be minimized. We can never permit it to become what Isaiah called "a commandment of men learned by rote." Our ritual cannot be routinized. Liturgy must possess splendor and majesty. A Hazzan, at every act of worship, be it at a *minyan* with only 10 people present in the house of mourners or at a magnificent Kol Nidre with thousands of people in attendance, marks each service with a dignity and a grandeur all its own.

Our congregation, like so many of the Conservative movement, has searched for new ritual forms and has attempted to rediscover and to embellish forgotten ones. This has indeed been a historic Jewish quest. In every age there were those splendid figures who tried to add to the effectiveness of worship as a means of lifting the spirits of the individual congregant. Our blessings go forth to those who have been so richly endowed with the natural talent and the skill to enhance, to beautify, to enrich the service of God.

A Hazzan is known by another name. He is the person who is *"Yored Lifne Hatevah,"* who goes down before the ark of the Torah. You will notice that in every Jewish synagogue, when one goes up to the Ark, one must always ascend several stairs. This is done to teach us that we must have humility when we pray. "Out of the depths I call to You." One of the greatest Hazzanim of this generation, Leib Glantz, recorded the Selihot prayer, "How can we open our mouth before You, dwelling on high: How shall we pour forth our prayers?" It takes courage to pray. We are mortal human beings, among the weakest of the creatures on earth. Jewish prayer seems to be an act of arrogance, a deed of presumption. The Rabbis spoke of the verse, "Worship the Lord in the beauty of holiness" and read not *hadrat* (beauty) but *herdat* (trembling). There is the element of trembling in prayer. "Serve the Lord in awe and rejoice with trembling." The words of the Hazzan give us courage to pray. It is only after he has chanted forth *"Hamelech—* the King" on festivals, or *"Shochen Ad—*You who lives in Eternity" on a Sabbath morning, that we are able to pray. Jewish prayer is a conversation with God. We speak to Him on the most personal of terms as You or *Du.* Jan Peerce has called one of his most beautiful recordings "A *Dudele* with God." We speak to Him in dialogue.

There is a great power in Jewish song to restore the hearts of our people and to bring those who have drifted away back into the fold of Jewish life. A very moving letter in Yiddish was written some time ago to our Eternal Light program office at the Seminary in New York. It came from a man who lived in the upper reaches of Canada, far away from other Jews. These were his words:

"Der brief iz geschriben in tint fun treren. . . . This letter is written in ink of tears. . . . I have not heard a Yiddishe Vort, a Jewish word, for the thirty-seven years that I have lived up here in this Hudson Bay northland. . . . I broke down and cried when I heard your program last Sunday, "Dos Lied Fun Berdichev." . . . It was my home town. . . . Your program has led me to decide to leave this place where I have been a trader all these years, to seek out a community where there are Jews. . . . Es is shoin tzeit tzu sitzen tzvischen Acheinu B'nai Yisroel. 'It's time to dwell with Brother Israelites.' " This is the power of Jewish song to bring people back to our midst.

An early rabbinic commentary on Leviticus observes regarding the words, "These are the commandments that the Lord gave Moses for the children of Israel at Mount Sinai," that Moses was the fitting messenger of our people. The commentary says, "May the messenger be worthy of the message and the message worthy of the messenger." Thank God, our Hazzan was worthy to carry the message of our people, the message that had been assigned to him. The message that he bore was carried proudly and reverently.

We are grateful to Hazzan Silverman for all that he has meant to this congregation and to the wider Jewish community and to his colleagues over the years. The Scots have a fine saying: *"Gratitude preserves auld friendships and begets new ones."*

In the splendrous tapestry of Anshe Emet there is a magnificent silver thread that was woven in strongly and lovingly for forty-six years. This silver thread helped to bind this congregation together in some of its most trying times. The shiny brightness of the thread gave lustre and color to our lives. We will always be grateful to Moses J. Silverman.